Perfect Deterrence

An important and timely contribution to international relations and political science, this is the first general analysis of deterrence since the end of the Cold War. Using non-cooperative game theory, the authors offer a new approach to deterrence – Perfect Deterrence Theory – which they apply to unilateral and mutual direct deterrence relationships, and to extended-deterrence relationships supported by deployment policies such as Massive Retaliation and Flexible Response. The authors focus on the relationship among capability, preferences, credibility, and outcomes to achieve a new understanding of threats and responses. Some surprising conclusions emerge, indicating that credible threats to respond to attack can sometimes make an attack more likely, and that incredible response threats can sometimes promote peace. With the application of deterrence theory in diverse social settings, and historical examples from before, during, and after the Cold War, this book provides a welcome new examination of the subject.

FRANK C. ZAGARE is Professor and Chair of the Department of Political Science at the University at Buffalo, State University of New York (SUNY). His books include *Modeling International Conflict* (Gordon & Breach, 1990), *The Dynamics of Deterrence* (University of Chicago Press, 1987), *Exploring the Stability of Deterrence* (Lynne Rienner Publishers, 1987), and *Game Theory: Concepts and Applications* (Sage Publications, 1984).

D. MARC KILGOUR is Professor of Mathematics at Wilfrid Laurier University in Waterloo, Ontario, Director of the Laurier Centre for Military Strategic and Disarmament Studies, and Adjunct Professor of Systems Design Engineering at the University of Waterloo. His recent books include *Designing Institutions for Environmental and Resource Management* (Edward Elgar, 1998), *Interactive Decision Making: The Graph Model for Conflict Resolution* (Wiley, 1993), and *Game Theory and National Security* (Blackwell, 1988).

CAMBRIDGE STUDIES IN INTERNATIONAL RELATIONS: 72

Perfect deterrence

Editorial Board

Cambridge Studies in International Relations is a joint initiative of Cambridge University Press and the British International Studies Association (BISA). The series will include a wide range of material, from undergraduate textbooks and surveys to research-based monographs and collaborative volumes. The aim of the series is to publish the best new scholarship in International Studies from Europe, North America and the rest of the world.

CAMBRIDGE STUDIES IN INTERNATIONAL RELATIONS

Series list continues at the end of the book

Perfect Deterrence

Frank C. Zagare

and

D. Marc Kilgour

CAMBRIDGE
UNIVERSITY PRESS

PUBLISHED BY THE PRESS SYNDICATE OF THE UNIVERSITY OF CAMBRIDGE
The Pitt Building, Trumpington Street, Cambridge, United Kingdom

CAMBRIDGE UNIVERSITY PRESS
The Edinburgh Building, Cambridge CB2 2RU, UK   www.cup.cam.ac.uk
40 West 20th Street, New York, NY 10011–4211, USA   www.cup.org
10 Stamford Road, Oakleigh, Melbourne 3166, Australia
Ruiz de Alarcón 13, 28014 Madrid, Spain

First published 2000

Printed in the United Kingdom at the University Press, Cambridge

Typeset in Palatino 10 /12.5pt   [CE]

A catalogue record for this book is available from the British Library

Library of Congress cataloguing in publication data
Zagare, Frank C.
Perfect deterrence / Frank C. Zagare, D. Marc Kilgour.
      p.   cm. – (Cambridge studies in international relations: 72)
Includes bibliographical references.
ISBN 0 521 78174 4 (hb) – ISBN 0 521 78713 0 (pb)
1. Deterrence (Strategy).   I. Kilgour, D. Marc.   II. Title.   III Series.
U162.6.Z34   2000
355.02′17 – dc 21   99–088000

ISBN 0521 78174 4 hardback
ISBN 0521 78713 0 paperback

To A. F. K. Organski and Anatol Rapoport,
who taught us so much.

Contents

Contents

Figures

Tables

Preface

Our purpose in this book is to develop a *general* theory of deterrence, applicable across the entire spectrum of human interactions, not restricted to any particular time period nor specific to any particular technology. Our starting point is the inadequacy of the standard formulation – classical deterrence theory – which we see as logically inconsistent, empirically inaccurate, and prescriptively deficient. All human conflict, we argue, shares a common dynamic that is best understood in terms of its inherent logic. We have tried to construct a theory of deterrence that balances parsimony with policy relevance, a theory that neither exaggerates nor understates critical variables. We believe that the theory of deterrence we develop in this book approaches this ideal.

Since classical deterrence theory is largely a byproduct of the Cold War era, it should be no surprise that its development has been inordinately influenced by the hostile relationship of the United States and the Soviet Union and by the haunting specter of nuclear weapons. But now that the Cold War has ended, it should be easier to see that deterrence is a universal phenomenon that operates across cultures, across technologies, and across millennia. As such, it requires a more general treatment than is typically found in the literature of international relations.

For reasons we explain later, we call our theory Perfect Deterrence. We do not claim, however, that Perfect Deterrence Theory addresses all of the inadequacies of classical deterrence theory, only its most glaring deficiencies. In particular, Perfect Deterrence Theory makes consistent use of the rationality postulate and is *prima facie* in accord with the empirical record. As well, it constitutes a framework that, with appropriate calibration, can be used to explain past, present, and future deterrence encounters, encounters that may occur in diverse social settings, in the marketplace, or on the world stage.

Our book has four parts. Part I (chapters 1–3) stakes out our theoretical position, explains why classical deterrence theory is flawed, and details Perfect Deterrence Theory's axiomatic base. Part II (chapters 4–5) applies Perfect Deterrence Theory to both mutual and unilateral direct deterrence relationships. In Part III (chapters 6–9) we turn to extended deterrence, evaluating several relevant deployment policies and delving into a number of questions associated with limited conflict and escalation spirals. Finally, Part IV (chapter 10) summarizes our theoretical results and discusses Perfect Deterrence Theory's most important policy implications, many of which run counter to conventional wisdom.

We believe that Perfect Deterrence Theory has many virtues. Unlike classical deterrence theory, which it partially subsumes, Perfect Deterrence Theory is logically consistent and empirically plausible. It is also completely general. It can be used to explore mutual, unilateral, and extended deterrence relationships. It provides useful and counter-intuitive insights into the impact of threats, showing that sometimes even credible threats can be destabilizing or that even incredible threats can be stabilizing. It offers new insights into the dynamics of interstate relationships, before, during, and after the Cold War. Perfect Deterrence Theory also provides a new and compelling assessment of extended deterrence deployment policies like Massive Retaliation and Flexible Response. Unlike classical deterrence theory, it can explain why policy-makers avoid proliferation policies. It offers a powerful perspective on the impact of force reductions and demonstrates the underlying logic of certain arms reduction initiatives. It produces a new understanding of escalation dominance and of the implications of no-first-use and warfighting deployments. And it sets a range of real-world outcomes, including limited conflicts and escalation spirals, within a coherent theoretical perspective.

As the reader will soon see, our preferred analytical tool is non-cooperative game theory. In particular, we make extensive use of the contemporary methodology of games of incomplete information. There is a long tradition of using game theory to understand deterrence, and rightfully so. Deterrence is essentially a strategic relationship, so game theory, the science of interactive decision-making, is the natural methodology for coming to grips with the dynamics of deterrence.

Throughout we have struggled with the tradeoff between theoretical rigor and accessibility. Most often we have compromised. All proofs, and the bulk of the technical material, have been relegated to a comprehensive series of appendices that can be read by themselves as a formal exercise. But the text is self-contained as well. All relevant definitions are described informally, and all important results sketched verbally. Readers who find the discussion in the text lacking in specifics will find the technical appendices helpful.

Despite its title, we readily acknowledge that our book is far from perfect. Undoubtedly, it would be even further from perfection were it not for the inspiration, assistance, and encouragement of a number of individuals and institutions. For reasons too personal to discuss fully, we dedicate this book to A. F. K. Organski and Anatol Rapoport. Until his untimely death, Ken Organski provided provocation and intellectual sustenance. His articulation of power transition theory in *World Politics* sensitized us to the empirical inadequacies of structural deterrence theory. Anatol Rapoport was among the first to explicate the fundamental logical problems that plague contemporary strategic thinking. Insights from his under-appreciated book, *Strategy and Conscience*, led to our critical assessment of decision-theoretic deterrence theory, and helped us to formulate Perfect Deterrence Theory. As well, we thank Jacek Kugler, who supplied both trenchant criticism and sound advice, Steven J. Brams, who has been the source of a wide range of interesting ideas, and Randolph Siverson and Bruce Bueno de Mesquita, who in one way or another have been especially supportive of our research program. We also thank the following individuals for their helpful suggestions regarding the manuscript: Claudio Cioffi-Revilla, Raymond Dacey, Vesna Danilovic, George Downs, Erick Duchesne, Frederic J. Fleron Jr., Frank Harvey, Michael Kraig, Douglas Lemke, Michael Nicholson, Stephen Quackenbush, William Reed, Paul Senese, Suzanne Werner, and Frank Zinni.

We thank John Haslam for unstinting editorial support, Jane Schmalz for typing the appendices, Maura Brown for preparing the index, and Ann McLellan for administrative assistance. Frank C. Zagare acknowledges the generous support of the National Science Foundation under grant no. SBR-9514160. Any opinions, findings, and conclusions or recommendations expressed in this publication are those of the authors and do not necessarily reflect the views of the National Science Foundation. D. Marc Kilgour acknowledges the research support of the Laurier Centre for Military Strategic and Disarmament Studies and the Social Sciences and Humanities Research Council of Canada. Finally, we thank Patricia Zagare and Joan Kilgour. While this book was in preparation, they were indeed perfect.

Part I
Theoretical underpinnings

1   Classical deterrence theory

International relations is a study that is plagued with platitudes.

A.F.K. Organski

For over forty-five years, the rivalry between the United States and the Soviet Union defined the world we live in. Civil wars in Africa, *coups d'état* in Latin America, revolutions in Asia, and small wars around the globe were filtered through the prism of the Cold War, not only in Washington and Moscow, but in just about every major capital on the planet.[1]

The global contest between the superpowers was both dramatic and dangerous. As is generally the case in hegemonic competitions, the stakes were high: control of the international system lay in the "balance." But for some, and later most, strategic thinkers, the dropping of atomic bombs on Hiroshima and Nagasaki instantly and permanently changed the nature of the international system and the laws that govern it. Bernard Brodie was the first to argue that the world before 1945 was fundamentally different from the world that would follow. Up to that point, he argued, "the chief purpose of our military establishment [had] been to win wars. From now on its chief purpose must be to avert them. It can have almost no other purpose" (Brodie, 1946: 76).

If the post-World War II world were truly *sui generis*, as Brodie and others argued, then a new theory would be needed to replace the conventional wisdom of the past. The enormous costs associated with warfare after 1945 would clearly be the cornerstone of this new theory. But there was another essential difference between the older and the

---

[1] This chapter is based on Zagare (1996a).

newer world order that any new theory would have to take account of.

Prior to 1939, the international system was decidedly multipolar as several great states, and a handful of lesser states, vied for power and influence around the globe. But after the defeat of Germany and Japan in 1945, this was no longer the case. The multipolar Eurocentric world had suddenly been transformed into a system dominated by two superpowers from the periphery of the European state system. The bipolar nature of the post-war period would also have to be considered by theorists trying to understand the inner workings of the new system.

It was in this context that *classical* (or *rational*) *deterrence theory* was born. Although Brodie is considered its father, the theory had a long and distinguished pedigree; as we will show, the conceptual break with past intellectual traditions was not as complete as is sometimes claimed.

As classical deterrence theory matured in the 1950s and early 1960s, many strategic thinkers nurtured its growth. Scholars like Herman Kahn, Thomas Schelling, Albert Wohlstetter, Oskar Morgenstern, William Kaufmann, and Glenn Snyder contributed mightily to its development and refinement. In time, the theoretical edifice they created came to be seen as the Rosetta Stone of the nuclear age. As a descriptive tool, it was used to explain the operation of the international system and its constituent parts; and, as a normative device, policy-makers in the United States and later the Soviet Union employed it as a guide to action. With seemingly good reason, the tenets of the theory became, in both academic and official circles, the conventional wisdom. Not only did classical deterrence theory purport to explain the absence of a US–USSR war after 1945 but, if properly heeded, could be used to all but eliminate the possibility of future superpower conflicts.

Deadly nuclear weapons and a carefully maintained strategic balance were the "twin pillars" upon which this global nirvana rested (Gaddis, 1986; Waltz, 1993). Each was seen as a necessary condition for peace and stability.[2] Thus, the superpowers were simultaneously

---

[2] As Levy (1985: 44) rightly observes, "'stability' is one of the more ambiguous concepts in the international relations literature." At one time Waltz (1964) equated stability with peace, and instability with war. But his definition left open the critical question of how to treat periods of crisis. As Lebow (1981) notes, crises fall between peace and war. This is perhaps why Mearsheimer (1990: 7) defines stability "as the absence of

enjoined not to "build down" by dramatically reducing their ability to inflict unacceptable damage on one another, and not to "build up" by seeking unilateral advantage. If ever there was a theory that enshrined the status quo, this was it.

In 1989 the Berlin Wall was torn down. A few months later the Soviet empire in Eastern Europe dissolved. By 1991 the Soviet Union itself was in tatters. Amidst the euphoria and astonishment that surrounded these events, many observers were sure that this *new* new world order, even as it evolved, would be inordinately peaceful. Indeed, some were ready to proclaim the "end of history" and, with it, the eradication of ideological struggles (Fukuyama, 1992). What was overlooked by all but a few (e.g., Huntington, 1989; Mearsheimer, 1990), however, was that this putatively ultra-stable environment differed markedly from the bipolar nuclear system that had been so widely credited with maintaining peace since the end of World War II.

Was the Cold War period, particularly after the Soviet Union achieved nuclear parity with the United States, as stable as classical deterrence theorists claimed? If so, it follows that the collapse of the Soviet Union was a destabilizing event that will shortly make us long for the "good old days" of the Cold War (Mearsheimer, 1990). But if not, then another new theoretical framework is needed, not only to explain the relative tranquillity of the past, but also to understand and manage the present and future world. In particular, if the bipolar nuclear relationship of the superpowers was as dangerous as some now assert, then the actual stability of the Cold War era remains the anomaly to be explained.

To cut to the chase: this book argues that classical deterrence theory is flawed, both empirically and logically. Moreover, this book seeks to provide a theoretical framework – Perfect Deterrence Theory – from which to view the world we are living in now. As well, by offering an explanation of the workings of bilateral conflict relationships, it attempts to come to grips with the old world order so recently left behind.

wars *and* major crises" (emphasis added). Later, Waltz (1993: 45) redefined the concept in terms of systemic durability: "systems that survive major wars thereby demonstrate their stability." To eliminate possible confusion we shall follow Mearsheimer and restrict our use of the term as follows: when we say that either a system or a deterrence relationship is stable, we mean that the status quo is likely to survive; and when we say that a system or a deterrence relationship is unstable, we mean to imply that *either* a crisis or a war is possible.

Unlike classical deterrence theory, Perfect Deterrence Theory is not confined to relationships between nuclear states. It is perhaps understandable that each generation of statesmen (and academics) sees its own era as unique. But this particular conceit, however comforting to those wishing to avoid the mistakes of their forebears, does not stand up to unimpassioned scrutiny. There is simply no compelling reason to believe that the prohibitively high costs of conflict are likely to inoculate contemporary states against warfare, no more so than there was when Sir Norman Angell (1910) made this very same argument just prior to World War I.

Because Perfect Deterrence Theory affords no special status to nuclear weapons, its logical and empirical domain is not confined to superpower relationships. Of course, this is not to say that nuclear weapons are necessarily "irrelevant," as Mueller (1988) and a few others have suggested. Rather our position is that if weapons – nuclear or otherwise – that alter the costs of war have an impact, we hope to ascertain what that impact is, and when it comes into play. But we do not believe that particularly powerful weapons necessarily require a theory unto themselves.

Put in a slightly different way, Perfect Deterrence Theory is completely general and should apply as well to conflict-of-interest situations between various combinations of large and small states, with or without nuclear capabilities. In fact, with the proper modifications and provisos, the set of interrelated models we develop may be used to explore contentious relationships between non-state actors, between organized groups, or even between individuals. We hold that the underlying dynamic of human strife, however aggregated, is fundamentally the same.

Nonetheless, because interstate conflict remains our principal focus, classical deterrence theory will be our point of departure. As Kenny (1985: ix) notes, "deterrence is the key concept for the understanding of the strategy and diplomacy of the age." And, as DeNardo (1995: 2) astutely observes, "as long as weapons of mass destruction and hostile relationships coexist in world politics, the question of deterrence will not go away." We begin, therefore, with a description of the underlying premises and principal conclusions of classical deterrence theory, detailing along the way some of its logical and empirical deficiencies.

1.1 Classical deterrence theory: assumptions and implications

Because there is no single, authoritative exposition of its major premises, an outline of classical deterrence theory must be pieced together from a variety of sources. Fortunately, there is wide consensus among theorists on both the provenance and the broad contours of the theory.[3] It is generally agreed that the roots of classical deterrence lie in the intellectual tradition that has variously been labeled "political realism," "*realpolitik*," or "power politics." This state-centric approach – which some trace back to Thucydides or earlier – posits egoistic, rational, and undifferentiated[4] units driven by their nature to maximize power (Morgenthau, 1948), or by their environment to maximize security (Waltz, 1979). When aggregated, these units constitute a self-help system that resembles Hobbes's "state of nature" where the life of man is "solitary, poore, nasty, brutish, and short." In the realists' paradigm, the international system, like Hobbes' anarchistic pre-societal state, is seen to lack an overarching authority or sovereign (Milner, 1991). Thus, each state in the system must "rely on [its] own strength and art for caution against all others" (Hobbes, 1968 [1651]: 224).

In a system where every state must provide for its own security, most realists hold that a *balance of power* is the most efficient mechanism for maintaining order (Morgenthau, 1948; Claude, 1962; Waltz, 1993; Kissinger, 1994). When power is equally distributed among actors in the system, or among the major partitions of actors – as the argument goes – peace is more likely since no one state has an incentive to upset the status quo and challenge another. By contrast, an asymmetric distribution of power provides no check on stronger states intent on enhancing their welfare. Or as Mearsheimer (1990: 18) puts it, "power inequalities invite war by increasing the potential for successful aggression; hence war is minimized when inequalities are least."

---

[3] Glaser (1989) subdivides the wider strategic literature into three categories. What we call classical deterrence theory corresponds most closely to what Glaser terms the punitive retaliation school.

[4] This is one reason why Waltz (1993: 47) goes out of his way to argue that "our conviction that the United States was the status quo and the Soviet Union the interventionist power distorted our view of reality." For Waltz and other classical deterrence theorists, *all* states are essentially the same; they are insecure, afraid, and protective of their vital interests.

Classical deterrence theory builds upon this theoretical base, and extends its domain, by considering the consequences of war in the nuclear age. In this regard, two distinct, yet compatible, strands of the theory can be discerned: *structural* (or *neorealist) deterrence theory* (Kaplan, 1957; Waltz, 1979; Mearsheimer, 1990) and what we shall refer to, for want of a better term, as *decision-theoretic deterrence theory* (Ellsberg, 1959, 1961; Schelling, 1960, 1966; Jervis, 1972; Snyder, 1972). As Allison (1971) clearly demonstrates, both of these complementary approaches to deterrence share a conceptual orientation with the realist approach to international politics. In the strategic literature, these two strands converge to form the pastiche of classical deterrence theory.

1.1.1   Structural deterrence theory

Like traditional balance of power theorists, structural deterrence theorists see the key to international stability in the distribution of power – within the system, in general, and among the great powers in particular. Most structuralists hold that when a parity relationship is combined with the enormous absolute costs of nuclear war, a deliberate (i.e., a "rational") war is at once unthinkable and virtually impossible. Those who subscribe to this view see the nuclear balance as unusually robust and stable, and credit the absence of a major superpower conflict in the post-war period directly to the enormous destructive power of nuclear weapons.

Structural deterrence theorists offer numerous explanations for the pacifying impact of bipolar structures. Waltz (1964: 882–886), for instance, argues that "the remarkable stability" of the bipolar post-war period derives from the absence of peripheries, the intensity of the competition, the "nearly constant presence of pressure and the recurrence of crisis," and the preponderant power of the two major contenders. Gaddis (1986: 105–110) cites different factors. For Gaddis, the "long-peace" of the post-war period can be traced to a "relatively simple structure" that at once reflected the realities of power, was easy to maintain, had a more stable alliance system, and could easily absorb shifts in alliance patterns. Mearsheimer (1990: 14) sees still other reasons why bipolar systems are, in general, more peaceful than multipolar systems: "First, the number of conflict dyads is fewer, leaving fewer possibilities for war. Second, deterrence is easier, because imbalances of power are fewer and more easily averted. Third, the prospects for deterrence are greater because miscalculations of relative power and of opponents' resolve are fewer and less likely."

While structural deterrence theorists may differ about exactly why bipolar systems are inherently more peaceful than multipolar systems, they are in almost unanimous agreement about the consequences of nuclear weapons.[5] Virtually every structural deterrence theorist believes that the high cost of war in the nuclear era has rendered states more prudent and, simultaneously, raised the provocation level necessary for outright conflict (Snyder and Diesing, 1977: 450–453). When these effects are combined with the pacifying tendencies of a bipolar system, a world order is produced that, *when properly managed,* is unlikely to be characterized by major interstate war.

Of course, this judgment is subject to many qualifications and provisos. Most important is the nature of current military technology. Specifically, when defensive aspects are ascendant, or are thought to be ascendant, the underlying stability of a parity relationship, be it bipolar or multipolar, is reinforced. But when offensive aspects predominate, as was *believed* to be the case in 1914, even a strict bipolar structure could witness war (Wohlstetter, 1959; Quester, 1977; Jervis, 1978; Snyder, 1984; Van Evera, 1984: 72).

The intricate relationship between system structure, the cost of war, and the characteristics of weapons systems is succinctly captured in a formal model of a missile war developed by Intriligator and Brito (1984, 1987). Since this model reflects the underlying assumptions of structural deterrence theory and highlights several of its important and non-obvious implications, we shall use its original graphical representation (figure 1.1) as an organizing device for summarizing the principal tenets of structural deterrence theory.[6] We realize that our tack is fraught with danger: we risk oversimplifying an extensive literature characterized by nuance and subtlety.[7] Nonetheless, undeterred, we shall proceed according to this plan. The reader should

---

[5] A concise summary of the debate about the war proneness of different systemic configurations can be found in Kegley and Raymond (1994). See also Sabrosky (1985).

[6] For an incomplete information game model that reaches similar conclusions about the conditions of war and peace, see Bueno de Mesquita, Morrow, and Zorick (1997). In this model, which is based on assumptions that are compatible with classical deterrence theory, the probability that the status quo will be challenged increases as the observable military advantage of one side or the other increases.

[7] See, for instance, the wide range of responses (and non-responses) to Vasquez's penetrating evaluation of the realist paradigm in the December 1997 issue of the *American Political Science Review.*

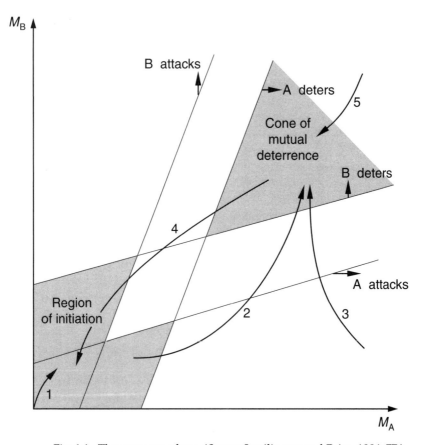

Fig. 1.1. The weapons plane. (*Source*: Intriligator and Brito, 1984: 77.)

keep in mind, though, that we are attempting to offer a *consensus* view of a diverse and multifaceted approach to international conflict.[8]

As one might expect, there are two actors (here called State A and State B) in this model. Like the individuals in Hobbes' state of nature, the states are linked in a hostile relationship characterized by mutual mistrust and fear. Both states are rational and their relationship is governed by the absolute cost each is capable of imposing on the other in a conflict. Note that the states are undifferentiated units: each considers attacking the other. They are also egotistical: each takes into

---

[8] For a balanced discussion of the varieties of structural realist thought, see Elman (1996).

account the costs it can impose on the other only to the extent that those costs alter the other's behavior and, consequently, its own payoff. Ethical, moral, and legal considerations do not enter into either state's decision-making framework.

War costs are determined by the number and characteristics of the weapons in each state's arsenal, and by the strategic choices of each state's decision-makers. Strategic decisions involve two critical choices: "First there is a choice of targets between counterforce targets of enemy weapons and countervalue targets of enemy cities and industrial capability ... Second, there is a choice of rate of fire between the extreme values of a maximum rate, i.e., firing all weapons as rapidly as possible, and a zero rate, i.e., holding weapons in reserve for later use" (Intriligator and Brito, 1987: 15). A state's choice of a target and rate of fire together constitute its *grand strategy*.[9]

In the model, the two states choose optimal grand strategies that will inflict certain costs on one another when and if a war occurs. The anticipation of these costs, in turn, drives each state's behavior. In particular, State A *attacks* State B "if it can launch a first strike on B ... and reduce the number of B weapons sufficiently that B does not have enough weapons left to inflict unacceptable casualties on A in a massive retaliation strike." By contrast, State A *deters* State B "if given a first strike by B ... A can absorb this strike and have enough weapons left to inflict an unacceptable level of casualties to B in a retaliatory massive retaliation strike" (Intriligator and Brito, 1987: 16, 18). Notice that the incentive to attack is presumed. Consequently, there is only one determining variable in each state's calculus – the cost of attacking.

Given optimal targeting and firing strategies, the costs and benefits of attacking depend on the absolute number of weapons in both arsenals. The consequences of the states' cost/benefit calculations can be determined by locating their combined arsenals in the *weapons plane* of figure 1.1. In this figure, the number of missiles available to State A, M_A, is measured along the horizontal axis, while the vertical axis measures the number of missiles possessed by State B, M_B.

Notice the four critical thresholds represented by the two sets of parallel lines. One line in each set represents the cost level beyond which A or B is deterred; the other represents the point below which

---

[9] Wagner (1991) uses game theory to evaluate the strategic implications of counterforce targeting options.

benefits outweigh costs so that either A or B is motivated to attack. The intersections of these lines define nine different regions in the weapons plane. (Ignore for now the curved arrows indicating movements on the plane.) The behavioral patterns anticipated in each region constitute the principal conclusions of the model. These conclusions are congruent with the major tenets of structural deterrence theory.[10]

1. *Parity relationships, when coupled with high war costs, are especially peaceful*. When war costs are mutually high, bilateral strategic relationships fall into the shaded region in the northeast section of figure 1.1 – called the *cone of mutual deterrence*. Clearly, relations within this cone reflect the MAD (Mutual Assured Destruction) condition: each state can inflict unacceptable costs on the other, regardless of which attacks first. All structural deterrence theorists (by definition), and most balance of power theorists, hold that as soon as this condition is met, peace is at hand (see, *inter alia*, Kaufmann, 1956; Brodie, 1959; Snyder, 1961; Glaser, 1990; Mearsheimer, 1990).

By contrast, when the cost of outright conflict is low, even parity may be insufficient to preclude confrontations, suggesting that "war is always possible among states armed only with conventional weapons" (Waltz, 1993: 77). In figure 1.1, the sawtooth-shaped region adjacent to the origin represents all strategic relationships characterized by low war costs. For obvious reasons, Intriligator and Brito call it the *region of initiation*. In the center section of the region, where parity reigns, neither side can deter the other; conflict is almost inevitable. Thus, "this portion is one of virtually forced preemption in which it is greatly advantageous to initiate rather than retaliate. The 'reciprocal fear of surprise attack' based on the tremendous advantage in striking first forces both sides to initiate, each trying to preempt the attack of the other" (Intriligator and Brito, 1984: 73–74).

2. *Asymmetric power relationships are associated with crises and war*. The most precarious form of asymmetry occurs when neither state can deter the other (i.e., when war costs are mutually low), but when one of them nonetheless calculates an advantage in attacking first. Thus, along with the center portion of the region of initiation (see above), both the lower right and upper left portions exhibit "instability against war outbreak" (Intriligator and Brito, 1984: 74).

Still, even when one state can deter the other, some form of conflict

---

[10] For the sensitivity of these results to the model's initial conditions, see Mayer (1986).

is likely. This conclusion follows from the assumption that all states have similar concerns and motivations (i.e., states are undifferentiated units). Consequently, general deterrence is unlikely to succeed[11] in the entire area of the weapons plane below the line labeled "A attacks" and to the left of the line labeled "B attacks." Whenever at least one state is undeterred, war remains a distinct possibility. Of course, outright conflict *might* be averted if the disadvantaged state follows a policy of appeasement and adjusts its policies to reflect the stronger state's interests (Kugler and Zagare, 1990: 60–63). In either case, though, the status quo is unlikely to survive.

3. *As the absolute costs of war increase,* ceteris paribus, *the probability of war decreases.* Or in Mearsheimer's (1990: 19) words, "the more horrible the prospect of war, the less likely it is to occur." In fact, with an overkill capability that places both states deep within the cone of mutual deterrence, the probability of war "may be reduced to virtually zero" (Intriligator and Brito, 1981: 256).

The functional relationship between war costs and war proneness can be observed by considering the strategic implications of various trajectories (represented by curved arrows) through the weapons plane of figure 1.1. As one moves northeast away from the region of initiation (trajectory 2) where each state can attack the other, or away from either asymmetric area in which only one state can attack (for

---

[11] Like "stability" (see footnote 2), deterrence "success" is an "essentially contested" concept (MacIntyre, 1973). One reason is that success and failure are relative terms (Levy, 1988: 498). If deterrence success is equated with the absence of war, deterrence can be said to have succeeded even when a crisis occurs, or when one state is able to win concessions from another by threatening war. Huth's (1988a: 25) coding scheme is consistent with this conceptualization. For example, Huth codes the Berlin crisis of 1948 and the 1954–55 confrontation between China and the United States over Quemoy and Matsu as successes. Since the domain of Huth's empirical study is restricted, in part, to "immediate" deterrence encounters in which one state is "seriously considering attacking" another (Morgan, 1977: 33), his definition is understandable. But in another sense, deterrence failed: a challenge occurred. To account for these subtleties, we reserve the term "deterrence success" to indicate situations in which the status quo is not disturbed. We use the terms "deterrence success" and "general deterrence success" synonymously. (The term "general deterrence" refers to hostile relationships in which no state "is anywhere near mounting an attack" against its opponent [Morgan, 1977: 28].) We take "immediate deterrence success" to imply that the status quo has been contested but that an all-out conflict (e.g., war) has been avoided. Clearly, immediate deterrence cannot succeed unless general deterrence has failed. Finally, we equate an "immediate deterrence failure" with all-out conflict. In chapter 9, we relax our qualifications to take into account a wider range of outcomes than we currently consider.

instance, trajectory 3), toward the cone of mutual deterrence where war costs are mutually prohibitive, the probability of war initiation decreases dramatically.[12] By contrast, movement downward through the cone (see trajectories 4 and 5) toward the origin of the weapons plane and the region of initiation (where war costs are lower) only increases the prospect of conflict, especially when such bilateral disarmament is "carried too far" (Intriligator and Brito, 1987: 22).

In sum, structural deterrence theory attributes the "long-peace" of the Cold War era to the *balance of terror*, that grizzly combination of rough parity and high destructiveness unique to the nuclear age. From this axiom flow several practical, policy-orientated, conclusions.

- *First, quantitative arms races, which serve to increase the cost of conflict, can help prevent wars* (Gray, 1974: 209).

Like the Roman military strategist Vegetius, then, most classical deterrence theorists hold that proper preparation for war reduces its likelihood. For this reason, they worked against the nuclear freeze movement during the 1980s, opposed all bilateral – or worse – unilateral efforts to disarm during the Cold War and, in the early days of the Reagan era, favored a shift to single-warhead missiles (Art, 1985; Aspin, 1986).

- *By contrast, qualitative arms races, which threaten to provide one side or another with a first-strike advantage, increase the probability of preemptive war.*[13]

This is one reason why most classical deterrence theorists opposed the development of more accurate delivery systems, resisted the deployment of missiles armed with multiple warheads (Jervis, 1978; Scoville, 1981), and disputed the implementation of counterforce targeting doctrines (Van Evera, 1984). Also related were worries about

---

[12] Trajectory 1, which begins at the origin of figure 1.1, is an exception to this statement. Clearly, when neither state has any weapons, outright conflict is impossible. Thus, any movement away from the origin into the region of initiation raises the probability of war.

[13] For a contrary view, see Huntington (1958). It is worth mentioning, however, that Huntington's argument that quantitative arms races increase the probability of war rests upon the supposition that they lead to an asymmetric distribution of power. In Huntington's view, qualitative arms races reinforce parity and, therefore, reduce war's likelihood.

a "window of vulnerability" in the late 1970s and early 1980s (Nitze, 1976/77; Johnson, 1983).

- *Comprehensive and effective defense systems make conflict more likely.*

Because of the purported consequences of strategic defense systems, most classical deterrence theorists in the United States worked against the Strategic Defense Initiative (or "Star Wars" program) of the Reagan administration (Bundy *et al.*, 1984/85), continue to oppose anti-ballistic missile (ABM) systems, and support the SALT I Treaty that first limited and eventually abolished them (National Academy of Sciences, 1997: 42–46).

- *The selective proliferation of nuclear weapons can help prevent war and promote peace.*

Although often unappreciated, this argument rests on, and indeed flows from, the supposition that nuclear deterrence is "very robust" (Berkowitz, 1985: 117). Recognizing the logical connection between premise and conclusion, many classical deterrence theorists have supported the "prudent" dissemination of nuclear technology.[14] Early in the nuclear age, for instance, Oskar Morgenstern (1959, 74–77) submitted that it was in the interest of the United States to provide the Soviet Union with an invulnerable strategic retaliatory force,[15] and Pierre Gallois (1961) defended the French decision to go nuclear because he believed that an independent nuclear force would reduce French vulnerability to political coercion and outright attack.

More recently, Mearsheimer (1990: 54) has suggested that a German nuclear capability is "the best hope for avoiding war in post-Cold War Europe" and argued that peace is much more likely if Ukraine retains its nuclear force (Mearsheimer, 1993). And, if former Soviet spymaster Pavel Sudoplatov (1994: 195) is to be believed, it was precisely the logic of proliferation that led several of the West's leading scientists to pass

---

[14] While this is a minority position, it is telling that support for controlled proliferation policies comes from writers (e.g., Waltz and Mearsheimer) whose work is most explicitly theoretical.

[15] Morgenstern was particularly concerned with the impact of an asymmetric strategic relationship that, paradoxically, might cause a weaker, more vulnerable state (i.e., the Soviet Union) to preempt a stronger, less vulnerable state (i.e., the United States). Note, however, that Morgenstern presumed that the chance of war between two states possessing an invulnerable second-strike nuclear capability was remote.

sensitive information derived from the Manhattan Project to the Soviets: "Since [J. Robert] Oppenheimer, [Niels] Bohr and [Enrico] Fermi were fierce opponents of violence, they would seek to prevent a nuclear war, creating a balance of power through sharing the secrets of atomic energy." Waltz (1981), Intriligator and Brito (1981), Bueno de Mesquita and Riker (1982), Van Evera (1990/91), and Posen (1993), *inter alia*, have also made the case for the discriminate distribution of nuclear technology.[16]

- *Accidental war is the gravest threat to peace.*

Here, too, the argument rests on the theoretical consequences of the confluence of parity and the high costs of nuclear war (see, for example, Morgenstern, 1959: 69; Smoker and Bradley, 1988). When both conditions are present, a deliberate (i.e., rational) war is improbable; hence, nuclear wars are most likely to occur by mistake (Abrams, 1988; Intriligator and Brito, 1981; Sagan, 1993; Brito and Intriligator, 1996). To prevent accidental nuclear war, classical deterrence theorists argue for redundancy in command, control, communication, and intelligence (C^3I) systems (Bracken, 1983) and against "launch on warning" doctrines (Blair, 1993: 174).

1.1.2 Decision-theoretic deterrence theory

Unlike structural deterrence theory, which finds the key to interstate stability in the structure and distribution of power, decision-theoretic deterrence theory focuses on the interplay of outcomes, preferences, and choices in determining interstate conflict behavior. The genre includes both formal and informal rational choice (expected utility) analyses and subsequent game-theoretic refinements. In the discussion that follows, we lump all these methodologies together, ignoring important differences. Right now our purpose is simply to highlight their common theoretical point of view.[17]

---

[16] Structural deterrence theorists do not, however, favor disseminating nuclear weapons to "crazy states" or their "irrational leaders." As we note below, however, this escape clause is inconsistent with two fundamental axioms of their approach; namely, the assumption that states are undifferentiated and rational. Thus, like Great Britain during the eighteenth and nineteenth centuries (Organski, 1958), Iraq, Libya, Iran, Cuba, and North Korea appear to be the current exceptions to the rule that *all* states are self-interested power maximizers.

[17] Our label for this group of theorists could be misleading. We do not include all expected utility and game-theoretic models of deterrence in this category, only those that share the modal assumptions discussed below.

	State B	
	Cooperate *(C)*	Defect *(D)*
Cooperate *(C)*	*Status Quo* (3,3)	*B Wins* (2,4)
State A		
Defect *(D)*	*A Wins* (4,2)	*Conflict* (1,1)

> (x,y) = payoff to A, payoff to B
> 4 = best; 3 = next-best; 2 = next-worst; 1 = worst

Fig. 1.2. Chicken as an informal model for deterrence.

Beginning where structural theorists leave off, the decision-making strand of classical deterrence theory posits a situation in which nuclear war is so costly that only an "irrational" leader could consider it a means of conflict resolution. Thus, a critical *deduction* of structural deterrence theory is accepted and embedded as an *axiom* by decision-theoretic deterrence theorists.

Since nuclear war was taken to be at once irrational and unthinkable, interstate crises came to be seen as its functional equivalent, that is, a contest for exhibiting and measuring power (Waltz, 1964: 884; Hoffman, 1965). To represent war's surrogate, most classical deterrence theorists used, as a formal or informal metaphor, the deceivingly simple game of *Chicken* (or a structural equivalent).[18]

Chicken is a stark model of the interaction of two decision-makers.

---

[18] As is well known, this game models a contest reportedly indulged in by reckless teenagers who would drive cars toward each other at high speed. The first driver to swerve was the "chicken," and was disgraced. Of course, not swerving was much worse – for both drivers. (For applications of Chicken to deterrence, see, *inter alia*, Kahn, 1960, 1962, 1965; Snyder, 1971; Hopkins and Mansbach, 1973; Brams, 1975, 1985; Jervis, 1979; Powell, 1987, 1990; Nicholson, 1989; and especially, Schelling, 1960, 1966.)

As before, call them State A and State B. Each state is seen as having two broad strategic choices: either to *cooperate* (*C*) by supporting the status quo, or to *defect* (*D*) from cooperation by seeking to overturn it. These alternative choices (or strategies) give rise to four broad outcomes: if both states cooperate, the *Status Quo* (outcome SQ) prevails; if one state cooperates and the other does not, the non-cooperator wins or gains an advantage (either *A Wins* [outcome DC] or *B Wins* [outcome CD]); and if neither state cooperates, *Conflict* (for now, read "nuclear war") occurs (outcome DD). By definition, in Chicken, each player most prefers to gain the advantage and "win" the game, next prefers mutual cooperation (i.e., the *Status Quo*), next prefers to concede the advantage to its opponent and, significantly, least prefers *Conflict*.[19]

The strategies, outcomes, and ordinal rankings are summarized in figure 1.2, which for now we treat as an informal model rather than as a *strategic-form* game.[20] Preference rankings are represented by an ordered pair in each cell of the matrix that indicates State A's (row's) and State B's (column's) preference ranking of the four outcomes. The most-preferred outcome is indicated by a rank of 4, the next most-preferred by 3, and so on. For example, in Chicken, outcome DC (*A Wins*) is State A's best outcome (i.e., rank 4 for A) and State B's next-worst outcome (i.e., rank 2 for B).

Chicken captures well the underlying assumptions of realism in general[21] and classical deterrence theory in particular. When analyzed as a *non-cooperative game* in which binding agreements are not permitted, it mirrors the anarchy condition; as a *non-zero-sum game*, it captures the general understanding among classical deterrence theorists that, in the nuclear age at least, states have a common interest in avoiding war;[22] and as a *two-person game*, it starkly reflects the bipolar post-war international system.

---

[19] We use a simple convention to distinguish between outcomes in a game model and real-world events with the same name: game outcomes are italicized; analogous real-world events are not.

[20] For a definition of strategic-form (or normal-form) games, see chapter 2. An informal treatment allows us to describe a wider range of decision-theoretic deterrence theory. As we move on, however, our analysis will become progressively more formal.

[21] For the general compatibility of game theory and realism, see Jervis (1988a).

[22] This consensus took some time to develop and was due, in no small part, to the work of Thomas Schelling. Reflecting perhaps the intensity of the McCarthy period in the United States of the 1950s, almost all of the early applications of game theory analyzed interstate conflicts as zero-sum games. (See, for instance, McDonald and

As well, the players are presumed to be undifferentiated (i.e., "billiard balls"), rational, and egotistical: each most prefers to gain an advantage. Most significant, though, from the point of view of theory construction, is Chicken's defining characteristic: conflict is the *worst* possible outcome for both sides.

Consider the theoretical implications of this critical, yet not clearly justified *assumption*: by accepting the Chicken analogy, decision-theoretic deterrence theorists perforce presume the "irrationality" of outright conflict;[23] they structure a model in which no "rational" leader would *ever* purposefully choose to resist aggression; and thereby, they presuppose that only irrational and accidental wars are possible. In other words, by uncritically embracing the Chicken analogy, this group of classical deterrence theorists takes as given many of the major *propositions* of structural deterrence theory!

At this juncture one might conclude that decision-theoretic deterrence theorists presume too much, that the assumptions embedded within a Chicken model are so prejudicial that an unimpassioned inquiry into the dynamics of interstate conflict is no longer possible. But such a judgment would be premature. Assumptions, even heroic assumptions, are simply useful devices for facilitating the construction and refinement of theories (Friedman, 1953). Rather, it is the collection of propositions that flows from such theoretical primitives that is telling. In the end, it is the empirical accuracy of these propositions, not the assumptions that led to them, by which a theory must be judged.

Viewed in this light, decision-theoretic deterrence theory serves a particularly useful purpose. By presupposing the world envisioned by structural deterrence theory, the models developed by decision-theoretic deterrence theorists help to specify the logical implications of structural deterrence theory. In other words, these models map out what optimal strategic behavior would be in the world implied by structural deterrence theory. Thus, an evaluation of the theoretical consequences and the empirical accuracy of the models of decision-

---

Tukey, 1949; McDonald, 1950; Haywood, 1954; Williams, 1954; and Morgenstern 1959, 1961a.) When *The Strategy of Conflict* was re-published in 1980 by Harvard University Press, Schelling remarked in a new preface that the idea that conflict and common interest were not mutually exclusive, so obvious to him, was among the work's most important contributions.

[23] For instance, a mutually worst outcome cannot be an equilibrium in any sense in any game with strict preference rankings over outcomes.

theoretic deterrence theorists can help put structural deterrence theory itself to a more refined test. It is with this noble purpose in mind, then, that we turn to a brief description of the conceptual model lurking beneath the decision-making strand of classical deterrence theory.

Perhaps the easiest way to describe the underpinnings of decision-theoretic deterrence theory is to consider Chicken in light of an expected utility model of blackmail developed by Daniel Ellsberg (1959). Ellsberg's *critical risk* model fully reflects Kissinger's (1994: 481) view that the "art of policy is to create a calculation of the risks and rewards that affect the adversary's calculations." Underlying this model is a set of assumptions common to many decision-theoretic deterrence theorists (Wagner, 1992a).

First is *strategic uncertainty*. Neither player knows for sure which strategy the other will choose. Without a doubt, this lack of information inordinately confounds the decision problem for the players in Chicken. For instance, say that State A knows for sure that State B plans to cooperate. Then its best choice is to defect, because defection yields A's most-preferred outcome and cooperation its second most-preferred outcome. Conversely, if A knows for sure that B plans to defect, then its best choice is to cooperate. (Defection gives A its worst outcome, cooperation its next-worst.) But without certain knowledge of B's choice, State A's optimal choice is unclear.

Second is the *subjectivity* assumption. Although the players are uncertain about each other's behavior, each makes a subjective estimate (based perhaps on intelligence reports, past experiences, prophecies, astrological readings or, as Hans Morgenthau once suggested, hunches) of the other's behavior, expressed as a subjective probability attached to each of the opponent's possible actions. Each player also assesses, again subjectively, the other's (cardinal) utilities for the possible outcomes, i.e., the worth of each outcome to the opponent.[24] Of course, a player knows its own utilities.

Finally, there is the *rationality* assumption. Using the probability estimates and the utility assessments, the players act *as if* they were expected utility maximizers. In other words, each player chooses its strategy so as to achieve the highest expected utility. For example, in

[24] By utility, we mean von Neumann–Morgenstern utility. (For a discussion, see Morrow, 1994a: ch. 2.) What is important is to be able to interpret the expected utility of a lottery over outcomes as the utility of the lottery itself. For examples, see footnote 25.

Chicken, a player cooperates when the expected utility of cooperation, $E(C)$, exceeds the expected utility of defection, $E(D)$, and defects otherwise.[25]

In Ellsberg's model, which is based on Chicken, each player's *critical risk* occurs when the expected utilities of its two strategies are equal, that is, when $E(C) = E(D)$.[26] This risk is critical in that it represents the maximum risk of conflict (DD) a defecting player is willing to tolerate. At any higher risk level, a rational player simply cooperates. Hence, the lower a player's critical risk, the more likely it is to cooperate; the higher a player's critical risk, the more likely it is to defect.

The calculations seem simple enough, but the choices facing decision-makers involved in a crisis clearly are not. Lurking in the background are two considerable dangers. The most obvious is the very real chance of disaster: if both players stand firm and defect, an "accidental" war (that no one really wants) results. But there is also the risk of losing the advantage by making unnecessary concessions. The rub, of course, is that to avoid one calamity, one must face the other. It is small wonder, then, that during the Cold War period, crises came to be seen as "competitions in risk taking." Everything else being equal, the player with the highest critical risk would "win" the contest.[27]

Given the risks, what is the best way to play this most dangerous game? Like latter day Machiavellis, decision-theoretic deterrence theorists were at the ready to provide policy-makers with answers to this question, proffering sage advice for managing acute interstate crises. The tactics they suggested were both novel and counter-intuitive. The prescriptions soon gained wide currency in both official

---

[25] To illustrate one way to make this calculation, assume that that the ordinal ranks in figure 1.2 represent utilities and that State A believes that there is a 40 percent probability that State B will defect. Then

$$E(C) = 3\,(.6) + 2\,(.4) = 2.6$$
$$E(D) = 4\,(.6) + 1\,(.4) = 2.8$$

Since $E(D) > E(C)$, State A should defect.

[26] In the previous example, A's critical risk is .5 because that is the "crossover" point where $E(C) = E(D)$. Any estimate of the probability that B plans to defect greater than .5 makes it rational for A to cooperate, and conversely. (This calculation follows a formula given by Jervis, 1972. For an alternative method of calculating a player's critical risk, see Snyder, 1972.)

[27] Powell's (1990) model reaches the opposite conclusion. For a discussion, see chapter 2.

(Kaplan, 1983) and academic circles in the United States, "even though there was little evidence for the validity of the propositions" and even though several recommended tactics were "contrary to common sense" (Jervis, 1979: 289, 292) or appeared "bizarre" (Rapoport, 1992). Indeed, despite empirical, logical, and ethical challenges (Rapoport, 1964; Green, 1966; Young, 1968; George and Smoke, 1974; Smoke, 1977; Snyder and Diesing, 1977; and Zagare, 1987, 1990a), the collected wisdom of decision-theoretic deterrence theory became the conventional wisdom, and remains so to this day.

It is important to keep in mind that all of the strategic imperatives discovered by these "Neo-Clausewitzians," as Rapoport (1968) pejoratively referred to classical deterrence theorists, flow from the confluence of Ellsberg's critical risk model and the structural dynamics of Chicken. Jervis (1979: 301), for example, once confessed that he gained insight into deterrence "only by deducing the bargaining tactics that should be effective in the game of Chicken."

To manage crises successfully, decision-makers were counseled to take actions that decreased the other player's critical risk, making it more likely that the other player would back down. Snyder (1972) provides an extensive list of manipulative bargaining tactics and a useful scheme for categorizing them. *Critical risk tactics* include both *accommodative moves* designed to make cooperation more attractive for an opponent, and *coercive moves* that make defection more costly and, hence, less attractive. Much more provocative, however, are *commitment tactics* that aim to alter an opponent's estimate of the probability that one intends to defect.[28] The appeal of committing, even probabilistically, to a hard-line strategy in Chicken is obvious: *ceteris paribus*, the higher an opponent's estimate of the probability that one intends to defect, the lower the opponent's critical risk and the higher the opponent's probability of concession – and conversely.

The best way to assure victory during a crisis, then, is to make the opponent believe that concession is impossible. Of course, the same incentive exists for the opponent so that movement from theory to practice is not altogether straightforward. Commitment is an art, not a science (Schelling, 1966: ch. 2). Nonetheless, in coercive bargaining situations, statesmen are counseled to "relinquish the initiative" by

---

[28] See Dixit and Nalebuff (1991: ch. 6) for an informal discussion and a more contemporary listing of commitment tactics.

making an "irrevocable commitment" not to back down. Schelling (1966: 43) succinctly explains why:

> If you are faced with an enemy who thinks you would turn and run if he kept advancing, and if the bridge is there to run across, he may keep advancing. He may advance to the point where, if you do not run, a clash is automatic. Calculating what is in your long-run interest, you may turn and cross the bridge. At least, he may expect you to. But if you burn the bridge so that you cannot retreat, and in sheer desperation there is nothing you can do but defend yourself, he has a new calculation to make. He cannot count on what you would *prefer* to do if he were advancing irresistibly; he must decide instead what he ought to do if you were incapable of anything but resisting him.

In an even more colorful example, Kahn (1962: 11) extols the benefits of ripping the steering wheel off the ship of state, a move that virtually forces the opponent to concede. (Rapoport [1968] calls this "Chicken à la Kahn.") Similarly Jervis (1972: 279) points out that a statesman could dramatically increase the probability of prevailing in a crisis by "making a commitment to stand firm," and Ellsberg (1959: 357) notes that there are advantages to be gained should a blackmailer "voluntarily but irreversibly give up his freedom of choice." Kissinger (1979: 622) puts it in slightly different language: "A leader must choose carefully and thoughtfully the issues over which to face confrontation. He should do so only for major objectives. Once he is committed, however, his obligation is to end the confrontation rapidly. For this he must convey implacability."[29]

A second type of commitment tactic involves a player manipulating its own payoffs (Schelling, 1960: 126–128). By making one's own defection less costly, or cooperation less attractive, for example by increasing domestic audience costs (Fearon, 1994b), one can make concession appear less probable to the opponent. Again, the opponent's defection would become less likely.

Decision-theoretic deterrence theorists have likewise offered numerous ways to change an opponent's perception of one's own evaluation of the outcomes. For example, statesmen (and stateswomen) could make a public pledge not to back down, or could attempt to "link" the present conflict to future confrontations (Jervis, 1970). Both these maneuvers are techniques to persuade the opponent that one's cost of backing down is high. The most provocative

---

[29] See Payne (1981) for a similar argument.

stratagem, though, is Schelling's (1966: 37–42) notorious suggestion (see also Ellsberg [1959: 360] and Jervis [1972: 285]) that a player feign "irrationality." By appearing oblivious to the obviously high cost of a collision, one might be able to induce an opponent to "chicken out."

Collectively, the prescriptions of decision-theoretic deterrence theory extend structural deterrence theory by considering the micro-level implications of international structure and the high costs of nuclear conflict. The clear emphasis of this influential sub-literature of deterrence is on devising mechanisms for dealing with the world as seen by structural deterrence theorists, a world in which all-out conflicts are at once unthinkable and virtually impossible, a world in which crisis replaces war, a world in which the greatest threats to peace are miscalculation, misperception, and accident, and, therefore, a world in which deft bargaining skills are essential. To deal with this world, decision-theoretic deterrence theorists urge not caution but abandon, not flexibility but implacability, and not rationality but irrationality.

1.2   Empirical anomalies

At first blush, the worldview of classical deterrence theory is compelling. After all, the theory seems to explain the most important empirical characteristic of the post-1945 period: the absence of major superpower war. Accepting this perfect congruence between fact and theory, it is little wonder that structural realism in general, and classical deterrence theory in particular, was, and is, "the dominant school of thought in International Relations theory" (Buzan, Jones, and Little, 1993: 1).

Still, there are some nagging doubts. As Jervis (1985: 6) – wearing a different theoretical hat – points out, "many events present unexplained puzzles for standard deterrence theory." Or as Mueller (1995: 47) writes, "This view of deterrence ... simply does not explain very well how states actually behave." Consider the following empirical anomalies:

- *A balance of power is not a good predictor of peace.*

Or as even Waltz (1993: 77) observes, "if Mearsheimer is right in believing that an 'equality of power ... among the major powers' minimizes the likelihood of war, World War I should never have been fought." Even more troubling is that precisely the opposite appears to be the case. World War I is not an anomaly. *All* major power wars for which there are reliable data have been fought under parity conditions, including the Franco-Prussian war, the Russo-Japanese war, World War II (Organski and Kugler, 1980: ch. 1), the Seven Weeks War (Bueno de Mesquita, 1990), the Crimean War, and the War of Italian Unification (Kim, 1989, 1991). As well, a growing empirical literature suggests that a rough equality of power resources is associated with other, lesser, types of militarized interstate disputes (Garnham, 1976; Weede, 1976; Siverson and Sullivan, 1983; Houwelling and Siccama, 1988a, 1988b; Gochman, 1990; Sullivan, 1990; Bremer, 1992; Bueno de Mesquita and Lalman, 1992; Geller, 1993; Leng, 1993; Lemke, 1996; and de Soysa, Oneal, and Park, 1997).

The alert reader will recall, however, that classical deterrence theorists consider a balance of capabilities as a necessary, though not a sufficient condition, for deterrence stability. For peace to reign, warfare must also be excessively costly. In this view, each of the "two pillars: bipolarity and nuclear weapons" (Waltz, 1993: 44) must be present before war can be considered untenable. To be sure, no major power war has, as yet, occurred under conditions of nuclear parity. But it is also entirely possible that this perfect correlation is spurious – that nuclear war has been avoided not because of nuclear weapons, but in spite of them.

How could we tell the difference? One indirect, albeit revealing, way to address this vexing epistemological problem is to examine the behavior of nuclear powers involved in major interstate disputes. If nuclear weapons have in fact altered the very fiber of international politics, some behavioral trace should be observable in those conflicts that have fallen short of outright warfare. In other words, conflicts involving a nuclear power should be resolved differently than disputes involving only non-nuclear states.

Surprisingly little data buttresses this proposition. In fact, there is a great deal of systematic empirical evidence to the contrary. For example, Huth (1990) reports an association between the possession of nuclear weapons and immediate deterrence success.[30] But Fearon's (1994a: 250) reanalysis of Huth's statistical study strongly suggests that the reported association can be explained by selection effects.

---

[30] We note that Huth, Gelpi, and Bennett's (1993: 618) finding that a "defender's possession of a second-strike capability has a powerful deterrent effect on the escalatory behavior of the challenger" is not inconsistent with the theory of deterrence to be developed in this work.

Specifically, threats to nuclear powers "will most often have been made with the initial belief that the defender was probably not willing to use force on the issue. Hence a costly signal in response will be comparatively likely to succeed."[31]

Likewise, after an analysis of fourteen intense post-war disputes, Kugler (1984: 479) finds "it difficult to conclude that nuclear weapons have directly affected the outcomes of extreme crises or deterred conflicts." In the same vein, Betts's (1987: 16, 20) study of those "East–West crises in which some sort of specifically nuclear threat was made" led him to observe that "both the balance of interests and balance of power theories prove useful for explaining either the threat or the response, but neither appears adequate to account for both sides' behavior at the same time." And, after examining fifty-four cases of extended deterrence, Huth and Russett (1984: 29) report that "the long-term balance of forces and the defender's possession of nuclear weapons make little difference" for whether deterrence fails or succeeds.

A number of other investigations strike the same cord (see, *inter alia*, Russett, 1963; George and Smoke, 1974; Blechman and Kaplan, 1978; Organski and Kugler, 1980; Huth, 1988a, 1988b; Huth and Russett, 1988; Geller, 1990; and Huth, Bennett, and Gelpi, 1992).[32] Taken as a group, these studies indicate that, in militarized interstate disputes at least, nuclear weapons do not afford any special advantage to states that possess them, whether or not another party to the dispute also has them. There is little empirical support, therefore, for the proposition that states deport themselves differently in the nuclear age than they did before it: factors other than nuclear capability continue to account for most observable conflict behavior.[33]

- *An asymmetric distribution of power is not a good predictor of major interstate war.*

Just as parity conditions are not associated with peace, there is no clear association of conflict with power asymmetries. Apparently, even when the motivation exists, states do not automatically jump through their "windows of opportunity" (Lebow, 1984; Jervis, 1985: 6). Indeed, the absence of a superpower conflict during the periods of

[31] For a model linking domestic political processes and audience costs, see Smith (1998a).

[32] For an illuminating review of this literature, see Harvey and James (1992).

[33] To some extent, this lack of evidence may also be attributable to selection effects.

American nuclear superiority constitutes the foremost empirical puzzle for classical deterrence theory. The abstract version of the theory clearly implies that the United States should have exploited the obvious strategic advantage it enjoyed throughout the 1950s and the early 1960s, not only against the Soviet Union but against lesser powers as well. As Jervis (1988a: 342) points out, realists are unable to "explain the fact that the United States did not conquer Canada sometime in the past hundred years." Or as Gaddis (1997: 88) puts it, "the actions the United States took [during the early Cold War years] failed to fit traditional patterns of great power behavior."

To explain away this glaring anomaly, classical deterrence theory, perforce, admits an exception to the standard realist assumption that all states are "undifferentiated" power or security maximizers, and its corollary that "*all* other states are potential threats" (Mearsheimer, 1990: 12, emphasis added). Like Great Britain during the heyday of nineteenth-century balance of power politics, the United States was considered exempt from Morgenthau's (1948) famous dictum that "statesmen think and act in terms of interests defined as power" (Organski, 1958). With more than a little legerdemain, the United States was characterized either as a status quo power that lacked the usual motivation to maximize its security interests, or as a self-deterred democracy unwilling to violate moral precepts by waging an unjust offensive war. While most Western observers lauded the United States for its self-restraint, others – more true to the realist paradigm – urged a preventive war and a "rollback" of the Iron Curtain (Kahan, 1975: ch. 1).

Ad hoc arguments like these are almost impossible to refute, and we shall not try. Note, however, the difficulty of sustaining a similar argument in the Chinese–Soviet case. Despite a highly contentious political relationship, the Soviet Union considered exploiting its preponderant position *vis-à-vis* China in the late 1960s and the early 1970s, but chose not to. For its part, China was *not* deterred from pressing its border claims along the Amur and Ussuri, from waging a war with Vietnam (a staunch Soviet ally), or from strongly opposing the Soviet invasion of Afghanistan in 1979. In this case, the restraint shown by the USSR surely cannot be attributed to either moral considerations or to political naïvety. It is also hard to believe that the opposition of the United States and its pledge of support for China (Kissinger, 1979: 764) was a critical determinant of Soviet behavior. After all, by the time the Soviet Union sounded out the US reaction to a possible preemptive strike against China, the credibility of the American promise to defend Europe and its NATO allies had already been called into question. If the United States was unwilling to risk Washington or New York for Paris or Bonn, how likely was it to wage a nuclear war to protect a communist state with which it too had an unsettled and stormy relationship?

Nor is such restraint unique to the nuclear age. In the years leading up to World War I, Germany enjoyed a decided (yet declining) military edge over France and Russia, its two principal continental adversaries. Still, despite the recommendations of the German General Staff to wage a preventive war, German leaders sought a political reconciliation with Germany's rivals during disputes in the Balkans in 1905, 1908, and again in 1912. As Lebow (1984: 151) observed about all three cases, "what is surprising *given the assumptions of deterrence theory* and the window of vulnerability thesis is not that Germany stumbled into a European war in 1914 but that it consciously rejected such a war on three previous and more favorable occasions" (emphasis added). Napoleon, then, is not the only world leader who "simply refused to play according to the rules of the balance of power" (Kissinger, 1957a: 131).

In hindsight, the decision of Kaiser Wilhelm and two German Chancellors (von Bülow and Bethmann-Hollweg) to reject the strategic imperative implicit in classical deterrence theory may not be so unusual. Most policy-makers instinctively spurn proliferation policies and the superpowers, at least, resisted transferring nuclear technology to third states, except in extreme circumstances. The reluctance of political leaders to accept this prescription is yet another indication that the underlying theoretical argument is spurious.

Some classical deterrence theorists, including those who support the selective proliferation of nuclear weapons, explain away this anomaly by exempting so-called crazy states from the behavioral tendencies of their models. After all, deterrence theory considers only the behavior of "rational" actors. At other times, however, these same theorists claim that nuclear weapons create their own logic, that the mere existence of these weapons is sufficient to induce extremely circumspect behavior (Waltz, 1993: 53–54; see also Bundy, 1983). But on this count, we feel, one cannot simply "have it both ways."

Another serious discrepancy between theory and practice is evident in the actual behavior of states during acute crises and other periods of intense conflict. If there is one characteristic of the post-war international system that most observers agree on, it is the absence of precipitous action by most states, especially the superpowers (see, *inter alia*, Gaddis, 1986: 23, or Waltz, 1993: 67). Apparently, states have not only eschewed commitment strategies like those highlighted by Ellsberg, Schelling, or Snyder, but they have also avoided those brinkmanship tactics that, by forfeiting control, unleash an autonomous risk of war. As Jervis (1988b: 80) observes: "although we often model superpower relations as a game of Chicken, in fact the United States and USSR have not behaved like reckless teenagers." Or as Betts (1987: 30) puts it, "the view that apparent recklessness and irrevocable commitment are more effective is usually more comfortable to pure strategists than to presidents."

For example, in an empirical examination of four intense post-World War II crises, Young (1968: 218) finds that in such situations decision-makers acted "to retain wide freedom of choice as long as possible and to avoid becoming boxed in to an irrevocable position." Similarly, Snyder and Diesing's (1977: 489–490) analysis of sixteen major interstate crises, including some dating back to the nineteenth century, reveals that "strongly coercive tactics such as physically 'irrevocable commitments' or severe committing threats are rarely used." (It is also telling that Snyder and Diesing could find but one instance of a political leader feigning "irrationality" [viz., Hitler in 1938] to gain a tactical advantage in a crisis.) Similarly, Deibel (1980: 58), in a legal review of post-war treaty obligations of the United States, notes that "even in that great era of supposed commitment after World War II, when American alliances with nearly fifty states were signed, the resultant treaties allowed the United States great flexibility in response. Indeed, their net effect was not one of restricting America's freedom of action but of extending its power to the farthest defense perimeter ever."[34] Along the same lines, Maxwell (1968: 4) observes that "international history yields no example of a state making such [an irrevocable] commitment." And finally, in a review of recent scholarship on deterrence, Huth (1999: 74) writes that

---

[34] A good example is what the *New York Times* (Erlanger, 1996) characterizes as the "intentionally vague commitment" of the United States as set forth in the Taiwan Relations Act of 1979. Here is how one senior US administration official described the Act when China sought to influence the 1996 presidential elections in Taiwan by testing missiles around Taiwan's main ports: "*Without pre-committing*, or allowing Taiwan to dictate our China policy, it's very important that China know it cannot act with impunity, and that we have options and can use them" (emphasis added).

"early arguments about the strategic advantages of the manipulation of risk and commitment strategies have not been fully supported by empirical research."

There is good reason for the reluctance of states cavalierly to employ coercive bargaining tactics, and to exhibit instead what Betts (1987: 29) calls "political leaders' universal penchant for keeping options open." More often than not, escalatory maneuvers culminate in war as opponents, rather than "chickening out," choose to stand firm and resist (Leng, 1993; Goldstein and Freeman, 1990; Kroll, 1995).[35] Thus, decision-theoretic deterrence theory suffers as a descriptive tool because it is unable to account for the behavior of either the challenger or the defender in precisely those dramatic and dangerous interactions it purports to explain. And, as Morgenstern (1961b: 105) so presciently observed, the prescriptions of these models "would appear dangerous should they have an influence upon policy."[36]

1.3 Logical problems

Empirical difficulties aside, decision-theoretic deterrence theory also suffers from a more fundamental deficiency: in its standard formulation, it is logically inconsistent. Or as Gaddis (1997: 101) tactfully puts it: "logic, in this field, was not what it was elsewhere."

To demonstrate the problem, consider again the Chicken model (see figure 1.2). Recall that Chicken encapsulates the underlying theoretical framework of classical deterrence theory. Especially noteworthy is the presumption that conflict in the nuclear age is at once unthinkable and irrational. This critical *assumption* is the defining characteristic of Chicken. *If* one accepts this characterization, and the presumption that Chicken accurately reflects the structural and psychological conditions of a bipolar nuclear relationship, then the problem with the theory is

---

[35] There may also be psychological reasons why statesmen avoid making "irrevocable choices." Janis and Mann (1977: 15), for instance, find that most decision-makers seek relief from "conflict, doubts, and worry (by procrastinating, rationalizing, or denying responsibility for [their] own choices." We hasten to add, however, that there is no necessary contradiction between the observation that statesmen shun commitment tactics because they involve risky and potentially costly actions and the claim that, psychologically, statesmen are risk-averse. We discuss the potential synergy of psychological and rational choice explanations in chapter 2.

[36] Leng (1993: 3) makes the same point.

clear: assuming (instrumentally) rational players,[37] the status quo should not often survive. Crises should be common and general deterrence should fail on a regular basis.

The reason is manifest. Given that one player cooperates by supporting the status quo, it is not in the other player's interest to also continue to cooperate and support the status quo. Cooperation results in the other player's next-best outcome. Non-cooperation, however, induces the other player's most-preferred outcome. Consequently, given rational actors with a mutual aversion to all-out conflict, general deterrence should not succeed on a regular basis.[38] All of which strongly suggests that the apparent faith that many strategic theorists place in the ability of nuclear weapons to secure the status quo rests on shaky theoretical grounds.[39]

Contrary to Miller (1993: 70) and others, then, it looks as if the logic of classical deterrence theory is not quite "impeccable," that there is an inherent contradiction between the precepts of rationality and the intuition of many classical deterrence theorists that nuclear weapons are stabilizing. Given these assumptions, Jervis (1984: 19) is quite correct in asserting that "a rational strategy for the employment of nuclear weapons is a contradiction in terms."

This logical inconsistency raises yet another empirical problem for decision-theoretic deterrence theory, namely, reconciling the persistence of the status quo throughout the Cold War with its theoretical instability in the underlying bargaining model.[40] Thus, like structural

---

[37] The qualification will be explained in detail in chapter 2.

[38] The informal discussion in the text implicitly assumes simultaneous choice. Technically, if Chicken is played simultaneously (each player chooses C or D without knowledge of the other player's choice, and they do this once and only once), then there are three patterns of behavior that are consistent with rational play (*i.e.*, Nash equilibria). Either one player wins; or the other player wins; or the mixed equilibrium is played. (Interestingly, Rapoport [1992: 483] associates the latter with Schelling's threat that leaves something to chance.) If the mixed strategy equilibrium comes into play, then all four outcomes occur with positive probability – in particular, one expects the survival of the status quo sometimes, but not necessarily often. This means that the mixed strategy equilibrium is also inconsistent with the observation that the status quo was generally maintained during the Cold War. (O'Neill [1992: 471–472] argues persuasively that the mixed strategy equilibrium in Chicken also fails as a normative device.) For a detailed discussion of the equilibrium structure of Chicken, under a variety of conditions, see Fink, Gates, and Humes (1998).

[39] This conclusion does not depend on the assumption of simultaneous choice. See chapter 3 for a demonstration.

[40] Downs and Rocke (1990: 76) encountered a similar theoretical problem in their study of arms races, i.e., the "difficulty of reconciling the existence of instances of arms

deterrence theorists, decision-theoretic deterrence theorists are hard put to explain the absence of chronic crises and persistent challenges to the status quo during the post-war period. In particular, extended periods of *détente* are clearly inconsistent with the core assumptions of decision-theoretic deterrence theory, suggesting perhaps that the theory's axiomatic base is too rigid to account for dynamic interstate relationships.

For some classical deterrence theorists, especially those who believe that the very existence of nuclear weapons is sufficient to stabilize a conflictual relationship (see, for example, Bundy, 1983), such logical contradictions are of little moment. Waltz (1993: 53–54), for one, simply brushes the problem aside: "Logic says that once the deterrent threat has failed, carrying it out at the risk of one's own destruction is irrational. But logic proves unpersuasive because a would-be attacker cannot be sure that the logic will hold."[41]

But others, untroubled by oxymorons and analytic incongruity, revel in the contradiction or embrace its implications. Schelling's suggestion that rational players feign irrationality is a case in point. Jervis's (1972, 1978, 1979, 1984, 1989) Janus-like musings, at once formulating and rebuking decision-theoretic deterrence theory, are another. Rhodes's (1989: 1) pithy observation that deterrence is "a relationship in which the rational and irrational are inherently linked" is a third. For Rhodes (1988), deterrence stability is enhanced by the *inability* of modern governments, with labyrinthine bureaucracies and unpredictable operating procedures, to guarantee that they will act rationally.

1.4 Coda

There are a number of ways to respond to the empirical and logical problems of classical deterrence theory: one could ignore the inconsistencies, as does Rhodes (1988), and construct a theory that requires actors to be, simultaneously, rational and irrational; alternatively, one could simply dismiss the theory as logically inconsistent, as does Achen (1987), and go on to propose the construction of a new

cooperation with the unique Nash equilibrium of mutual defection in the Prisoner's Dilemma."

[41] One might well wonder whether the logic supporting proliferation policies is subject to a similar caveat. Nonetheless, Waltz is on to something here. We defer a discussion of exactly what until chapter 3.

theory that relies on an altogether different conception of rationality; one could attempt to resolve the paradox, as do Howard (1971), Gauthier (1984), Nalebuff (1986, 1991), Powell (1987, 1990), and others, by trying to demonstrate that rational deterrence theory need not be a contradiction in terms; or one could retain the rationality assumption, and try to formulate a theory that respects logical analysis and empirical truth, as we shall do in the latter chapters of this book.

We reject the first option largely for scientific reasons: we hold that logical consistency and empirical accuracy are the *sine qua non* of good theory.[42] We have no *a priori* objection to the second tack, and in fact look favorably on attempts to construct alternative theories, including those that draw upon insights from the psychological literature. Nonetheless, rather than simply jettisoning the rationality assumption, we prefer to evaluate classical deterrence theory on its own terms. Accordingly, in the next chapter, we assess some prominent attempts to reconcile classical deterrence theory with the precepts of rationality, and explain why they are not successful. Then, in chapter 3, we propose our own reformulation – Perfect Deterrence Theory – using game theory. In our view, deterrence is fundamentally a strategic relationship in which state interests both clash and interact. Thus, game theory is the perfect tool for exploring the dynamics of deterrence across a variety of strategic settings.

Part II extends the analysis of chapter 3, focusing exclusively on direct deterrence situations. Chapter 4 examines the *Generalized Mutual Deterrence Game* wherein each of two states are potential threats to the other. Chapter 5, by contrast, explores the *Unilateral Deterrence Game* in which only one player has an incentive to upset the status quo. Particular attention is paid in these two chapters and those that follow to the impact of incomplete information on deterrence dynamics.

Extended deterrence relationships are analyzed in part III. In chapter 6, the *Asymmetric Escalation Game* model is described and explored under conditions of complete information. In this elementary escalation model, the initial choice of the challenger does not include a direct attack on the defender. Such a choice remains possible, but only as the game unfolds and the conflict escalates. Thus, unlike the treatment of direct deterrence relationships in part II, the formaliza-

---

[42] Walt (1999) downplays the importance of logical consistency in theory construction. See Zagare (1999) for the counter-argument.

tions in part III attempt to model situations in which the potential threat is to another player's secondary interest, such as a third party. Of course, this is not to suggest that extended deterrence threats are unimportant or lack saliency, just that they are different in scope and nature. As such, they present a defender with a distinct strategic conundrum.

In chapter 7, the efficacy of a defender's complete reliance on an all-or-nothing response to sub-strategic aggression is explored. The consequences of more flexible response options are evaluated in chapter 8. Chapter 9 develops the implications of the *Asymmetric Escalation Game* model more generally, seeking in particular to identify the conditions under which conflicts either remain limited or escalate to the highest level. In chapter 10 (part IV), Perfect Deterrence Theory is once again contrasted with classical deterrence theory. Its overall implications are discussed and its wider policy implications laid out.

In examining both direct and extended deterrence relationships our purpose is not necessarily to tease a set of testable hypotheses from our models, although we are clearly not averse to this enterprise. Nor is it our aim to put together a compendium of counter-intuitive insights into what we consider the most fundamental form of inter-state relationship. Indeed, our contention is that classical deterrence theory is suspect, in part, because its precepts all too often run counter to intuition. Rather our goal is to expound a common-sense theory of deterrence, and to lay out systematically the general dynamics of some basic deterrence situations in a way that is both logically consistent and empirically plausible. In this sense our analysis is theoretically prior to many recent game-theoretic treatments of the subject,[43] and especially to those studies that analyze the relationship between threat credibility and the management or resolution of international disputes.

For instance, Fearon's (1994b: 578) bargaining model of an interstate crisis effectively illustrates how "audience costs" may enable "a state to signal its true preferences ... more credibly and more clearly." Similarly, both Morrow (1994b) and Smith (1995, 1996, 1998b) construct models that map out the connection between deterrence and the costly signals implicit in alliance formation. In the same vein, Kim and Bueno de Mesquita (1995) demonstrate, both logically and empirically,

---

[43] For comprehensive reviews, see Nicholson (1989) and O'Neill (1989, 1994). See also Allan and Dupont (1999), Walt (1999), and Morrow (2000).

that perceptions about threat credibility can cut both ways, enhancing the prospects for peace in some cases while diminishing them in others. And Wagner's (1991) evaluation of the rational foundations of US and USSR targeting strategies during the Cold War links the credibility of a threat to use nuclear weapons to the availability of counterforce options.

But none of these studies, or related models of interstate conflict developed by Bueno de Mesquita and Lalman (1992), Morgan (1994), Kydd (1997), and several others,[44] systematically explores the *overall* relationship between uncertainty, threat credibility, and the outcomes of deterrence games. By contrast, the theory we develop – Perfect Deterrence Theory – explains both why and when credible threats matter.

Nor do any of these other works examine the strategic implications of competing extended deterrence deployment stances, as does Perfect Deterrence Theory. And lastly, unlike Perfect Deterrence Theory, none of these other formalizations have sought specifically to explicate the conditions that separate conflicts that remain limited from those that escalate to the highest level. In other words, the particular questions we address, and the answers we provide, set Perfect Deterrence Theory apart from other recent attempts to use game theory to understand international relations. It is our hope and belief that our theory both supplements and complements much of the recent formal work on interstate cooperation and conflict.

To put this in a slightly different way, Perfect Deterrence Theory is not aimed necessarily at filling any particular gap in the game-theoretic literature *per se*. We find, in general, that the latest wave of formal studies has greatly expanded the field's boundaries and extended our theoretical understanding of international politics. Downs and Rocke (1995: 6), for example, posit a number of closely related game models to explore the "expectations that domestic uncertainty creates and the consequences of that uncertainty" on interstate politics. Similarly, Milner (1997) analyzes how interstate cooperation is abetted by internal political competition. Powell (1996a, 1996b) models both the unsettling choice facing a state declining in power relative to its adversary, and the connection between the distribution of power and war. Carlson (1995, 1998) constructs and

---

[44] See, in particular, Ordeshook (1989); Zagare (1990c); Intriligator and Luterbacher (1994); and *Journal of Conflict Resolution*, vol. 41, no. 1 (February 1997).

tests an escalation model in which the players are uncertain of the opponent's cost tolerance. And Sorokin (1994) uses game theory to analyze the relationship between alliance formation and general deterrence in regional rivalries.

As important and as innovative as this recent literature is, however, it has not, as yet, had a significant impact in official and policy circles. By contrast, classical deterrence theory remains a potent intellectual force, shaping the policy debate in the United States (see, for example, National Academy of Sciences [1997]; Paul, Harknett, and Wirtz [1998]) and elsewhere (Singh, 1998). For this reason we focus on its logical structure, on classical deterrence theory's empirical accuracy, and on its policy implications.

This does not mean, however, that we consider Perfect Deterrence Theory simply a substitute theory of Cold War interactions. In our opinion, deterrence is a universal relationship that operates across time and space, and in a variety of settings. To accommodate this view, our modeling choices tend to favor simplicity over complexity, and generality over specificity. We believe that the purposefully austere models we explore apply, in principle, to deterrence relationships wherever and whenever they exist.

2   Rationality and deterrence

A rational strategy for the employment of nuclear weapons is a contradiction in terms.

Robert Jervis

The consensus view of classical deterrence theory is deficient, both empirically and logically. Empirically, the theory is hard put to explain, *inter alia*, the stability of the Cold War period before the Soviet Union achieved essential equivalence with the United States, the absence of an all-out conflict between the Soviet Union and China, especially during the most contentious stretches of this strategic relationship, and the historical tendency of major-power wars to occur under parity conditions. Logically, the theory is marred by a fundamental incompatibility between its tenets and the canons of rationality. This is the *paradox of mutual deterrence.*[1] More specifically, logic implies that the status quo should unravel as higher and higher costs render mutual conflict worse and worse for both sides. Classical deterrence theory, however, asserts the opposite.

States clearly do not always behave the way classical deterrence theory suggests they do or should. Waltz (1993: 53–54) notwithstanding, the glaring discrepancy between logic and fact, between prescription and description, is troubling. Accordingly, in this chapter and the next, we inquire whether classical deterrence theory can be resuscitated, that is, whether it can be rendered logically coherent and, ultimately, empirically accurate. To this end, we now explore the

---

[1] Van Gelder (1989: 159), who refers to this problem as one of two "credibility dilemmas," observes that it "threatens the very foundations of nuclear deterrence as a rational strategy."

merits of three potential resolutions of the paradox of mutual deterrence that attempt to explain general deterrence stability without violating the rationality postulate: deterministic threats, "threats-that-leave-something-to-chance," and a solution suggested by the theory of metagames. A fourth resolution, based on mutually credible threats, is examined in chapter 3. We begin by defining terms.[2]

2.1 On rationality

There is perhaps no concept in social science more misunderstood and more frequently misapplied than rationality; and nowhere is this problem more acute than in the field of security studies where reliance on ideas of rational action is fundamental to most analyses. The conceptual confusion is not difficult to explain. The idea of rational choice (or its absence) plays a central role in two progressive research traditions, both of which figure prominently in the scholarly literature of deterrence. Within the confines of each tradition, the concept is defined differently, serving two quite distinct theoretical purposes. Compounding the confusion is the lamentable fact that the two paradigms are generally perceived to be theoretically incompatible, or even mutually exclusive.[3] As a consequence, inter-paradigmatic communication is frequently muddled and rarely productive. What seems to have been lost in this dysfunctional discourse is the potential synergy of the concept of *procedural rationality*, which underlies the work of those who approach strategic behavior from the vantage point of individual psychology (Simon, 1976), with the more limited technical definition of *instrumental rationality* used by most rational choice theorists (Riker and Ordeshook, 1973).

2.1.1 Procedural rationality

The procedural definition of rationality corresponds closely to an everyday appreciation of the term. In this view, a rational choice is seen as a "cool and clearheaded ends–means calculation" (Verba, 1961: 95) made by a near omniscient actor who, before deciding, considers *all* possible courses of action and carefully weighs the pros and cons of each of them. A procedurally rational decision, then, requires that an actor have an accurate perception of the implications

---

[2] Portions of this chapter are based on Zagare (1990a).
[3] See, for instance, Leng (1993) or Kaufmann (1994).

of *all* conceivable alternatives and a well-defined set of preferences over the entire set. It also requires a decision-maker who can correctly and dispassionately assess the preferences of other relevant actors, their likely responses to his or her choices and, in particular, to concessions or threats. In the view of the proceduralist, misperceptions – or other deficiencies of human cognition – and rational decision-making are mutually exclusive. Rational agents – if they exist – begin by establishing an accurate understanding of their environment and by eliminating all conceptual impediments to sound choice. Moreover, procedurally rational decision-makers factor out of their decision calculus other, extraneous considerations stemming from psychological predispositions or emotional and affective deficiencies (de Rivera, 1968; Jervis, 1968; Steinbruner, 1976; Lebow, 1981).

Clearly there are few, if any, real world actors who satisfy the stringent requirements of procedural rationality, especially in crisis situations, which are generally characterized by inordinately high stakes, considerable stress, and intense time constraints. Why then define rationality in such a restrictive way? The short answer is that the notion of procedural rationality serves an important theoretical function. Theorists who rely on this definition of rationality to examine interstate behavior use it as a benchmark to identify and measure deviations from the ideal. If the behavioral consequences of misperceptions, beliefs, psychological idiosyncrasies, cognitive deficiencies, and the like are to be determined, some fixed point is required. The procedural definition of rationality serves this purpose well by facilitating the study of micro-level variables and their impact on decision-making.

2.1.2   *Instrumental rationality*

The concept of rationality serves a different purpose in rational choice theory. It should not be surprising, then, to find that decision theorists and game theorists offer an alternative definition: according to Luce and Raiffa (1957: 50), an (instrumentally) rational actor is one who, when confronted with "two alternatives which give rise to outcomes . . . will choose the one which yields the more preferred outcome."[4] As will be seen, this unexceptional definition is used by rational (*and* by psychological) choice theorists to make inferences about the logical

---

[4] Hargreaves Heap and Varoufakis (1995: 7) trace the tradition of instrumental thinking to David Hume's *Treatise on Human Nature*.

connection between preferences – which may, in principle, reflect perceptions (or misperceptions) or beliefs – and actual choice.

The definition of instrumental rationality is indeed straightforward. Only two axioms, each associated with the logical structure of an actor's preference ordering, are implicit in it. For an actor to be instrumentally rational, he or she must have a *complete* and *transitive* preference ordering over the set of available outcomes.[5]

Completeness of preferences simply means that the actor is able to compare any two outcomes and determine a relative preference. For example, given a choice between two alternatives, *a* and *b*, a decision-maker with complete preferences either prefers *a* to *b*, or *b* to *a*, or is indifferent between *a* and *b*. The behavior of an actor whose preferences are not complete may not be explicable or predictable by rational choice methods.

Transitivity means the following: for any alternatives *a*, *b*, and *c*, if an actor prefers *a* to *b*, and *b* to *c*, then the actor must also prefer *a* to *c*. The choices of an actor with intransitive preferences are logically incoherent and, consequently, best analyzed outside a rational choice framework.

It is a mathematical fact that an actor with complete and transitive preferences can arrange all alternatives in (ascending or descending) order of preference. The definition of instrumental rationality is then straightforward: an instrumentally rational actor is an actor with complete, transitive preferences over all alternatives, who always chooses the most-preferred alternative, or any one of the most-preferred alternatives if several are tied for this position.[6]

Complete and transitive preferences are surely minimal requirements for a definition of rationality. Yet without them, rational choice theory would be well-nigh impossible. In fact, *any* theory assuming *purposeful* action would be impossible. More to our purpose, these two assumptions are not only necessary for a theory of rational deterrence, they are also implicit, we submit, in what are frequently mistaken as incompatible theoretical constructs.

Consider, for example, the two conceptual models Allison offers as

---

[5] Hargreaves Heap and Varoufakis (1995: 6) include the *reflexivity* condition in their definition of instrumental rationality. Preferences are reflexive if each alternative is indifferent to itself.

[6] Technically, to ensure that a most-preferred alternative exists, one must also assume that the number of available alternatives is finite (or that the alternatives are bounded in some sense).

alternatives to the Rational Actor Model (I) in his classic study of the Cuban missile crisis: the Organization Process Model (II), and the Governmental Politics Model (III). Juxtaposing the three models, Allison (1971: 246) suggests an "incompatibility between the level of discourse in the Model I account and that of the Model II and Model III accounts."

If Allison's conceptual models are incompatible with one another, however, it is *not* because they make fundamentally different assumptions about the underlying nature of the choices made by the units, but because each model ascribes different motives to its principal unit of analysis. Indeed, *all* three models rely on the instrumental definition of rationality to make inferences about unit *choices*: the *states* of Model I are assumed to behave (rationally) so as to maximize their particular strategic objectives; the *organizations* in Model II are presumed to pursue (rationally) their parochial bureaucratic goals; and the *individuals* in Model III are assumed to act (rationally) on the basis of their largely idiosyncratic political agendas.

It is not generally appreciated, but many *psychological* theories of deterrence also depend on the notion of instrumental rationality for inferences about behavior. Consider, for example, de Rivera's (1968: 256) explanation of the uneasy interpersonal relationship of President Truman and General MacArthur that he attributes to their policy dispute over Korea. "After a person is publicly committed to an action," he writes, "he builds up a public following that supports the action for its own reasons. Once this occurs and persons expect one to advocate the action, it is difficult to change one's advocacy."

Even though de Rivera explains Truman's and MacArthur's rigidity in terms of "cognitive dissonance," his interpretation of their contentious relationship clearly rests on a calculation of costs (in this case psychological or public relations costs that may be no less real than more tangible costs) and benefits. Thus, de Rivera makes use, simultaneously, of both the instrumentalist's and the proceduralist's definitions of rationality – and there is nothing necessarily wrong with that. Interestingly, decision-theoretic deterrence theorists do the same when they underscore the effectiveness of a public commitment to a hard-line strategy as a potent manipulatory device (see chapter 1).

Similarly, Lebow (1984: 156) – a leading critic of "rational" deterrence theory – presumes instrumental rationality when he attempts to explain the stability of the US–USSR strategic relationship before essential equivalence: "the absolute cost of nuclear war was probably an important restraining factor for American policy-makers through-out the period of their nuclear superiority *vis-à-vis* the Soviet Union." Here and elsewhere (Lebow, 1981: 264 and *passim*), Lebow infers a connection between cost (psychological or otherwise), preference, and choice. And again, there is nothing necessarily wrong with that.

The two postulates that underlie the notion of instrumental ration-ality are neither heroic nor exceptional. To be sure, some individuals may not qualify as rational, even in the limited sense of the instru-mentalist. But while there are clearly instances of international deci-sion-makers suffering from mental illness, it is also probably the case that most of them, including Hitler and others with morally repugnant intentions, have coherent (not laudable, or sagacious, or even reason-able, but coherent) preference orders. In other words, the concept of instrumental rationality does *not* depend on any absolute evaluation of the particulars of a decision-maker's preferences. This minimalist definition merely requires that preferences be (logically) consistent, *whatever they are.* Thus, while the context in which choices are framed may have a dramatic impact on a decision-maker's preferences (Tversky and Kahneman, 1981), this observation does not preclude a rational choice model.

Given the above, one might well ask "where do preferences come from and how are they defined?" For the instrumentalist, who takes preferences as givens, they are defined subjectively by each indi-vidual decision-maker (Savage, 1954; Ellsberg, 1959: 347; Wagner, 1992a: 119). This is one reason why instrumentalists, in contrast to proceduralists, do not usually assess preferences, however bizarre, reprehensible, or ill-founded they may be. The question of what preferences and/or perceptions an actor *should* have is not relevant for a theorist using the instrumental definition of rationality to develop an explanatory or predictive (i.e., positive) theory of political behavior.[7]

For instance, consider a leader who prefers systematic genocide to the benign neglect of a minority population. If the actions of this leader are consistent (or are perceived by the actor to be consistent)

---

[7] It may even be true, as Jervis (1988b: 324) argues, that "by taking preferences as givens, we beg . . . the most important question on how they are formed." But this does not mean that other questions are unimportant. In our view, a fully articulated theory of interstate conflict resolution requires both a theory of preference formation and a theory, such as the one presented in this work, that maps the consequences of various preference orderings under a variety of environmental conditions.

with this repugnant preference ordering, then the leader is rational by the definition of the instrumentalist. The reason is manifest: *qua* scientist, the instrumentalist is primarily interested in theory construction, not in *a priori* judgments of the ethical or moral basis of choice. What is the best way to understand Hitler's behavior? Simply by understanding his goals. In other words, once preferences are taken as givens, actual or optimal behavior can be deduced.[8]

Instrumentally rational actors, then, can have preferences rooted in incomplete, imperfect, or even erroneous information (Wagner, 1992a). Variables that the proceduralist would reject as illegitimate influences on policy-making can also have an impact on the preferences of an instrumentally rational actor. As well, the distortions implied by the organizational context of policy-making and the imperatives of the political process are consistent with this notion of rationality. And even an individual whose vision is clouded by the pressures of time and stress in a crisis can be considered rational in the limited sense of the instrumentalist.

Putting this in a slightly different way, the instrumentalist's notion of rationality is quite restricted, and may even be consistent with conceptual models based on the notion of procedural rationality.[9] In fact, in some ways the instrumentalist's definition is nothing more than a convenient tautology.[10] Instrumentalists *and* proceduralists (like de Rivera and Lebow) use it not because it is the "correct" way of

[8] This is not to suggest that instrumentalists are uninterested in normative questions or that such issues lie outside the scope of legitimate inquiry. It is simply to say that, in general, instrumentalists examine these problems from a different vantage point than either political philosophers or political psychologists. It is also important to keep in mind that these two approaches to preferences are not necessarily inconsistent.

[9] To be sure, the proceduralists' view of rationality has predisposed them to develop a brand of theory that looks and feels much different than that produced by scholars who assume only instrumental rationality. The wise instrumentalist, however, would be ill-advised to ignore this strand of research since rational choice models are not only potentially consistent with models or theories stressing individual-level variables, but also presuppose them. In other words, one can interpret the work of micro-level theorists as exploring the causal field of cognitions and affectations culminating in preferences and the perception thereof. Similarly, one can interpret the work of rational choice theorists as exploring the strategic consequences of various sets of real or perceived preference rankings. Putting this in still another way, to flesh out a rational choice model fully, a theory of preference formation is required. And, as many proceduralists implicitly acknowledge, to understand the consequences of perceptions and misperceptions completely, a theory of strategic interaction, like game theory, is needed.

[10] See, for example, Samuelson (1938).

defining the term, but because the assumption of instrumental rationality is useful for constructing theories of rational and psychological choice.

The point, however, is that rational *choice* models, as opposed to the rational (or unitary) *actor* model in international politics, are not only consistent with, but are potentially synergistic with, models or theories that treat rationality in procedural terms (Downs, 1989).[11] As used by the instrumentalist, the term does *not* connote superhuman calculating ability, omniscience, or an Olympian view of the world, as some proceduralists have concluded.[12] The individual decision-makers analyzed by rational choice theorists can be, at one and the same time, rational in the limited instrumental sense, and irrational in the sense of the proceduralist.[13] Thus, to the extent that subjective interpretations of the world are built into the models of the instrumentalist,[14] rational choice models could also be used to describe the behavior of decision-makers suffering from cognitive closure, selective perceptions, misinformation, motivated error, and so on.[15]

2.2 Some implications of the assumption of instrumental rationality

Before turning to an assessment of proposals to resolve the paradox of mutual deterrence, it is useful to explore one development in non-cooperative game theory that deepened considerably our understanding of instrumental rationality, namely, Selten's (1975) concept of a *subgame-perfect equilibrium*. Until the specification of this concept, the

[11] Merely recognizing this potential compatibility, however, will not ease the task of theoretical integration. One important reason is that a parsimonious and coherent theory of preference formation based on micro-level variables does not yet exist (Jervis, 1985: 33).

[12] See, for example, Snyder and Diesing (1977: ch. 5).

[13] An important case in point is Schelling's notorious "rationality of irrationality" strategy (discussed in chapter 1) that turns on a denial of procedural, but not instrumental, rationality. The player feigning irrationality will appear to be procedurally irrational because that player's preferences will seem to be different than those deemed *reasonable* by most deterrence theorists; but this same player is, nonetheless, treated as an instrumentally rational agent who, presumably, acts consistently with these irrational *preferences*.

[14] Bueno de Mesquita's (1981, 1985a) expected utility model is a good example. In this model, different risk functions permit the analysis of decision-makers with different perceptions of objective reality. Also see Kugler and Zagare (1987b, 1990).

[15] See Stein (1982) for an explicit example of such a merger.

only widely accepted rationality requirement for players in a non-cooperative game was that their strategies form a *Nash equilibrium*.[16] What Selten did, in the context of some games, was to demonstrate that only Nash equilibria that are subgame-perfect can be defended in terms of the rationality principle. We will illustrate Selten's idea using Harsanyi's (1977) example.

Backtracking for a moment, let us define a few terms: a *game* is a model of an interactive situation in which the outcome depends on the choices of two or more actors. A *non-cooperative game* is one in which the players are either unable to communicate *or*, if they can communicate, are unable to commit themselves to any particular strategy (plan of action) because of the lack of any reliable enforcement mechanism. It is easy to see why non-cooperative game theory holds a particular attraction for theorists of interstate conflict. Because there is no overarching authority to enforce commitments or agreements, great power politics clearly meets the definitional requirements of a non-cooperative game.

At the heart of the theory of non-cooperative games lies Nash's equilibrium concept. A Nash equilibrium is a combination of strategies, one for each player, that produces an outcome from which neither player could gain, immediately, by unilaterally switching to another strategy. The reason for the centrality of this concept in non-cooperative game theory is transparent: Nash equilibria are associated with instrumentally rational choices by all decision-makers, so the associated outcomes are, in essence, *self-enforcing*. (No player has an incentive unilaterally to break the agreement implicit in any Nash equilibrium.) Hence, in an environment lacking an enforcement agent, only Nash equilibria can be considered rational outcomes. Outcomes that do not meet Nash's criteria must involve irrational behavior, because at least one player must have an instrumental reason to switch to another strategy in order to induce a more preferred outcome.

To illustrate these concepts, consider first figure 2.1, an *extensive-form game* originally given by Harsanyi (1977). The extensive-form (or *game tree*) summarizes the sequence of choices in a game, the possible outcomes, the players' utilities at those outcomes, and the information available to each player when a choice is to be made.[17] The collection

---

[16] See Nash (1951) for a discussion.
[17] We defer for now a full discussion of the latter two elements.

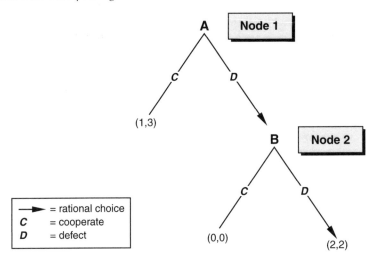

Fig. 2.1. Extensive-form representation of Harsanyi's game.

of choices available to a player at any one time is called a *move*. In the extensive-form, moves are represented by *nodes* on a game tree. The *branches* of the tree at any one node summarize the choices available to a player at a particular point in a game.[18] In an extensive-form game of *perfect information*, the players know where they are in the game tree whenever they are to make a choice.

For instance, in the game of figure 2.1, there are two players, A and B, and three possible outcomes. As before, the payoffs to the players at the terminal nodes are given by an ordered pair representing the payoffs to A and B, respectively. As usual, the players prefer higher payoffs to lower payoffs.

A begins play at node 1. The two branches at node 1 indicate that A has two choices at the start of the game: either to cooperate (i.e., choose *C*) or to defect (i.e., choose *D*). If A cooperates, the game ends and the payoff to A is 1 while the payoff to B is 3. If A defects, the game continues and B makes the next move. B also has two choices, represented by the two branches at node 2: either to cooperate or to defect. In either case, the game ends after B moves. If B cooperates, the payoff to each player is 0; if B defects, each player's payoff is 2.

Consider now figure 2.2, the *strategic-* (or *normal-*) *form representation*

---

[18] For an especially clear discussion of the extensive and strategic forms, see Morrow (1994a: ch. 2).

B

	Cooperate *(C)*	Defect *(D)*
Cooperate *(C)*	Outcome CC (1,3)*	Outcome CD (1,3)
Defect *(D)*	Outcome DC (0,0)	Outcome DD (2,2)*

A is labeled on the left side between the two rows.

(x,y) = payoff to A, payoff to B
* = Nash equilibrium

Fig. 2.2. Strategic-form representation of Harsanyi's game.

of the game of figure 2.1. In the strategic form, each player's strategies, or possible choices throughout the game, are shown as rows or columns. A *strategy*, then, is a complete contingency plan specifying a player's choice at every situation that might arise in a game, that is, at every node of the game tree where it is to make a choice. Thus, in the strategic form, the players have only one choice, namely to choose a strategy. Their choices are assumed to be made simultaneously. Note that in reducing sequences of moves to strategies, information about the order of play is no longer explicit, nor is information about what the players know about prior choices, that is, about their current position on the game tree.

In the strategic form of Harsanyi's game (figure 2.2), each player has two strategies. A's strategies are listed as the rows of the matrix, while B's strategies are given by the columns. Note that although the original game has only three outcomes, there are now four possible strategy combinations. Of these four combinations, two are Nash equilibria, indicated by the asterisks. Outcome DD is an equilibrium since either player would do worse by switching, unilaterally, to its other strategy. Specifically, were A to switch from its *D* strategy to its *C* strategy, which would induce outcome CD, A's payoff would go from 2 – A's best – to 1 – A's next-best. And if B were to switch to its *C* strategy, B's payoff would go from 2 – B's next-best – to 0 – B's worst. Thus neither player benefits by switching unilaterally to another strategy, so DD is a Nash equilibrium. For similar reasons, CC is also a Nash equilibrium; neither player would benefit by switching. By contrast, neither of the remaining two outcomes is stable in the Nash sense because at least one player would gain by changing to another strategy.

Selten's ideas demonstrate that the two Nash equilibria in the strategic form are not equally defensible as outcomes rational players would select. CC involves B's threat to do something irrational should its choice arise in the game tree, whereas DD does not depend on any such irrational threat.

Some differences between the Nash equilibria can be found simply by analyzing the strategic form. Specifically, since DD is the product of B's unconditionally best (or *dominant*)[19] strategy, and A's best response to B's unconditionally best strategy, compelling reasons exist to consider this equilibrium as the outcome that rational players would arrive at.

One might object, however, arguing that B could do better. Could B not threaten to choose C if A selects D, thereby inducing A to choose C and bringing about B's best outcome? The short answer is "no," because the equilibrium at CC is not perfect, that is, because it involves both "irrational behavior and irrational expectations by the players about each other's behavior" (Harsanyi, 1977: 332).

To see why CC can be eliminated as an outcome that (instrumentally) rational players would select, we must consider the original extensive-form representation of figure 2.1. In particular, consider the calculus of A at the first node of this tree. A can either select C and induce CC, A's second-best outcome, or select D, which might result either in A's best or A's worst outcome. Clearly, A should choose C if A expects B to select C also, since the choice of D would then result in A's worst outcome. Conversely, A should select D if A expects B to select D, since this induces A's best outcome, DD. The question is: what should A expect B to do?

If A assumes that B is (instrumentally) rational, then A expects B to

---

[19] Technically, B's choice of D is *weakly dominant*, that is, it provides B with a payoff that is at least as good as, and sometimes better than, any other strategy available to B (in this case B has only one other strategy), no matter what strategy A selects. By contrast, a *strictly dominant* strategy always provides a player with a strictly higher payoff than any other strategy, no matter what strategies other players select. For further discussion of this and related concepts, see Zagare (1984).

select *D* when B makes its choice at node 2, i.e., after A chooses *D*. To expect B to carry out the threat to choose *C* if A chooses *D* is to assume that B is irrational. It follows that for B to expect A to select *C* is to assume that B harbors irrational expectations about A. In other words, CC is not subgame-perfect in the game of figure 2.1. Knowing, then, that the game of figure 2.2 is a representation of the game of figure 2.1 provides us with another explanation of why CC is not an equilibrium rational players would select: it is not supported by rational choices at every node of the game tree. To repeat, the CC terminal node of figure 2.1 cannot be achieved by players who are rational and who expect each other to be rational.

Still, one might object a second time and argue that B could "irrevocably commit" herself to *C*, leaving A no choice. Might not such a commitment change the answer? This is a question we next consider in the context of the paradox of mutual deterrence, asking in particular whether irrevocable commitments provide a theoretically satisfying basis to explain deterrence. We are especially interested in asking whether such commitments can explain – consistent with the canons of rationality – the stability of the *Status Quo* in the Chicken game of figure 1.2 (reproduced here as figure 2.3). An intuitively plausible equilibrium supporting this outcome would resolve the paradox and bridge the gap between the expectations of the model world of decision-theoretic deterrence theorists and the real world of superpower politics.

2.3   Resolving the paradox I: deterministic threats

Before addressing this issue, however, we first distinguish two kinds of commitments. The first – a *pre*-commitment – is a commitment made to a strategy *before* the opponent selects a strategy; the second – a *post*-commitment – is executed *after* the other player makes a strategy choice.

Pre-commitments do not resolve the paradox of mutual deterrence; rather, they underscore it. If, in Chicken, a player were able to preempt the choice of an opponent, in effect making the first move, the preempting player would "win." If A defects, B is forced to choose between defecting and inducing its worst outcome, or cooperating and inducing its next-worst outcome. Similarly if B defects. Thus both players have an incentive to defect first, so the status quo is not stable, and the paradox stands.

	State B	
	Cooperate *(C)*	Defect *(D)*
Cooperate *(C)*	Status Quo (3,3)	B Wins (2,4)*
Defect *(D)*	A Wins (4,2)*	Conflict (1,1)

State A

(x,y) = payoff to A, payoff to B
4 = best; 3 = next-best; 2 = next-worst; 1 = worst
* = Nash equilibrium

Fig. 2.3. The game of Chicken.

Decision-theoretic deterrence theorists have well understood the strategic benefit of making the first move in a game with the structural characteristics of Chicken.[20] As discussed in chapter 1, strategic thinkers like Schelling, Ellsberg, and Kahn have concocted a multitude of mechanisms designed specifically to exploit the advantage of a preemptive choice. If nothing else, these provocative maneuvers highlight and reinforce the paradox: they presume, indeed require, that the player choosing second, being instrumentally rational, will concede.

It is, however, the second type of commitment that is frequently called upon to explain the stability of deterrence and resolve the paradox of mutual deterrence. It is easy to understand why such a contingent commitment, *if believed*, would deter an opponent from upsetting the status quo by defecting first. If a player believes an opponent will respond with certainty[21] to a choice of *D* by choosing *D* also, the player's alternatives are reduced to choosing *C* – which

---

[20] Technically, there is no first mover in Chicken since it is a strategic-form game. Hence the slight qualification.

[21] Or, as we show in chapter 3, with a "sufficiently" high probability.

would induce its next-best outcome – or *D* – which would induce its worst outcome. Given this choice, no player would rationally preempt its opponent. And if both players commit themselves to a *tit-for-tat* strategy of responding to *D* with *D*, then mutual deterrence is established.

But, and this is the crux of the matter, can a rational player make a commitment to retaliate given the costs of carrying out the retaliatory threat? Gauthier (1984) and other theorists argue "yes." To support this contention, Gauthier constructs an expected utility model of deterrence in which the costs of retaliation exceed the costs of capitulation, thereby making retaliation irrational or incredible. Next, he queries whether a utility maximizer can commit itself to retaliate, even when retaliation is inherently incredible. It can, Gauthier claims, but only if a commitment to retaliation provides the actor with a higher expected payoff than non-commitment. Then, not surprisingly, he shows that *under certain circumstances* such a commitment can indeed be rational, although Gauthier is fully cognizant that the absence of these conditions renders a retaliatory strategy irrational and deterrence unstable.

Note that Gauthier does not argue that it is rational to form the intention to retaliate if and only if it is utility maximizing to execute it. Rather, he argues that it would be rational to execute the commitment to retaliate if and only if it was utility maximizing to make it in the first place. Thus since it may be rational to form the intention to execute a retaliatory threat, it may also be rational to carry it out.[22] In fact, Gauthier – with laudable consistency – asserts that if the intention has been formed, and if deterrence fails, then a rational agent who intends to retaliate should do so, since acting on this intention is part of the behavior required of an expected utility maximizer.

---

[22] Gauthier's contention that a utility-maximizing agent may rationally choose to retaliate sets his argument apart from a similar one advanced by Brams and Kilgour (1988), who recognize that, if deterrence fails, it will always be irrational to retaliate. Other than this, however, Brams and Kilgour's work is similar in spirit, though not in detail, to Gauthier's. Brams and Kilgour begin with an underlying model of deterrence based on the structure of Chicken, but produce a qualitatively different game by permitting the players to commit themselves to retaliation that is based, for example, on automatic response procedures that may or may not work. Given these assumptions, they show that a *deterrence equilibrium* can emerge in the game they construct, along with other equilibria that involve preemption. It is precisely for this reason that Brams and Kilgour conclude that deterrence can constitute a rational and stable relationship.

There are, however, two problems with Gauthier's conclusion. First, since the stability of deterrence in this and similar models depends on each player's commitment to the (currently) irrational should deterrence fail, Gauthier's resolution of the paradox fails to satisfy Selten's perfectness criterion. This raises the question of why either player would believe that an opponent is actually committed to retaliation.

If it is (at least momentarily) irrational to retaliate in the event of a breakdown of deterrence, one can be deterred only if one believes that one's opponent is, or will be, instrumentally (and procedurally) irrational after an attack. But if a player is deterred because he believes his opponent will retaliate irrationally, how can he rely simultaneously on a policy justified by the assumption that the same opponent will be perfectly rational in being deterred? Or, put differently, why manipulate the costs of an opponent by threatening massive levels of destruction when the overall stability of the relationship can be explained *only* if each player, at some point, is assumed to be willing to disregard these costs completely and act irrationally? A rational choice theory of deterrence that explicitly rejects the perfectness criterion is a contradiction in terms. In effect, it explains deterrence stability by assuming, *concurrently*, that a player is rational (when the player is deterred) and irrational (when the player is deterring an opponent). Such intellectual sleight of hand is known as having it both ways.

Also problematic is the assumption that players can *commit* themselves to retaliate. Recall that such commitments are not a part of non-cooperative game theory, and that the paradox of deterrence rests upon the *inability* of the players to commit themselves to any particular strategy. Thus, Gauthier's type of resolution, relying on a commitment to a particular course of action regardless of its rationality, solves the paradox by assuming away the very source of the conundrum.

At this point one might respond "So what?" Granted, in the real world the preordained rules of non-cooperative game theory are not sacrosanct or inviolate. Let us assume for a moment a world in which such commitments are possible, or to use Schelling's (1960: 26) phrase, a world where "'cross my heart' is universally recognized as absolutely binding." It is clear that in such a world there would be no security dilemma. Deterrence policies would be unnecessary and military establishments superfluous.

To see why, assume for a moment that the players are able to commit themselves to a particular strategy in Chicken. Then each player could simply commit to the choice of C, maintaining the status quo. In so doing, each player would implicitly agree to forego its individual incentive to upset the status quo. There would be no problem with this agreement since, by assumption, it would be strictly enforceable. Thus, if strategy commitments are possible, there is no paradox.

Most classical deterrence theorists would categorically reject any proposal to stabilize a deterrence relationship that depends on an opponent ignoring its interests.[23] Such proposals would be regarded as hopelessly utopian or idealistic. Recall that a fundamental principle of political realism and classical deterrence theory is that states are self-interested power maximizers, i.e., they will *always* act in their own interest. But it is precisely this premise that Gauthier must discard in order to generate deterrence stability. Putting this another way, it is simply inconsistent to insist that states will *not* forego individual benefits and, at the same time, to hold that the stability of deterrence rests upon the willingness of each state to carry out a threat that is not only instrumentally irrational, but is also incompatible with the fundamental principle that states seek self-preservation first, and power maximization second.

In sum, either states can make commitments or they cannot. If they cannot, then arguments like those of Gauthier are not germane. But if commitments are permitted, then one cannot logically reject, *a priori*, other proposed solutions to international security – such as the Kellogg–Briand Pact renouncing war, or collective security organizations like the League of Nations – as hopelessly utopian.

Gauthier (1984: 494), much to his credit, maintains logical consistency by admitting other possible commitment strategies. "Rational nations," he writes, "recognizing the need to seek peace and follow it given the costs of war, can unilaterally renounce the first use of nuclear weapons and thereby end all strike policies." But *if* this prescription strikes the reader as hopelessly naïve, then so should the prescriptions of classical deterrence theory. Each rests upon what are, ultimately, self-abnegating choices (Wolfers, 1951, 1962). On the other hand, *if* this prescription strikes the reader as perfectly reasonable, the

---

[23] As Craig and George (1995: 171) note in the context of international negotiations, "self-enforcing agreements are generally preferred" to those that "depend on the good faith of each side."

reader has already rejected the underlying premises of political realism upon which classical deterrence theory depends.

2.4 Resolving the paradox II: the threat-that-leaves-something-to-chance

Recognizing the need to reconcile rationality and retaliation, Powell (1987, 1990: ch. 3) advanced a different line of reasoning to explain the rationality of deterrence. Like many others, Powell begins with an underlying Chicken model that is transformed, via assumptions, into a sequential game in which the players must decide whether to accept the status quo, to escalate the contest by challenging it, or to attack. If the first player chooses not to challenge the status quo or to attack, the game ends. But if escalation is chosen, the second player is faced with similar choices. The four possible outcomes are the same as in Chicken. If the player choosing first does not escalate or attack, the status quo prevails. If one player escalates and the other does not, the escalating player wins. If either player attacks, the game ends in disaster. And if both players escalate, the game continues until one player submits or until the game "gets out of control" and culminates in disaster. Powell assumes that by choosing to escalate, a player unleashes an autonomous risk, beyond its control, of disaster. Powell's model thereby provides a formalization of Schelling's (1960) "threat-that-leaves-something-to-chance." As such, it captures well the view that a nuclear crisis is a "competition in risk taking."

Given these assumptions, Powell shows that the existence of a crisis equilibrium, that is, a stable outcome that arises after a challenge by one player and resistance by the other, depends on incomplete information, that is, each side's lack of information about the values of its opponent.[24] Moreover, with regard to the purposes of this chapter, Powell demonstrates that, *under certain conditions,* no challenge will be made and, hence, deterrence can be stable. This suggests that even if each of two states knows the other prefers capitulation to disaster, neither would issue a challenge, provided that the resolve of each player to resist a challenge by the other exceeds a certain threshold. Interestingly, Powell's model reveals that when deterrence breaks

---

[24] When information is complete, deterrence is never stable. The player with the highest "effective" resolve simply escalates and wins. A similar conclusion is found in Zagare (1987: 53–54) and Fearon (1994b: 583).

down, the connection between resolve and victory in a crisis does not always depend on a greater willingness to risk war. This conclusion runs counter to the implications of Ellsberg's critical risk model.

One might think that this puts the issue to rest. Even in a world in which mutual defection is the worst of all possible outcomes, rational players can choose not to challenge each other since each obtains a greater expected utility by not challenging. Moreover, while the threat to unleash disaster is not seen to be credible, the threat to escalate and risk war satisfies the rationality and, hence, the perfectness criterion. Thus, Powell's model would seem to explain the stability of deterrence in the nuclear age. Each superpower may have been deterred from challenging the other simply because it feared that the other would, by resisting, unleash a process that would escalate and get out of control.

The problem with this seemingly seductive argument, however, lies in the assumptions necessary to support it. First, note that Powell assumes the players know each other's preference orders over the four outcomes, but not their cardinal utilities. Also note that the conclusions rest on the supposition that the choice of "attack" by one player *always* results in mutual disaster, presumably because the opponent will automatically counter-attack. At the highest rung of the escalation ladder, therefore, each player's threat to retaliate is afforded perfect credibility, even though it is instrumentally irrational to carry out. Thus it is not surprising that none of the equilibrium strategies identified by Powell involves a direct attack by one player against the other. This possibility is eliminated *by assumption*, because it always results in the attacker's worst outcome.

Powell is not the only theorist who assumes that attacks will inevitably be countered. Indeed, it is quite common in the game theory and deterrence literature. For instance, Fearon (1994b: 590), Bueno de Mesquita, Morrow, and Zorick (1997: 17), and Kydd (1997: 379), assume that a war will occur once one side initiates hostilities.[25] The assumption, however, is clearly problematic.

For one, it ignores the incontestable fact that "a war requires the participation of at least two states" (Wagner, 1991: 747). Worse still is its theoretical implication. As Bueno de Mesquita, Morrow, and Zorick (1997: 18) observe, when this assumption is coupled with

---

[25] For reasons that are unclear, Kim and Bueno de Mesquita (1995) also make this assumption, but only for one of the two players in the "crisis subgame" they explore.

another core assumption of classical deterrence theory – i.e., high war costs – "violence will never occur . . . and the problem will have been trivialized."[26]

As well, the assumption has been called into question by theorists who argue that deterrence becomes tenuous when a window of vulnerability opens and tempts one side to launch a limited first-strike to create and then exploit a strategic asymmetry.[27] But even more significant, it is precisely the opposite assumption (i.e., the assumption that states prefer *not* to retaliate) that gives rise to the paradox of mutual deterrence in the first place. Thus, at the strategic level, Powell's model in effect postulates, rather than derives, stability.[28]

Leaving aside for the moment the problem of strategic stability, one can ask whether deterrence can emerge at some lower level during a crisis in which at least one side has already challenged the status quo and the other has resisted the advance. More explicitly, given overall stability at the highest level, why does one side or the other not simply escalate to the penultimate stage of the game since, by assumption, each player is deterred in the next and last stage of the game? For instance, why did the Soviet Union not simply invade Western Europe during the Cold War, given that each side's strategic arsenal was mutually deterred?

The answer suggested by Powell's model is that such an escalatory process would not occur – under specified conditions – because of the fear by each side that the other might do something to cause the process to get out of control.[29] But why should either player fear that its opponent would unleash a process that would lead down the slippery slope toward a general nuclear war? Given the preference assumptions associated with Chicken, this fear is unfounded if the opponent is instrumentally rational. As Maxwell (1968: 12) astutely points out, "if the supposition that neither side believes the other

---

[26] To avoid this problem, Bueno de Mesquita, Morrow, and Zorick's crisis model restricts the cost of violence, keeping it *relatively* low. The restriction has implications for the model's generality. Specifically, the model does not apply to any relationship in which negotiations are preferred to a "favorable" outcome of an all-out war. Most, if not all, hostile nuclear relationships likely fall into this exempted category.

[27] See, for instance, Wohlstetter (1959), Nitze (1976/77), Gray (1979), and the discussion in chapter 1.

[28] To avoid *necessarily* reaching this conclusion, the models developed in this book assume that a state that is attacked may always choose not to resist.

[29] Nalebuff (1986) and many others depend on this assumption to generate a stable deterrence relationship.

would deliberately initiate nuclear war is accepted . . . neither side would have any reason to believe that there was a 'danger of things getting out of hand.'" Or as Wagner (1991: 747) argues, "anyone who is skeptical about the willingness of states to resort to nuclear war rather than accept defeat must also be skeptical about the possibility that a nuclear war will occur inadvertently."[30]

Powell's (and Schelling's) response is that such a process would not be selected by either player but by *Nature*, a "player" with no stake in the game, who imposes the sanction probabilistically. In this model, then, crisis stability depends not only on the stipulation of an irrational response at the highest rung of the escalation ladder, but also on the assumption that, at lower levels, the irrational will occur with some positive probability.[31] This dependence on the irrational is precisely why Achen (1987: 92) argues that "far from leaning too heavily on rational choice postulates, 'rational deterrence theory' necessarily assumes that nations are not always self-interestedly rational." The "strategy-that-leaves-something-to-chance," therefore, can explain deterrence stability, but only by standing the rationality principle on its head.

Powell (1987: 725) admits as much when he writes that "one might object that requiring the states' strategies to be sequentially rational and then relying on Nature to impose the irrational sanction does not really solve the credibility problem. I agree with this criticism." Powell goes on to note, however, that "it is important to realize that this is not so much a criticism of the model as it is a fundamental criticism of the way that the strategy-that-leaves-something-to-chance has attempted to overcome the credibility problem. The model only exposes this weakness." We agree.

---

[30] Wagner (1991) argues that the very availability of counterforce options enhances the credibility of a threat to use nuclear weapons. Wagner's model of extended deterrence, however, lacks generality. It presumes that the attacker (i.e., the Warsaw Pact) would win a conventional war, and that this fact is common knowledge. For other limitations, see O'Neill (1992). Also see our discussion of the efficacy of warfighting strategies in chapter 8.

[31] This is one reason why Fearon (1994b) concludes that Powell's model cannot "explain why states would *consciously* choose to abandon peace for war." Or as Wagner (1991: 742–743) puts it, since "the source of this autonomous probability of war is usually not specified . . . brinkmanship models [like Schelling's and Powell's] leave unclear how a war can occur without anyone's choosing to engage in it."

2.5   Resolving the paradox III: the metagame solution

Neither deterministic threats nor threats-that-leave-something-to-chance provide a satisfactory resolution of the paradox of mutual deterrence. To resolve the paradox by permitting players to commit to a retaliation strategy is necessarily to jettison the assumption of international anarchy, a core assumption of political realism. And the resolution that relies on a Schellingesque threat to abrogate control solves the paradox, in part, by assuming away the source of the contradiction.

In this section, we explore a third possible way to reconcile the instability of the status quo outcome in Chicken with the observed stability of the superpower relationship during the Cold War period. Based on an idea first suggested by von Neumann and Morgenstern (1944: 100–106), but more fully developed by Howard (1971), this resolution involves an alteration of the underlying game to take into account the possibility that the players might be able to anticipate each other's strategy choice. Presuming that each player bases its own strategy choice on the strategy it expects the other to select, a new game – Howard calls it a *metagame* – is rendered and played "in the heads" of the players prior to the play of the actual game. In the metagame, players choose *metastrategies* rather than strategies. A metastrategy can be thought of as a strategy for selecting a strategy. Stable outcomes of the metagame are termed *metaequilibria*.

To illustrate these concepts, consider once again the game of Chicken, but assume now that State B is able to predict – or thinks it can predict – State A's strategy choice. With this assumption, which is logically equivalent to the assumption that State B selects its strategy after learning A's choice, B's range of choices expands. Rather than having just two strategies (i.e., C or D), B now has $2 \times 2 = 4$ metastrategies:

1. C/C: choose C regardless of A's choice (*C Regardless*)
2. D/D: choose D regardless of A's choice (*D Regardless*)
3. C/D: choose C if A chooses C, D if A chooses D (*Tit-for-Tat*)
4. D/C: choose D if A chooses C, C if A chooses D (*Tat-for-Tit*),

which gives rise to the *first-level* metagame shown in figure 2.4.

Figure 2.4 can be interpreted in one of two ways: as the game that would be played if B were able to anticipate A's strategy choice (i.e.,

State B

		C/C *C Regardless*	*D/D* *D Regardless*	*C/D* *Tit-for-Tat*	*D/C* *Tat-for-Tit*
State A	C	(3,3)	(2,4)*	(3,3)	(2,4)
	D	(4,2)*	(1,1)	(1,1)	(4,2)*

(x,y) = payoff to A, payoff to B
4 = best; 3 = next-best; 2 = next-worst; 1 = worst
* = metaequilibria (Nash equilibria)

Fig. 2.4. A first-level metagame of Chicken.

the metagame), or as a sequential (extensive-form) game in which A selects its strategy first.

Notice that there are three metaequilibria in this first-level meta-game. Two correspond to equilibria in the original (simultaneous choice) game while the third – (D, D/C) – is strictly a product of the metagame structure. But this new metaequilibrium has a special property that distinguishes it from the other two and, therefore, gives it a singular status: it is the product of B's weakly dominant meta-strategy (i.e., D/C) and A's best response to B's dominant meta-strategy (i.e., D).[32] Should this equilibrium come into play – and there are good reasons to expect that it, rather than any other, would – A would get its best outcome, and B would get its next-worst outcome.

This preliminary result is interesting for two reasons. First, it shows that the ability to forecast an opponent's strategy does not always help. In Chicken, it actually hurts. And second, it formalizes the view of many decision-theoretic deterrence theorists that the player who seizes the initiative in Chicken wins. Recall that it is on the basis of this observation that decision-theoretic deterrence theorists counsel commitment and related manipulative bargaining tactics.

Metagames, however, do not stop here. Howard now proposes not only that B can anticipate A's strategy choice, *but that A bases its choice*

---

[32] Recall that a weakly dominant strategy (or metastrategy) is at least as good as, and sometimes better than, any other. For a detailed definition, see footnote 19.

on B's predictions of A's choice. If A conditions its strategy choice on B's metastrategy, it can choose either *C* or *D* for each of B's four metastrategies, which gives State A $2 \times 2 \times 2 \times 2 = 16$ *second-level* meta-strategies. For instance, the second-level metastrategy *D/D/C/D* requires A to

1. Choose *D* if B chooses *C/C* (*C Regardless*)
2. Choose *D* if B chooses *D/D* (*D Regardless*)
3. Choose *C* if B chooses *C/D* (*Tit-for-Tat*)
4. Choose *D* if B chooses *D/C* (*Tat-for-Tit*).

A's 16 second-level metastrategies and B's 4 first-level metastrate-gies imply a $16 \times 4 = 64$ outcome strategic-form game. An abbreviated version of this matrix, listing only non-repetitive metaequilibria, is given in figure 2.5. Notice the increased number of metaequilibria. Among them is one that corresponds to the *Status Quo* outcome CC with payoffs (3,3). This is a significant result because it suggests that if Howard's assumptions are satisfied, the status quo could survive and deterrence could succeed.

The operative word here is "could." There are other possibilities. Still, the metastrategies associated with the (3,3) metaequilibrium of figure 2.5 (i.e., the outcome CC) are explicitly suggestive of the conditions under which deterrence success might occur. Specifically, B's *C/D* metastrategy is a variant of tit-for-tat: cooperate if A coop-erates, defect if A defects. So is A's *D/D/C/D* metastrategy. It implies cooperation, but only in response to B's conditionally cooperative tit-for-tat strategy. All of which indicates that mutual cooperation is possible, but only when each player is prepared to cooperate condi-tionally, that is, when each intends to cooperate should the other player cooperate and – equally important – when each intends to defect should the other defect.

Observe that the metastrategies associated with mutual cooperation (i.e., with stable deterrence) are risky: each carries with it the possibility of a player's worst outcome, DD. But as Howard (1971: 184) argues, if the players are unwilling to run this risk, a compromise equilibrium is not possible. Brams (1975: 44) concurs, adding that the metagame analysis suggests "that a policy of deterrence, by which each side promises retaliation for any untoward acts by the other, is not only desirable from the viewpoint of the players, but stable as well."

If this conclusion holds, the paradox of mutual deterrence is solved. Whether it holds, however, depends on the interpretation given to the

State B

	C/C C Regardless	D/D D Regardless	C/D Tit-for-Tat	D/C Tat-for-Tit
C/C/C/C	(3,3)	(2,4)*	(3,3)	(2,4)
···	···	···	···	···
D/C/C/D	(4,2)	(2,4)*	(3,3)	(4,2)
State A ···	···	···	···	···
D/D/C/D	(4,2)	(1,1)	(3,3)*	(4,2)
···	···	···	···	···
D/D/D/D	(4,2)*	(1,1)	(1,1)	(4,2)*

(x,y)	= payoff to A, payoff to B
4	= best; 3 = next-best; 2 = next-worst; 1 = worst
*	= metaequilibria (Nash equilibria)
···	= unlisted metastrategies/outcomes

Fig. 2.5. A second-level metagame of Chicken (part).

metaequilibria. Howard's construction is strictly *descriptive*: metaequilibria are established as theoretical possibilities only, and the metastrategies are theoretical statements about the content of the communication necessary to lead to some outcome. In Howard's view, no particular metaequilibrium has special status. Each, therefore, describes a logical possibility in a game between rational players. Which metaequilibrium eventually comes into play depends on what the players expect from one another, or what they communicate to each other in pre-play bargaining and discussion. In the present example, then, mutual cooperation is possible, provided the players are both prepared to cooperate conditionally. But there are also other rational possibilities. For example, should B expect A to select metastrategy $D/C/C/D$ and should A expect B to choose metastrategy D/D (*D Regardless*), the metaequilibrium italicized in figure 2.5, CD, with payoff (2,4), will occur. This metaequilibrium is best for B and next-worst for A.

Notice that $D/C/C/D$ – or what Howard refers to as the "sure-thing" metastrategy – is weakly dominant for A, giving B good reason to suspect that A will choose it; and since *D Regardless* is B's best response to $D/C/C/D$, A has a good reason to suspect that B will choose it. All this suggests that the metaequilibrium associated with these two metastrategies might well evolve in a game between rational players.

Howard, however, rejects this outcome as *the* solution to the metagame, and denies that any particular reason exists for singling it out. In fact, he argues it would be *foolish* for A to select its sure-thing metastrategy because it induces a worse outcome for A than its "retaliatory" metastrategy $D/D/C/D$. Or in Howard's (1974a: 730) own words, the sure-thing metastrategy is "the strategy of a 'sucker' who invites, and is ready to yield before, the most extreme ultimatum in the possession of his opponent, and is thus willing to surrender his position before any bargaining begins."

But Harsanyi (1974b), hewing to a normative interpretation and insisting on the perfectness criterion, argues that the use of any dominated metastrategy is irrational and, hence, *incredible*.[33] Since a player with a dominant metastrategy always maximizes its expected utility by choosing it, there is no good reason for an opponent to believe that any other metastrategy would be chosen. This, in turn, implies that a player with a dominant metastrategy should choose it.[34] To do otherwise would be to invite calamity.[35] Specifically, if A were to select its retaliatory metastrategy $(D/D/C/D)$ and B, anticipating A's sure-thing metastrategy $(D/C/C/D)$, selects *D Regardless*, each player's worst outcome, DD, results.

Harsanyi's admonition not to abandon the use of a weakly dominant strategy, especially in a one-shot game, is difficult to ignore: dominant strategies are unconditionally best. But, then, what are we

---

[33] In chapter 3, we discuss in detail the connection between subgame-perfect equilibria and credibility.

[34] For the particulars of the debate, see Harsanyi (1973, 1974a, 1974b) and Howard (1973, 1974a, 1974b).

[35] It is worth pointing out that the lively three-way debate among Howard, Anatol Rapoport, and Richard Harris over whether the theory of metagames resolves Prisoners' Dilemma also turned on the proper interpretation of Howard's theory. Rapoport's (1967) argument that it does rests on a normative reading was similar to the one advanced by Harsanyi. Howard, refusing to claim anything but a descriptive status for his theory, rejected Rapoport's suggestion. For the full set of citations, see Brams (1975: 39).

to make of Howard's (1974b: 1693) observation that, in Chicken, "what is the *best* strategy from the viewpoint of rationality is the *worst* strategy from the viewpoint of inducement?" In our view, it is simply another way of stating the paradox of mutual deterrence: when conflict is a mutually worst outcome, deterrence stability can only be generated by assuming both "irrational behavior and irrational expectations by the players about each other's behavior" (Harsanyi, 1977: 332).

Rather than solving the paradox of mutual deterrence, then, Howard's methodology highlights it by reformulating it in a way that deepens our understanding. As Brams (1975: 44) adds, "metagame theory specifies precisely, if indirectly, the *content* of the communications and the *nature* of the bargaining necessary to reach compromise." This, of course, is no mean feat. But when interpreted normatively, the theory reveals that compromise, while potentially stable, has no rational basis. In fact, a normative interpretation suggests that B should win, given that B's best response (D/D) to A's dominant metastrategy ($D/C/C/D$) leads to a metaequilibrium at CD. This should be no surprise, since the assignment of a higher-order metastrategy to A is in some sense equivalent to the assumption that State A chooses its strategy with knowledge of B's choice. The observation that the player choosing second in Chicken will lose continues to be robust.

But what if one accepts Howard's strictly descriptive interpretation of metagame theory? In our opinion, the paradox remains unresolved. Without a normative foundation, one is left without an explanation of why, or when, players would transmit the statements necessary to induce and support mutual cooperation.[36]

2.6   Coda

In the previous sections we have examined three proposed resolutions of the paradox of mutual deterrence. Two in fact do resolve the logical

---

[36] The compromise outcome can be supported, however, if one accepts the "stability by simultaneity" criterion advanced by Fraser and Hipel (1984) in their refinement of Howard's *analysis of options* technique. An otherwise unstable outcome is rendered stable by simultaneity if both players do worse when they switch strategies at the same time. We believe the possibility of simultaneous strategy switches to be so remote that the resolution suggested by this rationality postulate is not germane to our discussion. Thus the puzzle of how to establish the stability of the status quo in Chicken-like contests is not resolved in Fraser and Hipel's system, nor in the more inclusive *graph model* of Fang, Hipel, and Kilgour (1993).

contradiction, but only at the expense of a core assumption of the realist paradigm. To wit, the logical and empirical inconsistency of classical deterrence theory is eliminated *if* the players are permitted to pre-commit to a retaliation strategy. But this presumption violates the precept that, in an anarchic world, "covenants, without the Sword, are but Words, and of no strength to secure a man at all" (Hobbes, 1968 [1651]: 223). Needless to say, most extant realist thinking, structural or otherwise, depends critically on this axiom. One must reflect deeply, therefore, before abandoning it.

Much the same could be said about Schelling's "threat-that-leaves-something-to-chance." In order to explain real-world deterrence stability in terms of this chance mechanism, however, one must cast aside the assumption that statesmen are rational utility maximizers. Again, while one might logically accept this explanation for the absence of a nuclear war between the United States and the Soviet Union during the Cold War period, one cannot do so within the confines of the realist paradigm.

The third proposal, Howard's metagame theory, provides no resolution at all. When interpreted normatively, it suggests behavior inconsistent with deterrence stability. And when interpreted descriptively – Howard's favored interpretation – it highlights and reinforces the paradox, but does not resolve it.

Once more we are led to ask whether classical deterrence theory can be rendered logically consistent and empirically accurate. In the next chapter we explore a resolution that we believe lays the foundation for an empirically plausible reformulation of deterrence theory, and does so without violating the postulates of individual rationality.

3 Credibility and deterrence

> A rational deterrent cannot be based on irrational responses.
>
> Richard Nixon

The fundamental tenets of classical deterrence theory are incompatible with models based on rational choice. Deterministic threats, which rest on the presumption that states can commit themselves to irrational actions, violate the canons of both classical deterrence theory and instrumental rationality. While the threat-that-leaves-something-to-chance maintains consistency with the rationality postulate, consistency is achieved only by assuming that irrational actions are carried out by a disinterested third party. And the resolution suggested by a metagame analysis serves merely to bring the paradox of mutual deterrence into sharper focus: when the costs of war are so high that all-out conflict is the worst outcome for both players, mutual deterrence is unlikely. It might appear, then, that there is no escape from this pernicious puzzle.

We believe otherwise. In this chapter we propose still another resolution. Our proposal is based on the concept of *perfectly credible* retaliatory threats. Like other attempts to eliminate the paradox, this resolution involves a modification of the underlying game form; but unlike other proposals, ours retains the core realist assumption of an anarchical international system while remaining faithful to the definition of instrumental rationality. In a narrow technical sense, then, the paradox of mutual deterrence stands. Technicalities aside, however, the resolution we propose permits an intuitively satisfying and empirically plausible respecification of classical deterrence theory that helps to explain the dynamics of a wide range of deterrence relationships, *including those that occur under the conditions that delimit the paradox*.

3.1   On credibility

Before demonstrating the above, however, we must pause once again to define an important term: *credibility*. Freedman (1989: 96) characterizes credibility as the "magic ingredient" of deterrence. And Gilpin (1981: 33), who equates credibility with "prestige," claims that it plays "a critical role . . . in the ordering and functioning of the international system." Yet for a concept so central to deterrence, it is surprising how little attention has been given in the traditional strategic literature to establishing a rigorous definition. The vast majority of strategic analysts appear to be of the opinion that the term is transparent enough that no formal definition is required. Threat credibility is generally taken to mean that the threat is believed – and left at that (Schelling, 1966; George and Smoke, 1974; Freedman, 1989; Jervis, 1985; Pruitt and Rubin, 1986; and Mueller, 1995). Typically, the next analytical step is to explore the underlying determinants of such beliefs.

Conversely, threats which are not believed are characterized as *incredible*. For example, consider the Eisenhower administration's threat to inflict nuclear devastation on the Soviet Union for even relatively minor transgressions of the status quo. Shortly after the policy of *Massive Retaliation* was formulated, it was widely criticized for being unbelievable and, consequently, lacking credibility (Kaufmann, 1956).[1] In Smoke's (1987: 88) words, "the threat was not credible in the face of growing Soviet strategic power. As the Soviet arsenal of atomic bombs, and of long-range bombers to deliver them, grew during [the mid- to late 1950s], it became less believable that the United States would actually launch an atomic war over some invasion in Asia or elsewhere."

Significantly, the credibility of threats is sometimes also closely linked with their rationality. Lebow (1981: 15), for instance, notes that the difficulty of imparting credibility to the threat to go to war in the nuclear age stems from the fact that "the adversary knows the inherent *irrationality* of such threats" (emphasis added). In the strategic literature, therefore, the notion of credibility is either directly or indirectly associated with rational or self-interested behavior (Betts, 1987: 12; Smoke, 1987: 93). Credible threats are threats that are

---

[1] We analyze this policy in detail in chapter 7.

believed; threats can be believed exactly when it is rational to carry them out; thus, only rational threats are credible threats.

But what constitutes a rational threat? The answer to this vexing question depends on the definition of rationality. There are two possibilities. In the tradition of *procedural* rationality, one could identify rational threats by carefully delineating the real-world conditions that would justify a retaliatory response by one state to an untoward action of another, thereby separating those situations in which a deterrent threat is credible from those in which it is not.[2] Colin Gray (1979: 55), for one, did just this some time ago when he argued that a massive nuclear assault on the Soviet Union "would likely trigger a Soviet response in kind" since, under these circumstances, the Soviets would have "nothing left to lose." Curiously, while Gray imputed almost perfect credibility to the Soviet threat to respond to an all-out American attack, he questioned the credibility of the US deterrent under exactly the same circumstances, seeing little "merit (let alone moral justification) in executing the posthumous punishment of an adversary's society." Gray's difficulty in maintaining consistent criteria for evaluating the rationality of these identical hypothetical choices underscores an inherent limitation of the procedural approach.[3]

Of course, at the level of policy determination, speculation about the conditions under which an adversary would either contemplate an attack, or respond to a challenge, is not only appropriate, but essential. Still, such speculation may be counter-productive at the level of theory construction. Rather than enter into a debate about what would, or would not, precipitate an attack or a response by some state – a question that in any case must ultimately be answered by those in policy-making positions – we take a second, more limited, approach to specifying credible threats. In the tradition of *instrumental* rationality, we define threat credibility as the extent to which a threatener is seen to prefer to execute the threat (should the

---

[2] For a useful summary of the contours of this and related debates, see Eden and Miller (1989).

[3] The secondary assumptions of models developed by Fearon (1994b) and Morrow (1994b) are consistent with this approach to credibility. Fearon suggests that "audience costs" may be the key for states attempting to signal a credible threat. Morrow argues that alliances augment credibility because they impose peacetime costs on their members.

appropriate contingency arise). We measure that extent as the subjective probability assigned to this event by the decision-makers. Like other instrumentalists, we assume that an actor prefers to execute a threat when the anticipated worth of doing so exceeds the anticipated worth of failing to do so. Otherwise, the threat is irrational and, hence, incredible.

It is important to emphasize that the connection we draw between credibility and rationality is operationally the same as insisting that equilibria satisfy Selten's (1975) perfectness criterion.[4] As Rasmusen (1989: 87) notes, "perfectness rules out threats that are not credible." By equating rational threats with credible threats, therefore, we maintain consistency not only with the informal strategic literature of deterrence, but also with the game-theoretic literature, where the credibility of threats is generally taken to be synonymous with subgame perfectness of Nash equilibria, that is, with equilibria that are consistent with rational choices on all possible paths of the game tree (Selten, 1975; Friedman, 1986: 80–82; Holler, 1988; and Zagare, 1990a). Or, in Gibbons's (1992: 57) words, some games "may have many Nash equilibria, but some of these may involve non-credible threats or promises. The subgame-perfect Nash equilibria are those that pass a credibility test."[5]

The approach we take is now all but standard in the formal literature of deterrence.[6] For instance, both Fearon (1990: 25) and Wagner (1991: 739) equate threat credibility with the probability that a threat is carried out. Given the widespread acceptance of this definition, it is somewhat surprising that no systematic formal analysis of the implications of this important element of the deterrence mixture

---

[4] This is why Harsanyi, in evaluating Howard's metagame analysis of Chicken (see chapter 2), argued that dominated metastrategies like "sure-thing" are inherently incredible.

[5] We note that subgame-perfect equilibria are associated with games in extensive-form and that Nash equilibria are associated with games in strategic form. Because any extensive-form game can be converted to strategic form, one can locate any subgame-perfect equilibrium in a strategic-form representation. Any subgame-perfect equilibrium corresponds to a Nash equilibrium, but there may be some Nash equilibria that do not correspond to any subgame-perfect equilibrium.

[6] To our knowledge, in the formal literature of deterrence, the linkage between credibility and rationality was first suggested by Zagare (1985), albeit in the context of games of complete information. Zagare (1987) and Langlois (1989, 1991) were the first to develop game models that fully incorporated the possibility of credible (i.e., rational) retaliatory threats.

has ever been attempted. There have been, however, some important partial attempts.

To wit: Fearon's (1990) signaling model affords a defender an opportunity to take a costly action that could enhance its credibility. But since these actions can take place only after aggression has occurred, Fearon's model does not speak directly to the role credibility plays in general deterrence relationships like those analyzed in this and the next chapter. (See also Fearon, 1994b, and Bueno de Mesquita, Morrow, and Zorick, 1997). Similarly, because Bueno de Mesquita and Lalman (1992) and Kim and Bueno de Mesquita (1995) focus attention on the "crisis subgame" of a more general "international interaction game," their most pointed conclusions about threat credibility concern its role in immediate deterrence situations. And finally, Morrow (1994b) and Smith (1995, 1996, 1998b) construct models that link threat credibility and alliance commitments. In consequence, the insights that can be drawn from these models pertain almost exclusively to situations of extended deterrence.[7] None of these studies, therefore, attempts to explain fully the dynamics of direct general deterrence relationships. Nor do they provide a definitive resolution of the paradox of deterrence – although they may be suggestive of, and potentially consistent with, the resolution we provide.

We should also make clear that this approach to credibility remains inconsistent with the underlying precepts of classical deterrence theory in general, and of brinkmanship models in particular. As already discussed, classic formulations of deterrence start with the presumption that *all* end-game deterrent threats are (both instrumentally and procedurally) irrational, but that they are nonetheless executed probabilistically by an impersonal force with no stake in the game. As we argued above, this approach bypasses the credibility problem – as even Powell (1987) admits – because it supposes that the players' risks are imposed on them by "nature," rather than as a consequence of the opponent's threat. Since the classic approach treats the credibility of end-game threats as a constant, the very possibility of exploring the relationship between threat credibility and stable deterrence is precluded. But even if credibility were to be treated as a variable, a fundamental problem would still exist: as long as incredible threats can be executed, no linkage can possibly be established between credibility and deterrence.

---

[7] We analyze extended deterrence relationships in part III.

All of which is not to say that we hold that nature plays no role in the way that conflicts, nuclear or otherwise, evolve. Rather than prejudge the question, however, we assume that the risks associated with war and other conflict outcomes are reflected in the values (utilities) of the players. As we hope to demonstrate, this approach permits a thorough evaluation of the connection between credibility and deterrence stability and, more importantly, leads to a theory of deterrence that is at once logically consistent and empirically plausible. Equally important are the policy implications of the theory we construct: they differ significantly from those that follow from classical deterrence theory (see chapter 1). We discuss these differences in detail in chapter 10.

3.2 Resolving the paradox IV: mutually credible threats

As a first step toward constructing a new general theory of deterrence, we now demonstrate that the paradox of mutual deterrence is resolved once each player's retaliatory threat is afforded perfect credibility. By resolving the paradox, we eliminate the logical contradiction inherent in decision-theoretic deterrence theory and lay the conceptual foundation for a reformulation of classical deterrence theory.

To this end, consider again the broad outlines of a typical mutual deterrence situation in which State A and State B are trying to prevent each other from upsetting the status quo. To maintain conceptual consistency, and to keep things as simple as possible, assume the same *initial* choices the players have in Chicken. Each player must decide whether to cooperate (C) with the other by supporting the status quo or to defect (D) from cooperation by attempting to overturn it. Also assume, for now, that the players make their initial choices *simultaneously*.[8] Thus, if both cooperate, the *Status Quo* (outcome SQ) ensues. (We represent A's *utility* for outcome SQ by a_{SQ} and B's by b_{SQ}. In general, A's and B's utilities at outcome K will be denoted (a_K, b_K).) Similarly, if both sides defect, all-out *Conflict* (outcome DD) results. In this case, the utility of A is a_{DD} and of B is b_{DD}. Here and hereafter we assume that the players' utilities (a_{SQ}, b_{SQ}, a_{DD}, b_{DD}, etc.) are von

---

[8] In chapter 5 we consider the consequences of sequential choice.

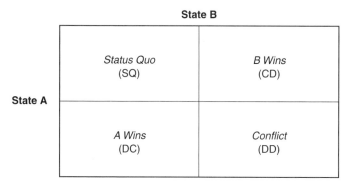

Fig. 3.1. Outcome matrix for the Generalized Mutual Deterrence Game.

Neumann–Morgenstern (1944) utilities.[9] Thus a player's utilities automatically represent both its relative preferences and its risk attitudes.

Now assume that if one player cooperates while the other defects, the cooperating player has another opportunity to choose *D*, that is, to retaliate; if the cooperating player decides *not* to retaliate (i.e., sticks with *C*), the other *Wins* or gains an advantage (either outcome DC or CD); but if the cooperating player retaliates, *Conflict* occurs. The four possible outcomes of this game, called the *Generalized Mutual Deterrence Game*, are summarized in the *outcome matrix* of figure 3.1.[10]

Before we get in over our heads, we remind the reader that game-theoretic models are, in essence, empty vessels: they can be filled with a wide variety of substantive liquids. And while the liquids largely take on the shape of their containers, they remain liquids: fluid and malleable. In the Chicken model, for instance, players may either cooperate or defect. But since both terms are operationally undefined, it is up to the modeler to ascribe meaning and draw distinctions. Thus, depending on the context, "to cooperate" might imply taking no action (i.e., doing nothing), or it could mean being proactive in

---

[9] Some conditions on preferences over lotteries (probabilistic packages of alternatives) are required to justify the von Neumann–Morgenstern utilities that we use below. For instance, preferences over lotteries are assumed to be continuous, which means that, if *a* is preferred to *b* and *b* to *c*, then there is some lottery involving *a* and *c* (say 50/50 or 60/40) that is indifferent to *b*. For a discussion and two different formulations of the other conditions, see Hargreaves Heap and Varoufakis (1995: 4–14) and Luce and Raiffa (1957: 23–31).

[10] We emphasize that this is an outcome matrix, not the strategic form of a game.

support of a collective goal. If the other player has already defected, "to cooperate" could also mean capitulating. Similarly, "to defect" might mean, *inter alia*, making a demand, issuing a challenge, precipitating a crisis, launching an attack or, if the opposing player has already defected, retaliating. Or as Bueno de Mesquita, Morrow, and Zorick (1997: 17) might put it, "the exact contents of the [defection] are exogenous to this model."

Similarly, the outcomes of any game model are protean concepts. A good example is the outcome we call *Conflict*. In some situations, *Conflict* could be taken to imply an all-out nuclear war. But the term need not be so restricted, or even confined to armed hostilities. In some contexts, it could imply a protracted confrontation, such as the Iranian hostage crisis that started in 1979 and did not end until early in 1981. In our models, therefore, as in the real world, the precise form of any *Conflict* outcome will depend on a number of factors, including the nature of the defection, the level of the response, etc. All of which is to explain why we will be, at times, intentionally vague about the empirical referents of the constituent parts of the models we construct and analyze.

Returning again to our previous discussion, consider now figure 3.2, a representation of the Generalized Mutual Deterrence Game in extensive or game-tree form. In this representation it might appear as if State A makes the first choice at node 1. But this is not the case. Notice the straight line – called an *information set* – connecting State B's choice at nodes 2a and 2b.[11] An information set provides a concise graphical summary of the knowledge each player has about all the choices made in a game *up to that point*. When two or more nodes are contained in a player's information set, the two nodes are indistinguishable to the player. Thus when B makes its initial choice, it does *not* know whether it is at node 2a or at node 2b, that is, it does not know what choice A has made.

Since A's choice is represented as the first choice in the game, there is, perforce, only one node in its information set.[12] But this is simply

---

[11] Technically, an information set is a set of nodes mutually joined by such lines. All nodes in the information set must belong to the same player, and must present that player with exactly the same number of choices, labeled in exactly the same way.

[12] Sets containing only one element are called *singletons*. If all information sets in a game are singletons, the game is said to be a game of *perfect information*. The game of figure 3.2, then, is not a game of perfect information. Perfect information should be distinguished from *complete information* which we discuss below.

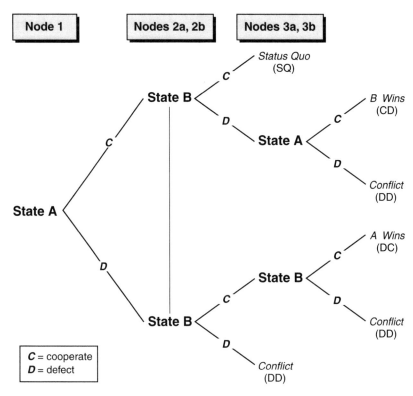

Fig. 3.2. Extensive-form representation of the Generalized Mutual Deterrence Game.

another way of saying that A's choice is made without prior knowledge of B's choice.

Notice that we have subtly changed the rules associated with the mutual deterrence game considered in chapter 1 to allow for the possibility of *retaliation*. At this point, the suspicious reader might think that our proposal to resolve the paradox of mutual deterrence depends on this modification of the underlying game form. This is only partly true. The rule change is motivated by a desire to represent better the dynamics of mutual deterrence relationships. In fact, the change is, by itself, insufficient to eliminate the paradox. Given the core assumptions of classical deterrence theory, the paradox stands.

To see this, assume for now that the *Conflict* outcome (DD) is mutually worst, as in Chicken. To maintain consistency with classical realism, also assume that each player is egotistical and (1) prefers winning (outcome DC or CD) to the *Status Quo* (SQ),[13] and (2) prefers the *Status Quo* to losing to the other side. These assumptions restrict the players' preferences over the four outcomes as follows:

$$\text{State A: } A \text{ Wins} >_A \text{ Status Quo} >_A B \text{ Wins} >_A \text{ Conflict} \qquad (3.1)$$
$$\text{State B: } B \text{ Wins} >_B \text{ Status Quo} >_B A \text{ Wins} >_B \text{ Conflict} \qquad (3.2)$$

where "$>_A$" means "is preferred to by A" and "$>_B$" means "is preferred to by B." In terms of utilities, these restrictions imply $a_{DC} > a_{SQ} > a_{CD} > a_{DD}$, and $b_{CD} > b_{SQ} > b_{DC} > b_{DD}$.

Notice that in this array neither player prefers to retaliate. A prefers *B Wins* to *Conflict* ($a_{CD} > a_{DD}$) while B prefers *A Wins* to *Conflict* ($b_{DC} > b_{DD}$). Thus, as in Chicken, neither player has a credible retaliatory threat.[14] Of course, the game is not Chicken. In Chicken, each player has only one move with two choices, while in the present example each player has two moves, each with two choices. In Chicken, then, each player has $1 \times 2 = 2$ strategies, to cooperate or to defect. By contrast, in the Generalized Mutual Deterrence Game, each player has $2 \times 2 = 4$ strategies:

1. *C Regardless* (C/C)
2. *Tit-for-Tat* (C/D)
3. *Tat-for-Tit* (D/C)
4. *D Regardless* (D/D).

Thus, the strategic-form of any game played under the rules of play summarized by figure 3.2 results in a 4×4 matrix. Figure 3.3 is the strategic-form representation of the ordinal game defined by the rules of figure 3.2 and the preference restrictions given by (3.1) and (3.2).

Selten's perfectness criterion can be applied to the extensive-form game of figure 3.2 at nodes 3a and 3b. Specifically, the requirement of rational choices throughout the *subgame*[15] beginning at node 3a means

---

[13] We modify this assumption from chapter 5 onward.

[14] Mansbach (1997) writes that "disaster occurs in chicken when both players believe the other is *bluffing*." In terms of our definitions, however, in Chicken and in the game of figure 3.2, both players *are* bluffing: each *prefers* to back down rather than endure conflict. Disaster occurs when both bluffs are called.

[15] The subgame beginning at a node of an extensive-form game is the extensive-form game obtained by deleting all nodes other than that node and its successors. (Note that the subgame is well-defined only if no information set of the original game

State B

	C/C	C/D	D/C	D/D
C/C	(3,3)	(3,3)	(2,4)*	(2,4)*
C/D	(3,3)	(3,3)*	(1,1)	(1,1)
D/C	(4,2)*	(1,1)	(1,1)	(1,1)
D/D	(4,2)*	(1,1)	(1,1)	(1,1)

State A

---

* = Nash equilibrium
(Shaded cells are consistent with the perfectness criterion.)

Fig. 3.3. Ordinal strategic-form representation of Generalized
Mutual Deterrence Game when neither player has a credible
retaliatory threat.

that State A must choose rationally either *C* or *D*, knowing that State B
has already chosen *D*. But here A is choosing between outcomes CD
(*B Wins*) and DD (*Conflict*), and (3.1) tells us that State A prefers CD,
i.e., that A should choose *C*. Thus behavior that calls for A to choose
anything other than *C* (i.e., *D*) at node 3a fails the perfectness criterion.
The argument is similar at node 3b, where perfectness demands that
State B choose *C* rather than *D*, based on (3.2).

In figure 3.3, Nash equilibria are indicated by asterisks. The shaded
cells are those outcomes consistent with the perfectness criterion.
Observe that there are five Nash equilibria in the strategic form, but
that only two are subgame-perfect. Specifically, the perfect equilibria
are (*D/C, C/C*), resulting in the DC outcome (A's most preferred and
B's next-least preferred), and (*C/C, D/C*), resulting in the CD

contains at least one node that is included in the subgame, and at least one node that
is not. In a game of perfect information, all information sets are singletons [i.e.,
contain only one node], so there is a well-defined subgame from every node. But in a
game with nontrivial information sets, some nodes will not correspond to a
subgame.)

outcome (A's next-least preferred and B's most preferred). There is one Nash equilibrium associated with the survival of the *Status Quo*, the "tit-for-tat" equilibrium (*C/D, C/D*), *but it is not perfect!* We conclude that if both sides have threats that lack credibility, the *Status Quo* cannot rationally survive – in other words, the precepts of rationality are inconsistent with general deterrence success.

To see why general deterrence fails, consider the Nash equilibrium with ordinal values (3, 3) shown in figure 3.3. The required tit-for-tat strategies require each player to choose *C* initially, but to plan to switch to *D* if the opponent's initial choice is *D*. If both choose *C* initially, the *Status Quo* results and the outcome is an equilibrium: neither can do better unilaterally by switching to another strategy. But, and this is a big "but," given each player's preferences, switching to *D* subsequently is irrational. For example, suppose that at the start of the game A chooses *D* and B chooses *C*. After these initial choices, B has an opportunity (at node 3b) to retaliate. B can stick with *C* – in which case *A Wins*, or choose *D* – in which case *Conflict* ensues. B, of course, preferring *A Wins* to *Conflict* ($b_{DC} > b_{DD}$), should – if it is rational – choose *C*.

All of which is another way of saying that when both players lack a credible retaliatory threat, the stability of the status quo is inconsistent with the canons of rational choice. Put in still different terms, general deterrence should not obtain when conflict is the worst outcome for both players. Thus, the alteration in the rules of play that we introduced is of little moment; given mutually incredible threats, the paradox of mutual deterrence stands.

All of this changes, however, when both State A and State B have *credible* retaliatory threats, *preferring* to retaliate if the other chooses *D* initially, that is, when:

State A: *A Wins* $>_A$ *Status Quo* $>_A$ *Conflict* $>_A$ *B Wins*   (3.3)
State B: *B Wins* $>_B$ *Status Quo* $>_B$ *Conflict* $>_B$ *A Wins*   (3.4)

or when $a_{DC} > a_{SQ} > a_{DD} > a_{CD}$ and $b_{CD} > b_{SQ} > b_{DD} > b_{DC}$.

It is particularly significant that these preferences are exactly the same as those of the players in game theory's most famous 2 × 2 game – *Prisoners' Dilemma*. The only structural difference between Prisoners' Dilemma and Chicken concerns the relative ranking of each player's two worst outcomes. In Chicken, each player prefers capitulation to conflict. In Prisoners' Dilemma, this ranking is reversed. As we show next, this simple difference has a very important implication for the dynamics of mutual deterrence relationships. When the preferences of expressions (3.3) and (3.4) hold, deterrence works.[16]

To see why, consider now figure 3.4, the strategic-form representation of the Generalized Mutual Deterrence Game (see figure 3.2) with preferences given by (3.3) and (3.4). Application of the perfectness criterion at nodes 3a and 3b imposes the requirement that both players choose *D* in this follow-up stage, because both now prefer conflict to capitulation. The outcomes consistent with this requirement, that is, with subgame perfection, are highlighted in figure 3.4.

The game of figure 3.4 has five Nash equilibria, but only two are perfect. One of them produces *Conflict*, but the other supports the *Status Quo*! This means that *when both players have a credible retaliatory threat, deterrence is not only stable, but rational as well.* Moreover, deterrence is more than just possible, it is likely; of the two perfect equilibria, only the deterrence equilibrium has a *Pareto-optimal* outcome.[17] In fact, the *Status Quo*, the outcome of the deterrence equilibrium, is *Pareto-superior* to *Conflict*, the outcome of the other perfect equilibrium. Thus, the criterion of perfectness reinforces the view of traditional strategic thinkers about the significance of credible threats in international affairs.

The intuition behind our conclusions about deterrence when both sides have credible threats is easy to grasp. If each player believes that, should it alone defect initially, the other would certainly retaliate (because it is instrumentally rational to do so), then each is better off by cooperating – and inducing its next-best outcome – than by defecting – and inducing its next-worst outcome. Given the emphasis on the importance of credible threats in the informal strategic literature, this result is hardly surprising. Most traditional deterrence theorists hold that deterrence works best when each side possesses a credible retaliatory threat. But, and this too is a big "but," since almost all decision-theoretic deterrence theorists start with the assumption

---

[16] This result should be contrasted with that of Bueno de Mesquita and Lalman (1992: 142, 167) who hold that Prisoners' Dilemma conditions encourage war and conflict. But their definition of these conditions within the context of their "crisis subgame" is suspect. (See Zagare [1993] for a detailed discussion.) More in line with our conclusion is Bueno de Mesquita and Lalman's (1992: 124) "cooperation proposition" which states that "if both parties to a conflict of interest are known to be prepared to retaliate, then cooperation or harmony is guaranteed."

[17] Outcome *K* is *Pareto-superior* to outcome *L* if all players find *K* at least as preferable as *L*, and at least one player strictly prefers *K* to *L*. Outcome *L* is *Pareto-optimal* if there is no outcome *K* that is Pareto-superior to *L*.

	State B			
	C/C	*C/D*	*D/C*	*D/D*
C/C	(3,3)	(3,3)	(1,4)	(1,4)
C/D	(3,3)	(3,3)*	(2,2)	(2,2)
D/C	(4,1)	(2,2)	(2,2)*	(2,2)*
D/D	(4,1)	(2,2)	(2,2)*	(2,2)*

State A

> * = Nash equilibrium
> (Shaded cells are consistent with the perfectness criterion.)

Fig. 3.4. Ordinal strategic-form representation of Generalized Mutual Deterrence Game when both players have a credible retaliatory threat.

that *all* retaliatory threats are inherently incredible (see chapter 1), this straightforward connection between credibility and deterrence stability is frequently obscured in the formal literature of deterrence. This is perhaps why there has been, as yet, no systematic analysis of the connection between threat credibility and the dynamics of deterrence across a range of strategic environments.

One aim of this book is to specify this connection, precisely, for a variety of deterrence relationships, mutual and unilateral, direct and extended. We believe that a significantly different theoretical structure emerges once the *possibility* is admitted that the players may prefer retaliation to capitulation – an assumption that is perforce eliminated by those classical deterrence theorists who begin with an underlying structure that reflects preferences similar to those in Chicken. In the rest of this chapter we lay the groundwork for this reformulation of classical deterrence theory.[18]

[18] Fearon's (1990, 1994b) crisis bargaining models are a hybrid of Perfect Deterrence Theory and the brinkmanship models discussed in chapter 2. Like Howard (1971), Gauthier (1984), Nalebuff (1986), and others, Fearon begins with a payoff structure in which neither player believes the other prefers war to backing down. But as the game

One implication, however, is immediate. If deterrence is unlikely when each player lacks a credible threat, then one would expect players involved in real-world mutual deterrence games to try to shore up the status quo by establishing credibility. Put another way, players have every incentive to manipulate the underlying structure of those mutual deterrence games that structurally resemble Chicken and attempt to transform them into games with preference configurations similar to Prisoners' Dilemma, as Fearon's (1994b) analysis of the impact of audience costs on crisis bargaining outcomes suggests. Thus, rather than by precipitous actions – which are clearly mandated in Chicken and its derivative games – one would anticipate that those acute interstate crises that are successfully managed to be characterized by verbal and nonverbal communication patterns like tit-for-tat – which are consistent with Prisoners' Dilemma games. Tit-for-tat strategies combine the carrot – "I'll cooperate if you will cooperate" – and the stick – "but otherwise I'll defect."

There is more than a modicum of empirical support for the proposition that conditionally cooperative strategies and reciprocal behavioral sequences are common patterns in international affairs (e.g., Snyder and Diesing, 1977; Walker, 1977; Huth, 1988a; Goldstein and Freeman, 1990; Leng, 1993). The theory we construct in this book is entirely consistent with these observations and, moreover, helps to explain why reciprocal actions are so frequently observed. By contrast, they are simply inexplicable within classical deterrence theory.

Parenthetically, we add that the connection we draw between deterrence stability, threat credibility, and tit-for-tat strategies is robust across a number of game-theoretic methodologies, including the theory of metagames,[19] the *analysis of options technique* developed by Fraser and Hipel (1984),[20] the *theory of moves* advanced by Brams

---

progresses, and as (audience) costs accumulate, one side is able to signal credibly that its preference is for war. In Fearon's formalizations and in the models developed herein (see figure 3.5), that side generally prevails. Since costly signals can be transmitted only after a threat has been issued, Fearon's models do not fully explain why and when general deterrence will succeed.

[19] The *Status Quo* (3,3) is a metaequilibrium in Prisoners' Dilemma. It is supported by one player's weakly dominant metastrategy ($D/D/C/D$) and the other player's best response to it (D/C). Both strategies are conditionally cooperative. See Howard (1971: 54–60) or Brams (1975: 30–39) for a discussion.

[20] Since movement away from (3,3) in Prisoners' Dilemma is "sanctioned" by both players, the Fraser–Hipel technique finds the *Status Quo* to be in equilibrium.

		State B		
		C/C	C/D	D/C	D/D

		C/C	C/D	D/C	D/D
State A	C/C	(3,3)	(3,3)	(1,4)	(1,4)
	C/D	(3,3)	(3,3)*	(2,1)	(2,1)
	D/C	(4,2)*	(2,1)	(2,1)	(2,1)
	D/D	(4,2)*	(2,1)	(2,1)	(2,1)

```
* = Nash equilibrium
   (Shaded cells are consistent with the perfectness criterion.)
```

Fig. 3.5. Ordinal strategic-form representation of Generalized
Mutual Deterrence Game when only one player (i.e., State
A) has a credible retaliatory threat.

(1994),[21] and the *evolutionary approach* taken by Axelrod (1984).[22] Significantly, *conditional cooperation* emerges as the key to deterrence stability in all of these approaches. This theoretical and empirical convergence on the efficacy of conditionally cooperative strategies strongly suggests the need to recast classical deterrence theory which, at the unit level, prescribes coercive bargaining behavior inconsistent with tit-for-tat. This is the task we have set out for ourselves in this work.

Finally, for the sake of completeness, we note that if credibility is asymmetrically distributed, that is, if one player has a credible retaliatory threat and the other player does not, the *Status Quo* is not

[21] The theory of moves assumes that if one player switches strategies and moves to another outcome, the other can then counter-move, the first can subsequently counter-counter-move, and so on. Given this possibility, the *Status Quo* (3,3) outcome emerges as a *nonmyopic equilibrium* in Prisoners' Dilemma. For an analysis of deterrence using this framework, see Zagare (1987).

[22] In Axelrod's "evolutionary approach," tit-for-tat is a "collectively stable" strategy provided that each player's value for future payoffs in an iterated Prisoners' Dilemma game is low enough.

consistent with rationality. (In this case, the underlying preference structure resembles the 2×2 ordinal game that Snyder and Diesing [1977: 46] label *Called Bluff*.) In this game, there is a single subgame-perfect equilibrium. The outcome associated with this equilibrium supports a win for the player whose threat is credible. (See figure 3.5, where State A's threat is credible, but where State B's threat is not.) Thus, when either one or both players' threats lack credibility, general deterrence does not stand a chance. But when both players have credible retaliatory threats, chances are good that deterrence will succeed.

3.3   On capability

While credibility is an important element in the deterrence mixture, it is, by itself, not sufficient to ensure a stable status quo. Like "Covenants without the Sword," such threats are "but Words, and of no strength to secure a man at all" (Hobbes, 1968 [1651]: 223). Most classical deterrence theorists have known for some time (e.g., Kaufmann, 1956) that successful deterrence requires both credible and *capable* retaliatory threats. The reason is simple. As we demonstrate below, a capable threat is a *necessary* condition for general deterrence stability (Zagare, 1987: ch. 4). Our primary purpose in showing this explicitly is to account for those general deterrence failures that occur when at least one side is intent on aggression. A secondary purpose is to illustrate that deterrence might fail even when threats are credible all around.

Like credibility, capability is an ill-defined concept in the security literature. Indeed, it is frequently the case that the two concepts are conflated. Consider, for example, Craig and George's (1995: 190) description of the strategic situation just prior to the 1967 war in the Middle East: "because of the distaste for foreign ground combat engendered by US involvement in Vietnam, President Johnson found himself *unable or unwilling* to honor Eisenhower's 1956 commitment in reference to the Straits of Tiran" (emphasis added).[23]

There is, however, a significant difference between being unwilling to do something and being unable to do something. The unwillingness to execute a threat has to do with the *preferences* of the party making a threat, and hence with threat credibility. But since the inability to carry out a threat has implications for the preferences of the party

---

[23] Also see Most and Starr (1989: 39).

being threatened, we associate it with threat capability. Following Schelling (1966), then, we define threat capability as the *ability* of the threatener to hurt its opponent.

When defined in this way, threats may be incapable for one of two reasons. First, a player may simply lack the physical ability to execute a threat (Kissinger, 1994: 478). Nuclear threats, for instance, require both nuclear weapons and the means to deliver them. Threats that cannot be carried out are not real and can safely be ignored, as we do in chapter 6 when modeling limited Soviet retaliatory capabilities during the early 1950s.

Second, threats lack capability if they would not "hurt" when executed. If a threat hurts, the target of the threat is worse off than if the threat had not been executed; if a threat does not hurt, the threatened side would be at least as well off, after the threat were executed, than had it not taken the prohibited action to begin with. Accordingly, we define threat capability in terms of the relationship between the outcome that results when no action is taken (i.e., the *Status Quo*) and the outcome that results when an untoward action is taken *and* the threat is executed (i.e., *Conflict*). A threat will be said to be capable, then, if and only if the threatened player prefers the *Status Quo* to *Conflict*; when this relationship is reversed, the threat will be said to lack capability.[24]

If words can be believed, the US threat to defend Taiwan against a Chinese invasion is a current example of a deterrent threat that lacks capability. Here is how one senior Chinese military officer put it in February 1997 shortly after the death of Deng Xiaoping: "if Taiwan became independent, we simply would have no room to back off and would resort to military force regardless of whether the United States interfered. If the Americans did not come, we would do it; if the Americans came, we would do it" (Tyler, 1997).

Similarly, in August 1995, neither a US threat to impose sanctions, nor a German threat to block Croatia's entry into the European Union, were judged capable of preventing Croatia from taking back Krajina from rebel Serbs. According to an account in the *New York Times*, "the consensus among most officials was that nothing the United States

---

[24] Thus, as in prospect theory (Kahneman and Tversky, 1979), the status quo is an important reference point in Perfect Deterrence Theory. We discuss the importance of this reference point below. For discussions of prospect theory and international relations theory, see Levy (1992a, 1992b, 1997). See also Downs and Rocke (1995: 15–18).

could do or say would dissuade [Croatian President Franco] Tudjman from attacking."[25] In consequence, perhaps, neither threat was made (Engleberg, 1995).[26]

The Belgian threat to resist a German invasion in 1914 is a good example of a threat that lacked both capability *and* credibility. The threat lacked credibility because Germany did not believe that Belgium would prefer to resist (Tuchman, 1962: 40). It lacked capability because the German preference for invasion did not depend on Belgian intentions – with or without Belgian resistance, the Germans preferred to invade.

By contrast, the British threat to defend Belgium was potentially capable, although some German strategists, including the architect of Germany's war plan, Count Alfred von Schlieffen, had previously discounted the impact of Britain's small expeditionary force (Kagan, 1995: 212). Unfortunately, the British threat almost certainly lacked credibility. The German High Command did not think Britain would fight (Massie, 1991). Had it been credible, it is very possible that German actions would have been more circumspect. The British threat to defend the Falkland Islands falls into the same category. According to US Secretary of State Alexander Haig (1984: 287), Argentine leaders did not expect the British to "go to war for such a small problem as these few rocky islands."

Threats, then, can be capable but not credible. Huth, Gelpi, and Bennett (1993: 612), however, argue that the converse cannot be true: "A credible threat implies that the deterring party has the military capabilities to impose high costs on a challenger and that the challenger perceives that the deterring party is willing to do so." In terms of our definitions, however, this is not so. Threats can be credible without necessarily being capable. The implicit Austrian threat to defend itself in 1866 is a case in point. Prussian minister Otto von Bismarck knew that Austria would fight back, but instigated a conflict with Austria anyway. Bismarck actually preferred a brief and decisive war to enduring an unsatisfactory status quo (Smoke, 1977). The Austrian threat to resist, credible as it might have been, was simply beside the point. Given Bismarck's preferences, Prussia could

---

[25] Apparently, the same threats *were* capable (and credible) in January 1995 when they were in fact issued. At that time, Croatia decided to hold off attacking.

[26] The US decision not to pressure Croatia may have turned on a reassessment of Serbia's position. Previously it was feared that Serbia would retaliate. By August, US intelligence officials were no longer certain that Serbia would intervene.

not be deterred. Much the same could be said about the Polish threat to defend itself against Germany in 1939 (Huth and Russett, 1990: 479), and numerous other cases in which an aggressor intended to attack no matter what the defender's intentions happened to be.

It is easy to demonstrate why capability is an absolutely *necessary* condition for deterrence success. To this end, assume now the following restrictions on the players' preferences:

$$\text{State A: } A \text{ Wins} >_A \text{Conflict} >_A \text{Status Quo} >_A B \text{ Wins} \quad (3.5)$$
$$\text{State B: } B \text{ Wins} >_B \text{Conflict} >_B \text{Status Quo} >_B A \text{ Wins} \quad (3.6)$$

which are the same as the preferences that define the 2×2 strict ordinal game Snyder and Diesing (1977: 124) call *Deadlock*. Note that both players have credible threats: both prefer *Conflict* to losing. But neither has a capable threat: each player's opponent prefers *Conflict* to the *Status Quo*.

Figure 3.6 is the strategic-form representation of the game defined by the model of figure 3.2 and the preference restrictions of expressions (3.5) and (3.6). There are eight Nash equilibria in this game, only three of which are subgame-perfect. All three are associated with *Conflict*, and all three involve initial defection by at least one player. Thus, even though both players have credible threats, the *Status Quo* is never stable, and deterrence is never rational.

It is easy to generalize this result: as long as at least one player lacks a capable threat, deterrence will fail. *A capable threat, therefore, is necessary, but not sufficient, for deterrence success.* Significantly, this conclusion sets Perfect Deterrence Theory apart from the position of some proponents of a "power politics" model who claim that a defender's possession of superior capabilities is a *sufficient* condition for deterrence success (Levy, 1988: 489).

3.4   Deterrence and uncertainty

So far we have shown that, provided both players possess capable retaliatory threats,[27] perfectly credible threats are sufficient to engender deterrence stability. Of course, in the real world, credibility is

---

[27] To focus attention on the most interesting and problematic cases, we henceforth take threat capability as given. In other words we shall ask, given capable threats, what is the impact of status quo assessments, threat credibility, and strategic uncertainty, *inter alia*, on deterrence relationships?

State B

		C/C	C/D	D/C	D/D
	C/C	(2,2)	(2,2)	(1,4)	(1,4)
	C/D	(2,2)	(2,2)	(3,3)*	(3,3)*
State A	D/C	(4,1)	(3,3)*	(3,3)*	(3,3)*
	D/D	(4,1)	(3,3)*	(3,3)*	(3,3)*

* = Nash equilibrium
(Shaded cells are consistent with the perfectness criterion.)

Fig. 3.6. Ordinal strategic-form representation of Generalized Mutual Deterrence Game when both players have a credible, but neither player has a capable, retaliatory threat.

usually less than perfect. Players in actual deterrence games may suspect that their opponent prefers retaliation to capitulation, or the other way around, but they rarely know this for sure. In this section, we provide a demonstration that credibility need not be perfect in order to ensure deterrence stability. In the process, we introduce the contemporary methodology of games of incomplete information. In the remaining chapters, the terminology and the methodology we introduce will be refined and extended as we more fully respecify classical deterrence theory.

To this end, consider the *Rudimentary Asymmetric Deterrence Game* depicted in extensive-form in figure 3.7: State A begins play by deciding whether to cooperate (C) and accept the status quo or to defect (D) and demand its alteration. If A chooses C, the game ends and the outcome is the *Status Quo* (SQ). But if State A defects, State B must decide whether to concede (C) the issue – in which case the outcome is *A Wins* (DC) – or deny (D) the demand and precipitate *Conflict* (DD).

To analyze this primitive model, we make several assumptions about the preferences, or the relative magnitudes of the players'

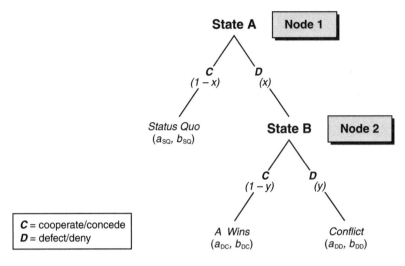

Fig. 3.7. Rudimentary Asymmetric Deterrence Game.

utilities, over the three possible outcomes, SQ, DC, and DD. To keep things simple, suppose that State A most prefers to win (*A Wins*). Also assume that State B's threat is capable: State A prefers the *Status Quo* to *Conflict*. Assume as well that State B prefers the *Status Quo* to all other outcomes. Rather than making a fixed assumption about B's preference between *A Wins* and *Conflict*, however, we assume that State B could be of one of two *types*:

1. *Hard*, preferring *Conflict* to *A Wins*, and
2. *Soft*, preferring *A Wins* to *Conflict*.

Thus, with respect to player preferences, we assume that:

State A:	*A Wins*	$>_A$	*Status Quo*	$>_A$ *Conflict*	(3.7)
State B (Hard):	*Status Quo*	$>_B$	*Conflict*	$>_B$ *A Wins*	(3.8)
State B (Soft):	*Status Quo*	$>_B$	*A Wins*	$>_B$ *Conflict*.	(3.9)

In terms of utilities, we assume $a_{DC} > a_{SQ} > a_{DD}$, and $b_{SQ} > b_{DD} > b_{DC}$ if State B is Hard, or $b_{SQ} > b_{DC} > b_{DD}$ if State B is Soft.

3.4.1 Rudimentary Asymmetric Deterrence Game with complete information

For the moment, assume that all information about preferences is *common knowledge*, that is, not only does each player know its own preferences, but State B knows State A's preferences, and State A knows State B's preferences, including State B's type. In other words, consider the Rudimentary Asymmetric Deterrence Game *with complete information*. We will now show that there is always a unique subgame-perfect equilibrium for the Rudimentary Asymmetric Deterrence Game, although what strategies that equilibrium prescribes depends on State B's type.

Consider first the case in which State B's type is *Soft*. Working backward up the tree of figure 3.7, State B will rationally concede at node 2 since a Soft B prefers *A Wins* to *Conflict* (i.e., $b_{DC} > b_{DD}$). Given this choice what should A do at node 1? If A cooperates, the outcome is *Status Quo*, A's next-best outcome. But if A defects, the outcome will be *A Wins*, A's best outcome. Clearly, State A should defect. The unique subgame-perfect equilibrium, then, is for A to choose *D*, and then B to choose *C*, resulting in outcome DC. Neither player can do better by unilaterally changing its decision.

Now suppose that State B is *Hard*. Again, working backward up the game tree, B's rational choice at node 2 is to defy A and choose *D*, since $b_{DD} > b_{DC}$ when B is Hard. Given this choice, it is clear that State A should cooperate at node 1 because cooperation leads to the *Status Quo*, A's next-best outcome, while defection leads to *Conflict*, A's worst outcome. Thus, the unique subgame-perfect equilibrium is for State A to cooperate and for State B to plan to defy A if A were to defect; the resulting outcome is *Status Quo*.

In the notation introduced in figure 3.7, x and y are strategic variables representing the players' decisions. Specifically

x = probability that A chooses *D*
y = probability that B chooses *D*.

Table 3.1 describes the unique subgame-perfect equilibrium of the Rudimentary Asymmetric Deterrence Game with complete information.

3.4.2 Rudimentary Asymmetric Deterrence Game with one-sided incomplete information

Assume now a game of *one-sided incomplete information* in which State A does not know State B's type or, in practical terms, State A does not know B's order of preference between *A Wins* and *Conflict*. Note that all information except State B's type is still common knowledge, so B knows State A's preferences, and A knows that B prefers SQ to either

Table 3.1. *Forms of subgame-perfect equilibria for the Rudimentary Asymmetric Deterrence Game with complete information*

	Subgame-perfect equilibrium	
	x	y
State B is Soft	1	0
State B is Hard	0	1

DD or DC.[28] To model State A's lack of information about State B's type, B's utility for *Conflict* (outcome DD) is treated as an independent binary random variable (which we indicate with an upper-case letter) with a known distribution:

$$B_{DD} = \begin{cases} b_{DD+} \text{ with probability } p_B \\ b_{DD-} \text{ with probability } 1-p_B \end{cases}$$

where the numbers b_{DD+}, b_{DD-}, and p_B satisfy $b_{DD+} > b_{DC} > b_{DD-}$ and $0 < p_B < 1$.

In words, this means that with probability p_B, State B will be of type Hard (i.e., prefers *Conflict* to *A Wins*), and with the complementary probability $(1-p_B)$, State B will be of type Soft (i.e., prefers *A Wins* to *Conflict*). Put in a slightly different way, with probability p_B State B's utility for *Conflict* will exceed its utility for *A Wins* ($b_{DD+} > b_{DC}$); otherwise, its utility for *A Wins* will exceed its utility for *Conflict* ($b_{DC} > b_{DD-}$). With these modifications, the following restrictions on utilities apply:

$$\text{State A: } a_{DC} > a_{SQ} > a_{DD} \tag{3.10}$$
$$\text{State B: } b_{SQ} > b_{DD+} > b_{DC} > b_{DD-}. \tag{3.11}$$

In a game of incomplete information, rational behavioral possibilities are summarized by the set of *perfect Bayesian equilibria* (or PBE), the natural extension of subgame-perfect equilibria. A perfect Bayesian equilibrium consists of a plan of action (i.e., a strategy) for each player, plus a set of beliefs about (i.e., subjective probabilities over) the other player's type (one for each player), such that each player (1) always

---

[28] We assume that both players know all the utilities, including the utilities that B would have if it were Hard, and the utilities that B would have if it were Soft. In fact, the only uncertainty, which is suffered by A alone, is *whether* B is Hard or Soft.

acts to maximize its expected utility given its beliefs, and (2) always updates those beliefs rationally (i.e., according to Bayes' rule) given the actions it observes during the play of the game. A perfect Bayesian equilibrium, therefore, specifies a rational action choice for every type of every player at every decision node or information set belonging to the player; as well, it must indicate how each player updates its beliefs about other players' types after observing their choices.

Because the Rudimentary Asymmetric Deterrence Game with incomplete information is quite austere, the perfect Bayesian equilibria are relatively easy to specify. First, note that condition (2) does not apply. In this simple game, since State A's preferences are presumed to be common knowledge (i.e., known to both players), State B has no need to update its beliefs. And since State A makes no move after State B, A has no opportunity to update its beliefs before acting. Thus, for this game, a perfect Bayesian equilibrium consists of a three-tuple specifying a single action choice for State A and two action choices for State B (one choice for each possible type). Extending the notation for strategic variables in a natural way, let

x = the probability that State A chooses D
y_H = the probability that State B chooses D, given that it is Hard
y_S = the probability that State B chooses D, given that it is Soft.

A perfect Bayesian equilibrium for the game of figure 3.7, then, will specify values for these three variables which we write as: $(x; y_H, y_S)$.[29]

In the Rudimentary Asymmetric Deterrence Game with incomplete information, State B makes its move after, and is fully informed about, State A's choice. As a consequence, State B's choices are strictly determined by its type: y_H *always* equals 1 and y_S *always* equals 0. In other words, if State B is Hard, preferring conflict to capitulation, it should always choose D; but if it is Soft with the opposite preference, it should always choose C. It remains to be shown, then, what choice maximizes State A's utility.

State A's choice depends on two variables. One is the intensity of its preference (i.e., its utility) for outcome DC. *Ceteris paribus*, the higher the value that State A places on winning, the more likely it should be to defect at node 1. The other determinant of State A's optimal strategy

---

[29] Since there is no opportunity for updating, this is in fact a *Bayesian equilibrium* (Fudenberg and Tirole, 1991: ch. 6). We do not emphasize the simpler Bayesian equilibrium because we wish to introduce the somewhat more elaborate perfect Bayesian equilibrium, which we will use later.

is its *belief* about B's type, since B's type will determine whether initiation results in *A Wins* or *Conflict*. The higher the credibility of State B's threat (i.e., the higher the probability that State B is Hard), the higher the probability that State A will cooperate at node 1, and conversely.

It is not difficult (see appendix 3) to show that State A maximizes its expected utility by choosing C if and only if the probability that State B is Hard (p_B) exceeds a threshold a_m defined as follows:

$$a_m = \frac{a_{DC} - a_{CC}}{a_{DC} - a_{DD}} \tag{3.12}$$

and maximizes its expected utility by choosing D when $p_B < a_m$. (We do not consider the possibility that $p_B = a_m$, which "almost never" occurs.) Thus, there is exactly one perfect Bayesian equilibrium in this game, which must take one of two forms. Table 3.2 summarizes its technical details:

1. A *Deterrence Equilibrium* $(x; y_H, y_S) = (0; 1, 0)$ in which State A always chooses to cooperate at node 1 and State B plans to defect at node 2 if it is Hard and plans to cooperate at node 2 if it is Soft. This equilibrium exists if and only if State B's threat is credible enough (i.e., $p_B > a_m$). The outcome under this equilibrium will always be the *Status Quo*.

2. An *Attack Equilibrium* $(x; y_H, y_S) = (1; 1, 0)$ under which State A always chooses to defect at node 1. The Attack Equilibrium exists as long as State B's credibility falls below the threshold required to support the Deterrence Equilibrium. The actual outcome, of course, depends on State B's type. If State B is Hard, it defects and *Conflict* occurs. But if State B is Soft, it cooperates and *A Wins*.

Note that despite its extreme simplicity, the Rudimentary Asymmetric Deterrence Game with incomplete information provides an explanation of how *Conflict* can sometimes occur in a deterrence situation. This is an important question because (1) the decision-makers are assumed to be rational, and (2) the *Conflict* outcome is Pareto-inferior – both players prefer the *Status Quo*, and each knows that its opponent prefers it too.

Furthermore, the model suggests that *Conflict* occurs only when State B is unexpectedly Hard. To be more specific, State A compares its beliefs (likelihood that State B is Hard, p_B) with a threshold that

Table 3.2. *Forms of equilibria and existence conditions for the Rudimentary Asymmetric Deterrence Game with one-sided incomplete information*

Equilibrium	Strategic variables			Existence condition
	State A	State B		
	x	y_H	y_S	
Deterrence	0	1	0	$p_B > a_m$
Attack	1	1	0	$p_B < a_m$

Key:
x = probability that State A chooses D
y_H = probability that State B chooses D given that it is Hard
y_S = probability that State B chooses D given that it is Soft
p_B = probability that State B is Hard
a_m = deterrence threshold

depends on its preferences (a_m); *Conflict* is not possible, according to the model, unless the likelihood that State B is Hard is low enough. Conversely, when this likelihood is high, deterrence is obtained.

The deterrence threshold (a_m) specified by expression (3.12) provides important information about the strategic implications of three of the model's variables: as one might expect, *ceteris paribus*, the greater State A's utility for the *Status Quo* (a_{SQ}) relative to its utility for the other outcomes, or the greater the cost of conflict (a_{DD}), the lower a_m and the easier it is for State B to deter State A. Conversely, the more State A values *A Wins* (a_{DC}), the higher a_m and the higher must be State B's credibility to deter State A.

What status should be given to these two perfect Bayesian equilibria? As noted, perfect Bayesian equilibria delimit the contours of rational play in a game of incomplete information. Thus, they are a model's predictions about likely behavior. In the particular case of the Rudimentary Asymmetric Deterrence Game of figure 3.7, a reasonable interpretation is that the behavioral pattern associated with one of the two perfect Bayesian equilibria would manifest itself in a real-world interaction between rational players. Which one would depend primarily on State A's beliefs about State B's type. If State B's threat is credible enough, State A is deterred; if not, the *Status Quo* should not survive.

Additionally, when such expectations are supported empirically, the relationship between the premises and the conclusions of a model provides a potent causal explanation of actual behavior. It is important, therefore, to know the perfect Bayesian equilibria of a game of incomplete information; they are the foundation upon which a model's predictions are made and its explanations constructed.

In this context, it is worth pointing out that in this example the behavioral possibilities are quite sparse. For one thing, there are only two perfect Bayesian equilibria, making explanations and predictions relatively uncomplicated. Most real-world interactions and all of the models we subsequently develop involve more complex choice sequences, and this complexity confounds theory construction. As will be seen, in some games there may be a large number of perfect Bayesian equilibria, and hence, a large number of possible rational behavioral patterns.

But it is not simply the limited number of equilibria that makes it easy to develop an explanation, or to make predictions, about play in the Rudimentary Asymmetric Deterrence Game with incomplete information. In addition to being few in number, the two perfect Bayesian equilibria are also mutually exclusive, that is, they never coexist. Either there is a Deterrence Equilibrium or an Attack Equilibrium, never both. This will not always be the case in the models developed in the remaining chapters of this book: more than one perfect Bayesian equilibrium may well exist at the same time and under the same conditions, and when this happens we will sometimes be hard put to specify likely behavior. In practical terms, this means that the explanations we provide, or the predictions we make, will be weaker than those that could be developed when, as in the present example, the perfect Bayesian equilibria are unique.

For some, the absence of a definitive result may be disappointing, an indication that the model is underspecified. While we are always happier with a point prediction, and confess to mild disappointment when our model is ambiguous about the behavioral possibilities, the existence of multiple coexisting perfect Bayesian equilibria is a reality that, at times, we have come to accept – grudgingly – and, at other times, to embrace. As Michael Bacharach (1977: 5–6) points out, "the failure of game theory to give unambiguous solutions to certain classes of games does not necessarily imply that the theory is flawed, or inadequately developed. It may be in the nature of things." In other words, it is entirely possible that a model with multiple equilibria accurately reflects the complexity of the real world where more than one rational possibility exists.

This should not be taken to mean that we are satisfied with indeterminate results, but that we are comfortable with limitations to our understanding of complex social events. The reader should also keep in mind that even when a model is ambiguous, insight into human affairs is gained as long as some behavioral possibilities can be ruled out. This will generally be the case for most of the models we subsequently construct.

It is also worth mentioning that the reality of multiple behavioral possibilities has a distinct upside: it suggests that, while constrained, human interactions are not necessarily fully predetermined by the calculations of individual self-interest. This leaves open the possibility that skillful diplomacy and adroit statesmanship can save the day.[30] Thus, the good news associated with the existence of multiple equilibria is that individuals, despite the constraints placed on them by their environment and their rationality, may still exercise some control over their fate, or the fate of their countries.

3.5 Coda

In this chapter we propose a resolution to the paradox of mutual deterrence based on mutually credible retaliatory threats. Unlike other proposed solutions, this resolution is consistent with the notion that the international system is fundamentally anarchistic, and with the assumption that choices are in some sense rational. Nonetheless, it is important to note that it is inconsistent with what is for some classical deterrence theorists a critical deduction and, for others, a protected assumption. More specifically, this denouement depends on a stipulation that when information about preferences is common knowledge, neither player considers conflict to be the worst possible outcome. Stated in a slightly different way, Perfect Deterrence (PD) depends on an underlying preference structure similar to that of Prisoners' Dilemma (also PD) *and* rules of play that permit retaliation. When these conditions are satisfied so that both players have capable and credible threats, retaliation is rational, and so is deterrence.

---

[30] The last thing we wish to suggest here is that negotiations are irrational or not driven by self-interest. Rather, our point is just the opposite: at times, rational calculations can support more than one outcome, and our framework does not always allow us to discriminate among the rational possibilities. For that, more specific bargaining models (e.g., Downs and Rocke, 1990) are required. We eschew complicating our models, however, in order to maximize generality.

This is no small or trivial point. We contend that a theory of deterrence that flows from it is radically different than the extant theory that takes the fixed preference structure of Chicken as its starting point. The remaining chapters of this work demonstrate our contention. In what follows, we explore the theoretical implications of this divergent axiomatic base under a variety of environmental conditions, and argue that the empirical and theoretical conclusions we draw are at once more general and more intuitively satisfying than those that follow from decision-theoretic deterrence theory. In the end, we hope to derive the conditions associated with stable deterrence, rather than postulate them.

Given the above it is appropriate to ask whether the core assumption that undergirds the subsequent analysis is defensible. Can a threat to retaliate against, say, a nuclear attack be made credible? Was it ever better to be dead than red, rather than the other way around? Or as Ellsberg (1959: 358) poses the question, "Whose reputation for honesty is so great that to wager it would make it actually rational to carry out such a threat? And who, with such issues at stake, would really . . . carry out a suicidal punishment?"

The short answer to these and similar questions is that no one, including analysts or even statesmen, knows. To be sure, many of us have opinions. But most of these opinions are beside the point, and may even lead to essentially irresolvable disputes. Ellsberg (1959: 358), for one, presumes the credibility of a threat to retaliate against an all-out attack while Gray (see section 3.1) questions the rationality of such a reprisal, but only for the United States. Who is right? To put the question in another way, is it *procedurally* rational to carry out a deterrent threat after, say, a nuclear attack and, if so, when and under what conditions? Again, our answer or your answer is not particularly relevant.

The beliefs and answers that do matter, though, are those of real-world actors who are involved in an actual deterrence game. In other words, what is important are the perceptions and the beliefs of those who have a finger on a button that can launch an attack or respond to one. Note, however, that typically even these individuals are uncertain about the preferences and, hence, intentions, of their opponent(s). It seems reasonable to suppose that such uncertainty about an opponent's preferences, especially the critical preference between conflict and capitulation, has important strategic consequences. Accordingly, we turn next to developing a new theory of bilateral deterrence. The theory we construct treats credibility as a (continuous) variable, gives a prominent place to the role of uncertainty in the strategic equation, remains true to the assumption of international anarchy, maintains consistency with the precepts of instrumental rationality, and does not presume an answer to the most critical questions of deterrence theory.

Part II
Direct deterrence

4 Uncertainty and mutual deterrence

> Uncertainty is a synonym for life, and nowhere is uncertainty greater than in international politics.
>
> Kenneth Waltz

> Certainty as to whether an adversary will stand firm is rare. Statesmen have to deal with probabilities.
>
> Robert Jervis

> In war the chief incalculable is the human will.
>
> Lidell Hart

When information is complete, when players are rational, and when binding agreements are precluded, perfect deterrence requires perfect credibility. This maxim, which we refer to as the *credibility principle*, is the rock upon which we construct a new theory of rational deterrence – *Perfect Deterrence Theory*. In this chapter and the next, we explore the implications of this strategic and political law for *direct deterrence* relationships in which at least one state must rely on its own strength and art to deter another. The present chapter examines those direct deterrence situations in which each of two states feels threatened. Chapter 5, by contrast, posits a unilateral (or asymmetric) deterrence game in which the players have analytically distinct roles: one player, content to preserve the status quo, harbors no significant aggressive desire while the other, unsatisfied with the existing distribution of benefits, is motivated to upset it. In part III, we turn away from direct deterrence relationships to explore situations of *extended deterrence* and the dynamics of the escalation process.

We call those direct deterrence relationships in which each of two states feels threatened by the other, *mutual deterrence*. With the exception of the Rudimentary Asymmetric Deterrence Game, the discussion of deterrence theory in part I of this book presumes a situation of mutual deterrence. Mutual deterrence relationships conform most closely to the set of assumptions that demarcates realism and classical deterrence theory. Indeed, our principal justification for examining mutual deterrence games in detail is the presumption by many prominent realists that *all* states are similarly motivated: most traditional realists assert that states think and act in terms of interests defined as power (Morgenthau, 1948), while neo-realists presume that states uniformly seek security (Waltz, 1979). In mainstream realist thought, there is simply no room for differentiated actors with distinguishable preferences. As well, some important strategic conundrums (e.g., the reciprocal fear of surprise attack) arise only in the context of mutual deterrence relationships. In our opinion, then, powerful theoretical reasons exist for examining the full range of behavioral possibilities for those games in which the deterrence problem is symmetric.[1]

Mutual deterrence relationships include most situations Morgan (1977) terms *general deterrence,* in which two states feel threatened by each other, but there is no immediate danger of attack by either state.[2] By most accounts, the strategic relationship of the superpowers during the Cold War period would qualify as mutual deterrence (Waltz, 1993). For much of this period, the United States and the Soviet Union sought to deter each other from a wide range of offensive actions. More recent examples arguably include the rivalries between Iran and Iraq, North and South Korea, Israel and Syria, Greece and Turkey, Egypt and Sudan, Yemen and Saudi Arabia, Ethiopia and Eritrea, Serbia and Croatia, Armenia and Azerbaijan, Peru and Ecuador, Rwanda and Burundi, and India and Pakistan – to name just a few. Thus, there are also compelling empirical reasons for explicating the inner workings of mutual deterrence games in detail.

Mutual deterrence relationships include, but are not limited to, general deterrence. For example, France and Prussia were involved in an intricate *immediate deterrence* relationship in July 1870: each actively

---

[1] O'Neill (1992) offers additional theoretical reasons for examining simultaneous choice deterrence games.

[2] Morgan (1977: 40–41) admits the possibility that general deterrence relationships may be one-sided or asymmetric, so the correspondence with our definition of mutual deterrence is not exact. Nonetheless, Morgan notes that in the most severe general deterrence situations, it is likely that each side sees the other as motivated to contest the status quo.

considered attacking the other. But for both political and strategic reasons, the Prussian Minister-President, Otto von Bismarck, provoked the French to attack first (Smoke, 1977: ch. 6).

The strategic backdrop to some preemptive wars might also qualify under our definition as a mutual deterrence situation. In a preemptive war, one side strikes first because it fears an attack by the other and wishes to gain a tactical advantage. For instance, King William of Prussia agreed to initiate a conflict with Austria in 1866, thereby precipitating the Seven Weeks War, but only after Bismarck convinced him that an Austrian attack was imminent (Massie, 1991: 59). Similarly, conflicts like the 1967 Middle East war, for which there is some dispute over exactly which side was the initiator, likely evolved from an unstable mutual deterrence relationship.

As well, even certain *extended deterrence* relationships can plausibly be interpreted as a mutual deterrence situation.[3] For example, when Great Britain and France squared off in Fashoda in 1898, much more than control of the Upper Nile was at stake. Many historians believe that a general war between the two European powers was likely if neither backed down. At a severe local disadvantage, the French gave way in the end and war was averted.

4.1 Capability, credibility, and mutual deterrence

A great deal is already known about the dynamics of mutual deterrence under complete information. (Table 4.1 summarizes the relationship between threat characteristics and the likelihood of deterrence success when the players know each other's preferences.) For example, from the discussion in chapter 3, we can infer that differences in perceptions, or what Jervis (1968) terms "misperceptions," that stem from incomplete information are neither necessary nor sufficient for a failure of mutual deterrence, and similarly, that shared assessments of the strategic environment are neither necessary nor sufficient for the success of mutual deterrence.[4] We also know that stable mutual deterrence absolutely requires that both sides possess a

---

[3] Indeed, we will draw on some extended deterrence relationships to illustrate a number of technical points later in this chapter and in the next. Nonetheless, not all extended deterrence relationships can be fully captured by simple models of mutual (or unilateral) deterrence. We explicitly model extended deterrence in part III.

[4] See Kim and Bueno de Mesquita (1995) for a similar observation. See also Bueno de Mesquita and Lalman (1988).

Table 4.1. *Mutual deterrence under complete information*

Threat characteristics	Preferences based on	Deterrence success
Both capable, both credible	Prisoners' Dilemma	*Status Quo* is always a subgame-perfect equilibrium, so deterrence is perfectly rational, but not certain.
Both capable, one credible	Called Bluff	*Status Quo* is never a subgame-perfect equilibrium; side with credible threat wins; deterrence rationally fails.
Both capable, neither credible	Chicken	*Status Quo* is never a subgame-perfect equilibrium; deterrence rationally fails.
At least one player lacks a capable threat	Deadlock and its variants (Zagare, 1987: ch. 4)	*Status Quo* is never a subgame-perfect equilibrium; deterrence rationally fails.

capable retaliatory threat. In the absence of capability, even perfect credibility is insufficient to stabilize a mutual deterrence relationship.

Most real-world deterrence failures, mutual or otherwise, are likely traceable to the absence of a retaliatory threat that hurts enough. In practical terms, this means that deterrence is almost certain to break down when one or both sides in a dispute believes that pressing a demand will result in a net gain, *even if the other side resists or fights back*. A possible example is the relationship of the United States and Japan in 1941 (but see section 4.3.1.1). According to Snyder and Diesing (1977: 124–127), both sides preferred war to capitulating *and* to compromising with the other. Such preferences correspond to the 2×2 strict ordinal game called Deadlock.[5]

As Snyder and Diesing (1977: 124) point out, games like the one the United States and Japan played in 1941 are theoretically "uninteresting, since there are no mixed motives. There is nothing to bargain about; the necessary outcome is *DD*, and no maneuvers can make any

---

[5] Mansbach (1997: 301), by contrast, argues that "by late 1941, US–Japanese relations had become a game of *Chicken*. Each side blustered, threatened, and took steps to convince the other that it was willing to go to war rather than back down." But Mansbach's interpretation does not hold up empirically. If war was in fact the worst outcome for the United States, it would have rationally sued for peace after the attack on Pearl Harbor.

difference." For this reason, we focus attention in the remainder of this book on those deterrence relationships in which both sides have capable retaliatory threats. Perforce, the theory we construct will be most relevant to hostile parity relationships.[6] The range of games we explore, then, are those that fall within the "cone of mutual deterrence." But contrary to classical deterrence theory, we show that, in a variety of strategic settings, parity and high conflict costs do not necessarily guarantee peace.

To be sure, deterrence equilibria, which are equilibria under which no player *ever* initiates conflict, frequently exist in the games we study, but these equilibria are generally flawed: sometimes they are imperfect; sometimes they are based on implausible beliefs; and sometimes they coexist with other, less hospitable, equilibria. While the game models we develop in this and subsequent chapters will become progressively more complex, the fundamental picture of deterrence relationships that will emerge from our analyses is simple, and at odds with the conventional wisdom of classical deterrence theory: deterrence is no sure thing, even when both players have capable and credible retaliatory threats. Our point is that the line between war and peace will oftentimes be thin, and that war is not always easy to eliminate as a rational possibility. Policy implications of this view of deterrence are discussed in detail in the concluding chapter.

Like capability, credibility is a necessary but not a sufficient condition for successful deterrence in a mutual deterrence game with complete information. Additionally, the stability of deterrence is completely undermined when one player, or both, lacks a credible retaliatory threat. In the former case, when the underlying preference structure mirrors that of the 2×2 strict ordinal game Called Bluff, the player whose threat is credible should win. And when neither player's threat is credible, the outcome is uncertain (because there are two subgame-perfect equilibria, one associated with a win for each of the players). But since in this instance the *Status Quo* is *never* a subgame-perfect equilibrium, it is very unlikely to survive rational play.

---

[6] This is not to suggest that Perfect Deterrence Theory's domain is restricted to parity relationships. Under certain conditions, or over certain issues, even a small cost could render a deterrent threat capable.

4.2   Credibility, uncertainty, and mutual deterrence[7]

The real world, of course, is neither as simple nor as transparent as table 4.1 might suggest. Most, if not all, interstate relationships are characterized by, among other things, nuance, ambiguity, equivocation, duplicity, and ultimately, uncertainty. Policy-makers, especially those involved in hostile deterrence relationships, are typically unable to acquire complete information about their opponent's preferences; at best, they can hope for probabilistic knowledge of these key determinants of interstate behavior. Colin Gray's speculation about the "likely" Soviet response to various US initiatives (see chapter 2) is a case in point. Clearly, Gray's analytic uncertainty stems from lack of information about Soviet preferences – with rational actors and complete information, the likely response of an opponent is easy to determine.

The same applies to other long-standing strategic conundrums. Would the United States have risked Washington or New York for Paris or Bonn during the darkest days of the Cold War, as de Gaulle once asked rhetorically? Given the uncertain nature of interstate politics, the only possible answer to this question is "perhaps." What about Toronto? Maybe. San Francisco or Boston? Probably. But not certainly. If one could answer "certainly" (or "certainly not") to such questions, a deterrence game would be completely specified and the stability of mutual deterrence apparent (see section 4.1). But when players have only uncertain knowledge of an opponent's preferences, they cannot tell much about the underlying structure of the game they are playing, which may be based on Chicken, Called Bluff, Prisoners' Dilemma, or even Deadlock. Of course a player generally knows its own preferences, and can therefore eliminate some possibilities, but uncertainty remains integral to most real-world deterrence situations, and this fact is strategically crucial.

Players with real-life deterrence problems, however, can make estimates about the likely motives of an opponent. Sometimes these estimates lead to correct inferences about actions, but frequently they do not. For example, Chamberlain was wrong about Hitler's intentions in 1938; many historians believe that Hitler seriously misjudged the willingness of the British to fight in 1939; and Argentina completely underestimated British resolve in 1982. Such guesses, right or

---

[7] The remainder of this chapter draws on Kilgour and Zagare (1991).

wrong, concern the likely preferences of the opponent and, consequently, the probable structure of the game the players are involved in.

Behind these estimates lies what Joynt and Corbett (1978: 94–95) call the *curve of credibility*. This curve "begins with defense of the homeland, descends to clearly defined spheres of influence or the territory of allies and then drops to near zero for the defense of other interests." In other words, states are more likely to respond to certain kinds of challenges than to others, so credibility will vary across the range of conflict issues.

What is significant about the curve of credibility, however, is not its existence but its effects on behavior. Since credibility obviously has important implications for deterrence in an uncertain world, we now begin to explore systematically its strategic implications. In the end, we aim to specify explicitly the connection between deterrence, preferences, and threat credibility.

To model the role played by uncertainty in bilateral strategic relationships, we return to the *Generalized Mutual Deterrence Game* originally given by figure 3.2, and reproduced here as figure 4.1. Recall that the two players in this game, State A and State B, each have the same initial choices, which are made simultaneously at the start of the game: to cooperate (*C*) and support the *Status Quo* or to defect (*D*) and demand its change.[8] If both cooperate, the *Status Quo* (outcome SQ) prevails. If both defect, *Conflict* (outcome DD) ensues. But when one player cooperates and the other defects, the player that cooperates has an opportunity to retaliate by switching from *C* to *D*. Retaliation also leads to *Conflict*. When the cooperating player capitulates (i.e., sticks with *C* and does not retaliate), the defecting player wins (outcome DC or outcome CD). This game is the simplest model of mutual deterrence we can imagine that takes account of the possibility of retaliation.

Parenthetically, we add that throughout this work we make every effort to keep things as uncomplicated and parsimonious as possible. We agree with Bennett (1995: 39) that "simplicity has much to commend it." By avoiding the temptation to complicate or even fine-tune our models, we hope to focus on the critical variables that

---

[8] State A makes this choice at node 1; and State B makes its choice at either node 2a or 2b. But since nodes 2a and 2b are in the same information set, they are indistinguishable to State B. State B's choice is effectively simultaneous with State A's – each choice is made without the knowledge of the other.

Direct deterrence

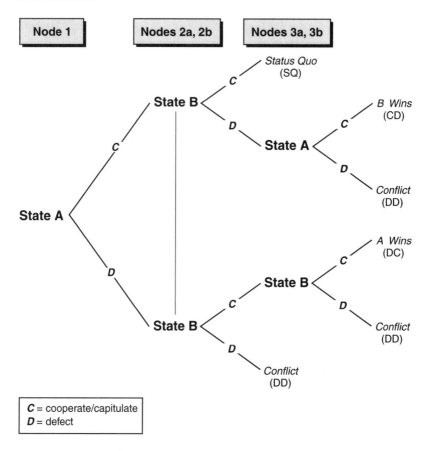

Fig. 4.1. Generalized Mutual Deterrence Game.

determine the underlying dynamic of a wide variety of deterrence relationships. For this reason, all the models we develop are discrete. We make no attempt to model variations and gradations in action choices, such as levels of cooperation or defection. By using discrete models, we are able to keep the number of possible choices and the number of possible outcomes to a manageable minimum. In other words, this mutual deterrence model does not distinguish among various kinds of confrontations, crises or not, initiated in different ways – we are working in broad brush-strokes, and our objective is simply to predict, *inter alia*, under what general conditions the status quo will be contested. A model that represents decision options and outcomes in finer detail would be required to address more specific aspects of mutual deterrence relationships.

For similar reasons, we are oftentimes imprecise, perhaps infuriatingly so, about the empirical domain of our models. We emphasize that this is intentional. Our motivation is to develop models that are at once more general and easier to interpret than would be the case if they contained more detailed choices or were specific to a limited range of interstate competitions, such as trade or military relations. In fact, as we mention in chapter 1, the family of interrelated models we construct in this work is not necessarily restricted to international affairs. The players could be taken as individuals, groups, or even institutions, and the models, because they are general, apply to deterrence games played out in a variety of settings with an assortment of players.

With these caveats in mind, we now continue with our discussion of the Generalized Mutual Deterrence Game with incomplete information. The four possible outcomes of this game, and the notation for the (von Neumann–Morgenstern utility) payoffs, are summarized in figure 4.2. We assume payoffs that are consistent with any *mutual* deterrence game. Specifically, we assume that each prefers to win, thereby gaining an advantage, rather than endure the *Status Quo*, but prefers the *Status Quo* to losing to its opponent. We continue to assume, here and throughout, that each player has a capable retaliatory threat, that is, each prefers the *Status Quo* to *Conflict*. No fixed assumption is made, however, about either player's preference between *Conflict* and capitulation (i.e., losing to the opponent).[9] More formally, we always place the following restrictions on preferences:

$$\text{State A: } A \text{ Wins} >_A \text{ Status Quo} >_A [\text{Conflict and } B \text{ Wins}] \qquad (4.1)$$
$$\text{State B: } B \text{ Wins} >_B \text{ Status Quo} >_B [\text{Conflict and } A \text{ Wins}]. \qquad (4.2)$$

The relative preferences of the outcomes enclosed in brackets are unspecified, i.e., they are the parameters of our model.[10]

Why do we leave these particular preferences open? The short answer is that we believe that they are *the* critical determinants of most deterrence games, mutual or otherwise.[11] As explained above,

---

[9] Classical deterrence theory, by contrast, takes as axiomatic each player's preference for capitulation. As Downs and Rocke (1990: 194–196) point out, such a restrictive assumption severely limits any theory's generality.

[10] In terms of utilities, we assume that $a_{DC} > a_{SQ} > \{a_{DD}, a_{CD}\}$ and $b_{CD} > b_{SQ} > \{b_{DD}, b_{DC}\}$.

[11] This is not to say that other variables are unimportant. For example, a player could

State B

Status Quo (SQ) (a_{SQ}, b_{SQ})	B Wins (CD) (a_{CD}, b_{CD})
A Wins (DC) (a_{DC}, b_{DC})	Conflict (DD) (a_{DD}, b_{DD})

State A (label at left of table)

Fig. 4.2. Outcome and utility notation for Generalized Mutual Deterrence Game.

we take each player's estimate of the other's preference for *Conflict* over capitulation as a measure of the other player's credibility. As well, these critical preferences determine each player's *type*: a *Hard* player prefers to retaliate (i.e., prefers *Conflict* to losing the advantage) while a *Soft* player prefers to capitulate.[12] Thus, we assume that there are two types of the two players in the game, characterized by the following preferences:

State A (Hard): *A Wins* $>_A$ *Status Quo* $>_A$ *Conflict* $>_A$ *B Wins*   (4.3)
State A (Soft): *A Wins* $>_A$ *Status Quo* $>_A$ *B Wins* $>_A$ *Conflict*   (4.4)
State B (Hard): *B Wins* $>_B$ *Status Quo* $>_B$ *Conflict* $>_B$ *A Wins*   (4.5)
State B (Soft): *B Wins* $>_B$ *Status Quo* $>_B$ *A Wins* $>_B$ *Conflict*.   (4.6)

Finally, we assume that each player knows its actual type (i.e., its own preferences) and has probabilistic knowledge of its opponent's type. We also assume these probabilities are common knowledge – both players know them, know they know them, and so on.

---

also be uncertain about its ability to prevail in a conflict, about its opponent's relative evaluation of the status quo, or an opponent's capitulation costs. For an examination of uncertainty stemming from lack of information about an opponent's capability, see Altfeld (1985), Morrow (1989a, 1989b), and Bueno de Mesquita, Morrow, and Zorick (1997). For the impact of uncertainty about an opponent's satisfaction with the status quo, see Kydd (1997). And for an analysis of the implications of "audience costs" and other costly signals, see Fearon (1994b).

[12] The terms for player types, *Hard* and *Soft*, are not necessarily game-theoretic. For example, just two days before Germany attacked Poland in 1939, a German general summarized the British position as follows: "General impression, England 'soft' on the issue of a major war" (quoted in Jervis, 1976: 60).

Our approach allows for several conceptually compatible ways to interpret uncertainty. For example, not knowing an opponent's preference between *Conflict* and capitulation implies uncertainty about an opponent's intention to execute a threat. This is conceptually equivalent to saying that there is uncertainty about likely choices at a particular node of the game tree. Similarly, lack of knowledge about an opponent's preference between *Conflict* and capitulation could stem from not knowing the value an opponent places on the issue in dispute (is it worth fighting for?) or the costs it attaches to conflict.

In the real world there may be many reasons for lack of complete information about an actor's type. For instance, governments may be divided.[13] After a crisis has erupted, one faction (i.e., the hard-liners) typically favors a strong response while another (i.e., the soft-liners) prefers a weak response, or no response at all. Thus, uncertainty about an opponent's preferences could stem from inadequate intelligence about the relative political standing of the various coalitions comprising an opponent's government. Other sources might include a country's inability to see itself as the other sees it, a lack of appreciation of political pressures within an opponent's society, insensitivity about the symbolic value of contested issues, or simply cognitive limitations associated with high stress. In the end, uncertainty abounds.

To model uncertainty about preferences, the players' utilities for *Conflict* (A_{DD} and B_{DD}) are treated as independent binary random variables (indicated with upper-case letters) with known distributions. Specifically, it is common knowledge that

$$A_{DD} = \begin{cases} a_{DD+} & \text{with probability } p_A \\ a_{DD-} & \text{with probability } 1 - p_A \end{cases}$$

$$B_{DD} = \begin{cases} b_{DD+} & \text{with probability } p_B \\ b_{DD-} & \text{with probability } 1 - p_B \end{cases}$$

where $a_{DD+} > a_{CD} > a_{DD-}$ and $b_{DD+} > b_{DC} > b_{DD-}$. In other words, with probabilities p_A and p_B, State A and State B, respectively, are seen as willing to retaliate (i.e., as Hard), and with probabilities $1 - p_A$ and $1 - p_B$, A and B, respectively, are seen as unwilling to retaliate (i.e., as

---

[13] A good example is the US government during the early years of the Cold War. At the time, proponents of the so-called "Riga Axioms" saw "the USSR as a revolutionary state with unbounded ideological ambitions [intent] to achieve world hegemony." By contrast, for adherents of the "Yalta Axioms," the Soviet Union was simply "a conventional great power in the international system" (Brecher 1993: 85).

Soft). Because we assume that both players know these probability distributions, there is inter subjective agreement about the credibility of each player's threat. However, only State A knows the actual value of A_{DD} and only State B knows the actual value of B_{DD}, suggesting, for example, that the players will understand that a real or intended threat may not be fully appreciated, or that a bluff may work. The realization of these values occurs just prior to play of the game.[14]

The credibilities of the players' threats to retaliate, then, are reflected in the values of p_A and p_B. The higher the value, the more credible the player's threat. Overall, State A's and, respectively, State B's threats will be credible and their preferences like those of both players in a Prisoners' Dilemma game, with probability p_A and p_B; conversely, State A's and State B's threats will be incredible, and their preferences like those of players in a Chicken game, with probability $1 - p_A$ and $1 - p_B$.

The process we are attempting to model, then, goes like this: first, something exogenous happens (first stage) that determines, *a priori*, the probability that each player would prefer to respond to a non-cooperative act by the other. We remain silent, however, on exactly what this "something" might be – perhaps a significant change in the underlying power relationship of the two nations (Organski and Kugler, 1980); or an internal power shift like the one which occurred in the Soviet military prior to the 1962 Cuban missile crisis (Allison, 1971); or a shock like the 1973 Middle East war, that embroiled the two superpowers in a tricky deterrence game. Thus this model could apply to immediate or to general deterrence, or to an international crisis.

In any event, after the (first) stage has been set, each player makes a strategic choice based on its own evaluation of the outcomes (i.e., the stakes) and its estimate of the preferences of its opponent. This choice constitutes the second stage of our model. For example, in June 1948, Soviet decision-makers decided to clamp a blockade around Berlin in the belief that the Western powers would have little choice but to accept this as a *fait accompli*. The Soviets were obviously mistaken, however, since the Western powers chose to resist the Soviet move by launching an airlift of food and other supplies to Berlin. Such a retaliation opportunity, should it arise, constitutes the third and final stage of the game.

---

[14] Technically, these probabilities will be assumed to satisfy $0 < p_A < 1$ and $0 < p_B < 1$.

4.3 Perfect Bayesian equilibria of the Generalized Mutual Deterrence Game

To this point our examination of mutual deterrence games presumes players with complete and accurate information about each other's preferences, that is, when p_A and p_B equal either one or zero. But what happens when each player simply does not know what its opponent will prefer in the case of a defection? In other words, in a mutual deterrence game, what are the strategic implications of *incomplete information* about the credibility of the other's threat? How credible must a threat be in order to deter? What is the precise connection between the credibility and magnitude of a retaliatory threat?

To answer these questions, we now identify all perfect Bayesian equilibria of the Generalized Mutual Deterrence Game with incomplete information in which the parameters p_A and p_B have values somewhere between 0 and 1, that is, where the players have probabilistic knowledge of each other's preference between capitulation and retaliation. Recall that the perfect Bayesian equilibria encompass all possible patterns of behavior consistent with basic rationality assumptions. In other words, they stipulate for each player a strategy and a set of beliefs, such that each player always acts to maximize its expected utility, given its beliefs and the actions it observes during the play of the game. In the particular case of the Generalized Mutual Deterrence Game with incomplete information, a perfect Bayesian equilibrium will specify an action choice for each type of each player at every node or decision point: for State A at nodes 1 and 3a, and for State B at nodes 2a, 2b, and 3b.[15]

We begin our analysis by using backward induction to examine State A's choice at node 3a and State B's choice at node 3b. These choices are easy to determine since each player always has complete information about its own payoffs. These payoffs strictly determine each player's choice at these two decision points. Thus, this determination is essentially an application of the perfectness criterion.

---

[15] As with the Rudimentary Asymmetric Deterrence Game with incomplete information, players can update their beliefs about the other's type before making a subsequent choice, but neither player needs to, as the node 3 choice that maximizes utility depends on the player's own preferences only. Hence, perfect Bayesian equilibria in the Generalized Mutual Deterrence Game with incomplete information do not specify updated probabilities.

For example, assume that State A finds that it is to make a choice at node 3a. Since the information set of node 3a is a singleton and is, therefore, distinguishable from all other possible decision points, A will be able to determine all the choices that led up to this choice. Specifically, A will know that it chose *C* initially and that State B chose *D*. State A will also know its own preferences. If A is Hard, its utility for *Conflict*, $A_{DD} = a_{DD+}$, is greater than its utility for *B Wins*, a_{CD}. Similarly, if A is Soft, its utility for *Conflict*, $A_{DD} = a_{DD-}$, is less than a_{CD}. State A's choice is clear. Its uncertainty over whether $B_{DD} = b_{DD+}$ or $B_{DD} = b_{DD-}$ is of no strategic significance. If A is Hard, it should always choose *D*; if A is Soft, it should always choose *C*.

Similarly, State B's choice at node 3b is always strictly determined by its type. If State B is Hard, i.e., prefers *Conflict* to *A Wins*, it should choose *D*. But if it is Soft, i.e., prefers *A Wins* to *Conflict*, it should capitulate (i.e., choose *C*).

Because the players' choices at nodes 3a and 3b can be determined, their strategic decisions are reduced to initial choices of *C* or *D*, which *do* depend on their state of knowledge when they make this selection. It follows that a perfect Bayesian equilibrium of the Generalized Mutual Deterrence Game with incomplete information will consist of a four-tuple of probabilities, one probability for each type of each player. Extending the notation from chapter 3 a bit further, let

x_H = the probability that State A chooses *D*, given that it is Hard
x_S = the probability that State A chooses *D*, given that it is Soft
y_H = the probability that State B chooses *D*, given that it is Hard
y_S = the probability that State B chooses *D*, given that it is Soft.

A perfect Bayesian equilibrium for the Generalized Mutual Deterrence Game with incomplete information, then, will specify a value for these four variables, which we will write as $[x_H, x_S; y_H, y_S]$.

These probabilities can be thought of as each player's "defection" policy for each of the two situations that can arise in a deterrence situation: if the player is Hard and prefers to resist if challenged (i.e., $A_{DD} = a_{DD+}$ or $B_{DD} = b_{DD+}$), it will defect initially with probability x_H or y_H; or if the player is Soft and prefers to capitulate rather than resist (i.e., $A_{DD} = a_{DD-}$ or $B_{DD} = b_{DD-}$), it will defect initially with probability x_S or y_S. Thus, the two types of State A defect initially with probabilities x_H and x_S, and the two types of State B with probabilities y_H and y_S.

The expected payoffs to each type of each player can now be determined. If State A is Hard, then A's expected payoff is $E_{A|H}(x_H; y_H, y_S)$, where:

$$E_{A|H}(x_H; y_H, y_S) = p_B \left[(1-x_H)(1-y_H) a_{SQ} + (x_H + y_H - x_H y_H) a_{DD+} \right]$$
$$+ (1-p_B) \left[(1-x_H)(1-y_S) a_{SQ} + x_H(1-y_S) a_{DC} + y_S a_{DD+} \right].$$

If State A is Soft, its expected payoff is:

$$E_{A|S}(x_S; y_H, y_S) = p_B \left[(1-x_S)(1-y_H) a_{SQ} + (1-x_S) y_H a_{CD} + x_S a_{DD-} \right]$$
$$+ (1-p_B) \left[(1-x_S)(1-y_S) a_{SQ} + x_S(1-y_S) a_{DC} \right.$$
$$\left. + (1-x_S) y_S a_{CD} + x_S y_S a_{DD-} \right].$$

B's expected payoffs, $E_{B|H}(y_H; x_H, x_S)$ and $E_{B|S}(y_S; x_H, x_S)$, are analogous.

Next, we inquire which of the strategy combinations $[x_H, x_S; y_H, y_S]$ are in equilibrium.[16] The perfect Bayesian equilibria of the Generalized Mutual Deterrence Game with incomplete information are determined in appendix 4. As it turns out, all but fourteen strategy combinations can be eliminated immediately. Of these, four are *transitional equilibria* that occur under only a very limited set of conditions and will not be discussed here.[17] This leaves but ten perfect Bayesian equilibria to be described. Table 4.2 provides summary information about them.

The equilibria can be grouped into four distinct categories. In what follows, we describe the equilibria within each group, explain the

[16] Technically, the equilibria we identify are *subgame-perfect Bayesian equilibria*. They are subgame-perfect because at nodes 3a and 3b we are able to apply (non-trivially) Selten's (1975) perfectness criterion. They are *Bayesian equilibria* (Harsanyi, 1967–68; Fudenberg and Tirole, 1991: ch. 6) because players' actions are rational given their initial beliefs about their opponents' types. Later we will use the concept of perfect Bayesian equilibrium (Fudenberg and Tirole, 1991: ch. 8) in games where it is meaningful for a player to update its beliefs about its opponent's type after observing an action choice by that opponent. (Here, the players can update their beliefs about types, but this information is not relevant to their choices at nodes 3a and 3b.) Throughout, we will restrict attention to the conceptually simpler perfect Bayesian equilibrium, rather than the many refinements, including *sequential equilibrium* (Kreps and Wilson, 1982b) and *trembling-hand perfect equilibrium* (Selten, 1975), that impose additional requirements on the updating of beliefs.

[17] An equilibrium is transitional if it exists only when the parameters of a model satisfy a specific functional relationship (i.e., an equation). Thus we concentrate on equilibria that exist when (for instance) $p_A \leq a_2$ or $p_B \geq b_2$, to the exclusion of an equilibrium that exists only when, say, $p_A = a_2$. Here parameters such as a_2 and b_2 are fixed numbers. The justification for ignoring transitional equilibria, here and elsewhere in this book, is that, however the parameter values are obtained, they are very unlikely to satisfy any specific equation, so that any equilibrium that does not exist unless, say, $p_A = a_2$, is unlikely to be sustained in actual play.

Table 4.2. *Perfect Bayesian equilibria and existence conditions for Generalized Mutual Deterrence Game with incomplete information*

Class	Equilibrium		State A		State B		Existence conditions		
			x_H	x_S	y_H	y_S	on p_A		on p_B
1	Sure-Thing	STDE	0	0	0	0	$\geq b_2$	*and*	$\geq a_2$
	Separating	SE	1	0	1	0	$\geq b_u$	*and*	$\geq a_u$
	Hybrid	HE	u	0	v	0	$\geq b_2$	*and*	$\geq a_2$
2A	Attack$_{1A}$	AE$_{1A}$	1	1	0	0			$\leq a_1$
	Attack$_{2A}$	AE$_{2A}$	1	1	v	0			$< a_u$
	Attack$_{3A}$	AE$_{3A}$	1	1	1	0			$\leq a_u$
2B	Attack$_{1B}$	AE$_{1B}$	0	0	1	1	$\leq b_1$		
	Attack$_{2B}$	AE$_{2B}$	u	0	1	1	$< b_u$		
	Attack$_{3B}$	AE$_{3B}$	1	0	1	1	$\leq b_u$		
3	Bluff	BE	1	u	1	v	$\leq b_u$	*and*	$\leq a_u$

conditions under which they might come into play, and highlight their theoretical implications.

4.3.1 Class 1 equilibria

We begin our discussion with *Class 1 equilibria*, the most diverse and interesting family of perfect Bayesian equilibria of the Generalized Mutual Deterrence Game with incomplete information. As table 4.2 indicates, there are three equilibria in this category: a *Sure-Thing Deterrence Equilibrium*, a *Separating Equilibrium*, and a *Hybrid Equilibrium* that shares characteristics of the first two. All three equilibria take the form $[\cdot, 0; \cdot, 0]$, where $(\cdot)$ signifies any value. In other words, under any Class 1 equilibrium, a Soft player *never* defects initially (i.e., $x_S = y_S = 0$). Hard players, by contrast, may behave differently under each perfect Bayesian equilibrium in Class 1. In particular, under either the Hybrid Equilibrium or the Separating Equilibrium, a Hard player either sometimes or always chooses D initially. But under the Sure-Thing Deterrence Equilibrium, a Hard player never defects initially. Thus, while the equilibria of Class 1 share some characteristics, they are also distinct in ways that have important theoretical implications. For this reason we now describe their strategic characteristics in some detail, beginning with Sure-Thing Deterrence.

4.3.1.1 The Sure-Thing Deterrence Equilibrium

The *Sure-Thing Deterrence Equilibrium* (or *STDE* in appendix 4) is the strategy combination [0, 0; 0, 0], where $x_H = x_S = y_H = y_S = 0$. Under the Sure-Thing Deterrence Equilibrium, then, neither player, regardless of its type, *ever* defects. Both Hard and Soft players always cooperate initially. And since each player's policy is never to confront the other, no matter what its retaliation/non-retaliation preferences might be, peace is at hand.

Obviously, the status quo is particularly secure under the Sure-Thing Deterrence Equilibrium. Unfortunately, this equilibrium occurs only under very stringent conditions. As demonstrated in appendix 4, for Sure-Thing Deterrence to be a perfect Bayesian equilibrium, both of the following inequalities must hold:

$$p_B \geq a_2 = \frac{a_{DC} - a_{SQ}}{a_{DC} - a_{DD+}}, \quad p_A \geq b_2 = \frac{b_{CD} - b_{SQ}}{b_{CD} - b_{DD+}}. \qquad (4.7), (4.8)$$

To explain the strategic significance of these inequalities, it is best to refer to figure 4.3. The horizontal axis of this figure represents p_A, the probability that State A is Hard, or the probability that $A_{DD} = a_{DD+}$; similarly, the vertical axis represents p_B, the probability that State B is Hard, or that $B_{DD} = b_{DD+}$. Recall that these probabilities can be interpreted as the players' credibilities. Thus, the higher p_A, the more credible State A's threat to retaliate, and the higher p_B, the more credible State B's threat.

Several constants, such as a_2 and b_2, are also indicated along the two axes of figure 4.3. These constants, which are defined and discussed in detail in appendix 4, are convenient thresholds for categorizing and interpreting the equilibria of the Generalized Mutual Deterrence Game with incomplete information.

Notice from figure 4.3 that both a_2 and b_2 are plotted fairly close to $p_B = 1$ and $p_A = 1$, respectively. Thus, the Sure-Thing Deterrence Equilibrium is to be found only in the extreme northeast region of the figure, above and to the right of these threshold values. That these two parameters are close to 1 means that for the Sure-Thing Deterrence Equilibrium to exist, each side must place a relatively large probability on the other's willingness to retaliate against any attempt to upset the status quo. Put in a slightly different way, Sure-Thing Deterrence requires two players with highly credible threats. But perfect credibility, $p_A = p_B = 1$, is not necessary for mutual deterrence to occur.

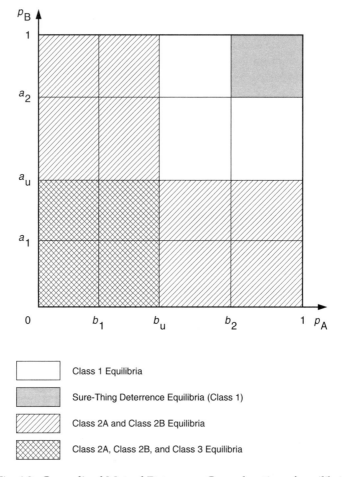

Fig. 4.3. Generalized Mutual Deterrence Game: location of equilibria.

Going beyond the obvious, notice from (4.7) and (4.8) that a_2 and b_2 are defined in terms of the magnitude of each player's evaluation of the *Status Quo* (a_{SQ} and b_{SQ}), of winning (a_{DC} and b_{CD}) and of *Conflict* (a_{DD+} and b_{DD+}), but in the latter case only when the players are Hard. Thus, we can observe that:

- *As the values of a_{SQ} and b_{SQ} increase, the threshold values a_2 and b_2 decrease.*

This means that, *ceteris paribus*, the higher each player's evaluation of the *Status Quo*, the larger the region of Sure-Thing Deterrence, the more likely this equilibrium form to exist, and the more likely the *Status Quo* to survive.

The relationship between deterrence success and satisfaction with the *Status Quo* provides a theoretical justification for policies based on *détente* or reconciliation. For example, during the Nixon administration, the United States attempted to draw the Soviet Union into a more lucrative economic and political relationship. The aim was to reduce the possibility of conflict and war by enhancing the benefits the Soviet Union received from the current order. In peripheral areas especially, the United States hoped that lower levels of threat credibility could be offset by increasing the Soviet Union's stake in the system. The hope is certainly understandable. As our simple model demonstrates, mutual deterrence is more likely when the value of the *Status Quo* is high.

This is not to say, however, that such policies are always prudent. Even though *"all* wars can be prevented by raising the potential aggressor's estimation of the status quo" (Mueller, 1995: 31), such policies frequently fail, as both Britain and France learned the hard way in 1939. Hitler could not be bought off. The attempt to appease him at Czechoslovakia's expense did not bring "peace in our time," despite guarantees to Poland and a British decision to rearm shortly after the occupation of Prague in March 1939. With the benefit of hindsight, it is easy to understand why. As Kagan (1995: 412) explains:

> Perhaps the most important reason for the failure of this belated attempt at deterrence was that it lacked credibility. Whatever its military capabilities, would Britain have the will to use them? Whatever their commitments, would the British have the courage to honor them? Even after Prague and the shift to a policy of deterrence in the political and military spheres [British Prime Minister Neville] Chamberlain continued to employ appeasement by offering economic and colonial concessions. Small wonder that Hitler never seems to have taken his opponent's warning seriously. As he laid plans for the attack on Poland he discounted the danger from the leaders of Britain and France. "I saw them at Munich," he said. "They are little worms."

All of which serves to remind us that all things are never equal in interstate politics and that, by itself, a highly valued status quo is insufficient to eliminate conflict possibilities.[18] The "carrot" is only

---

[18] Bueno de Mesquita and Lalman (1992: 135–137) reach a similar conclusion.

part of a successful deterrent. A credible "stick" is also required. Thus, despite the inverse relationship between the value of the status quo and the likelihood of war, credibility remains critical to the success of mutual deterrence.

- *As the values of a_{DD+} and b_{DD+} decrease, the threshold values a_2 and b_2 also decrease.*

This means that, *ceteris paribus*, deterrence stability is also enhanced by increasing the costs associated with mutual punishment.

Here we find a clear illustration of the standard device used to bolster military deterrence, and an explanation of why some arms competitions have been resolved peacefully. As the cost of *Conflict* increases, the credibility requirements of a deterrent threat become less onerous, and deterrence becomes more likely. In other words, when the costs of mutual punishment go up, so that its value goes down, deterrence can be achieved with less credible threats. This is fortunate indeed since there is almost certainly an inverse relationship between the credibility of threats and the costs associated with their execution.[19]

Significantly, however, our analysis reveals that there is a point at which such a strategem becomes ineffective, and may even be counter-productive. Note that the Sure-Thing Deterrence Equilibrium depends only on the value of a_{DD+} and b_{DD+}, and *not* on a_{DD-} and b_{DD-}. Recall that we assume that each player's utility for *Conflict* and, therefore, the player's type, is established *before* the actual play of the game. Thus, given that p_A and p_B are fixed, if $A_{DD} = a_{DD-}$, or if $B_{DD} = b_{DD-}$, so that at least one player is Soft, then deterrence success is not made more probable by further decreases in the utility (payoff) of the conflict outcome to the Soft player. Notice that this conclusion applies specifically to the set of conditions presumed by classical deterrence theorists: by postulating players with inherently incredible retaliatory threats, classical deterrence theory perforce assumes Soft players.

But now let us compare deterrence problems with different values of the credibility parameters, p_A and p_B. If these parameters are significantly reduced, and this reduction is not more than offset by an increase in the costs associated with *Conflict*, then mutual deterrence

---

[19] See Van Gelder (1989) for a thoughtful discussion of the tradeoff between the credibility of nuclear threats and the costs associated with their use.

becomes relatively more difficult to establish, suggesting a reason why some arms races terminate in war.[20] For example, under most circumstances, the threat to use nuclear weapons is inherently less credible than are lesser threats. And if the dramatic increase in the cost of warfare associated with nuclear weapons is assumed to all but eliminate the credibility of retaliatory threats, deterrence would actually be more likely to fail.[21] In other words, *if* classical deterrence theorists are correct, and strategic nuclear weapons make war at once excessively costly and minimally credible, the status quo should not likely survive (see section 4.3.3).

Thus, in this, our initial foray into the dynamics of deterrence relationships, we find little theoretical support for the argument of Intriligator and Brito (1984) and other classical deterrence theorists that mutual overkill necessarily adds to the stability of deterrence. Rather, our model suggests that for crises in core areas, where credibility is naturally highest, a *minimum deterrent posture*, which relies "on the retention of only enough nuclear weapons to provide an assured destruction capability" (Kegley and Wittkopf, 1989: 351), is better. As both China and India profess to have realized, such a policy, if properly implemented, would not make a retaliatory threat incredible, but would impose significant costs on an aggressor and, therefore, should suffice for deterrence stability.[22]

- As the value of a_{DD+} approaches a_{SQ}, and as the value of b_{DD+} approaches b_{SQ}, a_2 and b_2 approach 1.

This means that, *ceteris paribus*, deterrence is *less* likely as each player's utility for *Conflict* approaches its utility for the *Status Quo*. Under these conditions, a player will be almost as satisfied fighting as not fighting and, therefore, more likely to defect.

The connection between these two parameter values (a_{DD+} and a_{SQ}, or b_{DD+} and b_{SQ}) can, perhaps, shed some theoretical light on the reasoning behind the Japanese attack on Pearl Harbor in 1941.

---

[20] For a more pointed discussion of why some arms races are stabilizing, while others are not, see Downs and Rocke (1990) and Downs (1991).

[21] If either p_A or p_B is small, so that at least one side lacks credibility, there is no deterrence equilibrium. More specifically, general deterrence fails when $p_A < b_2$ or $p_B < a_2$.

[22] Our model, therefore, is an exception to O'Neill's (1992: 459) sweeping charge that "game deterrence models have tended to support excessive arming." Our model uncovers significant "reasons for restraint."

Historians seem to agree that this particular breakdown in the international system did not occur because Japan placed a high probability on a military victory, or because American credibility was low. While some Japanese leaders hoped that the United States might not fully resist, most believed otherwise. In either event, however, most also believed that suffering the consequences of a military defeat was not much worse than enduring an unsatisfactory and humiliating status quo. Parenthetically, we note that it is not necessary to assume, as do Snyder and Diesing (1977: 124–127), that Japan actually preferred *Conflict* to the *Status Quo* in order to explain its behavior. In an uncertain world, deterrence may collapse, and a war may occur, when the players' relative evaluations of these two outcomes are close.

The comparative closeness of these two values, at least for US decision-makers, might also explain the build-up in both conventional and nuclear forces during the early years of the Reagan administration. One explanation offered for that build-up was that it was driven not so much by the structural determinants that lie behind many arms races (Baugh, 1984), as by the perception of the President that the weakness of the Soviet economy would eventually cause the Soviet Union to falter and perhaps even drop out of the race altogether (Bailer and Afferica, 1982/83). In other words, because the United States placed a high probability on success, its evaluation of the outcome it associated with mutual defection (i.e., a Soviet Union defeated and demoralized by an expensive arms race) increased and began to approach the value of a relatively unsatisfactory status quo, and made it less likely that the United States would fully cooperate with the Soviet Union to cap military spending.

Contrariwise, one might further speculate, as many did at the time, that it was the cost to the Soviet Union imposed by this build-up that induced its later cooperation in negotiating the 1987 Intermediate Nuclear Force (INF) disarmament agreement. This assertion, however, depends on the assumption that, unlike China today, the Soviet Union and the Warsaw Pact were committed to keeping pace with any and all US and NATO strategic initiatives. Our model shows that this proviso is necessary, for if the USSR preferred otherwise, then the imposition of additional costs would be unrelated to the calculus of deterrence.[23]

---

[23] Current Chinese policy is directed toward acquiring "an arsenal large enough to give them global status and deter the potential for nuclear blackmail, but small enough to avoid the Soviet Union's mistake – a military force so expensive that it sped the bankruptcy of the nation" (Sanger and Eckholm, 1999).

- *As the values of a_{DC} and b_{CD} increase, the threshold values a_2 and b_2 increase.*

Not surprisingly, the probability of deterrence success is *inversely* related to the value the players attach to winning. *Ceteris paribus*, the more value attached to a prize, the less likely deterrence. For this reason it is likely that the discovery of significant reserves of oil and natural gas in the South China Sea will only make it more difficult for the smaller states in the region to fend off China's claims to the Spratly Islands. Conversely, the less valuable the prize, the easier it is to defend. For example, as Berlin's symbolic value waned during the Cold War, so did the probability that it would be the locus of a deterrence breakdown.

Finally, we should note that the Sure-Thing Deterrence Equilibrium might just as well be called the "tit-for-tat cooperative equilibrium" since it involves initial, yet conditional, cooperation by both players at the start of the game. Its existence depends on each player's perception that the other intends to retaliate with a very high probability in response to any defection. This equilibrium can, therefore, be considered a one-shot game analogue of the cooperative equilibrium supported by tit-for-tat strategies that can emerge when Prisoners' Dilemma is iterated (Axelrod, 1984). It is also akin to the cooperative equilibrium that emerges from the application of Howard's (1971) metagame theory, of Fraser and Hipel's (1984) analysis of options technique, of most medium- and long-horizon stability definitions in the graph model (Fang, Hipel, and Kilgour, 1993), or of Brams's (1994) theory of moves, to the Prisoners' Dilemma game (see chapter 3 for a discussion). Thus, as before, we find an implicit association between stable mutual deterrence and *conditional* cooperation, that is, an initial decision to cooperate, buttressed by an intention to retaliate (defect) with high probability should the opponent abandon cooperation.

4.3.1.2 The Separating Equilibrium and the Hybrid Equilibrium

Before euphoria sets in, however, it is important to emphasize that the mere existence of a Sure-Thing Deterrence Equilibrium does not guarantee that the *Status Quo* will survive. Sure-Thing Deterrence is never unique. It generally coexists with the Separating Equilibrium and *always* coexists with the Hybrid Equilibrium. Thus, even among rational players, other behavioral patterns are possible under precisely those conditions that give rise to Sure-Thing Deterrence.

The *Separating Equilibrium* (or *SE* in appendix 4) consists of the strategy combination [1, 0; 1, 0]. This means that when State A or State B is Hard, it *always* defects initially.[24] The *Hybrid Equilibrium* (or *HE* in appendix 4), which is a cross between the Sure-Thing Deterrence and the Separating Equilibria is the combination [u, 0; v, 0], where u and v are specific probabilities.[25] This means that if State A is Hard, it defects initially with probability u, and if State B is Hard it defects initially with probability v. The only difference between these two equilibria, then, is that under the Hybrid Equilibrium, Hard players defect probabilistically rather than with certainty.[26] In both cases, Soft players *always* cooperate.

The *Status Quo* is not nearly as robust under either the Hybrid Equilibrium or, especially, the Separating Equilibrium, as it is under the Sure-Thing Deterrence Equilibrium. Under these equilibria, Hard players defect initially, either sometimes or always, whereas under the Sure-Thing Deterrence Equilibrium, no player of any type ever defects first. Compounding the instability problem is the fact that all three Class 1 equilibria occur precisely when both players are very likely Hard. Thus all-out conflicts are distinct possibilities when either the Separating or Hybrid Equilibria are in play, especially as the credibilities approach 1.

As discussed in appendix 4, the existence conditions for the Separating Equilibrium are somewhat different from those for the Sure-Thing Deterrence Equilibrium and the Hybrid Equilibrium, so that it is possible for the Separating Equilibrium to be the only equilibrium. (Figure 4.3 shows this case.) If this happens, the *Status Quo* will survive only if both players are actually Soft, i.e., prefer not to retaliate if attacked. At the same time, however, each player must

---

[24] Any *separating* equilibrium separates players by type. Hard players *always* act one way, and Soft players *always* act another way. Under any separating equilibrium, then, a player can infer its opponent's type by observing its action choices. By contrast, under a *pooling* equilibrium, such as the Sure-Thing Deterrence Equilibrium, all types of every player always play the same strategy.

[25] Formulas for u and v can be found in appendix 4.

[26] One way to think of the Hybrid Equilibrium is as a traveler between the Sure-Thing Deterrence Equilibrium and the Separating Equilibrium. As the credibility parameters p_A and p_B get closer and closer to 1, the Hybrid Equilibrium becomes more and more similar to the Separating Equilibrium, that is, x_H and y_H also approach 1, so that defection becomes more and more likely. And as p_A approaches b_2 and p_B approaches a_2, moving away from 1, the Hybrid Equilibrium gets more and more similar to the Sure-Thing Deterrence Equilibrium, that is, x_H and y_H approach 0, and defection becomes less and less likely.

believe that its opponent is likely Hard. Clearly, this combination of beliefs and preferences is somewhat unlikely. Thus, even when both players have highly credible threats, the stability of the *Status Quo* is not assured. In fact, when the Separating Equilibrium is the only equilibrium, *Conflict* is to be expected.[27]

On the other hand, if the Sure-Thing Deterrence Equilibrium exists, then the Hybrid Equilibrium also exists and the Separating Equilibrium generally does too. But despite the fact that the Sure-Thing Deterrence Equilibrium is Pareto-superior (indeed, it is strictly preferred by both types of both players) to either of the other two (see appendix 4 for the details), deterrence remains problematic. There is simply no guarantee that the players will settle on Sure-Thing Deterrence.

Put in a slightly different way, the conditions for war and peace generally coexist in our model of mutual deterrence and, as will be seen, in many of the other models we develop in this book. This finding is at odds with the tenets of classical deterrence theory and has important theoretical consequences. Under parity or balance of power conditions, even highly credible retaliatory threats and high conflict costs do not eliminate (and may not even significantly reduce) the risk of intense conflict. In our view, then, all-out war is a possibility even in the most favorable circumstances, contrary to the arguments of Intriligator and Brito (1981: 265) and other classical deterrence theorists. If anything, our model suggests the opposite, which helps explain why a balance of power is not a good predictor of peace (see chapter 1). Thus, unlike classical deterrence theory, our model is consistent with the lack of a strong association between parity and the absence of war.

4.3.2 Class 2A and 2B Attack Equilibria

The second major family of perfect Bayesian equilibria in the Generalized Mutual Deterrence Game with incomplete information is the

---

[27] The zone of existence of the Separating Equilibrium depends on the logical structure of the deterrence model. Here the two sides choose their actions simultaneously, which means that each side must make its choice without knowledge of the choice of the other. The Separating Equilibrium exists even when both sides have very high credibility. In chapter 5, a Separating Equilibrium appears in a sequential model, but its zone of existence does not include situations of very high credibility on both sides. This is a significant difference between the two models and provides further justification for an examination of both mutual and unilateral deterrence.

Attack Equilibria. There are two sets of three equilibria in this family, each a mirror image of the other. *Class 2A* consists of equilibria of the form [1, 1; ·, 0], while *Class 2B* corresponds to [·, 0; 1, 1], where (·) represents any value. In Class 2A, which is composed of Attack Equilibria AE_{1A}, AE_{2A}, and AE_{3A}, State A's strategy is *always* to defect; this is similarly true of State B in Class 2B, which consists of Attack Equilibria AE_{1B}, AE_{2B}, and AE_{3B}. Since all six Attack Equilibria involve certain defection by one player (for now, the "attacker"), and certain submission by the other player (for now, the "target") when the target is Soft, there is *no chance* of general deterrence succeeding when any of these equilibria are in play.

The equilibria within each class differ, however, with respect to the target's initial policy given that it is Hard and prefers to retaliate. As indicated in table 4.2, State B's strategy associated with AE_{1A}, and State A's with AE_{1B}, involve the target's certain choice of C; both AE_{2A} and AE_{2B} involve probabilistic defection by the target; and AE_{3A} and AE_{3B} are associated with the target's certain choice of D. No matter what the target's *initial* choice, however, the *Status Quo* will be violated. But it is unlikely that the target is Hard, so in any case *Conflict* is likely to be avoided.

As one might expect, Class 2 Attack Equilibria exist when either p_A or p_B is sufficiently low. (See appendix 4 for details.) This means that a calculated rupture of deterrence becomes much more likely as the probability increases that one player prefers to "chicken out"; the low probability of retaliation provides the other player with a strong incentive to risk conflict in order to gain an advantage. Specifically, for equilibria of Class 2A or 2B to exist requires either $p_A \leq b_u$, or $p_B \leq a_u$, or both. As indicated in appendix 4, these threshold values depend on the values of b_{SQ} and b_{DD-}, and a_{SQ} and a_{DD-}, respectively. For small negative values of either b_{DD-} and a_{DD-}, the Attack Equilibrium region covers almost the entire square of figure 4.3. Under these conditions, the breakdown of deterrence is almost certain. Conversely, as the values of b_{DD-} or a_{DD-} decline (i.e., as the costs associated with unwanted *Conflict* increase), the zone of existence of Class 2 Equilibria shrinks, making the behavioral patterns associated with other equilibria more likely. Figure 4.4 shows a typical case.

One implication is that, in situations where at least one player's retaliatory threat is *not* very credible, increasing the cost of unwanted conflict can make successful deterrence more likely. It would appear that under such conditions nuclear weapons can have a salutary

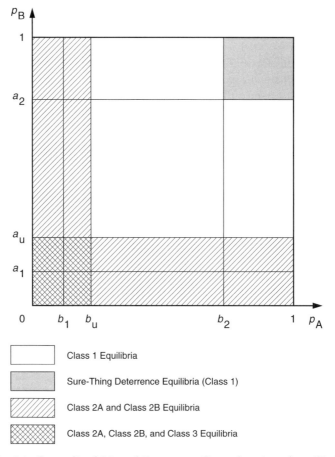

Fig. 4.4. Generalized Mutual Deterrence Game: location of equilibria when the costs of unwanted conflict are high.

effect: *ceteris paribus*, as the price of underestimating an opponent's resolve increases, the probability of deterrence success increases. We re-emphasize, however, that it is seldom the case that all things are equal in politics.

We also stress that the most likely outcome under any Class 2A equilibrium is *A Wins* and, under any Class 2B equilibrium, *B Wins*. It is easy to explain why. Note that except in the area around the origin of figure 4.3, where they overlap with the Class 3 Bluff Equilibrium (see below), Class 2 Attack Equilibria occur when one player's credibility is relatively high and the other's relatively low. In such cases, the subjective "balance of resolve" favors one player or the other, and so does the game. Our analysis, therefore, helps to specify the conditions under which an "imbalance of resolve" may overtake a "balance of power" as the best predictor of interstate behavior (Betts, 1987: 479). Specifically, when a player with a highly credible threat believes its opponent to be very likely Soft and, therefore, likely to concede if challenged, the favored player will defect.

For similar reasons, the disadvantaged player tends not to defect initially. Its opponent is probably Hard and, therefore, likely to retaliate if confronted. Thus when any Attack Equilibrium is in play, one player will certainly contest the *Status Quo*, and the other, unlikely to initiate itself, will probably capitulate, which helps to explain why a great power (such as the United States in the Americas or the former Soviet Union in Eastern Europe) might enjoy free rein in its sphere of influence, and may help to explain why a weaker state, like Finland, might adjust its policies to accommodate a feared neighbor.[28]

Finally, we should observe that it is possible for some Attack Equilibria to coexist with the Sure-Thing Deterrence Equilibrium (see appendix 4 for details), so that the mere existence of an Attack Equilibrium does not altogether eliminate the possibilities for peace. But the reverse remains true as well: the fact that the Sure-Thing Deterrence Equilibrium exists is no guarantee that the *Status Quo* will survive. Even then, deterrence remains a "sometimes thing."

4.3.3   Class 3 Bluff Equilibrium

But what if *both* p_A and p_B are so low that *neither* player's threat is particularly credible? Under these conditions, an additional equilibrium outcome, the *Bluff Equilibrium* (*BE*), may be possible in addition to the equilibria of Classes 2A and 2B.

The Bluff Equilibrium, which uniquely constitutes Class 3, takes the form $[1, u; 1, v]$. This means that the choice of a Hard player is always to defect immediately. Of course, neither player is very likely to be Hard when the Bluff Equilibrium exists.

Soft players defect too, but probabilistically rather than with certainty. Given that a player is Soft, this defection constitutes a bluff,

---

[28] Of course, less powerful states tend to lack capable threats, which is why we qualify somewhat our explanation of Finland's behavior.

albeit calculated, since its opponent is also likely to be Soft and, hence, unlikely to call the bluff. Such bluffs become more and more likely as a player's credibility decreases.[29] At higher credibility levels, a player is more likely to be Hard and, therefore, less likely to be bluffing.

It is interesting to observe that the overall probability that either player defects initially under a Bluff Equilibrium is constant (i.e., always equals a_u or b_u) throughout the entire Class 3 region. In other words, as a player becomes more likely to be Soft, i.e., as p_A or p_B decreases, the player compensates by *increasing* the probability of bluffing when Soft, and conversely. By sometimes defecting when Soft, a player conceals its type and avoids exploitation. All of which suggests that under the credibility conditions that give rise to the Bluff Equilibrium, a crisis could be instigated as a purely defensive measure, that is, as a way of fending off pressure for concessions. One could plausibly interpret the series of incidents between the United States and China during the late 1950s in terms of just such a consideration. By acting Hard and making Quemoy and Matsu an issue, an underdeveloped China could avoid giving the impression that it may have been Soft, thereby helping to deter unwanted future demands by the United States or other powers. Similar considerations might also explain what Kagan (1995: 449) characterizes as the Soviet Union's "aggressive policy of bluff" that targeted West Berlin during the late 1950s and very early 1960s.

Finally, note that the Bluff Equilibrium exists under precisely those fixed conditions presumed by classical deterrence theorists, that is, antagonists with low credibility. Thus, the model of interstate conflict we develop in this chapter, and extend in subsequent chapters, subsumes most models developed by classical deterrence theorists and, in this sense, is more general. More important, however, is the fact that the implications of our model differ substantially from those of classical deterrence theory. In our model, when threat credibility is mutually low, players are prone to bluffs, probes, or even outright attacks. As a consequence, deterrence is unlikely to succeed, the status quo is extremely fragile, and conflict can hardly be ruled out. All of which serves to underscore the extreme dependence of classical deterrence theory on special assumptions, assumptions that are either

---

[29] Appendix 4 gives formulas for the bluff probabilities x_S and y_S in terms of the players' own credibilities and payoff parameters.

at odds with basic rationality postulates, or that require divine intervention to save the players from themselves.[30] Worse yet, these special assumptions lead to empirically dubious propositions about the conditions under which the status quo is most likely to survive, and a bevy of policy prescriptions that court disaster.

4.4   Coda

In this chapter we examine the theoretical connections between deterrence stability and threat credibility in mutual deterrence situations. We do this by formulating as a model of mutual deterrence a game of incomplete information in which each player is not only dissatisfied with the status quo, but also uncertain about how its opponent would respond to a challenge. By identifying the credibility of each player's threat to retaliate with the probability that a player prefers retaliation to capitulation, we maintain consistency with both the traditional strategic literature, in which credibility is usually equated with believability, and with the literature of game theory, in which credibility is taken to be a prerequisite for rational behavior.

Perhaps the signal contribution of the model is to provide a precise measure of the circumstances under which mutual deterrence can emerge in an uncertain world, and of the conditions likely to lead to a breakdown of deterrence. Specifically, when the credibility of each player's threat is sufficiently high, deterrence is possible, perhaps even likely, but by no means certain, as some classical deterrence theorists have speculated. The credibility threshold for the existence of the Sure-Thing Deterrence Equilibrium depends on each player's evaluation of the status quo and the costs associated with conflict. Contrary to Lebow (1984: 181) and most classical deterrence theorists, however, we found no linear or other simple relationship between the costs of warfare and deterrence stability. In fact, our model indicates that in core areas, where both players likely have inherently credible threats, increasing the costs of mutual punishment past a certain point does little to enhance deterrence stability. And if there is, as we suspect, an inverse relationship between these costs and threat credi-

---

[30] Perhaps suggesting that there is more ideologizing than theorizing taking place, some classical deterrence theorists seem to recognize that mutual nuclear deterrence is, at best, a fragile relationship – but only when they are discussing relationships between non-Western states such as India and Pakistan.

bility, then increasing the costs of war at this level may even make deterrence less likely, not more likely.

For this reason we recommend for the security of any country's homeland a policy of deterrence that aims for a capability that is sufficient to inflict unacceptable damage on an opponent, yet is able to survive preemption to deliver a retaliatory attack. An "overkill" capability is just that – overkill. For the nuclear powers, then, we favor continuing arms reductions, single-warhead missiles, and hardened silos. A thin "defensive" system around second-strike forces is also consistent with the spirit of our findings, provided that such a system does not trigger a nullifying compensatory reaction by another party. *Ceteris paribus*, building down is better than building up, suggesting that it is preferable that the United States meets China at the lower Chinese deployment level rather than the other way around.

The policy implications of our model for conflict areas where inherent credibility is mutually low are not so clear. Even small increases in the costs the players associate with conflict will decrease the probability that the status quo will survive rational play, so the best hope would appear to lie with diplomatic initiatives that, simultaneously, bolster or enhance extant credibility levels and, by adjusting the status quo, reduce the temptation to defect. Such policies, of course, are fraught with danger, especially against an ambitious adversary looking for trouble in all the wrong places. Moreover, given the probabilities, these tactics are unlikely to be successful on a fairly regular basis, especially during expansionary periods such as the nineteenth century when imperial urges were strong. In today's world, a saving grace could be that in truly peripheral areas, no major power has a meaningful incentive to defect.

Much the same can be said of conflict in those tangential areas where an asymmetry of credibility exists. Under these conditions, deterrence of an unsatisfied player is most unlikely. Over the long haul, the status quo is unlikely to survive when one player's credibility is negligible and the other's is not.

We believe that the history of the post-war period conforms roughly to the expectations of our model. In core areas, where credibility is by definition highest, deterrence has indeed prevailed and war has, fortunately, been avoided. The principal breakdowns of deterrence have come in areas where only one superpower had a vested interest and, consequently, a higher level of credibility. When deterrence failed in Hungary or Czechoslovakia because of Soviet actions, or in

Vietnam because of a US decision to re-establish a deteriorating status quo, the locale was such that the core interests of the other superpower were not at risk.

To be sure, there are exceptions to this statement. But it is telling that the exceptions include all of the dramatic cases in which strategic deterrence almost evaporated. In Cuba, for instance, the Soviet Union directly challenged the interests of a stronger and more highly motivated United States and, perhaps not surprisingly, eventually backed down after its bluff was called. In Berlin, starting in 1948 and continuing until the mid-1960s, persistent Soviet challenges very nearly upset the foundations of the European equilibrium. Finally, the two superpowers came close to war again during the 1973 Middle East war when the Soviets threatened to intervene to protect Egypt's Third Army and President Sadat's pro-Soviet regime. It is consistent with our model that in the latter two cases, where the interests of the two sides were seriously at risk, deterrence prevailed because the threats of relatively severe retaliation offset the concomitant decline of each side's credibility.

If strategic deterrence has been the rule, and small breakdowns of deterrence the exception, since 1945, the question arises of how the strategies pursued by the superpowers brought this state of affairs into being. Or, put another way, what is the nature of the equilibrium which characterized superpower behavior from the dawn of the nuclear age to the collapse of the Soviet Union? It is possible, both empirically and logically, for each superpower sometimes to have selected strategies consistent with the Sure-Thing Deterrence Equilibrium: never behave aggressively, and always threaten harsh retaliation. But, the absence of war is also consistent with other equilibria under which the survivability of the status quo is no sure thing. The most disturbing of these is clearly the Bluff Equilibrium which exists under precisely those conditions presumed by classical deterrence theorists, i.e., mutually incredible retaliatory threats.

Obviously, our formal analysis can shed no light on transcendental questions such as which equilibrium was in play during the Cold War, or how one equilibrium could shift to another, or how any particular equilibrium could be changed. Still, the theoretical possibility, slight as it may be, that deterrence could succeed under a Bluff Equilibrium requires that, at minimum, we outline some possibilities. There are at least two.

One is that the axiomatic base that delimits classical deterrence theory was realized during the Cold War, but that no superpower was in fact willing to endure actual conflict.[31] To sustain this argument, however, one must also assume, as do some strategic thinkers who are skeptical about the persistence of mutual deterrence (e.g., Jones and Thompson, 1978), or even some who are not (e.g., National Academy of Sciences, 1997: 16), that more than just a modicum of luck was involved. How else can one explain why, over a span of almost half a century, no simultaneous defection ever occurred? We observe, however, that any explanation of post-war stability that depends upon good fortune is inconsistent with a characterization of the superpower relationship as robustly stable.

If this description of the basis of the "long peace" rings true, then the prescriptions of classical deterrence theory follow. States should, *inter alia*, aim for an overkill capability, eschew significant arms reductions, pursue proliferation policies and, in crisis, seek advantage by reducing flexibility or by behaving recklessly. On the other hand, if this explanation of the post-war period strikes the reader as either inconsistent or implausible, then a different axiomatic base is required. Perfect Deterrence Theory is our preferred theoretical alternative.

Perfect Deterrence Theory starts with the assumption that threats, including some nuclear threats, can indeed be credible. From this perspective, the stability of the Cold War period is (perhaps too) easily explained: each side's retaliatory threat was sufficiently credible to deter the other from attacking.[32] While this explanation might appear unexceptional, it runs counter to the conventional wisdom. As well, Perfect Deterrence Theory's policy implications stand in stark contrast to classical deterrence theory's: states should, *inter alia*, develop a minimum deterrent capability, pursue arms control agreements, cap military spending, avoid proliferation policies and, in crisis, seek compromise by adopting firm-but-flexible negotiating stances and tit-for-tat military deployments.

To conclude, we observe that Perfect Deterrence Theory's dramatically different policy recommendations obtain when classical deterrence theory's core assumptions are disturbed, but ever so slightly. Specifically, our alternative prescriptions require the possibility that

[31] Under a Bluff Equilibrium, Hard players always defect.
[32] In our opinion, this explanation does not adequately account for the absence of a US challenge to the Soviet Union in those periods during the Truman, Eisenhower, and Kennedy administrations when the United States enjoyed a clear-cut strategic advantage. We address this deficiency in the next chapter.

states prefer retaliation to capitulation. This theoretical modification does not strike us as exceptional, especially for direct, general, deterrence relationships – even when nuclear weapons are involved.

Still, there is no reason to stop here. Accordingly, we next examine the theoretical implications of adjusting another of classical deterrence theory's core assumptions, undifferentiated actors. By dropping this assumption we are able to connect our decision-making theory with a conceptually compatible structural theory – power transition – and examine Perfect Deterrence Theory's implications under a slightly different set of initial conditions. As we will argue, this additional theoretical tweaking is required to take fuller account of credibility asymmetries that arguably existed until the Soviet Union achieved essential equivalence with the United States sometime in the early 1970s.

5   Unilateral deterrence

It is only in equilibrium that the world will find peace.

Charles de Gaulle

For logically consistent realists, mutual deterrence games (or larger *n*-actor variants) are the only games in town. Realism, classical or neo-, loses much of its explanatory power if only some states are taken to be power maximizers, or if only some states are motivated by structural insecurity. As we have seen, however, logical consistency is not a hallmark of classical deterrence theory. Thus, conceptual and logical models of unilateral deterrence stand side by side in the strategic literature with models of mutual deterrence.[1] Daniel Ellsberg's (1959: 358–359) critical risk model is a good example. In it, deterrence is seen as essentially a one-sided problem: how to deter a blackmailer, via threats, when the cost of executing the threat is prohibitive.

But Ellsberg is not alone, and it is easy to understand why: the foundations of modern deterrence theory were laid against the backdrop of the Cold War. Most strategic thinkers of that era were understandably preoccupied with the question of how the Soviet Union might be deterred from attacking Western interests (and not vice versa). Thus, it should not be surprising that the assumption of asymmetry in offensive motivation figures prominently in the strategic literature. In fact, Jervis (1979: 297) reports that "most of the literature is written from the standpoint of the country resisting change."

For instance, the theoretical distinction between unilateral (asym-

---

[1] It should be emphasized that the lack of consistency pertains only to those realists and classical deterrence theorists who otherwise presume actors to be undifferentiated.

metric) and mutual (symmetric) deterrence is implied in Morgan's (1977: 28) well-known definition of "immediate" deterrence as a relationship in which "one side is seriously considering an attack while the other is mounting a threat to prevent it." Such deterrence situations are almost always one-sided. Rarely do two states simultaneously plan to attack one another, save for those circumstances in which one state expects the other to attack first and so launches a preemptive war.

Likewise, unilateral deterrence is presupposed in the literature of acute international crises. The standard definition depicts a crisis as a situation characterized, *inter alia*, by shortness of decision time and strategic surprise (Hermann, 1969). Such conditions are likely to be satisfied only when one state has already directly challenged the interests of another, suggesting once again differences in motivation and circumstances between the states involved in the crisis. Snyder and Diesing's (1977) now classic description of the anatomy of a crisis is unambiguous: crises are the direct result of a decision by one state to challenge the security interests of another.

As well, the literature of interstate war often posits an asymmetric, hierarchically structured international system. While realists and balance of power theorists view states as undifferentiated actors, other system-level theories, such as the theory of long cycles (Modelski, 1983; Modelski and Thompson, 1989), power cycle theory (Doran, 1989a, 1989b), hierarchical equilibrium theory (Midlarsky, 1988), and hegemonic stability theory (Kindleberger, 1974, 1976; Gilpin, 1975, 1981; Krasner, 1976), distinguish between the positions occupied by, and the situations faced by, states in the system. Organski and Kugler's (1980) power transition theory explicitly envisions an environment that could disintegrate as a consequence of a challenge made by a dissatisfied state to a satisfied status quo power defending an institutionalized order.[2]

In the more descriptive literature of interstate conflict, there is also widespread consensus that certain states, at specific times, have had either expansive or defensive orientations. In his well-known study of the Concert of Europe, for instance, Kissinger (1957a: 270, 321) saw Prussia and Russia as essentially revisionist states. By contrast, both Great Britain and Austria – "the epitome of the status quo powers" –

---

[2] In section 5.5 we explicitly discuss the connection between the model we explore in this chapter and power transition theory.

are characterized as being content with the Congress system. Likewise, Craig and George (1995: 32) assert that "after 1856, Russia, France, Prussia, and the rising power of Piedmont could all be considered as revisionist powers, and only Austria and Great Britain as supporters of the existing order." Similarly, Kagan's (1995) discussion of the origins of the Peloponnesian War, the Second Punic War, and World War I, respectively, takes as axiomatic Sparta's, Rome's and Great Britain's conservative policies and general satisfaction with the status quo.

5.1   Game form[3]

Since one-sided deterrence relationships have obvious empirical and theoretical import, we now explore their underlying properties game-theoretically. One purpose is to gauge the sensitivity of the conclusions drawn from an analysis of the Generalized Mutual Deterrence Game to the assumption of simultaneous choice. Another is to explore more thoroughly the theoretical consequences of positing undifferentiated actors. And finally, we wish to connect Perfect Deterrence Theory with those structural theories that distinguish between states with offensive and defensive orientations.

To these ends we posit a simple two-person game, called the *Unilateral Deterrence Game*, in which one player, *Challenger*, decides whether to challenge the other, *Defender*, but not vice versa.[4] Figure 5.1 depicts this game in extensive form.

In the Unilateral Deterrence Game, Challenger begins play at node 1. Challenger can either initiate a conflict (by defecting and choosing D), or not (by cooperating and choosing C). If Challenger cooperates, the game ends, the outcome is *Status Quo* (SQ), and the payoffs to Challenger and Defender are c_{SQ} and d_{SQ}, respectively; if Challenger defects initially, the game continues and Defender moves next at node 2.

Defender's choices are either to concede (i.e., choose C) or to defy Challenger (i.e., choose D). Concession results in outcome DC (*Defender Concedes*) and payoffs c_{DC} and d_{DC} to Challenger and Defender, respectively. Defiance leads to a second and final choice by Challenger

---

[3] The rest of this chapter draws on Zagare and Kilgour (1993a) and Zagare (1996b).

[4] Our convention for specific references to the players in our game model, Challenger and Defender, is to capitalize their names. We drop the capitals when referring to their real-world analogues.

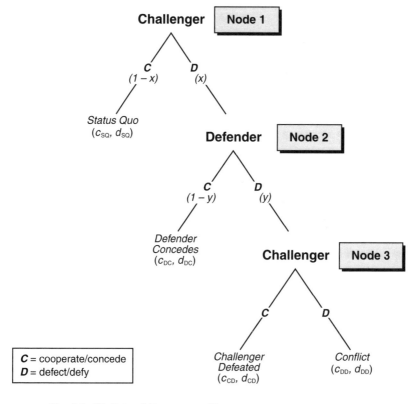

Challenger | Node 1 |

C
(1 − x)

D
(x)

Status Quo
(c_{SQ}, d_{SQ})

Defender | Node 2 |

C
(1 − y)

D
(y)

Defender
Concedes
(c_{DC}, d_{DC})

Challenger | Node 3 |

C

D

C = cooperate/concede
D = defect/defy

Challenger
Defeated
(c_{CD}, d_{CD})

Conflict
(c_{DD}, d_{DD})

Fig. 5.1. Unilateral Deterrence Game.

at node 3. If Challenger chooses *C* and concedes, the outcome is CD (*Challenger Defeated*); if Challenger defies Defender by sticking with its previous choice of *D*, *Conflict* (outcome DD) occurs. In the former case the payoffs are c_{CD} and d_{CD} to Challenger and Defender, respectively; and in the latter case the payoffs are c_{DD} and d_{DD}.

For convenience, the four possible outcomes of the asymmetric deterrence model, as well as the notation for the (von Neumann–Morgenstern) utilities associated with them, are summarized in figure 5.2. Payoffs are represented by an ordered pair in each cell of the matrix, the first entry being Challenger's utility, and the second Defender's. Notice that except for the changes made to accommodate the new player names, the outcomes and payoffs in the Unilateral Deterrence Game are the same as those of the Generalized Mutual

Defender

	Status Quo (SQ) (c_{SQ}, d_{SQ})	Challenger Defeated (CD) (c_{CD}, d_{CD})
Challenger	Defender Concedes (DC) (c_{DC}, d_{DC})	Conflict (DD) (c_{DD}, d_{DD})

Fig. 5.2. Outcome and utility notation for Unilateral Deterrence Game.

Deterrence Game. This is no accident. In developing these models we have tried to keep things as uncomplicated and as comparable as possible.

Notice as well that the Unilateral Deterrence Game is a straightforward extension of the Rudimentary Asymmetric Deterrence Game (see figure 3.7). The one difference is that Challenger has an additional choice (at node 3) in the Unilateral Deterrence Game. This extra move means that the game no longer ends after Defender's response. Because Challenger is afforded an opportunity to retaliate should Defender resist, the possibility for coercive bargaining and tacit negotiation, or what George (1993) calls "forceful persuasion," exists. The Unilateral Deterrence Game, therefore, is a more elaborated model.

To add some real-world structure to the model, we place some reasonable restrictions on each player's preferences: first, we assume Challenger strictly prefers *Defender Concedes* to the *Status Quo* and the *Status Quo* to *Challenger Defeated*. This axiom is necessary since, without it, deterrence is spurious. On the other hand, we place milder restrictions on the preferences of Defender, who could most prefer either the *Status Quo* or *Challenger Defeated*, but is assumed to prefer both to *Defender Concedes*. As it turns out, Defender's relative evaluation of the first two outcomes is without strategic import.

We take all threats to be capable in the sense discussed in section 3.3. Thus, we presume Challenger prefers *Status Quo* to *Conflict*, and so does Defender. Again, we make this assumption because deterrence is impossible without it. As before, however, we make no fixed assumption about either player's preference between *Conflict* and conceding to the other player. These crucial relationships remain at the core of our model.

Challenger's preference between *Conflict* and *Challenger Defeated*, and Defender's preference between *Conflict* and *Defender Concedes*, then, establish their types. In the simplest possible discrete model, Challenger and Defender may be of one of two types, Hard or Soft, each with the following preferences:

Challenger (Hard):   *Defender Concedes* $>_{Ch}$ *Status Quo* $>_{Ch}$
                      Conflict $>_{Ch}$ *Challenger Defeated*   (5.1)

Challenger (Soft):   *Defender Concedes* $>_{Ch}$ *Status Quo* $>_{Ch}$
                      Challenger Defeated $>_{Ch}$ *Conflict*   (5.2)

Defender (Hard):   [*Challenger Defeated* and *Status Quo*] $>_{Def}$
                      Conflict $>_{Def}$ *Defender Concedes*   (5.3)

Defender (Soft):   [*Challenger Defeated* and *Status Quo*] $>_{Def}$
                      Defender Concedes $>_{Def}$ *Conflict*   (5.4)

where "$>_{Ch}$" means "is preferred to by Challenger," "$>_{Def}$" means "is preferred to by Defender," and where the relative values of the payoffs enclosed in brackets remain open.

We continue to assume that each player knows its own utilities (preferences) but has only probabilistic knowledge about its opponent's type. To model this uncertainty, the players' payoffs at outcome DD, C_{DD} (Challenger) and D_{DD} (Defender), are treated as independent binary random variables – indicated by upper-case letters – with known distributions. More specifically, both players know that

$$C_{DD} = \begin{cases} c_{DD+} \text{ with probability } p_{Ch} \\ c_{DD-} \text{ with probability } 1-p_{Ch} \end{cases}$$

$$D_{DD} = \begin{cases} d_{DD+} \text{ with probability } p_{Def} \\ d_{DD-} \text{ with probability } 1-p_{Def} \end{cases}$$

where $c_{DC} > c_{SQ} > c_{DD+} > c_{CD} > c_{DD-}$, $d_{CD} > d_{DD+} > d_{DC} > d_{DD-}$, $d_{SQ} > d_{DD+}$, $0 < p_{Ch} < 1$, and $0 < p_{Def} < 1$.

In the Unilateral Deterrence Game, p_{Ch} and p_{Def} are the credibility parameters for Challenger and Defender, respectively. This means that Defender sees Challenger as Hard with *a priori* probability p_{Ch} and as Soft with *a priori* probability $1-p_{Ch}$. Similarly, Challenger believes Defender Hard with probability p_{Def}, and Soft with probability $1-p_{Def}$. Recall that the larger p_{Ch} and p_{Def}, the more credible the player's threat (to choose D) is, and conversely. At the extremes, as these values approach 1 or 0, the corresponding threat becomes either completely credible or completely incredible.

5.2   Unilateral deterrence under complete information

Under what conditions will Challenger initiate a confrontation? When will Defender resist? When will war result? What is the connection between deterrence success and threat credibility? We address these and related questions, first in the simpler case when the players have complete information about each other's preferences, and then in the more complex setting of incomplete information.[5]

When information is complete, players have accurate and full information about each other's preferences. Because we define credible (i.e., rational) threats in terms of one player's belief about the other's preference for executing the threat, it follows that, under complete information, a player's threat is either perfectly credible (when $p_{Ch}=1$ or $p_{Def}=1$) or perfectly incredible (when $p_{Ch}=0$ or $p_{Def}=0$). In other words, when both players' types are common knowledge, each knows for sure whether the other is Hard or Soft, i.e., whether C_{DD} equals c_{DD+} or c_{DD-} and whether D_{DD} equals d_{DD+} or d_{DD-}.

Given the restrictions placed on the preferences of the players (see 5.1–5.4 above), there are only four strategically distinct Unilateral Deterrence Games with complete information. These games differ only with respect to the credibility of the players' threats: either both players are known to have a credible threat (i.e., $p_{Ch}=1$ and $p_{Def}=1$), only Challenger has one ($p_{Ch}=1$ and $p_{Def}=0$), only Defender has one ($p_{Ch}=0$ and $p_{Def}=1$), or neither player has a credible threat ($p_{Ch}=0$ and $p_{Def}=0$).

Table 5.1 summarizes the distinguishing characteristics of the four games. Using backward induction, it is easy to determine the subgame-perfect equilibrium of each game. Consider, for example, the first game (first and second columns) of table 5.1, which is represented in extensive-form in figure 5.3. In this game $p_{Ch}=1$ and $p_{Def}=1$. Both players are Hard, i.e., both have completely credible threats. In other words, $C_{DD}=c_{DD+}$ and $D_{DD}=d_{DD+}$, and both players know this. As

[5] For the interested reader we summarize the intermediate case of one-sided incomplete information in footnote 7.

Table 5.1. *Subgame-perfect equilibria for Unilateral Deterrence Games with complete information*

	Game 1		Game 2		Game 3		Game 4	
	Ch	Def	Ch	Def	Ch	Def	Ch	Def
p_{Ch} and p_{Def}	1	1	1	0	0	1	0	0
Type	Hard	Hard	Hard	Soft	Soft	Hard	Soft	Soft
Credible threat	Yes	Yes	Yes	No	No	Yes	No	No
Strategy	C/D	D	D/D	C	C/C	D	C/C	C
Subgame-perfect equilibrium outcome	*Status Quo*		*Defender Concedes*		*Status Quo*		*Status Quo*	

Key:
Ch   = Challenger
Def = Defender
p_{Ch} = probability that Challenger is Hard
p_{Def} = probability that Defender is Hard
C   = *Cooperate/Concede*
D   = *Defect/Defy*
x/x = Challenger's equilibrium choice at node 1/node 3

the arrows in figure 5.3 (representing rational choices) reveal, and as table 5.1 shows, the unique subgame-perfect equilibrium of this game produces the *Status Quo* as the outcome, so deterrence succeeds.

Application of backward induction explains why this is so. At node 3, Challenger can either choose C (concede) and bring about outcome CD (*Challenger Defeated*) or choose D (defy) and induce *Conflict*. Since Challenger is Hard, $C_{DD} = c_{DD+}$, and $c_{DD+} > c_{CD}$. At node 3, therefore, Challenger should choose D.

At node 2, Defender has choices similar to Challenger's at node 3. If Defender chooses C, the outcome is *Defender Concedes*; if Defender chooses D, then Challenger's choice at node 3 determines the outcome. Given complete information, Defender can anticipate that a Hard Challenger will choose D (see above) and that the outcome will be *Conflict*. Since Defender is also Hard and actually prefers *Conflict* to *Defender Concedes* ($D_{DD} = d_{DD+} > d_{DC}$), Defender should choose D at node 2.

Finally, at node 1, Challenger can either cooperate or defect. If Challenger cooperates, the game ends and the outcome is *Status Quo*. But if Challenger defects, Defender makes a choice at node 2. As just

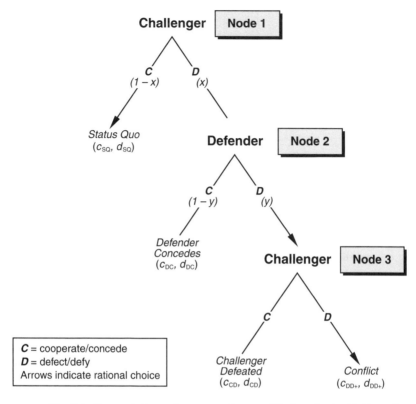

Fig. 5.3. Determining subgame-perfect equilibrium in the Unilateral Deterrence Game with credible threats and complete information using backward induction.

determined, a Hard Defender defects, leading, in turn, to Challenger's defection at node 3 and *Conflict*. Consequently, Challenger's node 1 choice reduces to C – in which case the outcome is *Status Quo* – or D – in which case the outcome is *Conflict*. By assumption, $c_{SQ} > c_{DD+}$, so Challenger should choose C initially. In equilibrium, then, Challenger chooses C at node 1 and intends to choose D at node 3, while Defender intends to choose D at node 2. The outcome is *Status Quo*. Thus, when each player has a credible threat, deterrence reigns.

Interestingly, as table 5.1 indicates, the *Status Quo* also survives rational play whenever (1) Defender's threat is credible, or (2) Challenger's threat is incredible. In the Unilateral Deterrence Game, then, mutually credible threats are sufficient, but not necessary, conditions for successful deterrence. But this is as it should be. Since Unilateral Deterrence Games are asymmetric, it should not be surprising that the conditions required for deterrence are somewhat different from those for symmetric games of mutual deterrence.

The asymmetric nature of the Unilateral Deterrence Game explains why the *Status Quo* is stable when Challenger lacks a credible retaliatory threat. When Challenger is known to be Soft, Challenger is unable to deter Defender from planning to choose *D* at node 2, and is therefore itself deterred from choosing *D* at node 1. In this sense, then, deterrence fails when credibility is absent. Fortunately, for Defender, this failure guarantees that the *Status Quo* will remain intact.

There is, however, one case in which the *Status Quo* is unstable, namely when Challenger is Hard and Defender is Soft. In this instance, Challenger deters Defender from planning to choose *D* at node 2; hence, Defender is unable to deter Challenger from choosing *D* at node 1. The end result is *Defender Concedes*.

Notice that deterrence succeeds in the Unilateral Deterrence Game when *both* players are Soft and lack a credible threat. One might argue, therefore, that this game model provides an alternative resolution to the paradox of deterrence. And indeed it does. But keep in mind that this resolution rests on a core assumption that lies outside the confines of classical deterrence theory: differentiated actors. In the Unilateral Deterrence Game, the players have distinct roles and distinct motivations. In classical deterrence theory, however, all states are considered alike. Thus, in order to accept this resolution, one must necessarily cast off yet another element of the axiomatic base of classical deterrence theory.

Nonetheless, this is an important and unanticipated result that clearly distinguishes the Unilateral Deterrence Game from the Generalized Mutual Deterrence Game. In the latter, the *Status Quo* is unstable when both players lack credible retaliatory threats: neither can deter the other. Just the opposite occurs, however, when deterrence is one-sided. As just mentioned, whenever Challenger's threat lacks credibility, Challenger cannot deter retaliation by Defender, and this fact has a significant strategic consequence: the *Status Quo* survives rational play and deterrence prevails.

The result is important for a number of reasons. For one, it illustrates once again the danger of accepting, uncritically, seemingly innocuous assumptions embedded in the very fabric of classical deterrence theory. More importantly, it sensitizes us to the possibility that the key to deterrence success may not lie in the specific properties of *Defender's* threat. In some deterrence situations, threat characteristics can have an interactive effect so that, in the end, it is the nature of Challenger's threat that determines whether or not a challenge is issued. Additionally, this result clearly demonstrates that the four conditions that Lebow (1981: 93) and many others postulate to be "necessary for successful deterrence" simply are not, illustrating yet another way in which the findings of Perfect Deterrence Theory run counter to more standard formulations.[6] And finally, the finding provides additional theoretical justification of our decision to explore the dynamics of both mutual and unilateral deterrence games.

5.3   Unilateral deterrence under incomplete information

So far we have demonstrated that the credibility of each player's threat completely determines the outcome of any Unilateral Deterrence Game with complete information. But what happens under incomplete information? Under these conditions, rational behavior depends on two kinds of information: a player's own preferences and its *beliefs* about its opponent's preferences.

Challenger's preferences are critical at the last node (3) of the tree where a Hard Challenger *always* chooses D to achieve $C_{DD} = c_{DD+}$ rather than $c_{CD} < c_{DD+}$, and a Soft Challenger *always* chooses C to achieve c_{CD} rather than $C_{DD} = c_{DD-} < c_{CD}$. Similarly, if there is a challenge to the *Status Quo*, a Hard Defender *always* chooses D at node 2 because both possible outcomes associated with this choice – *Challenger Defeated* and *Conflict* – are preferred by a Hard Defender to *Defender Concedes*, the outcome that would follow if Defender were to choose C.

This choice is not so automatic, however, when Defender is Soft. A Soft Defender prefers *Challenger Defeated* to *Defender Concedes*, but *Defender Concedes* to *Conflict*, so its choice rationally depends on its estimate of the likelihood of *Challenger Defeated*, as opposed to *Conflict*,

---

[6] According to Lebow (1981: 85), "Four conditions emerge as crucial to successful deterrence. Nations must (1) define their commitment clearly, (2) communicate its existence to possible adversaries, (3) develop the means to defend it, or to punish adversaries who challenge it, and (4) demonstrate their resolve to carry out the actions this entails." Of the four conditions, only the third, which we interpret as threat capability, emerges as a necessary condition in Perfect Deterrence Theory.

if it defies Challenger. This estimate depends, in turn, on its estimate of Challenger's type because, as noted above, Challenger's type directly determines the final outcome – if and when Defender chooses D. At node 2, therefore, a Hard Defender always defends, but a Soft Defender's rational choice might be either to defy or to concede.

Given that Challenger initiates, what information should Defender use to estimate the probability that Challenger is Hard? It is reasonable for Defender to update its initial estimate, p_{Ch}, in light of the new information it has received. Specifically, Defender now knows that Challenger has defected (at node 1), and this knowledge may rationally change Defender's beliefs about Challenger's type. One aspect of the equilibrium concept we apply, perfect Bayesian equilibrium, is the requirement that Defender rationally updates its beliefs about Challenger's type on the basis of the behavior it observes at node 1.

Finally, what choice should Challenger make at node 1? A Challenger of either type could rationally cooperate or defect. This decision depends on its estimates of Defender's type *and* Defender's anticipated behavior. With probability p_{Def}, Defender is Hard and will defy with certainty. But because the choice of a Soft Defender is uncertain (see above), Challenger must estimate the probability that Defender is Soft but will defend nonetheless.

In summary, rational choices in the Unilateral Deterrence Game with incomplete information are determined by the players' preferences for *Conflict* (DD) versus capitulation (either CD or DC), and also by each player's probability estimates, updated as and when appropriate, of the credibility of the other's threat.

5.4 Perfect Bayesian equilibria of the Unilateral Deterrence Game

To this point we have shown the implications of threat credibility for the stability of the *Status Quo* in a game of complete information. We have also discussed what rational players would need to consider when information is uncertain, and hence credibility is not perfect. Now we determine fully the rational choices for each player in the Unilateral Deterrence Game with incomplete information as defined by the perfect Bayesian equilibria.

The results are shown in figure 5.4, which graphs the credibility parameters, p_{Ch} and p_{Def}, on the horizontal and vertical axes, respectively. Along these two axes are indicated three constants, d_n, c_s, and

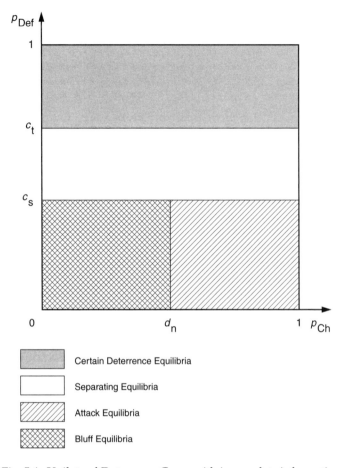

Fig. 5.4. Unilateral Deterrence Game with incomplete information: location of equilibria.

c_t, that are fully defined and discussed in appendix 5. These constants are threshold values that help distinguish the existence regions of the perfect Bayesian equilibria of the Unilateral Deterrence Game with incomplete information.[7]

---

[7] In fact, two of the three thresholds are characteristic of *one-sided* games of incomplete information as follows:

   a. When Defender's preferences are common knowledge, but not Challenger's, the *Status Quo* is stable if Defender is Hard, or if Defender is Soft and Challenger's threat is not credible enough to dissuade Defender from choosing D at node 2

The credibility parameters range from 0 to 1, as the corresponding threats range from perfectly incredible to perfectly credible. The four corners of this figure thus correspond to the four games of complete information discussed previously. Specifically, the northeast (respectively, northwest, southeast, and southwest) corner represents the situation where each player (only Defender, only Challenger, and neither player) has a credible threat. Recall that the *Status Quo* is stable in all but the southeast corner (where only Challenger's threat is credible).

It is proven in appendix 5 that four major types of perfect Bayesian equilibria are possible for intermediate values of threat credibility.[8] These equilibria can be represented by probability combinations $[x_H, x_S; y_H, y_S, p]$ where:

x_H = probability that a Hard Challenger will choose D at node 1
x_S = probability that a Soft Challenger will choose D at node 1
y_H = probability that a Hard Defender will choose D at node 2
y_S = probability that a Soft Defender will choose D at node 2
p = Defender's conditional probability that Challenger is Hard, given that Challenger chooses D at node 1.

The first four probabilities are strategic variables describing Challenger's and Defender's choices, contingent on type. As noted above, a Hard Defender always rationally chooses D at node 2, i.e., $y_H = 1$. The fifth probability is the *a posteriori* probability, updated by Defender once Challenger's choice of D at node 1 has been observed. Equilibrium values for p are reported in appendix 5 but are discussed below only when relevant. Perfect Bayesian equilibria will often be denoted $[x_H, x_S; y_H, y_S]$.

Table 5.2 summarizes the important strategic properties of each major equilibrium category. (Additional details about the perfect Bayesian equilibria of the Unilateral Deterrence Game with incomplete information can be found in appendix 5, table A5.1.) As the

$(p_{Ch} < d_n)$. But when Defender is Soft and Challenger's threat is sufficiently credible $(p_{Ch} > d_n)$, Challenger will defect at node 1 and the outcome will be *Defender Concedes*.

b. When only Challenger's preferences are common knowledge, deterrence succeeds when Challenger is Soft, or when Defender's threat is credible enough $(p_{Def} > c_t)$ to deter a challenge of any type. But if Challenger is Hard and Defender's credibility falls below this threshold $(p_{Def} < c_t)$, then the outcome is *Defender Concedes* when Defender is Soft and *Conflict* when Defender is Hard.

[8] There is also another equilibrium type but it is transitional so, as explained in appendix 5, we can ignore it as it "almost never" occurs.

Table 5.2. *Perfect Bayesian equilibria and existence conditions for the Unilateral Deterrence Game with incomplete information*

Equilibrium	Strategic variables				Existence conditions
	Challenger		Defender		
	x_H	x_S	y_H	y_S	
Certain Deterrence	0	0	1	unrestricted	$p_{Def} \geq c_t$
Steadfast Deterrence	0	0	1	u	$p_{Def} < c_t$
Separating Equilibrium	1	0	1	0	$c_s \leq p_{Def} \leq c_t$
Bluff Equilibrium	1	v	1	u	$p_{Def} < c_s$ and $p_{Ch} \leq d_n$
Attack Equilibrium	1	1	1	0	$p_{Def} < c_s$ and $p_{Ch} \geq d_n$

reader will no doubt notice, these equilibria are similar, but not identical, to those of the Generalized Mutual Deterrence Game with incomplete information, explored in chapter 4. This should be no surprise, as the two games are closely related. The main difference concerns the logical sequence of choices. In the Generalized Mutual Deterrence Game, the players make simultaneous initial choices. In the Unilateral Deterrence Game, Defender's initial choice, if it is made at all, comes only after Challenger has moved.

Despite the similarity of the perfect Bayesian equilibria in these two direct deterrence games, there are a number of good reasons for examining in detail the equilibria of the Unilateral Deterrence Game. For one, the equilibrium structure of the Unilateral Deterrence Game is less complicated, i.e., there are fewer equilibria and fewer overlaps of equilibria. Thus, the Unilateral Deterrence Game not only brings the range of possible behavioral patterns into sharper focus, but also helps to strengthen and refine our understanding of the dynamics of this important class of deterrence relationships.

There are also some significant differences between the perfect Bayesian equilibria of the incomplete information versions of the Generalized Mutual Deterrence Game and the Unilateral Deterrence Game. These differences help us to understand the extent to which our conclusions are driven by assumptions about the sequence of play. Moreover, the Unilateral Deterrence Game models a strategic relationship that is theoretically and empirically distinct. As such, it deserves special focus. Finally, the Unilateral Deterrence Game serves as a theoretical bridge between the Rudimentary Asymmetric Deterrence Game – which it subsumes – and the family of strategically more complex extended deterrence games explored in part III – which subsume it. A thorough understanding of the equilibrium structure of the Unilateral Deterrence Game, therefore, will be especially helpful in penetrating these more complex strategic structures.

5.4.1   Deterrence equilibria

Deterrence equilibria constitute the first major equilibrium category of the Unilateral Deterrence Game with incomplete information. These are equilibria in which Challenger *never* defects initially, that is, $x_H = x_S = 0$. At a deterrence equilibrium, therefore, the *Status Quo* is the only possible outcome. Challenger's decision is independent of its type, but it *may* be contingent on the strategy of a Soft Defender, i.e., on y_S. Although the *Status Quo* can sometimes result when other equilibria are in play, all remaining equilibria carry with them the possibility of different outcomes, depending on the players' types, beliefs, and choices. Thus, the *Status Quo* is fully robust under a deterrence equilibrium, but not under other equilibria.

A deterrence equilibrium is a plausible description of a strategic relationship between allies – such as Canada and the United States – or even between two hostile powers during periods of relative *détente*.[9] Under such circumstances, any challenge to the status quo would, at best, gain little and, at worst, risk a great deal.

On the other hand, the existence of a deterrence equilibrium is also

---

[9] During the first half of the nineteenth century, the United States and Canada invaded each other. As recently as 1920, the United States was seen by some within the Canadian defense establishment as its principal external threat (Jervis, 1976: 62). At the time, a top-secret contingency plan was reportedly developed for invading the United States (Vogel, 1995). Even more recently, there was speculation among some Canadians that a "rapid deployment force of the US Army's 10th Mountain Light Infantry Division [was] secretly being held in readiness at Fort Drum, in Watertown [NY], to seize the region from the Thousand Islands to Ottawa in the event of a Canadian breakup" (Clairborne, 1992). Of course, we do not mean to suggest that either side is currently considering the use of force against the other. Still, in the economic arena, an implicit threat of retaliation (by both sides but on different issues) helps support the North American Free Trade Agreement. Our model, which is completely general and therefore not limited to relationships in which the use of force is under active consideration, can help to explain even this very peaceful relationship.

consistent with the survival of the status quo under less benevolent conditions, such as those associated with the most heated periods of the Cold War. One superpower might have been deterred from directly attacking the other, but only after seriously considering a challenge. Similarly, a deterrence equilibrium could even describe a strategic relationship characterized by clear-cut military superiority – assuming that the defender is the more powerful player – while a more tenuous status quo might persist for a time in a contentious parity relationship such as that of Great Britain and Germany early in the twentieth century.[10]

Significantly, deterrence equilibria can come into play under *any* set of conditions describing the players' beliefs about threat credibility, save for the one pure case of complete information (discussed above) in which Challenger's threat is perfectly credible and Defender's is not. This means that deterrence could conceivably emerge under (almost) any conditions in a one-sided deterrence relationship. As discussed below, the key to this stability may be the willingness of a *Soft* Defender to resist with sufficiently high probability. (Recall that a Hard Defender always resists.) To support this willingness, Defender must believe, even after a challenge has been issued (i.e., after Defender observes Challenger's initial defection), that Challenger is unlikely to be Hard.

Although deterrence is (almost) always possible, it is not so often inevitable. In this regard, we distinguish two types of deterrence equilibria: *Certain* and *Steadfast*. We next discuss their distinguishing characteristics.

5.4.1.1 Certain Deterrence Equilibrium

When Defender's credibility (i.e., p_{Def}) is high, the sole equilibrium of the Unilateral Deterrence Game is a deterrence equilibrium. We call this equilibrium *Certain Deterrence*; when it exists, the *Status Quo* is the only rational outcome. The reason is simple: when a Certain Deterrence Equilibrium exists, it uniquely exists. There are no other rational behavior possibilities.

Certain Deterrence Equilibria occupy the entire upper region of the unit square in figure 5.4. Notice that the existence of a Certain Deterrence Equilibrium does not depend on the *a priori* credibility of Challenger's threat. In other words, this equilibrium is invariant with

---

[10] See Powell (1996a) for an alternative perspective on this relationship.

respect to Challenger's credibility: when a Certain Deterrence Equilibrium occurs, no rational Challenger – Hard or Soft – chooses to defect.

Although the existence of a Certain Deterrence Equilibrium does not depend on Challenger's credibility, Defender's credibility is critical. As shown in appendix 5, for a Certain Deterrence Equilibrium to exist, Defender's *a priori* credibility must exceed a threshold, namely

$$p_{Def} \geq c_t = \frac{c_{DC} - c_{SQ}}{c_{DC} - c_{DD+}} \tag{5.5}$$

The alert reader will recognize the similarity of the credibility threshold c_t to thresholds a_2 and b_2 that delineate the existence region of the Sure-Thing Deterrence Equilibrium in the Generalized Mutual Deterrence Game with incomplete information. In fact, the two equilibria are simple analogues. The main difference is that in the (symmetric) case of the Sure-Thing Deterrence Equilibrium, both players must take on the role of Defender. Thus, most of what has already been said about the Sure-Thing Deterrence Equilibrium can also be said about the Certain Deterrence Equilibrium:

- As the value Challenger places on the *Status Quo* increases, the minimum value for p_{Def} decreases, thereby making it more likely that Certain Deterrence will occur.
- The prospects of Certain Deterrence can also be enhanced by decreasing the value a Hard Challenger places on *Conflict*.
- Certain Deterrence becomes more likely as the value Challenger places on winning is reduced.
- Under certain conditions, (i.e., when Challenger is Soft and prefers not to engage Defender in *Conflict*), further increases in the cost of conflict (i.e., reductions in c_{DD-}) are redundant and irrelevant.

It is important to note that the existence of a Certain Deterrence Equilibrium does *not* depend upon any particular behavior plans a *Soft* Defender may have (i.e., on y_S).[11] Intuitively, the reason is that Certain Deterrence occurs only when Challenger believes it likely that Defender is Hard. In effect, Challenger assigns very little weight to the

---

[11] More technically, y_S is unrestricted.

benefits it might receive for challenging a Soft Defender. As we indicate below, however, the weight assigned these benefits may be crucial to the Challenger's optimal strategy under other conditions.

Similarly, to say that Challenger's credibility is of little moment when a Certain Deterrence Equilibrium exists is not to say that it is unimportant at other times. Nonetheless, when Defender's credibility is sufficiently high, the stability of the *Status Quo* is absolute and does not hinge on Challenger's willingness to fight.

5.4.1.2 Steadfast Deterrence Equilibrium

A deterrence equilibrium may still exist even when Defender's credibility falls below the threshold required for Certain Deterrence. But then a deterrence equilibrium cannot occur alone – it coexists with equilibria of other types (see below), so its occurrence in actual play is far from certain. Moreover, for this type of deterrence equilibrium to occur, Defender must be steadfast in the sense of being committed to defend with a certain probability, *even when it is Soft*.

A *Steadfast Deterrence Equilibrium* may come into play even when a Challenger places a relatively low value on the *Status Quo*, or a relatively high value on winning, or sees low costs at *Conflict*. This form of deterrence occurs only when Defender's threat is less credible than required for a Certain Deterrence Equilibrium. The difference is that with Steadfast Deterrence, Defender's threat to defend when Hard is not, in itself, sufficient to sustain the *Status Quo*. Further commitment is necessary. Specifically, to offset the relative decline in Defender's credibility, Challenger must believe there is a high enough probability ($y_S > u^*$; see appendix 5) that even a Soft Defender will resist. To support this intention rationally, Defender must believe that it is fairly likely that any Challenger who initiates is Soft, and will concede if Defender chooses D at node 2. Thus, while the *a priori* credibility of Challenger's retaliatory threat is unimportant to the existence of a Steadfast Deterrence Equilibrium, Challenger's *a posteriori* credibility is critical.

The irrelevance of Challenger's *a priori* credibility explains why a Steadfast Deterrence Equilibrium can be found anywhere below the threshold required for a Certain Deterrence Equilibrium. As can be seen from figure 5.4, other equilibria – all of which include the possibility of *Conflict* – also occupy this area. There are other rational possibilities, and the selection of a Steadfast Deterrence Equilibrium is far from certain.

In our opinion, Defender's *a posteriori* belief about Challenger's credibility is plausible, but only when the *a priori* probability that Challenger is Hard, p_{Ch}, is low. We find it difficult to fathom that a Challenger, who was initially thought to be likely Hard, will be perceived as likely Soft after a challenge has been issued. For this reason we are skeptical of the descriptive accuracy of the Steadfast Deterrence Equilibrium when and if Challenger is initially believed to be Hard.

Nonetheless, under proper conditions, a Steadfast Deterrence Equilibrium might evolve quite naturally. Suppose, for instance, that a highly dissatisfied Challenger is considering contesting the *Status Quo*. Defender may be Soft, yet Challenger may be convinced that Defender doubts Challenger's resolve and will defy any challenge with high probability, even if Defender is Soft. Faced with this likelihood of resistance, Challenger may now find its second-best outcome, the *Status Quo*, very appealing.

By their very nature, actual examples of deterrence equilibria (Certain or Steadfast) are difficult to identify.[12] Nevertheless, one indication that a Steadfast Deterrence Equilibrium may be in play, or that a Defender is trying to induce one, is a public denigration of the capability and, by extension, the credibility of Challenger's threat. For example, in the 1950s, when Mao repeatedly expressed reservations about US resolve, he might have been trying to deter a coercive move by the United States. From China's point of view, it was strategically immaterial whether the United States was, or was not, a "paper tiger," or whether US decision-makers thought China to be Soft. What was important to the Chinese was that US leaders believe that China thought the United States to be very likely Soft. Similarly, early in the post-war period, Soviet declaratory policy denying the strategic significance of nuclear weapons might have been consistent with actual Soviet beliefs. But if not, strategic considerations probably dictated its content. Under certain conditions, then, undermining an opponent's credibility may be as effective a tactic for stabilizing the status quo as is bolstering one's own.

---

[12] Achen and Snidal (1989: 161) give as some possibilities "the first Soviet–American War which erupted over Hungary in 1956 . . . the second one (over Chile) in the early 1970s . . . the US–China War, which began when the United States bombed the North Vietnamese dikes . . . [and] the second Korean War." For a debate on this issue, see Huth and Russett (1990) and Lebow and Stein (1990).

5.4.2 *Other equilibria*

In addition to the deterrence equilibria, three other non-transitional equilibria can occur in the Unilateral Deterrence Game with incomplete information: *Separating*, *Bluff*, and *Attack*. We now consider their logical and strategic properties serially.

5.4.2.1 Separating Equilibria

As figure 5.4 shows, *Separating Equilibria* lie between Certain Deterrence and Attack and Bluff Equilibria. At a Separating Equilibrium, the players' preferences are fully revealed by their strategy choices: a Hard Challenger always defects initially, and a Soft Challenger never does. Likewise, if challenged, a Hard Defender always defies and a Soft Defender always capitulates. The *Status Quo* may remain stable, therefore, when separating strategies are selected, but only when Challenger is Soft.[13] When Challenger is Hard, it gains an advantage if Defender is Soft (i.e., *Defender Concedes*) but precipitates *Conflict* if Defender is Hard. Thus, three of the four possible outcomes of the Unilateral Deterrence Game (see figure 5.2) can arise under a Separating Equilibrium.

Separating Equilibria separate the players by type.[14] Under a Separating Equilibrium, more so than any other, the stability of the *Status Quo* depends on Challenger's actual preferences. One might expect, therefore, that when a Separating Equilibrium is about to come into play, Defender would be tempted to manipulate Challenger's type by trying to influence the domestic political process of Challenger. The Vietminh did just this in late 1953 in order to force France to the negotiating table (Zagare, 1979). But the converse is also true. When Challenger is Hard, the *final* outcome of the game will be determined by Defender's type. Challenger will then have an interest in promoting soft-liners in Defender's bureaucracy, because Soft Defenders will appease Challenger while Hard Defenders will willingly endure *Conflict* (Snyder and Diesing, 1977).

It is noteworthy that Separating Equilibria are the only perfect Bayesian equilibria that do not correspond to one of the four games of

---

[13] Note that the survival of the *Status Quo* does not depend on a deterrence equilibrium coming into play.

[14] Cf. the Separating Equilibrium of the Generalized Mutual Deterrence Game with incomplete information described in chapter 4.

complete information discussed above (see table 5.1). Thus our examination of the Unilateral Deterrence Game with incomplete information has uncovered a qualitatively different strategic environment and identified prototypical strategies associated with it.

A stable *Status Quo* may indicate a Separating Equilibrium, or a Deterrence Equilibrium, or even a Bluff Equilibrium (see below). One empirical hint that a Separating Equilibrium might be in play, however, would be a simultaneous change in Challenger's regime and its policy orientation, but little else. The reason is that under a Separating Equilibrium, strategy choices depend on player types in the extreme. A possible example was the abrupt, albeit temporary, shift of Soviet policy in 1953, away from Stalin's confrontational stance, toward the new collective leadership's policy of *détente* with the West (Zagare, 1979). Similarly, during the 1967 crisis in the Middle East, Israel's attitude changed dramatically, from submission to confrontation, when Moshe Dayan, a hard-liner who was known to favor military action, replaced Prime Minister Levi Eshkol as Defense Minister (Zagare, 1981).

Separating Equilibria occur in an intermediate range of Defender's credibility, not high enough to render deterrence certain, but not low enough to make the preservation of the *Status Quo* unlikely. The upper bound of the region of Separating Equilibria (c_t) coincides with the lower bound of the Certain Deterrence region. The lower bound of the Separating region is the threshold

$$p_{Def} > c_s = \frac{c_{DC} - c_{SQ}}{c_{DC} - c_{CD}} \tag{5.6}$$

Thus the initial credibility requirements on Defender's threat are directly related to Challenger's evaluation of the *Status Quo*, c_{SQ}. As this value increases, approaching that of Challenger's best outcome, the lower bound of the region of Separating Equilibria moves downward, shrinking the region of Attack and Bluff Equilibria where *Conflict* is more likely (see below). Of course, the converse is also true. As Challenger's evaluation of the *Status Quo* decreases, the lower boundary of the region of Separating Equilibrium rises, increasing the probability that a Bluff or Attack Equilibrium will come into play. Equally, the lower threshold for Separating Equilibria can be reduced by decreasing Challenger's value for winning (c_{DC}) or decreasing Challenger's value for losing (c_{CD}).

5.4.2.2 Bluff Equilibria

When Defender's credibility is relatively low, that is, below c_s, the lower boundary for Separating Equilibria, then, depending on how credible Challenger's threat is, new equilibria arise: *Bluff* and *Attack*.

As figure 5.4 reveals, *Bluff Equilibria* occur when Defender's and Challenger's credibilities are *both* relatively low, that is, when both players believe the other probably prefers to capitulate rather than fight. In the case of complete information, when each player's threat is simply not credible, the *Status Quo* is stable and Challenger is deterred. Such is not necessarily the case, however, when the players are uncertain of each other's preferences.

At a Bluff Equilibrium, players' behavior depends upon their types. Challenger initiates for certain in the unlikely event that it is Hard. (After all, chances are that the Defender is Soft and likely to capitulate.) But if Challenger is Soft, it adopts a mixed strategy, initiating with some positive probability. The more credible Challenger is, the greater this probability.

The equilibrium choice of a Hard Defender is, as always, to defend. But at a Bluff Equilibrium, even a Soft Defender defends with some positive probability. This conditional probability, y_S, is a function of Defender's initial credibility, just as Challenger's conditional probability, x_S, is a function of Challenger's credibility. *But the lower Defender's credibility, the greater its tendency to bluff and resist a challenge when Soft*!

In fact, the family of Bluff Equilibria is pooling for Defender – the unconditional (i.e., without regard to Defender's type) *a priori* probability that Defender chooses to defend does not depend on its credibility (see appendix 5). In other words, Defender's overall probabilities of capitulating or defying are always the same, regardless of the value of p_{Def}. The Bluff Equilibria do not present this property from Challenger's point of view – in fact, the overall probability of a challenge increases with Challenger's credibility, p_{Ch}.

The logic of this equilibrium configuration guarantees that Challenger always faces the same probability that Defender will stand firm. Defender's policy serves to conceal its type – it is not possible to infer whether a Defender who resists is likely or unlikely to be Hard. As a consequence, Challenger is less and less willing to risk a challenge as its own credibility decreases – after all, the probability that it will have to back down if it challenges becomes greater and greater as its credibility drops. But the only way that Defender can achieve this constant level of defense readiness is to be prepared to defend when Soft more frequently as its credibility falls.

More than at any other equilibrium, then, play under a Bluff Equilibrium is likely to be a "competition in risk-taking" (Schelling, 1960, 1966). In one sense, this should be no surprise since the complete information analogue of such games resembles structurally the game of Chicken. Nonetheless, our model provides additional insight into the conditions under which "manipulative bargaining tactics" (Young, 1975) are relevant to the behavior of states in an acute crisis (Snyder and Diesing, 1977).

In contrast to the conventional wisdom, however, our model reveals an advantage for Defender, since Defender's type and, ultimately, its choice, is critical in determining the actual outcome. Of course, if Challenger does not defect initially, a crisis never occurs; and if it does, and Defender does not resist, the bluff will have succeeded and Challenger will have gained an advantage. But if Defender resists, a rational Soft Challenger will back down, so that Defender will win. In neither case, though, will a conflict result unless Challenger is prepared for it. Thus, given the postulated sequence of choices, Challenger will not necessarily win, even if it defects initially. This may be one reason why "commitment" and related bluffing tactics, although seductive, have rarely been used by challengers in precipitating a crisis and why, at least in the nuclear age, decision-makers have sought "to retain wide freedom of choice as long as possible and to avoid becoming boxed into an irrevocable position" (Young, 1968: 218; see also George and Smoke, 1974: 531).

As noted, the *Status Quo* is stable in the Unilateral Deterrence Game when both players have completely incredible retaliatory threats. Without a credible threat Challenger cannot deter Defender from resisting, forcing Challenger to back down. In the end Challenger is better off doing nothing. Under these circumstances, the lack of a credible threat actually fosters stability.

By contrast, in the region where Bluff Equilibria exist, and where both Challenger and Defender have a modicum of credibility, both players may be led, by their own rationality, to gamble. Challenger could rationally decide to rock the boat – just a little bit. After all, the odds of success are reasonably high. For similar reasons Defender could sometimes rationally run the risk of an all-out conflict. All of which demonstrates that credibility is a lot like knowledge: a little bit of it may be a bad thing.

With the benefit of hindsight, it is plausible to associate many of the events punctuating the US–Soviet relationship during the 1950s and 1960s with bluff conditions. Starting with the Berlin crisis of 1948, the Soviet Union and China precipitated a number of confrontations designed to probe the limits of US resolve. When the United States stood firm, they backed down (Gaddis, 1997: 31). While one cannot say for sure what actual US preferences were, the challengers' preferences for capitulation were revealed by their choices. In these cases at least, they were simply bluffing (Betts, 1987: 108).

5.4.2.3 Attack Equilibria

Like Bluff Equilibria, *Attack Equilibria* occur only when Defender's credibility is low. What distinguishes the two equilibria is Challenger's perceived credibility. When it is relatively low – like Defender's – a Bluff Equilibrium arises. But when Challenger's credibility exceeds a certain threshold, the Attack Equilibrium forms.

At an Attack Equilibrium, Challenger – whatever its type – *always* defects initially, and a Soft Defender *always* capitulates. Thus, because a Hard Defender always defends, war will occur if and only if a Hard Challenger attacks a Hard Defender. Although unlikely under these conditions, *Conflict* is possible. Typically, Defender has few options and little defense. Like the United States during the crises in Hungary in 1956 and Czechoslovakia in 1968, and the Soviets during the 1956 Suez crisis, a Defender unwilling to resist can only accept the inevitable; any other reaction would be contrary to its interests.

Deterrence is *never* stable under an Attack Equilibrium. Defender prefers *any* other equilibrium to *Attack*, as its expected utility is usually least at this equilibrium. In particular, the Attack Equilibrium is the only equilibrium where there is no chance that the Challenger will accept the *Status Quo*.

There are essentially two ways Defender can shift the game toward another equilibrium region: by taking measures that either shore up the credibility of its deterrent threat or enhance Challenger's evaluation of the *Status Quo*. If either measure is successful, a Separating Equilibrium is induced. But no matter what equilibrium is in play, these tactics are always available and never disadvantage Defender. Alternatively, a Defender wishing to avoid an Attack Equilibrium could try to induce a Bluff Equilibrium by reducing its conflict costs. As figure 5.4 indicates, if $p_{\text{Def}} < c_s$, then there will be a Bluff Equilibrium if Challenger's *a priori* credibility, p_{Ch}, falls below

$$d_n = \frac{d_{CD} - d_{DC}}{d_{CD} - d_{DD-}} \tag{5.7}$$

otherwise an Attack Equilibrium will come into play. (See appendix 5 for details.)

Note that an Attack Equilibrium is more likely the more costly conflict is to a *Soft* Defender. Thus, the higher the costs of confrontation to a Soft Defender, the more likely an Attack Equilibrium; the lower, the more likely a Bluff Equilibrium. Note also that the Attack Equilibrium becomes more likely as Defender's value for winning decreases and as Defender's value for capitulating increases.

This observation is consistent with the argument of some strategic thinkers that one consequence of nuclear weapons has been to make conflicts more likely in areas peripheral to a defender's interests. In this sense, at least, nuclear weapons can be considered destabilizing. For instance, the Soviet Union might have been less willing to invade Afghanistan in 1979 if the world were not nuclear, simply because the United States would have been more likely, *ceteris paribus*, to offer resistance were it not facing a nuclear power. Much the same could be said about US involvement in Vietnam. Thus the Unilateral Deterrence Game model explains why nuclear weapons may contribute, simultaneously, to the stability of "basic," "passive," or "Type I" deterrence, and to the instability of "extended," "active," or "Type II" deterrence (Kahn, 1960; Betts, 1987).[15]

5.5 The Unilateral Deterrence Game and power transition theory

The Unilateral Deterrence Game explores the connection between threat credibility and deterrence stability in one-sided or asymmetric deterrence relationships. Specifically, it models the choices of a Challenger and a Defender to foment or to avoid a crisis. Unlike the players in the Generalized Mutual Deterrence Game, then, the players in the Unilateral Deterrence Game have distinct and recognizable

---

[15] The models developed in part III shed additional light on extended deterrence relationships.

roles. As a consequence, the underlying conceptualization is at odds with the axioms of balance of power and classical deterrence theory, which take as given the non-differentiation of actors.

By contrast, the view of deterrence embodied in the Unilateral Deterrence Game is *prima facie* consistent with a number of theories of interstate conflict initiation that presume that states may play different roles in the international system.[16] Indeed, the Unilateral Deterrence Game was originally developed as a decision-theoretic extension of one such theory, *power transition* (Organski, 1958; Organski and Kugler, 1980).[17] Our purpose in this section, however, is not to model the transition process *per se*.[18] Rather, it is simply to suggest some important parallels between this dyadic, state-centric model of major-power war and what we consider its decision-theoretic analogue. Since the perfect Bayesian equilibria of the Unilateral Deterrence Game with incomplete information describe rational behavior as a function of credibility, they provide additional information about the range of behavioral possibilities during a transition period.

Unlike classical deterrence theory, which is riddled with logical inconsistencies and empirical inaccuracies (see chapter 1), power transition theory offers a theoretically rich and empirically consistent perspective from which to view the dynamics of interstate conflict. Like balance of power theory, power transition is structurally based. But unlike balance of power, power transition argues that parity is a necessary – though not sufficient – condition for major-power war. Put another way, power transition theory contends that major-power wars occur only when two great states are approximately equal in strength.

The power transition perspective helps to explain, therefore, the absence of war between the United States and the Soviet Union during the most heated days of the Cold War, and between the Soviet Union and China during the most intense period of that bitter rivalry; it also helps to explain the instinctual rejection of proliferation policies by most statesmen and strategic analysts, and the deep concern of decision-makers with marginal disadvantages and "windows of vulnerability."

---

[16] Nonetheless, the Unilateral Deterrence Game stands on its own and does not depend on any underlying structural model.

[17] For the original discussion, see Kugler and Zagare (1990).

[18] For explicit attempts to model power transition theory, see Kim and Morrow (1992), Powell (1996a), and Alsharabati (1997). Also see Kugler and Lemke (1996).

Power transition theory, however, is not a completely specified theory of interstate conflict initiation. While it provides a more thorough account of the outbreak of major-power wars during the last two centuries than does balance of power theory (Organski and Kugler, 1980; Kugler and Lemke, 1996), the power transition perspective leaves some important questions unanswered. In particular, it provides only a set of necessary conditions for the onset of major interstate wars, so it cannot distinguish, *a priori*, those transitions that culminate in war from those that do not. Why, for example, did Germany, Great Britain, and their allies fight two global wars while, under similar parity conditions, the United States and Great Britain avoided major catastrophe? Why did the United States and the Soviet Union not wage a strategic war as the Soviets moved toward nuclear parity at the end of the 1960s? Although the empirical record associated with these and related riddles is consistent with the power transition perspective, these questions have not yet been answered adequately within its theoretical confines.

We do not claim that the game model of this chapter eliminates all these ambiguities. Still, some additional precision about the conditions necessary for peaceful and non-peaceful transition can be derived from the perfect Bayesian equilibria of the Unilateral Deterrence Game with incomplete information. Specifically, transitions are most likely to be peaceful when Defender's credibility is unquestionably high, that is, when a Certain Deterrence Equilibrium exists. But the converse is not true. War is not a high probability event when Defender's retaliatory threat is minimally credible – although such circumstances are not particularly conducive to general deterrence stability. Rather, all-out conflicts are most probable for mid-ranges of Defender credibility, which are the conditions consistent with the existence of a Separating Equilibrium. As one might expect, then, non-peaceful transitions are most likely to occur precisely when Challenger is least certain about Defender's intentions.

As well, the strategic properties of the perfect Bayesian equilibria of the Unilateral Deterrence Game help to corroborate the importance power transition places on the role of the status quo in peace and war decisions (Kugler and Werner, 1993). Most balance of power and classical deterrence theorists tend to fixate on the high costs of nuclear war, ignoring this other critical variable. In the incomplete information model, both the value of the *Status Quo* and the players' evaluation of *Conflict* are strategically significant.

For instance, in the Unilateral Deterrence Game, the threshold value for Certain Deterrence depends, in part, on Challenger's evaluation of the *Status Quo*. Challenger's evaluation of the *Status Quo* is also critical in determining the threshold value at the lower bound of the region of Separating Equilibria.

All of which is consistent with power transition's auxiliary hypothesis that a Defender can enhance the prospects of a peaceful transition by making systemic adjustments that alleviate Challenger's dissatisfaction.[19] Notwithstanding the numerous caveats discussed in chapter 4, manipulation of the status quo remains a potentially potent diplomatic device for avoiding hostility and conflict. George and Smoke (1974: 531) are right, therefore, to emphasize that "accommodative moves" can reduce the need for overt deterrent threats, and increase the likelihood that more traditional policies focusing on raising the cost of conflict will succeed, when and if they are pursued. The analysis of this chapter adds precision to this debate by specifying why and when these stratagems work.

Contrariwise, policies that needlessly antagonize a potential opponent may significantly decrease the prospects for peace, especially when these policies are part of a general pattern of neglect or insensitivity. For example, recent attempts to expand NATO to include states bordering Russia are both risky and potentially disruptive of the underlying dynamic of the post Cold War European security system. Much the same could be said about ongoing efforts to develop an anti-missile defense system. In this case, both Russia's and China's level of frustration will likely grow should the drive continue. In the long run, their discontent will likely constitute a far greater threat to the United States than the current and future threat posed by lesser nuclear powers.

This does not mean that states should ignore their own interests when formulating policy. Initiatives that aim to increase a potential opponent's satisfaction with the status quo are not necessarily self-abnegating. Trade agreements or arms limitation accords can sometimes benefit both parties simultaneously, thereby making peace a little more likely.

In this context it seems reasonable to suggest that, overall, the break-up of the Warsaw Pact and the dissolution of the Soviet Union has been accompanied by Russia's increasing acceptance of the

---

[19] Powell (1996a) formally derives this proposition.

prevailing order. It is interesting to observe that, in consequence, many strategic analysts now believe that the probability of a major war is lower than at any time since the end of World War II. If so, the analysis of the Unilateral Deterrence Game suggests why. It is also clear that, if real, the enhanced stability of the post Cold War period, at the strategic level at least, is entirely independent of any significant increases in the costs of war.[20]

If the lower bounds of the regions of Certain Deterrence and Separating Equilibria are currently lower, and their areas significantly larger, it follows that the converse was likely true during most of the Cold War period. In other words, the regions of Bluff and Attack Equilibria likely occupied a relatively much larger area of the unit square of figure 5.4 than when the Soviet Union was largely dissatisfied with the distribution of rewards in the international system. Perfect Deterrence Theory, therefore, helps explain why, at certain times, this period of intense rivalry was punctuated by a series of acute superpower crises, in Berlin, in Cuba, in Asia, and elsewhere.

It should be emphasized that manipulation of the status quo is not generally advanced as a stratagem for practitioners of deterrence. One reason is the absence of this variable in most variants of classical deterrence theory.[21] Since all states are taken as essentially the same, dissatisfaction with the status quo is a constant in classical deterrence theory. As a rule, therefore, the emphasis of the traditional security literature has been on the strategic consequences of the vast destructive power of nuclear weapons. While the focus is understandable, the obsession of classical deterrence theorists on the absolute costs of war – to the exclusion of other variables – explains the obvious oversight.

This is not to say that either power transition theory or Perfect Deterrence Theory sees nuclear weapons as magic bullets. In fact, it is this issue more than any other that separates these approaches from classical deterrence theory. Both Perfect Deterrence Theory and power transition theory see limits to the stabilizing properties of nuclear weapons. Specifically, by taking account of both the absolute costs

---

[20] The states of the former Soviet Union, including Russia, are certainly militarily weaker today than in the 1980s.

[21] Another is the clear failure of the French and British attempt to appease Hitler. That such a policy failed, however, does not necessarily imply that all such policies are inherently flawed. It is likely the case, however, that they are extremely difficult to implement properly. But the same could also be said about deterrent policies based solely on establishing a credible nuclear threat.

associated with warfare and the marginal advantages of challenging the status quo, power transition theory concludes that conflict between nuclear powers is a distinct possibility. By contrast, classical deterrence theory sees a monotonic relationship between the absolute costs of war and deterrence stability. The greater these costs, *ceteris paribus*, the more stable deterrence.

Perfect Deterrence Theory corroborates and refines power transition theory's conclusions about the relationship between the costs of conflict and deterrence stability. To be sure, the prospects of Certain Deterrence are enhanced by decreasing the value a *Hard* Challenger associates with *Conflict*. As this value approaches the value Challenger associates with capitulation, the lower bound of the region of Certain Deterrence Equilibria moves downward, making Certain Deterrence more probable, and conversely. As one might expect, then, when conflict offers minimal advantages, deterrence becomes more robust.

Nonetheless, indiscriminate increases in the cost of conflict do not necessarily contribute to the likelihood of deterrence. In the Unilateral Deterrence Game with incomplete information, when Challenger is Soft, i.e., already prefers capitulation to conflict, further increases in the cost of conflict have no effect on the overall likelihood of deterrence success.[22] Like George and Smoke (1974: 507) then, Perfect Deterrence Theory finds that deterrent "threats are often irrelevant or dysfunctional." Again, this suggests that prudent defenders have no reason not to pursue a policy of minimum deterrence. It is on this point, especially, that the normative implications of Perfect Deterrence Theory – which is rooted in beliefs and perceptions about the nature of deterrent threats – are at odds with classical deterrence theory, where subjective variables are generally ignored in favor of more objective factors (like the cost of conflict) and fixed credibility assumptions.

While the absolute costs of conflict do have implications for the robustness of Certain Deterrence, they do *not* play a role in determining the boundary that distinguishes the region of Separating Equilibria from the more unstable areas associated with Bluff and Attack Equilibria. As noted above, the determinants of this threshold are Challenger's evaluation of the *Status Quo*, winning, and capitulating, suggesting once again that, under certain conditions, increasing

---

[22] The same conclusion applies to both players in the Generalized Mutual Deterrence Game with incomplete information.

war costs may contribute little to deterrence. One of the hidden benefits of the present analysis is that it specifies the circumstances under which this conclusion applies, again augmenting the theoretical implications of power transition theory.

The costs of conflict to a *Soft* Defender (relative to capitulation and the *Status Quo*) do, however, determine the boundary between Bluff and Attack Equilibria. But here the relationship operates in an unexpected way. The greater the costs of confrontation to a Soft Defender, the more likely an Attack Equilibrium; the lower, the more likely a Bluff Equilibrium. This indicates that under the shared conditions associated with the existence of these two equilibrium types (i.e., low Defender credibility), the high costs normally associated with nuclear warfare actually make a status quo less stable. While it is true, then, that under somewhat restricted conditions, nuclear weapons may enhance central deterrence, they may also have the opposite effect in more peripheral conflict venues.

5.6   Coda

In this chapter we conclude our examination of direct deterrence relationships. We explore the connection between threat credibility and deterrence stability in a simple one-sided deterrence game, and model the choices of both a Challenger and a Defender of the existing order. We focus especially on the case in which the players are uncertain about each other's willingness to fight rather than capitulate.

Because we make no fixed behavioral assumption about the strategy choices of the players at any stage of the game, or about either player's preferences, we are able to explore the full range of potential crisis situations, to offer a general assessment of the conditions under which the status quo is likely to persist, and to present a more complete description of the circumstances and consequences of a unilateral deterrence failure than is otherwise possible. As well, we connect the implications of our model to those of an influential state-centric explanation of major-power wars, power transition theory.[23]

Our analysis reveals that it is possible for the status quo to persist under most conditions included in our model, although a stable status quo is more likely to persist in some circumstances than others. In

---

[23] The implications of both direct deterrence models – mutual and unilateral – for the theory of the democratic peace are discussed in Kilgour (1991).

general, unilateral deterrence success becomes more probable as the Challenger's evaluation of the status quo increases, as its perception of the Defender's credibility grows, and as the benefits of conflict decline. Like power transition theory, the incomplete information model of unilateral deterrence finds that the conditions of war and peace may be present simultaneously. It also finds, however, that certain conditions may exist in which deterrence is the only rational outcome. Specifically, when a Defender's initial credibility is sufficiently high, a Certain Deterrence Equilibrium uniquely exists, and the survival of the status quo is assured.

At other times, under other conditions, the persistence of the status quo is more problematic. At intermediate levels of Defender credibility, under a Separating Equilibrium, the critical variable is Challenger's preference between confrontation and capitulation. Hard Challengers rationally initiate conflict; Soft Challengers refrain. If the status quo is upset, and Defender is Hard, war is inevitable. Otherwise, the Challenger will be appeased and its demands satisfied.

Although war is less likely, the status quo is more likely to be contested when Defender's credibility is low and either a Bluff Equilibrium or an Attack Equilibrium exists. A Bluff Equilibrium will exist when both Challenger and Defender are likely Soft. An Attack Equilibrium will exist when Challenger is perceived Hard and Defender's credibility is low. A stable status quo is unlikely under either of these equilibrium types. Nevertheless, peace remains a (remote) theoretical possibility, at least under the Bluff Equilibrium.

What then explains peaceful power transitions such as that from Great Britain to the United States, or the absence of a superpower war once the Soviet Union attained nuclear parity with the United States? The incomplete information model suggests several possibilities.

One is that the defender in each of these cases was able to project unusually high credibility, thereby ensuring a Certain Deterrence Equilibrium. Another possibility is that in these and related cases, the challenger was in fact soft and that the games were played in the region of Separating Equilibria. Finally, it is even possible that some peaceful power transition games were played out under a Bluff Equilibrium; but if so, the players were extremely lucky that no calculated risk ever ended in disaster.

Like power transition, the incomplete information model of unilateral deterrence finds that increasing the costs of conflict does not necessarily lead to greater strategic stability. Under some conditions, such increases are either unnecessary or counter-productive, leading us once again to recommend minimum deterrent policies that are effective and costly enough to ensure deterrence, while not so incredible as to undermine it. Policies that promote an overkill capability, or those aimed at proliferating nuclear weapons, do not emerge as stabilizing choices in our model.

Finally, as in power transition, the incomplete information model finds that Challenger's evaluation of the status quo is a critical determinant of its decision to initiate conflict. When this value is very high, deterrence becomes virtually certain. As it increases, the likelihood of conflict decreases. It is perhaps this variable, more than anything else, that accounts for successful transition periods. It is unfortunate indeed that most modern deterrence theorists have ignored its stabilizing possibilities, concentrating instead on the more dangerous – and more limited – tactic of manipulating the absolute costs of warfare.

Part III
Extended deterrence

6   Modeling extended deterrence

Equilibrium was the name of the game.

Henry Kissinger

The decision to escalate . . . is a strategic issue, involving not only assessment of the immediate advantage to one's own side, but also difficult and often painfully uncertain calculation of the possibilities for counterescalation by the enemy.

Richard Smoke

By design, the deterrence models explored in part II are extremely austere. To be sure, the "no-fat" modeling approach we adopt allows us to focus directly on the role of uncertainty and credibility in both mutual and unilateral deterrence games. But axiomatic austerity cuts both ways. The ability to penetrate core theoretical structures and analyze the role of a few fundamental variables is not altogether costless. Parsimony is inversely related to the complexity and range of questions that a model can fruitfully address. For example, in the simple models developed in part II, conflict is an all-or-nothing proposition. As a consequence, these models are unable to shed any light on the conditions associated with either limited conflicts or escalation spirals. Nor do our rudimentary models capture well the subtleties of some more complex deterrence situations. Thus, to address these and related limitations, we now begin to complicate, ever so slightly, our bare-bones deterrence models and to explore a number of questions associated specifically with *extended* deterrence relationships.

In this chapter we begin by describing a generic *two-level* extended deterrence/escalation model and discuss its characteristics under complete information. Chapter 7 begins an investigation into the model's implications under incomplete information and evaluates the efficacy of all-or-nothing extended deterrence deployment policies like *Massive Retaliation*. Chapter 8 assesses a competing deployment policy called *Flexible Response*. And in chapter 9, we examine an important special case covered by the model that helps shed light on the circumstances associated with both limited conflicts and escalation spirals.

6.1   Preliminaries

In contrast to direct deterrence relationships, where there exists a perceived threat to the homeland of at least one state, extended deterrence applies to situations in which one state – the defender – perceives an indirect threat against a third party – the *target*, or as Russett (1963) calls it, the *pawn* (or *protégé*). The pawn need not be a formal ally of the defender, but the defender must have a real interest in protecting the pawn, either for the pawn's own sake, or for the defender's overall security interests, or, more likely, for some combination.

In the post-war period, NATO's defense of Western Europe is the prototypical example. From the earliest days of the Cold War, the principal fear was of a Soviet blitzkrieg across the North German plain. Given such an attack, the Western democracies would have to decide how to respond. There were, practically speaking, only three options: NATO could *do nothing*, in essence conceding world leadership to the Soviet Union; or it could *respond-in-kind* and fight yet another debilitating ground war in Europe; or it could deliberately *escalate* by directing an all-out attack against the Soviet Union itself. Since these three generic response options constitute the core of the extended deterrence/escalation model developed in this chapter, we believe it closely approximates the essence of NATO's strategic predicament.

Similar tripartite choices are embedded in many other extended deterrence games. For example, after Archduke Franz Ferdinand was assassinated in 1914, Germany had to decide whether to back Austria and, if so, how. Doing nothing risked the loss of German influence and control in the Balkans, and was therefore rejected. Still, there was a great deal of debate in German official circles about the extent to which Austria should be supported in its conflict with Serbia. Germany could, by providing limited support, restrain Austria; or it could escalate the crisis by providing full support. Unfortunately, by issuing a "blank check," it chose the latter.[1]

According to Danilovic (1998), there have been forty-seven observable attempts at extended (immediate) deterrence among major powers since 1895 (see table 6.1). Cases included in this list occur in the context of an overt threat by a challenger to a third party, and an explicit attempt by a defender to deflect the threat.[2] Clearly there is case selection bias at work here.[3] Danilovic's list does not pick up cases in which either the initial challenge or the protective threat is itself deterred. Still, it provides a useful empirical referent for the underlying conceptualization of this and subsequent chapters of our book.[4]

Compared to direct deterrence – mutual or unilateral – extended deterrence is the problematic case.[5] As Quester (1989: 63) notes, direct (or basic) "deterrence is very easy to accomplish . . . Where there is much more doubt comes in 'extended deterrence.'" Thus, it should

---

[1] States face similar generic choices in other venues. For instance, "when a nation initiates an arms race, it sets up a challenge to the status quo that can be accepted, resisted with violence, or met by a corresponding arms increase" (Downs, 1991: 77). Thus, the model we next develop may also shed light on why some arms competitions never occur, why others reach stasis, and why still others spiral on and on.

[2] Alternative listings are provided by Huth and Russett (1990) and Huth, Gelpi, and Bennett (1993). Danilovic (1998) discusses the differences in detail.

[3] Selection bias is an unavoidable characteristic of all deterrence data sets – direct or extended (Morrow, 2000). For a further discussion, see Reed (1998).

[4] To facilitate the connection between Danilovic's innovative empirical work and the formalizations developed below, we have taken some liberties with her nomenclature. Specifically, we label as *Defender Wins* those cases in which she judges the Challenger has acquiesced. Similarly, we use the term *Challenger Wins* to describe cases in which the Defender is seen to have acquiesced. In Danilovic's coding scheme, "compromise" is a catch-all category that includes both negotiated outcomes and standoffs. This category corresponds, roughly, to events we will term *Limited Conflicts*. But the correspondence is not exact. We also include in this category wars that do not escalate. Since Danilovic makes no attempt to distinguish between limited and all-out wars, we have not altered her coding of those events that she simply calls "war." We would label some of the wars (e.g., World War II) identified by Danilovic as *All-Out Conflicts*. Others could, arguably, be identified as *Limited Conflicts*. Vasquez (1993: 73), for instance, offers the Russo-Japanese War of 1904 as an example of a limited war. As well, the Korean War is often given as an instance of a limited war. To capture fully all these empirical subtleties, a more complex escalation model, with finer distinctions and a wider range of mutual conflict outcomes (e.g., Zagare, 1992) is required.

[5] At least in disputes that involve one or more major powers (Danilovic, 1998).

171

Table 6.1. *Cases of immediate extended deterrence among major powers, 1895–1985*

Year	Challenger	Defender	Third party	Outcome	Crisis name
1895–96	Germany	UK	South Africa	Defender Wins	Delagoa Bay & Jameson Raids
1897	Germany	Russia	China	Limited Conflict	Kiao-Chow (German occupation)
1897–98	France	UK	Nigeria	Limited Conflict	Niger Dispute
1898	Russia	UK	China	Limited Conflict	Anglo-Russian Crisis
1898–99	UK, USA	Germany	Samoa	Limited Conflict	Samoan Islands Dispute
1898–99	France	UK	Sudan	Defender Wins	Fashoda
1899–00	Russia	Japan	Korea	Defender Wins	Masampo Episode
1902	UK, Germany	USA	Venezuela	Defender Wins	Venezuelan Crisis
1903	Russia	Japan	Manchuria	Challenger Wins	Manchurian Evacuation
1904–05	Russia	Japan	Korea, Manchuria	War	Russo-Japanese War
1905–06	Germany	France	Morocco	Defender Wins	First Moroccan (Tangier) Crisis
1908	A-H, Germany	Russia	Serbia	Challenger Wins	Annexation of Bosnia and Herzegovina
1911	Germany	France	Morocco	Defender Wins	Second Moroccan (Agadir) Crisis
1912	A-H, Germany	Russia	Serbia	Challenger Wins	First Balkan War
1914–17	A-H, Germany	Russia	Serbia	War	World War I
1914–18	Germany	UK, France	Belgium, France	War	World War I
1920–23	USSR	UK	Iran, Afghanistan	Limited Conflict	Anglo-Russian frictions in Central Asia
1932	Japan	UK	China	Defender Wins	Shanghai Incident
1935–36	Italy	UK	Ethiopia	Challenger Wins	Italo-Ethiopian (Abyssinian) War
1935–36	Japan	USSR	Outer Mongolia	Defender Wins	Outer Mongolian Frontier Dispute
1937	USSR	Japan	Manchuria	Defender Wins	Amur River Incident
1938	USSR	Japan	Manchuria	Challenger Wins	Changkufeng
1938	Italy	France	Tunisia	Defender Wins	Italian colonial claims
1938	Germany	UK, France	Czechoslovakia	Challenger Wins	Sudetenland Problem
1939	Italy	UK, France	Greece	Defender Wins	Italy's invasion of Albania
1939	Japan	USSR	Mongolia	War	Nomonhan Incident
1939–45	Germany	UK, France	Poland	War	World War II

1945	USSR	USA, UK	Iran	Defender Wins	Azerbaijan Issue
1945–46	France	UK	Syria	Defender Wins	Levant
1946	USSR	USA	Turkey	Defender Wins	Turkish Straits
1948–49	USSR	USA, UK, France	West Germany	Defender Wins	Berlin Blockade
1950–53	USA	China	North Korea	War	Korean War
1954–55	China	USA	Taiwan	Defender Wins	Chinese Offshore Islands
1956	UK, France	USSR	Egypt	Defender Wins	Suez Canal
1956	USSR	USA	France, UK	Defender Wins	Suez Canal (Soviet retaliatory threat)
1957	USA	USSR	Syria	Defender Wins	Turkish–Syrian Frontier Dispute
1957	USSR	USA	Turkey	Defender Wins	Turkish–Syrian Frontier Dispute
1958	China	USA	Taiwan	Defender Wins	Quemoy–Matsu
1958–59	USSR	USA	West Germany	Defender Wins	Berlin Deadline
1961	USSR	USA	West Germany	Limited Conflict	Berlin Wall
1962	USSR	USA	Cuba	Defender Wins	Cuban Missile Crisis
1967	USA	USSR	Israel, Syria	Challenger Wins	Six Day War
1970	Syria, USSR	USA	Jordan	Defender Wins	Black September
1971	USA	USSR	Bangladesh	Defender Wins	Bangladesh
1973	USSR	USA	Israel	Limited Conflict	Yom Kippur War
1973	USA	USSR	Egypt, Syria	Limited Conflict	Yom Kippur War
1975	USSR	USA	Angola	Challenger Wins	Angolan Civil War

Source: Based on Danilovic (1998).

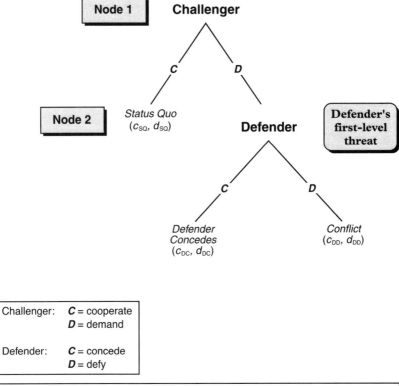

Fig. 6.1. Containment *circa* 1947.

come as no surprise that, with the exception of the Franco-Prussian war, all nine major-power wars since the Congress of Vienna have involved the failure of extended deterrence (Danilovic, 1995). Clearly, there are important empirical and theoretical reasons for turning our attention specifically to those deterrent relationships in which one state faces the difficult task of shielding another from an attack.[6]

6.2   The Asymmetric Escalation Game

To study the dynamics of extended deterrence relationships, we now explore a generic escalation model we call the *Asymmetric Escalation Game* (see figure 6.3). Although a simple model, the Asymmetric Escalation Game is considerably richer and more complex than any of the direct deterrence models developed earlier.[7] The choices available to the players are more varied; there are more outcomes; and, although it may not be immediately apparent, there are now two levels of play.

The two levels represent empirically possible *and* psychologically distinct forms of conflict. This criterion simply means that the players agree that there is a clear and recognizable difference between a constrained conflict and a conflict that escalates to some higher level. By incorporating different conflict levels into our model, we are able to expand the range of questions we can address, to explore the relationship between deterrence and escalation, to inquire into the conditions associated with limited conflicts, and to evaluate alternative extended deterrence defense postures.

The Asymmetric Escalation Game of figure 6.3 reflects a number of important modeling choices. Partly to explain these choices, and partly to motivate our analysis, however, we begin with the more basic structure given by figure 6.1 and a real-life example. Specifically, we interpret figure 6.1 in terms of the Truman administration's view of the US–USSR strategic relationship in 1947. Then we discuss how, beginning in 1952, changes in the global strategic environment transformed this unassuming structure first into the slightly more elaborate game represented by figure 6.2, and, eventually, into the Asymmetric Escalation Game of figure 6.3. The strategic characteris-

---

[6] We make no attempt to model all aspects of extended deterrence relationships. For a model that explicitly examines the relationship between extended deterrence and alliance formation, see Smith (1998b). Wagner (1991) uses game theory to explore the rational basis of counterforce strategies in the context of extended deterrence. The role of the pawn in extended deterrence relationships is modeled by Kilgour and Zagare (1994).

[7] See Zagare (1990b) for an analysis of a symmetric version of this game.

tics of the Asymmetric Escalation Game are then discussed in the next section.[8]

Figure 6.1 is an old friend. Except for minor notational changes, it is the Rudimentary Asymmetric Deterrence Game – discussed in detail and analyzed in chapter 3. Here, however, we eschew analysis in favor of description and (re)interpretation.

As before, there are two players in this game, but now we call them *Challenger* and *Defender*. Challenger begins play at node 1 either by *cooperating* (C) and accepting the *Status Quo* (outcome SQ), or by *defecting* (D) and demanding a change in the existing order. Challenger's demand could range from a simple request for special consideration to a direct military strike at Defender's client or ally. But since we will be modeling extended deterrence, we do not think of this demand as a frontal attack on Defender. The models explored in part II apply to those deterrence situations in which one state seeks to deter another from attacking directly. Thus we now think of Challenger's initial demand as restricted to a level short of an all-out assault against Defender.

If Challenger cooperates and no demand is made, the game ends, the *Status Quo* persists, and the payoffs (utilities, as usual) to Challenger and Defender are c_{SQ} and d_{SQ} respectively. But if Challenger defects, Defender must decide how to react. At node 2, Defender can either *concede* (C) the issue or *defy* (D) Challenger. Concession leads to outcome DC (*Defender Concedes*) while defiance results in outcome DD (*Conflict* or, more mnemonically, *Defender Defies*). Defender's choice at node 2 constitutes its *first-level* threat. There are, of course, no escalation choices in this rudimentary game model and, hence, no possibility of a conflict spiral.

To ensure that this simple model represents deterrence, we make three assumptions about the players' preferences. First, we assume Challenger prefers *Defender Concedes* to the *Status Quo*, i.e., prefers DC to SQ. This restriction on preferences is necessary to provide Challenger with an immediate incentive to defect. Second, we assume

---

[8] Clearly, in the context of extended deterrence relationships, the games depicted in figures 6.1 and 6.2 are anomalous. They are byproducts of the collapse of Germany and Japan in 1945 and the nuclear monopoly enjoyed by the United States in 1947 and shortly thereafter. We contend that the game depicted in figure 6.3, which evolved quite naturally from these two rump games, more fully captures the logic of extended deterrence situations, both before and after Hiroshima.

Defender prefers the *Status Quo* to all other outcomes, i.e., prefers SQ to DC and DD. This assumption, in effect, makes deterrence Defender's principal objective. Finally, to provide Defender with a capable threat, we assume that Challenger prefers the *Status Quo* to *Conflict.*

No fixed assumption is made, though, about Defender's preference between *Defender Concedes* and *Conflict.* As before, this preference relationship is critical to the model. But under complete information, which we assume for now, there are only two possibilities:

1. Defender prefers DD to DC (i.e., is Hard). Defender's threat is completely credible: Challenger knows that it is rational for Defender to carry out its threat should Challenger defect at node 1. As shown in chapter 3, deterrence succeeds (i.e., the outcome is SQ) when Defender has a credible threat and is known to be Hard.

2. Defender prefers DC to DD (i.e., is Soft). In this case, Defender's threat lacks credibility: Challenger knows that Defender would prefer *not* to carry out the threat. As shown in chapter 3, when Defender is known to be Soft, deterrence fails and the outcome is DC.

Given the above, it is easy to understand why, during the early years of the Cold War, containment of the Soviet Union was seen as a straightforward engineering problem. After all, until 1949 the United States had a monopoly on atomic weapons, and was clearly the world's dominant industrial and political power. The credibility of the US threat to defend itself, or its most important allies, was taken to be almost self-evident; and if there was doubt, US credibility was easily shored up by words, or deeds, or both.

For example, in 1947 Greece and Turkey were thought to be threatened, so the Truman Doctrine was proclaimed: military and economic help was to be provided to any country resisting outside (i.e., "communist") aggression. During the Berlin crisis of 1948, a more forceful message was sent when the United States transferred several B-29s, the so-called atomic bombers, to British and German bases. The intent of this signal was obvious: the US was Hard.

For a while containment worked, or at least it seemed so. Berlin was saved, and Greece and Turkey protected. In 1950, however, after South Korea was invaded, the Chinese were clearly not deterred from intervening on behalf of North Korea. By the time Eisenhower took office in 1952, American credibility was ebbing. Making matters worse, Eisenhower – who had campaigned on a pledge to end the war – publicly vowed to avoid future land wars in Asia. Evidently, the threat to resist communist expansion anywhere and at any time was no longer the cornerstone of US foreign policy. Thus the crucial question arose: how could the United States protect its interests abroad when it was apparently known to be unwilling to use military force in peripheral arenas?

The Eisenhower administration's response was its *New Look* defense policy that de-emphasized conventional forces and relied instead on atomic and, later, nuclear weapons to protect the status quo. At the heart of the New Look was the doctrine of *Massive Retaliation*. As enunciated by Secretary of State John Foster Dulles, the US notion of Massive Retaliation depended "primarily on a great capacity to retaliate, instantly, by means and at places of our own choosing."

The idea was to deter the Soviet Union from fomenting crises in out of the way places by threatening to transform local conflicts into strategic confrontations. Since the United States maintained a distinct strategic advantage over the Soviet Union in 1952, this threat was inherently more credible than a threat to intervene in a more limited way in less important venues.

In game-theoretic terms, the New Look sought to transform the game of figure 6.1 to the game of figure 6.2, where Defender has a third response option at node 2, to *escalate* (E). Defender's additional choice implies another possible outcome: *Defender Escalates* (DE). Presumably, unilateral escalation would lead to a clear-cut victory for Defender (i.e., the United States) while a non-escalatory response-in-kind (i.e., a choice of *D*) would result in a protracted crisis or other *limited* conflict in which neither side enjoyed an obvious advantage.

Dulles' new strategic doctrine rested on a number of assumed preference relationships. First, the threat of Massive Retaliation is unnecessary unless Defender's threat to respond-in-kind is seen to lack credibility. Hence, when analyzing this particular deployment policy in the next chapter, we assume Defender prefers (or at least is seen to prefer) DC to DD. We assume the opposite in chapter 8 when we analyze the policy of Flexible Response.

Similarly, Massive Retaliation as a strategic doctrine is incoherent unless Defender prefers to escalate unilaterally, i.e., prefers DE to DD. After all, limited conflicts take place on Challenger's terms, while any conflict that occurs after Defender escalates unilaterally would be on Defender's. Thus, we always presume Defender prefers DE to DC and

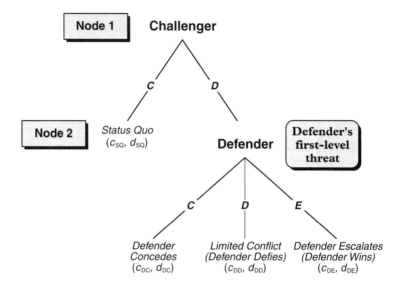

Fig. 6.2. Massive Retaliation *circa* 1952.

DD. For similar reasons we presume Challenger prefers *Limited Conflict* (DD) to *Defender Escalates* (DE).

Given these assumptions, it is easy to understand the reasoning behind the Massive Retaliation doctrine. Given the underlying strategic assumptions about both Challenger's and Defender's preferences, the *Status Quo* is stable, and deterrence should work.

Game-theoretically, the logic was impeccable. Unfortunately, the long-term structural viability of the game being played seems to have been overestimated. Before very long, critics like William Kaufmann (1956: 21) were charging that "if we are challenged to fulfill the threat of massive retaliation, we will be likely to suffer costs as great as those we inflict." In other words, the game envisioned by Eisenhower and Dulles appeared to be deteriorating rapidly.

In June 1955, in the now famous "fly-by" of long-ranged Bison bombers during an Aviation Day parade in Moscow, the USSR ostensibly demonstrated the capability of delivering repeated intercontinental attacks against American industrial and population centers. Shortly thereafter thermonuclear weapons were introduced into the Soviet arsenal (Quester, 1970: 126–129). In 1957, Sputnik, the first artificial earth satellite, was put into orbit by the Soviet Union, leading to the perception of a missile gap and a possible Soviet strategic advantage. Understandably, many observers came to believe that the Soviet Union was fully capable of responding to any strategic attack by the United States with a strategic strike of its own. This capability was certainly realized eventually.[9]

This important development is reflected in the Asymmetric Escalation Game of figure 6.3. Note in particular Challenger's node 3a option to escalate (first), and its option at node 3b to (counter-) escalate;[10] note as well Defender's option to counter-escalate at node 4. These additional choices give rise to two additional outcomes. Specifically, if Challenger escalates and Defender does not, *Challenger Wins* (outcome ED). And if both escalate, *All-Out Conflict* (outcome EE) occurs.[11]

The expanded set of choices also introduces two additional threats into the Asymmetric Escalation Game. Challenger now has a threat – to counter-escalate at node 3b. Defender's *first-level* threat to respond-in-kind at node 2 remains, but Defender now has a *second-level* threat as well: to counter-escalate at node 4, should Challenger escalate first

---

[9] Most strategic analysts now hold that the Soviet Union did not have an assured second-strike capability until sometime after 1965.

[10] Wagner (1991: 748) has argued that "in the case of extended deterrence of conventional attack, the defender, not the challenger, must be the first to launch a nuclear attack." Our model is consistent with this claim, but only to the extent that Defender has the first opportunity to escalate.

[11] To keep the model simple, we do not distinguish between all-out conflicts precipitated when Defender escalates first and those that arise as a consequence of Challenger's decision to escalate at node 3a.

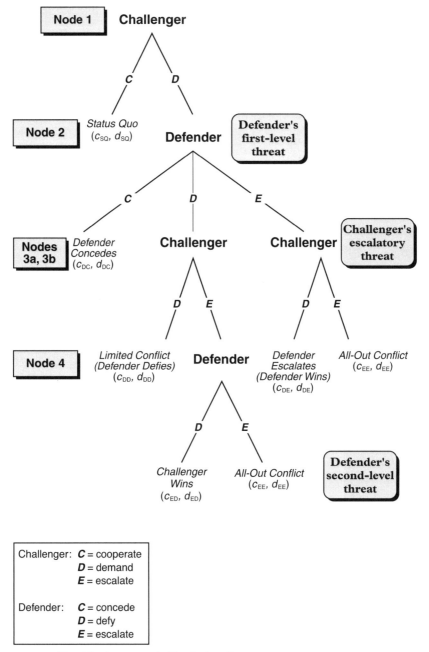

Fig. 6.3. Asymmetric Escalation Game.

at node 3a.[12] As one might expect, these additional threats play an important role in stabilizing or destabilizing the *Status Quo* in the Asymmetric Escalation Game; they have also been pointed to as key determinants of *intra-war* deterrence (Schelling, 1966). We henceforth assume that both of these threats are capable in the sense discussed above (i.e., each player prefers the *Status Quo* to *Limited Conflict*, and *Limited Conflict* to *All-Out Conflict*).

As a consequence of the additional choices, conflict spirals become distinct possibilities in the Asymmetric Escalation Game. Both players can make decisions that culminate in disaster. It is no accident that it was around the mid-1950s that the strategic literature on conflict escalation began to grow and, shortly thereafter, bifurcate (Smoke, 1977: ch. 2). Classical deterrence theorists, fixating on stability, modified their analyses to take account of the evolving realities. Eventually, most counseled more varied response options than those envisioned in the New Look.

The so-called spiral theorists, on the other hand, contended that the prescriptions associated with classical deterrence theory could lead to a vicious cycle of reciprocated and escalating conflict (Jervis, 1976). Believing, as did Eisenhower and Dulles, that war could not be contained, they opposed increased defense spending in general, and a limited war capability in particular (Gacek, 1994). As time passed, spiral theorists developed "action–reaction" models that illustrated how even purely defensive actions could easily develop into all-out conflict (e.g., Richardson, 1960; Wright, 1965; Holsti, North, and Brody, 1968; Pruitt, 1969). In chapter 9 we return to this debate to evaluate the conflicting claims of classical deterrence theory and proponents of the spiral model.

Our analysis of the Asymmetric Escalation Game is based on certain fundamental assumptions. We assume that players always prefer winning to losing. To reflect the costs of conflict, we assume that players prefer to win or, if it comes to it, lose, at the lowest level of conflict.[13] Thus Challenger prefers *Defender Concedes* to *Challenger Wins* – and so does Defender.

---

[12] Depending upon the specific empirical referent we have in mind at a particular moment, we may also refer to these two choices as either Defender's tactical (or sub-strategic) and strategic level threats, or as Defender's conventional and nuclear threats.

[13] This is a standard assumption of crisis escalation models. See, for example, Fearon (1994b).

Of course, we leave open each player's preference for executing its threat(s). This means that Challenger may be one of *two* types (Hard and Soft) and that Defender may be one of *four*:

- type HS (i.e., Hard at the first level, but Soft at the second)
- type SH (i.e., Soft at the first level, but Hard at the second)
- type HH (i.e., Hard at both levels)
- type SS (i.e., Soft at both levels).

In this chapter we assume complete information: players know their own types, and each other's. In subsequent chapters we assume incomplete information: each player has only probabilistic knowledge of its opponent's type.

In summary, we make the following assumptions about the players' preferences:

Challenger: *Defender Concedes* $>_{Ch}$ *Status Quo* $>_{Ch}$ *Challenger Wins* $>_{Ch}$ *Limited Conflict* $>_{Ch}$ *[Defender Escalates, All-Out Conflict]* (6.1)

Defender: *Status Quo* $>_{Def}$ *Defender Escalates* $>_{Def}$ *[Defender Concedes, Limited Conflict]* $>_{Def}$ *[Challenger Wins, All-Out Conflict]*. (6.2)

6.3 Extended deterrence and the dynamics of escalation

In the previous section we described how changes in both US and Soviet doctrine and capabilities brought about fundamental structural changes in the strategic relationship of the superpowers. In particular, we traced the evolution of the elementary extended deterrence problem facing the United States in 1947 to the much more complex structure we call the Asymmetric Escalation Game. In doing so, however, we did not restrict the generality of the model. The underlying escalation model, we believe, is generic – applicable to a wide range of human conflicts. Our description and interpretation of the Asymmetric Escalation Game, and our views about the origins of the decision problems it encapsulates, generally focus on the exercise of nuclear options. But alternative interpretations remain possible.

Consider, for example, our distinction between first-level (or limited) conflict and second-level (or all-out) conflict. In terms of the strategic relationship of the superpowers, the facile interpretation would be to associate the first level with conventional conflict and the

	Defender					
	C/D	*C/E*	*D/D*	*D/E*	*E/D*	*E/E*
C/D/D	SQ	SQ	SQ	SQ	SQ	SQ
C/D/E	SQ	SQ	SQ	SQ	SQ	SQ
C/E/D	SQ	SQ	SQ	SQ	SQ	SQ
C/E/E	SQ	SQ	SQ	SQ	SQ	SQ
D/D/D	DC	DC	DD	DD	DE	DE
D/D/E	DC	DC	DD	DD	EE	EE
D/E/D	DC	DC	ED	EE	DE	DE
D/E/E	DC	DC	ED	EE	EE	EE

(row label at left: **Challenger**)

Challenger:	**C** = Cooperate	Defender:	**C** = Concede
	D = Demand		**D** = Defy
	E = Escalate		**E** = Escalate

Fig. 6.4. Strategic-form representation of Asymmetric Escalation Game.

second with nuclear war. But the distinction could also be taken to separate conflicts in which only tactical (or theater) nuclear weapons are used from those in which strategic nuclear weapons are employed as well. Or the two levels could represent the distinction between conventional and chemical (or biological) weapons, between a localized limited-scale encounter and a broader more intense conflict, and so on. In other words, the two-level game model applies to *any* conflict in which the players share a common belief that a saliency (in the sense of Schelling [1960]) exists, and that crossing this threshold is irrevocable, and implies a serious escalation of the conflict. Although the implications of our model are particularly relevant to extended deterrence situations, they pertain as well to many bilateral conflicts, interstate or otherwise, extended or not, both before and after 1945.

Figure 6.4 is a strategic-form representation of the Asymmetric Escalation Game. But neither the strategic- nor the extensive-form representation of the Asymmetric Escalation Game reveals its underlying structural similarity to the two direct deterrence models developed previously. For this purpose we require figure 6.5, a graphical

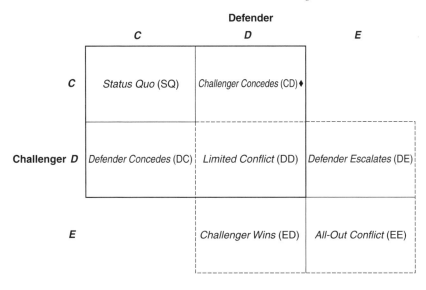

Defender

Fig. 6.5. Outcome array of Asymmetric Escalation Game.

summary of both the outcomes and the structural dynamic of the Asymmetric Escalation Game.

The outcome array of figure 6.5 is composed of two distinct 2×2 structures linked by a common outcome (i.e., *Limited Conflict*). The common outcome (DD) plays a role in both components: it is the mutual conflict outcome of the first-level deterrence game, and the revised status quo of the second-level deterrence game.[14]

Both the four northwest cells (enclosed in a solid border) and the four southeast cells (marked off by a broken border) of figure 6.5 correspond to the outcome matrix associated with the Generalized Mutual Deterrence Game (figure 4.2) or the Unilateral Deterrence Game (figure 5.2). This is no accident. In formulating the Asymmetric Escalation Game our intent was to extend the underlying logic of the

---

[14] With complete information about relative preferences, figure 6.5 constitutes a graph model (Fang, Hipel, and Kilgour, 1993).

direct deterrence models to extended deterrence and to limited and escalated conflicts.[15]

The reader with a vivid imagination may notice that figure 6.5 resembles a ladder – or at least a very short staircase. Again, this is not an accident. Our model of extended deterrence and the escalation process was inspired by Kahn's (1965) now-standard metaphor of an escalation "ladder." The specific sequence of moves and counter-moves in the Asymmetric Escalation Game was also influenced by an informal escalation model developed by Snyder and Diesing (1977: 61–63) in their classic study of interstate crises. As well, the Asymmetric Escalation Game is compatible with Smoke's (1977) character-ization of escalation as a choice that involves crossing a plateau (or saliency), and with Huth and Russett's (1988) "two-phase" conceptu-alization of escalation.

We concede that in developing the Asymmetric Escalation Game (and its symmetric variant) we have, somewhat arbitrarily, restricted the choices available to the players after both choose *D*, i.e., during *Limited Conflict*. This does not mean that we believe that other choices are impossible, either theoretically or empirically, but merely that we have (conceptually) folded all other choices into escalation. Our conception is that a limited conflict that persists in equilibrium might, eventually, evolve into a prolonged stalemate or a chronic crisis if both players hold firm, a clear victory for one of the players after the other backs down,[16] or a negotiated settlement if the players decide to mediate their differences, and so on. But we ignore these complexities to focus exclusively on the process of escalation and the dynamics of limited conflicts. To do otherwise would unduly complicate our still

---

[15] Seven different outcomes are listed in figure 6.5, even though there are only six distinct outcomes in the Asymmetric Escalation Game. The seventh and final outcome (*Challenger Concedes*) arises only in a symmetric version of this game in which both players have the opportunity to be Challenger (see Zagare 1990b for a discussion). It is included here only to enhance conceptual clarity and create visual symmetry. For all other purposes, it should be ignored. There are no interesting or meaningful distinctions between the symmetric and asymmetric versions of the game. We have chosen to explore the asymmetric variant to focus on extended deterrence relationships.

[16] Our model, however, does afford both players an opportunity to capitulate. Defender capitulates by not counter-escalating at node 4. Challenger capitulates by not counter-escalating at node 3b. As well, Defender can, by offering no resistance, accede to Challenger's demand at node 2. (See figure 6.3.)

simple model, with no sure prospect of a commensurate analytical payoff.

6.4 The Asymmetric Escalation Game under complete information

We begin by exploring the Asymmetric Escalation Game under complete information. We do so for two reasons. First, such an analysis serves as a benchmark for the evaluation of the game under incomplete information; second, the conclusions under complete information are interesting in their own right: they provide important, albeit provisional, insights into the dynamics of the escalation process and of extended deterrence. We will build on these insights in subsequent chapters.

We begin with an examination of the extensive-form Asymmetric Escalation Game depicted by figure 6.6, which is defined by the ordinal values given in figure 6.7. The northwest section of figure 6.7 shares the structural characteristics of Chicken: of the four outcomes, conflict is mutually worst. Thus, Defender's threat to respond-in-kind lacks credibility.

Much the same can be said about the southeast 2 × 2 component of figure 6.7: neither player's second-level threat is credible since neither prefers to match an escalatory choice of the other; Challenger prefers *Defender Escalates* (its next-worst outcome) to *All-Out Conflict* (its worst outcome) and Defender prefers *Challenger Wins* (its next-worst outcome) to *All-Out Conflict* (its worst outcome). Therefore, the underlying structure of the extensive-form game of figure 6.6 is composed of two 2 × 2 components that, structurally, resemble Chicken. All threats at every level for both players are inherently incredible.

Using backward induction, it is easy to determine the subgame-perfect equilibrium of this "double Chicken" variant of the Asymmetric Escalation Game. As the arrows indicating rational choices show, at node 4 Defender sticks with its previous choice of *D* in order to avoid its worse outcome, *All-Out Conflict*. For similar reasons, Challenger rationally chooses not to escalate at node 3b.

Challenger's choice at node 3a turns on Challenger's expectation that Defender will rationally choose *D* at node 4 (see above). Challenger's calculation is, therefore, that choosing *D* results in a *Limited Conflict* while choosing *E* leads to *Challenger Wins*. Clearly Challenger induces a more preferred outcome by escalating.

Extended deterrence

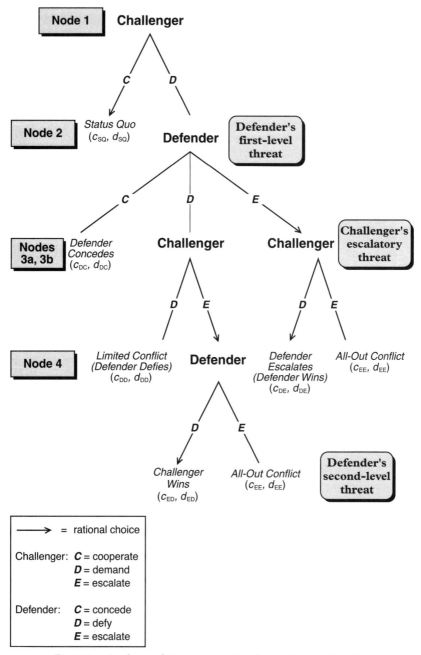

Fig. 6.6. Analysis of Asymmetric Escalation Game when threats are incredible

Defender

	C	D	E
C	Status Quo (6,6)	Challenger Concedes♦ (4,7)	
Challenger D	Defender Concedes (7,4)	Limited Conflict (3,3)	Defender Escalates (2,5)
E		Challenger Wins (5,2)	All-Out Conflict (1,1)

♦ = precluded
7 = best; 6 = next-best, etc.

Fig. 6.7. Outcome array of Asymmetric Escalation Game when threats are incredible.

Given these expectations, Defender should escalate at node 2. Escalation leads to *Defender Escalates* (*Wins*), defiance to *Challenger Wins*, and concession to *Defender Concedes*. Of these three outcomes, Defender prefers the first.

Anticipating Defender's escalatory response, Challenger's rational choice at node 1 is to cooperate. Cooperation implies Challenger's next-best outcome, the *Status Quo*; defection leads to its next-worst outcome, *Defender Escalates*. Thus, when threats are incredible all around, the *Status Quo* survives rational play: it is the outcome of the unique subgame-perfect equilibrium of this version of the Asymmetric Escalation Game.

6.4.1   Stability–instability paradox

Intuition might suggest that the stability of the *Status Quo* in this game turns on the postulated sequence of choices that apparently favors

Defender: simply by escalating, Defender can force Challenger to make the last choice in the Asymmetric Escalation Game. Being able to impose an unpalatable choice on an opponent is generally considered a significant tactical advantage. For example, one explanation frequently offered for the success of the Kennedy administration's tactic of blockading Cuba is that the blockade forced the Soviets to make the final choice between (nuclear) war and peace (Allison, 1971: 61). The supposition was, of course, that the Soviets would back down.

Intuition, however, can be misleading. The stability of the *Status Quo* is easily eroded in the Asymmetric Escalation Game. In fact, even when changes in the preference structure of the game that ostensibly favor Defender are made, the *Status Quo* can be destabilized.

To see this, assume now the ordinal utilities summarized in figure 6.8. These utilities reveal that both players have credible second-level threats. Challenger prefers *All-Out Conflict* to *Defender Escalates* and Defender prefers *All-Out Conflict* to *Challenger Wins*. All remaining preferences are the same as those assumed previously. Thus, while Defender's first-level threat remains incredible, both players now have credible escalatory threats.

Surprisingly, the *Status Quo* does not survive rational play in this game, even though Defender's *end-game* threat is now perfectly credible. *Defender Concedes* is the outcome of the unique subgame-perfect equilibrium! Counter-intuitively, the instability of the *Status Quo* can be traced to the modification of the credibility of each player's second-level (or end-game) threat, as all other preferences are the same as in figure 6.7. Under certain conditions, then, credibility is a double-edged sword, helping to promote deterrence success in some instances, but undercutting it in others.[17]

Glenn Snyder (1965) calls this phenomenon the stability–instability

---

[17] We do not mean to imply that the instability of the *Status Quo* is *solely* a function of the credibility characteristics of the players' second-level threats; it depends equally on the nature of Defender's first-level threat. For instance, the *Status Quo* is part of a subgame-perfect equilibrium in a game in which both players have credible threats at both levels of play (as discussed below). In this case, the stability of the *Status Quo* would be undermined if Defender's first-level threat were to suddenly lose its credibility. In other words, the make-up of Defender's first-level threat is as important in determining the outcome of this game as are the characteristics of the players' second-level threats. Our point here, however, is simply that there are times at which the credibility of an escalatory threat may actually undermine deterrence. We elaborate on this point below.

Defender

	C	D	E
C	Status Quo (6,6)	Challenger Concedes ♦ (4,7)	
Challenger D	Defender Concedes (7,4)	Limited Conflict (3,3)	Defender Escalates (1,5)
E		Challenger Wins (5,1)	All-Out Conflict (2,2)

♦ = precluded
7 = best; 6 = next-best, etc.

Fig. 6.8. Preferences associated with the stability–instability paradox.

paradox: credible threats at higher levels may lead to instability at lower levels. The fact that similar paradoxes occur in symmetric two-level escalation games (Zagare, 1990b), and in asymmetric three-level escalation games (Zagare, 1992), leads us to conjecture that the paradox is not simply an artifact of the Asymmetric Escalation Game. In fact, it seems plausible to attribute the series of superpower crises over Berlin in the late 1950s and early 1960s to this paradoxical feature of multi-level deterrence games. Quester (1970: 212), for instance, notes that one problem associated with the Eisenhower administration's policy of Massive Retaliation and its almost total reliance on nuclear deterrence was that the nuclear threat "might indeed be credible all around." Thus, in a setting like Berlin "where any military initiative had to fall to the West rather than the Soviet bloc," Western leaders might be presented with the unpalatable choice between all-out conflict and capitulation.

Within the context of Berlin, Quester's assessment might well be correct. Note, however, the critical role played by the characteristics of the players' second-level threat: when each player's end-game threat is incredible, Defender is advantaged (see the discussion above); when both players have credible second-level threats, the *Status Quo* becomes unstable, to the benefit of Challenger.

6.4.2 Escalation dominance

What happens when only one player has a credible end-game threat, creating an imbalance of resolve? The answer depends on the credibility of the players' first-level threats, and on which player lacks a credible second-level threat. The general idea, however, can be discerned in the variant of the Asymmetric Escalation Game with preferences as summarized in figure 6.9. Defender's first-level threat is credible; Challenger's threat is credible at the second level, but Defender's is not. As one might surmise, the unique subgame-perfect equilibrium under these credibility conditions produces *Defender Concedes*. The *Status Quo*, then, is unstable and Challenger, whose higher-level threat is credible, should prevail.

This example illustrates a dynamic that Kahn (1965) and others call *escalation dominance* (also see Freedman, 1987),[18] which we associate with an asymmetry of credibility in the second level of a two-level game or, if both players have credible second-level threats, in the first level. Clearly, credibility asymmetries in a multi-stage deterrence game are potentially destabilizing forces in interstate politics. But, and this is a big "but," they are neither necessary nor sufficient for destabilizing the *Status Quo*. We demonstrate this in the next section, showing that the *Status Quo* is highly sensitive to the specifics of the asymmetry.

6.5   Subgame-perfect equilibria

Given the restrictions on preferences in (6.1) and (6.2), there are precisely eight different two-level Asymmetric Escalation Games.

---

[18] Kahn (1965: 290) defines escalation dominance to be "a capacity, other things being equal, to enable the side possessing it to enjoy marked advantages in a given region of the escalation ladder . . . It depends on the net effect of the competing capabilities on the rung being occupied, the estimate by each side of what would happen if the confrontation moved to these other rungs, and the means each side has to shift the confrontation to these other rungs."

Defender

	C	*D*	*E*
C	Status Quo (6,6)	Challenger Concedes♦ (3,7)	
Challenger *D*	Defender Concedes (7,3)	Limited Conflict (4,4)	Defender Escalates (1,5)
E		Challenger Wins (5,2)	All-Out Conflict (2,1)

♦ = precluded
7 = best; 6 = next-best, etc.

Fig. 6.9. Preference assumptions illustrating escalation dominance

They are distinguished only by variations in the credibility of the states' deterrent threats, that is, by the players' types. Table 6.2 lists the games and, in each case, the outcomes of the unique subgame-perfect equilibrium.

A number of insights into the dynamics of escalation can be gleaned from table 6.2. First, notice that two conditions are sufficient for the stability of the *Status Quo*. Deterrence works when either (1) Challenger is Soft or (2) Defender is of type Hard/Hard (H/H). These conditions together are, in fact, necessary and sufficient. For deterrence to fail, Challenger *must* be Hard *and* at least one of Defender's two threats *must* lack credibility.

Interestingly, the *Status Quo* is stable in the two games in which *neither* player possesses a credible escalatory threat (see games 4 and 7). As our previous discussion of the double Chicken game (7)

Table 6.2. *Subgame-perfect equilibrium outcomes in Asymmetric Escalation Game*

No.	Challenger's type (2nd level)	Defender's type (1st level)	Defender's type (2nd level)	Subgame-perfect equilibrium outcomes
1	Hard	Hard	Hard	SQ
2	Hard	Hard	Soft	DC
3	Soft	Hard	Hard	SQ
4	Soft	Hard	Soft	SQ
5	Hard	Soft	Soft	DC
6	Hard	Soft	Hard	DC
7	Soft	Soft	Soft	SQ
8	Soft	Soft	Hard	SQ

illustrates,[19] the absence of mutually credible threats at the highest rung of the escalation ladder may *sometimes* be a stabilizing force in a deterrence relationship. Thus, in the nuclear age at least, *extended* deterrence success may depend less on the players' fear that their opponent will respond irrationally, as many classical deterrence theorists suggest, than on the expectation by each side that the other will respond optimally and escalate right up to the final rung of the escalation ladder.[20]

All of which might suggest that two-level games are more conducive to the long-term viability of the *Status Quo* than are one-level games. Indeed, the stated rationale for "flexible response" deployment postures rests, in part, on this very premise: additional response options are required to deter an opponent when end-game threats are inherently incredible. While the expected success of deterrence in games 4 and 7 is consistent with this conclusion, the conclusion does not generalize. Expanding response options and levels of play may either foster or destroy stability, depending of course on the way credibility is subsequently arrayed; moreover, as we show later, if the *Status Quo* is destabilized, *both* players could end up worse off.

Besides these two games, there are three other extended deterrence games in which the *Status Quo* is stable. In all three games (1, 3, and 8), Defender's end-game threat is credible. But this condition is

---

[19] See figure 6.7 for the defining preferences of game 7. Figure 6.8 summarizes the preferences associated with game 6. Game 2 is defined by figure 6.9.

[20] Which may explain Dulles's penchant for brinkmanship or Soviet Premier Nikita Khrushchev's "Sputnik Diplomacy" (Kahan, 1975: 54).

neither necessary nor sufficient for the long-term stability of extended deterrence. Defender's end-game threat is inherently credible in game 6, but the *Status Quo* does *not* result from a subgame-perfect equilibrium. And as noted above, the *Status Quo* is stable in game 7 in which no player's threat is credible at any level. Note that in game 1, a "double Prisoners' Dilemma," threats are credible all around. It should not be surprising that the *Status Quo* is stable in this game.

There are five games in which one player enjoys escalation dominance. In four of these games, one player possesses a credible threat in the second stage while its opponent does not (games 2, 3, 5, and 8). When Defender enjoys this advantage (games 3 and 8), the *Status Quo* is stable. But when Challenger alone has a credible end-game threat (games 2 and 5), *Defender Concedes* is the anticipated outcome under rational play. Thus, escalation dominance confers an important strategic advantage on the player who possesses it. In every case, the dominant player can expect its most-preferred outcome, irrespective of the credibility characteristics of Defender's first-level threat.

Escalation dominance also plays a role in the resolution of game 6. In this game both players have credible end-game threats; Defender's first-level threat, however, lacks credibility. Consistent with the above, it should be no surprise that the *Status Quo* is unstable; Challenger should prevail.

Finally, it is worth pointing out that, under complete information, neither limited nor all-out conflicts occur, and escalation spirals are impossible. Defender never has a reason to respond-in-kind to Challenger's demands, and neither player ever has the opportunity and the willingness to escalate, even though there is a built-in dynamic in the Asymmetric Escalation Game toward higher and higher conflict levels. Put in a slightly different way, in no case is it rational for the players to move very far along the escalation ladder when preferences are common knowledge.

6.6   Coda

In this chapter we describe the underlying structure of the Asymmetric Escalation Game, and show that the rules of play that define the model are essentially congruent with the broad parameters of the strategic relationship of the superpowers once the Soviet Union acquired a second-strike capability. This relationship was the prototype of extended deterrence situations throughout the Cold War period. We then argue that the structure of the Asymmetric Escalation Game generally applies to extended deterrence situations, and explore the model's implications under complete information.

Interestingly, the *Status Quo* is stable in the Asymmetric Escalation Game as long as *neither* player has a credible second-level threat. No such pattern occurs, however, when both players have credible end-game threats: under these conditions, deterrence succeeds or fails, depending on Defender's lower-level credibility. When Challenger's second-level threat is credible, stability requires that *both* of Defender's threats be credible as well.

Within the context of the Asymmetric Escalation Game, escalation dominance – defined as an asymmetry of credibility at the second level of a two-level game, or as the absence of a credible first-level threat for Defender when both players have credible end-game threats – emerges as a natural concept. Our analysis indicates, not unexpectedly, that escalation dominance confers a distinct advantage on the player who has it. In all five games in which one player has a credibility advantage, the advantaged player benefits, either, in Defender's case, when the *Status Quo* prevails or, in Challenger's case, when Defender capitulates and accepts an adjustment in the *Status Quo* that satisfies Challenger's demands.

Limited Conflict is never a subgame-perfect equilibrium in the Asymmetric Escalation Game; nor is *All-Out Conflict*. In fact, even though the assumptions (6.1 and 6.2) defining the Asymmetric Escalation Game generally give the players an immediate incentive to intensify their interaction, movement past the very first rung of the escalation ladder is never rational, no matter what assumptions are made about threat credibility. When information is complete, there is no "slippery slope."

We should caution the reader, however, that this and the other observations we make about the Asymmetric Escalation Game are tentative. The complete information assumption is strong. In politics, certainty about one's adversary is rare. Accordingly, we now turn to an examination of the Asymmetric Escalation Game with incomplete information. Our purpose is to discern whether these general patterns hold up when the complete information condition is relaxed, to determine what overall defense posture is most conducive to the success of extended deterrence, to learn if and when limited conflicts might rationally occur, and to specify the conditions that lead to escalation spirals and unconstrained conflict.

7 Modeling Massive Retaliation

> The ability to get to the verge without getting into the war is the necessary art.
>
> John Foster Dulles

> In war there is no substitute for victory.
>
> General Douglas A. MacArthur

The key to extended deterrence, at least under parity, lies in the way threat credibility is arrayed. This much is clear from our discussion of the Asymmetric Escalation Game with complete information. But many important questions about extended deterrence remain unanswered: in an uncertain world, how should multi-level threats be fashioned to best ensure the survival of the status quo? What is the best way to connect lower-level (or tactical) threats and higher-level (or strategic) threats? Are limited wars possible between two equally capable states and, if so, can threats be configured to ensure that they remain limited? Under what conditions are extended deterrence relationships likely to spiral to the highest level and culminate in an all-out conflict?

Historically, two broad schools of thought exist with respect to these and related questions: the *all-or-nothing approach* and the *limited-war approach*. In an insightful discussion of post-war American defense policy, Gacek (1994) traces the origins of the all-or-nothing school to a set of strategic principles enumerated by the Swiss military writer Henri Jomini. Drawing on Napoleon's legacy, Jomini argued that success in battle came from the decisive application of superior force with the purpose of confronting and exploiting an opponent's greatest vulnerability. Purely defensive actions, artificial (i.e., political) restraints on either military means or ends, and protracted wars of attrition all ran counter to Jomini's "principles of war." Anything that slowed war down was "condemned in principle, doomed in practice" (Shy, 1986: 179).

By contrast, members of the limited-war school draw intellectual sustenance from the work of the Prussian military philosopher Carl von Clausewitz. Like Jomini, Clausewitz understood that warfare has a built-in escalatory dynamic. But the natural tendency of conflicts to spiral out of control is effectively dampened by a number of factors, the most important, of course, being political considerations. After all, war is merely the continuation of politics by other means. Indeed, for Clausewitz and his intellectual descendants, this is as it should be: military objectives *ought* to be subordinate to political goals. Means and ends are symbiotic; nuanced political objectives require measured applications of force. In consequence, military forces should be deployed in a way that provides political decision-makers with maximum tactical and strategic flexibility. For proponents of more varied battlefield deployments, therefore, the all-or-nothing approach that relies exclusively on massive applications of force is too blunt to provide the appropriate bargaining leverage necessary to wage war successfully and, simultaneously, conduct political negotiations.

The substantial differences between the all-or-nothing approach and the limited-war school are reflected in a distinction that Glenn Snyder (1961) drew some time ago between defense postures that attempt to deter by *punishment* and those that rely on *denial*. According to Snyder, a punishment posture relies primarily on a *strategic* capability to inflict high costs on an aggressor. By contrast, more measured (i.e., *tactical*) response options are required to deter an opponent by denying possible gains. The punishment approach, therefore, depends primarily on increasing an opponent's estimate of the costs of aggression, while a denial policy seeks to deter by decreasing an opponent's estimate of the likelihood or extent of success. With regard to the current discussion, Snyder writes that the former is inherently more credible in response to an all-out frontal attack (i.e., direct deterrence), while the latter is more credible in response to lesser challenges, such as an attack on an ally (i.e., extended deterrence).

The Eisenhower administration, however, did not see it this way. Its *New Look* defense policy, which was decidedly Jominian, was developed to "deter both large- and small-scale Communist aggression. [It was] not just a doctrine of strategic deterrence" (Wells, 1981: 38, 34). The principal objective of the new policy, of course, was to deter a direct attack on the United States. But it also aimed to deter land wars in Europe and Asia.

At the heart of the New Look policy was the doctrine of *Massive Retaliation*. As enunciated by United States Secretary of State John Foster Dulles on January 12, 1954 in a speech to the Council on Foreign Relations, the New Look's aim was to deter Soviet expansion by depending "primarily upon a great capacity to retaliate, instantly, by means and at places of our choosing."

Interpretations of this doctrine vary. Freedman (1989) argues persuasively that the policy was considerably more subtle than the caricature painted by critics of the Eisenhower administration. And Wells (1981) suggests that many elements of the New Look were already in place before Eisenhower took office. Most analysts agree, though, that the cornerstone of the new strategic doctrine was the preeminent role *strategic* nuclear weapons were to play in defending the interests of the United States and its allies. Punishment, rather than denial, was clearly the new Republican president's approach to deterrence.

At the time it was developed, the doctrine made perfect sense. First, Massive Retaliation was consistent with the administration's generally conservative approach to budgetary matters. After all, nuclear weapons were cheaper than conventional forces, so Massive Retaliation delivered "a maximum deterrent at a minimum price." Second, this new approach to containment exploited the huge United States lead over the Soviet Union in nuclear capability. Finally, Dulles argued, Massive Retaliation would deny the Soviet Union the initiative in future confrontations, depriving it of the ability to determine the time and the place of the next crisis.

It would be wrong to conclude from the above, however, that the strategic philosophy that informed the New Look was simply a byproduct of strategizing at the dawn of the nuclear age. To be sure, in the world of the early 1950s, nuclear weapons were the weapons of choice, especially for a near-nuclear monopolist. But the underlying approach was more general than this, and its implementation did not depend on any particular weapon. As Gaddis (1982: 147) observes, "the central idea [of Massive Retaliation] was that of asymmetrical response – of reacting to adversary challenges in ways calculated to apply one's own strengths against the other side's weakness, even if this meant shifting the nature and location of the confrontation." Or as Gacek puts it, "the New Look should be understood as a threat to escalate low-level conflicts to the advantage of the United States, but it *did not require* nuclear war as an immediate or eventual response to aggression" (1994: 129, emphasis in original).[1]

In this light, it is not difficult to identify other historical manifestations of the doctrine of Massive Retaliation. For example, prior to both world wars, Great Britain's deployment posture was essentially the same as that of the United States during the Eisenhower years. Rather than conscript and maintain a large standing army to defend its continental allies, the Britain of the late nineteenth and early twentieth centuries relied on an escalatory threat (i.e., its fleet) to deter Kaiser Wilhelm's Germany. And, as Huth and Russett (1988: 34) point out, at the time of the Munich crisis in 1938, Britain lacked any military capacity "to defend Czechoslovakia short of engaging in an extended war." Thus, British deployments just prior to both world wars were, *de facto*, all-or-nothing postures.

During the inter-war years, the French also relied on an all-or-nothing posture. The French plan was to depend on the defensive advantages provided by "massive firepower" to deter attacks. Their "only plan of action called for a general mobilization of all forces" (Kagan, 1995: 356). In other words, rather than "a kind of military flyswatter, supple and relatively unmenacing ... [French] ... military doctrine prescribed a sledge hammer" (Young, 1978: 119). Much the same could be said about Russian defense policy in the 1990s. The essential difference, of course, is that the current Russian threat is primarily nuclear, while the French threat throughout the 1930s was conventional.

7.1   Modeling all-or-nothing deployments[2]

To better understand the dynamics of those extended deterrence relationships that are governed by all-or-nothing deployments, we return to the Asymmetric Escalation Game model (see figure 6.3), but now we explore it under *incomplete* information.[3] There are at least

---

[1] See also George and Smoke (1974: 563).

[2] The remainder of this chapter is based on material first developed in Zagare and Kilgour (1993b).

[3] As noted above, we assume two states with capable threats, that is, threats that hurt. The asymmetry in our model relates to a difference in motivation. One player, Challenger, is motivated to upset the status quo; the other, Defender, is intent on protecting it.

three reasons why a better understanding of the Massive Retaliation deployment stance would be valuable. First, a simple model that takes into account a defender's reliance on escalatory threats will allow a deeper understanding of many important periods of world politics, including the early Cold War. Second, our conclusions will serve as benchmarks for a comparison with other strategic doctrines, such as Flexible Response (see chapter 8), that encompass more limited responses to aggression. These conclusions have implications for such issues as the proliferation of nuclear weapons and the downsizing of conventional forces. Finally, we hope to demonstrate explicitly the dynamics of an important strategic situation, a situation that – for better or worse – will characterize many hostile interstate relationships in the future.

To model a strategic relationship consistent with a defender's reliance on escalatory options, we begin with the same preference restrictions as before (see expressions [6.1] and [6.2]), except that now we assume that Defender has a *known* preference for *Defender Concedes* (outcome DC) and *Defender Escalates/Wins* (outcome DE) over *Limited Conflict* (outcome DD). This is a strong assumption, but it is precisely the motivation for the reorientation of US defense policy during the Eisenhower administration. As noted above, Eisenhower and Dulles preferred to avoid engaging an enemy in a costly and protracted land war, such as the costly ground war waged in Korea from 1950 to 1953, or the potential war in Vietnam in 1954 (Zagare, 1979). This is exactly why the New Look policy de-emphasized the role of conventional or tactical forces in US defenses, emphasizing instead strategic nuclear weapons to deter Soviet and Chinese expansion and to protect US allies. We add that this assumption is wholly consistent with the claim that the New Look was flawed because, in a crisis, it left the United States with an unappealing choice – either precipitate an all-out nuclear war or capitulate.

We are not suggesting that all, or even most, defenders prefer, or should prefer, both unilateral escalation and capitulation over limited conflict. Rather, our argument is that such a preference is implied by all-or-nothing defense doctrines like Massive Retaliation. As Kahan (1975: 17) observes, "military planning under the New Look . . . yielded a US military posture with neither the plans nor the capacity for coping with even moderately large non-nuclear conflicts."

Given the above, it should be no surprise that the New Look policy touched off a heated debate within the US defense establishment. It is also telling that when the Democrats came to power in 1961, non-strategic US forces were strengthened significantly. The intent was to demonstrate both the ability and the willingness to defend Europe conventionally. In terms of the model, the Flexible Response deployment policy introduced by the Kennedy administration was designed to provide the United States with a credible tactical (i.e., local) threat and establish, minimally, a preference for *Limited Conflict* over *Defender Concedes*. This is why we associate this particular preference relationship with Flexible Response deployments, which are examined in chapter 8.

In sum, to model Massive Retaliation and related all-or-nothing defense postures, we place the following restrictions on the players' preferences:

Challenger: *Defender Concedes* $>_{Ch}$ *Status Quo* $>_{Ch}$ *Challenger Wins* $>_{Ch}$ *Limited Conflict* $>_{Ch}$ [*Defender Escalates, All-Out Conflict*] (7.1)

Defender: *Status Quo* $>_{Def}$ *Defender Escalates* $>_{Def}$ *Defender Concedes* $>_{Def}$ *Limited Conflict* $>_{Def}$ [*Challenger Wins, All-Out Conflict*]. (7.2)

We continue to assume that each player knows its own preference between capitulating to its opponent at the highest conflict level and *All-Out Conflict*, but has only probabilistic knowledge of its opponent's preferences. Thus, the payoffs to Challenger and Defender at outcome EE, C_{EE} and D_{EE}, are treated as binary random variables with known distributions. Each player knows the realized value of only its own variable. More specifically, it is common knowledge that

$$C_{EE} = \begin{cases} c_{EE+} & \text{with probability } p_{Ch} \\ c_{EE-} & \text{with probability } 1 - p_{Ch} \end{cases}$$

$$D_{EE} = \begin{cases} d_{EE+} & \text{with probability } p_{Def} \\ d_{EE-} & \text{with probability } 1 - p_{Def} \end{cases}$$

where $d_{SQ} > d_{DE} > d_{DC} > d_{DD} > d_{EE+} > d_{ED} > d_{EE-}$, $c_{DC} > c_{SQ} > c_{ED} > c_{DD} > c_{EE+} > c_{DE} > c_{EE-}$, $0 < p_{Ch} < 1$, and $0 < p_{Def} < 1$.

In words, we assume that Defender believes Challenger to be *Hard* with probability p_{Ch} and *Soft* with probability $1 - p_{Ch}$. Likewise, Challenger believes Defender to be *Hard* with probability p_{Def} and *Soft* with probability $1 - p_{Def}$. Now, however, these beliefs are measures of the credibility of each player's *strategic* (or second-) level threat. As usual, all threats are assumed to be capable.

7.2   Perfect Bayesian equilibria under Massive Retaliation

What are the effects of uncertainty on the escalation process when Defender's first-stage threat is known to lack credibility, that is, when Defender's only real response option is to escalate? In these circumstances, what is the connection between credibilities and deterrence success? How credible must each side's end-game threat be in order to deter escalation – or retaliation?

To answer these questions we identify the perfect Bayesian equilibria of the *Asymmetric Escalation Game with incomplete information*. We begin with the observation that under the preference restrictions of (7.2), Defender *never* rationally responds-in-kind at node 2 (see figure 6.3). Thus, an inherently incredible threat to respond-in-kind is tantamount to no such threat at all. This should be no surprise: Defender prefers the outcome it induces by not responding (*Defender Concedes*) to any of the three possible outcomes associated with its choice of D (i.e., *Limited Conflict*, *Challenger Wins*, and *All-Out Conflict*). Both sides know this, so the Asymmetric Escalation Game reduces to the game shown in figure 7.1. Notice that there are now four, rather than six, possible outcomes in the reduced version of the Asymmetric Escalation Game.

One aspect of the analysis of figure 7.1 is straightforward. Backward induction at node 3 is easy since Challenger always knows whether it prefers *Defender Escalates* (outcome DE) or *All-Out Conflict* (outcome EE), and has no reason to conceal this preference. A Hard Challenger, preferring *All-Out Conflict* to *Defender Escalates*, always escalates at node 3, while a Soft Challenger, with the opposite preference, rationally chooses D and does not escalate at node 3.

Because Challenger's behavior at node 3 is strictly determined by its type, strategic decisions are reduced to Challenger's node 1 choice of C or D, and Defender's node 2 choice, C or E. Unlike the node 3 choice, these decisions can depend on the state of knowledge of the decision-maker. We denote the probabilities of these choices as follows:

x_H = probability that Challenger chooses D, given that it is Hard
x_S = probability that Challenger chooses D, given that it is Soft
z_H = probability that Defender chooses E, given that it is Hard
z_S = probability that Defender chooses E, given that it is Soft.

Given the preference restrictions associated with all-or-nothing

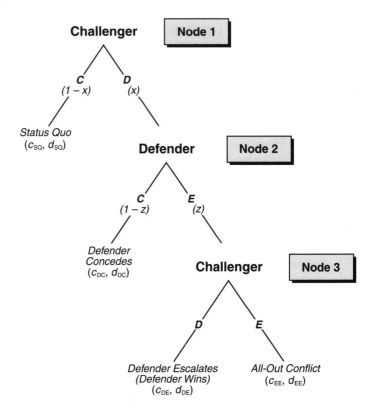

Fig. 7.1. Asymmetric Escalation Game when Defender lacks a credible first-level threat.

deployments, then, a perfect Bayesian equilibrium for the Asymmetric Escalation Game with incomplete information will specify a value for each of these four variables, plus a fifth belief variable (r) – *Defender's revised probability that Challenger is Hard, given that Challenger has*

Table 7.1. *Perfect Bayesian equilibria and existence conditions for Asymmetric Escalation Game when Defender's first-level threat lacks credibility*

Equilibrium	Strategic variables				Existence conditions
	Challenger initiates		Defender escalates		
	x_H	x_S	z_H	z_S	
Challenger-Soft Deterrence Equilibria	0	0	–	–	$r \leq d_2$
No-Response Equilibrium	1	1	0	0	$p_{Ch} > d_2$
Form I No-Limited-Response Equilibrium	1	1	1	0	$d_1 \leq p_{Ch} \leq d_2$ $p_{Def} \leq c_1$
Form II No-Limited-Response Equilibrium	1	u_3	1	v_3	$p_{Ch} \leq d_1$ $p_{Def} \leq c_1$
Form III No-Limited-Response Equilibrium	1	u_4	v_4	0	$p_{Ch} \leq d_2$ $p_{Def} \geq c_1$

Key: – = value not fixed although some restrictions may apply.

initiated. Thus, a perfect Bayesian equilibrium is described by a 5-tuple of probabilities $(x_H, x_S; z_H, z_S, r)$. The belief variable r is treated in detail in appendix 6; it will generally be suppressed in the discussion below.

Under an all-or-nothing policy,[4] there is always a Deterrence Equilibrium and, except on lines of transition, precisely one other perfect Bayesian equilibrium, which must belong to one of four categories. Table 7.1 summarizes the action choices associated with each equilibrium. Appendix 6 provides the technical details; here we restrict ourselves to an informal characterization. To facilitate the discussion, the equilibria are grouped into three categories: *Deterrence Equilibria, No-Response Equilibria,* and *No-Limited-Response Equilibria.*

7.2.1 Challenger-Soft Deterrence Equilibrium

Recall that a Deterrence Equilibrium is an equilibrium in which there is no initiation (i.e., $x_S = x_H = 0$). Under a Deterrence Equilibrium, Challenger – whether Hard or Soft – *never* defects. When any Deterrence Equilibrium is in play, then, the *Status Quo* is never disturbed.

---

[4] All conclusions reached in this chapter are subject to this restriction. For brevity, we will drop the proviso until we analyze limited-war deployments in chapter 8.

Only one form of Deterrence Equilibrium, the *Challenger-Soft Deterrence Equilibrium*, exists when Defender adopts an all-or-nothing policy.[5] Significantly, this equilibrium form may *not* depend on either player's *initial* belief about the other's type. It does, however, require that Defender believe that any Challenger who initiates is likely to be Soft. In consequence, under any Challenger-Soft Deterrence Equilibrium, both types of Defender intend to escalate at node 2 with a sufficiently high probability. Put differently, a Challenger-Soft Deterrence Equilibrium is possible as long as z_H and z_S are large enough and r, Defender's updated belief about Challenger's type given that Challenger selects D at node 1, is small enough.

Because the Challenger-Soft Deterrence Equilibrium may be independent of any (initial) beliefs the players have about each other's type, there are circumstances under which this equilibrium form lacks plausibility.[6] For instance, it is difficult to imagine that a Defender who believes a Challenger is likely Hard would, after observing an unexpected hostility, conclude that the Challenger is likely Soft. For this reason we consider the behavioral pattern associated with this form of Deterrence Equilibrium to be implausible when Challenger's initial credibility is high.

On the other hand, the Challenger-Soft Deterrence Equilibrium may well be plausible when Challenger's initial credibility is low to begin with. In fact, this particular form of Deterrence Equilibrium, and the beliefs associated with it, are consistent with the stability of the superpower relationship during the Eisenhower administration and with Dulles's brinkmanship strategy. Indeed, it is the most plausible explanation of the stability of the European status quo during this period. It may also help explain the absence of war in Europe until 1914, despite intense crises in the Balkans in 1905, in 1908, and again in 1912. Parenthetically, we observe that under the Challenger-Soft

---

[5] In subsequent chapters we distinguish other forms of deterrence equilibria.

[6] Extensive-form games of incomplete information (like the Asymmetric Escalation Game) take initial beliefs as given (i.e., as components of the model, like utilities for outcomes). The rational (Bayesian) updating requirement for perfect Bayesian equilibria links beliefs on later information sets to prior beliefs, but only on those information sets that are reached with positive probability at equilibrium. We are interested in identifying those beliefs that can give rise to particular perfect Bayesian equilibria, notably those with $x_H = x_S = 0$. It may happen that the only beliefs consistent with such an equilibrium are implausible in the sense that the initial beliefs and the beliefs on subsequent information sets (which happen to be "off the equilibrium path") lack consistency. Such is the case here.

Deterrence Equilibrium, Defender's beliefs about Challenger's type, were Defender to observe initiation by Challenger, are "off the equilibrium path." In other words, this is a belief about an event that never occurs, so it can never be tested against actual events.[7]

Even though the Challenger-Soft Deterrence Equilibrium is implausible under certain conditions, it is a perfect Bayesian equilibrium, and satisfies some equilibrium refinements (Fudenberg and Tirole, 1991).[8] And at least one Challenger-Soft Deterrence Equilibrium *always* exists.[9] (See appendix 6 for details.) Of course, this does not mean that deterrence success is a "sure thing." Indeed, the stability of the status quo will always be less than certain: at least one of four other perfect Bayesian equilibria, each of which involves certain initiation when Challenger is Hard, always coexists with a Challenger-Soft Deterrence Equilibrium.

Unlike the Challenger-Soft Deterrence Equilibrium, the other equilibria always exist under specific conditions depending on the initial beliefs of the players about each other's type (i.e., on p_{Ch} and on p_{Def}). Figure 7.2 summarizes the connection between these beliefs and the four other perfect Bayesian equilibria.[10]

7.2.2 No-Response Equilibrium

The second major form of perfect Bayesian equilibrium in the Asymmetric Escalation Game is the *No-Response Equilibrium*. A No-Response Equilibrium (NRE) is an equilibrium in which there is some possibility of initiation ($x_H + x_S > 0$) but there is *never* any response, either in-kind or escalatory, that is, where $y_H = y_S = z_H = z_S = 0$.

As shown in appendix 6, Challenger *always* defects (i.e., $x_H = x_S = 1$) when a No-Response Equilibrium is in play. Since the *Status Quo* never results from a No-Response Equilibrium, deterrence never succeeds, although (limited or unlimited) conflict and escalation

---

[7] For an illuminating discussion of the theoretical utility of off-the-equilibrium-path expectations, illustrated with an analysis of the German invasion of Poland in 1939, see Bueno de Mesquita (1996). For an explicit analysis of deterrence and off-the-path behavior, see Weingast (1996).

[8] For a discussion of three of these refinements in the context of deterrence theory, see Nalebuff (1991).

[9] This equilibrium is referred to as $CSDE_1$ in appendix 6. It is independent of either player's *initial* beliefs about the other's type. Defender's *a posteriori* estimate of Challenger's credibility is critical. This equilibrium will exist as long as $r \leq d_1$.

[10] Several constants, which are thresholds separating the equilibria, appear in figure 7.2. These constants are defined and discussed fully in appendix 6.

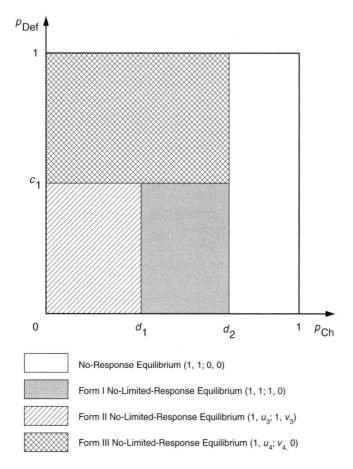

Fig. 7.2. Location of No-Response Equilibrium and No-Limited-Response Equilibria.

spirals cannot occur. Challenger always gets its way and the outcome is always *Defender Concedes* (DC). Under a No-Response Equilibrium, Challenger acts with impunity, as Hitler did in 1936 when he remilitarized the Rhineland, or as Ethiopia did in 1998 when it invaded Eritrea.

A No-Response Equilibrium is found in the eastern region of figure 7.2, where p_{Ch} is large. For an equilibrium of this form to exist, therefore, Challenger's credibility must be high enough that Defender is forever deterred from escalating. (Note that it is under these circumstances that we question the plausibility of the coexisting Challenger-Soft Deterrence Equilibrium.) In fact, it is precisely the high probability that Challenger will counter-escalate that dissuades even a Hard Defender from offering any resistance at all.

When a No-Response Equilibrium is in play, Defender simply stands aside after Challenger acts, as the British navy did in 1935 when Italian transport ships used the Suez Canal to prepare for war in Abyssinia. Since Defender is completely deterred under a No-Response Equilibrium, while Challenger is entirely undeterred, it should not be surprising that the existence of this equilibrium form depends on Challenger's credibility being high, but is unrelated to Defender's credibility. More specifically, Challenger's *a priori* credibility must exceed the threshold

$$p_{\text{Ch}} \geq d_2 = \frac{d_{\text{DE}} - d_{\text{DC}}}{d_{\text{DE}} - d_{\text{EE+}}}. \tag{7.3}$$

With respect to this threshold we make two observations. First, as Defender's immediate payoff from escalating (d_{DE}) increases, or as its payoff from immediate capitulation (d_{DC}) decreases, the threshold at d_2 moves to the right in figure 7.2, reducing the area of the region corresponding to the No-Response Equilibrium. As one might expect, then, the more Defender values unilateral escalation, or the less it values immediate capitulation, the higher must be Challenger's credibility to dissuade a Hard Defender from resisting.

As well, the threshold d_2 rises as the value a Hard Defender places on *All-Out Conflict* increases. In other words, as a central or strategic war becomes *less* onerous to Defender, the higher must be Challenger's *a priori* credibility to induce a No-Response Equilibrium. Clearly, Challenger can make it more likely that even a Hard Defender will capitulate simply by increasing Defender's costs for *All-Out Conflict*. Under the conditions that define a No-Response Equilibrium, then, weapons that increase the cost of conflict may make the status quo *less* likely to survive! On the other hand, if Defender is already Soft, such increases are devoid of strategic implications. In general, when Challenger can threaten an all-out war with even moderate credibility, Soft Defenders will not rationally resist.

7.2.3 No-Limited-Response Equilibria

In addition to the Challenger-Soft Deterrence Equilibrium and the No-Response Equilibrium, there are three other perfect Bayesian equilibria that can exist when Defender adopts an all-or-nothing defense posture. Together they constitute a family of equilibria we call the *No-Limited-Response Equilibria* (NLRE). A No-Limited-Response Equilibrium occurs when there is some possibility of Challenger initiating (i.e., $x_H + x_S > 0$), some possibility of Defender escalating (i.e., $z_H + z_S > 0$), but no possibility that Defender will respond-in-kind (i.e., of choosing D at node 2) should Challenger initiate. Hence its name.

There are three distinct forms of No-Limited-Response Equilibria. When a No-Limited-Response Equilibrium is in play, Hard Challengers *always* defect (i.e., $x_H = 1$) and there is always some possibility that Soft Challengers will defect as well (i.e., $x_S > 0$). Since Defenders either escalate or do not respond at all, limited conflicts cannot emerge under any No-Limited-Response Equilibrium.

7.2.3.1 Form I No-Limited-Response Equilibrium

Like the No-Response Equilibrium, the *Form I No-Limited-Response Equilibrium* involves certain initiation by all Challengers – regardless of type – and certain capitulation by a Soft Defender. When a Form I No-Limited-Response Equilibrium is in play, Hard Defenders escalate with certainty (i.e., $z_H = 1$). Soft Challengers then suffer a humiliating defeat, capitulating after Defender's harsh reaction, while Hard Challengers set in motion a process that culminates in *All-Out Conflict*. Thus a wider range of outcomes is possible than under a No-Response Equilibrium.

One additional important difference between No-Limited-Response Equilibria, including Form I, and the No-Response Equilibrium is that the NLRE family depends on both Challenger's and Defender's credibility. Specifically, the credibility thresholds for Challenger and Defender, respectively, defining the region of existence of a Form I No-Limited-Response Equilibrium are

$$d_1 = \frac{d_{DE} - d_{DC}}{d_{DE} - d_{EE-}} \leq p_{Ch} \leq d_2 \tag{7.4}$$

$$p_{Def} \leq c_1 = \frac{c_{DC} - c_{SQ}}{c_{DC} - c_{DE}}. \tag{7.5}$$

As figure 7.2 reveals, a Form I No-Limited-Response Equilibrium exists for intermediate levels of Challenger credibility, and lower levels of Defender credibility. A Form I NLRE occurs when Challenger's *a priori* probability of being Hard is high enough to deter a Soft Defender from retaliating, yet not so high that a Hard Defender capitulates. At the same time, Defender's credibility must be low enough that even a Soft Challenger would not hesitate before testing the water. It is important to note that it is the interaction of these credibility levels that produces the behavior associated with a Form I No-Limited-Response Equilibrium. At either a higher (than d_2) or a lower (than d_1) level of Challenger credibility, or a higher (than c_1) level of Defender credibility, other behavior patterns emerge.

The right-hand border of the zone of a Form I No-Limited-Response Equilibria is the threshold d_2, and its left-hand border is d_1. Like d_2, the location of threshold d_1 depends on Defender's payoff from both unilateral escalation (d_{DE}) and immediate capitulation (d_{DC}). More specifically, as Defender's payoff at *Defender Escalates* increases, or as its payoff at *Defender Concedes* decreases, both d_1 and d_2 move to the right, in tandem. Consequently, changes to Defender's payoff at these outcomes will affect the likelihoods of both a No-Response Equilibrium and a Form I No-Limited-Response Equilibrium. What depends on the specific values of these payoffs, though, is the extent to which Challenger's threat must be credible in order to induce Form I equilibrium behavior. As the net difference between Defender's payoffs at *Defender Concedes* and *Defender Escalates* increases, higher and higher levels of Challenger credibility are required for a Form I No-Limited-Response Equilibrium.

The value of the threshold d_1 also depends on the utility a Soft Defender receives from *All-Out Conflict* (d_{EE-}). As this value decreases, d_1 moves to the left, increasing the region of a Form I No-Limited-Response Equilibrium, and decreasing that of the Form II No-Limited-Response Equilibrium (to be discussed below). While Hard Defenders resist under either a Form I or Form II No-Limited-Response Equilibrium, Soft Defenders capitulate with certainty only when a Form I NLRE is in play. Thus, by manipulating a Soft Defender's payoff for *All-Out Conflict*, Challengers can increase the likelihood that a Soft Defender will capitulate.

The upper bound of the region of a Form I No-Limited-Response Equilibrium is the threshold c_1, given by (7.5); below c_1 lie the Form I and Form II NLRE, and above it lies the Form III NLRE. As will be seen, a Form I No-Limited-Response Equilibrium is distinguished from a Form III NLRE by the behavior of Soft Challengers and Hard Defenders, both of whom act less aggressively under a Form III

NLRE. But since c_1 depends on Challenger's payoffs, only Defender has an incentive and an opportunity to attempt to induce a Form III No-Limited-Response Equilibrium under which it is more likely to deter Challenger.

To decrease the probability that a Form I equilibrium comes into play, Defender could try to convince Challenger that it is likely Hard or, by manipulating the payoffs that define c_1, contract the region of the Form I equilibrium. Specifically, Form I (and Form II) equilibria become less probable (i.e., c_1 decreases) as Challenger's evaluation of the *Status Quo* increases, or as its payoff from either *Defender Concedes* or *Defender Escalates* decreases.

7.2.3.2 Form II No-Limited-Response Equilibrium

As with all perfect Bayesian equilibria other than the Challenger-Soft Deterrence Equilibrium, the two remaining No-Limited-Response Equilibria (Form II and Form III) involve certain initiation by a Hard Challenger. But unlike the No-Response Equilibrium and the Form I NLRE, Form II and Form III No-Limited-Response Equilibria are associated with probabilistic (as opposed to certain) initiation by a Soft Challenger.

Under a *Form II No-Limited-Response Equilibrium*, Hard Defenders always resist and Soft Defenders resist sometimes. But at a Form III No-Limited-Response Equilibrium, Defenders resist only when Hard, and only probabilistically at that. Under either of these equilibria, then, a Challenger unwilling to wage war might rationally precipitate a crisis; but only in the region of a Form II NLRE might a reluctant (i.e., Soft) Defender rationally call a Soft Challenger's bluff.

A Form II No-Limited-Response Equilibrium is to be found near the origin in figure 7.2, at the lowest levels of Challenger and Defender credibility. It should not be surprising, therefore, that rational behavior in this region involves the possibility of bluffing by *both* players.[11]

While all-out wars can transpire anywhere save for the region of the No-Response Equilibrium, it is only in the region of the Form II NLRE that a Soft Defender can find itself involved in a war it would prefer to avoid, for only in this region is it rational for a Soft Defender sometimes to defy Challenger by escalating. Each player's credibility

[11] Indeed, the Form II No-Limited-Response Equilibrium is a kind of Bluff Equilibrium – see chapters 4 and 5.

is lowest in the area of region II, which is why a Soft Defender can be tempted to resist and escalate. If Challenger happens to be Hard, the unthinkable happens.

The rightmost bound of the Form II No-Limited-Response Equilibrium region is the threshold d_1, given by (7.4), that separates a Form I from a Form II NLRE. As already noted, d_1 increases, expanding the area of Form II equilibria, as Defender's payoff from *Defender Escalates* increases, as its payoff from unwanted war (d_{EE-}) increases, or as its payoff from *Defender Concedes* decreases.

As is clear from figure 7.2, the upper bound of this region is c_1. The variables that affect the threshold separating Forms I and II from Form III No-Limited-Response Equilibria are Challenger's evaluation of the *Status Quo*, *Defender Concedes*, and *Defender Escalates*, as has already been discussed.

Hard Challengers always initiate in the Form II region, while Soft Challengers initiate with probability u_3, which is given by

$$u_3 = \frac{p_{Ch}(1 - d_1)}{d_1(1 - p_{Ch})}. \tag{7.6}$$

This probability increases steadily as one moves from the left-hand border ($p_{Ch} = 0$) of the region, where $u_3 = 0$, to the right-hand border ($p_{Ch} = d_1$), where $u_3 = 1$. In other words, under a Form II NLRE, as Challenger's credibility rises, so does its tendency to test Defender's resolve, even when Challenger is Soft.

By contrast, a Soft Defender's optimal response strategy in the Form II region is v_3, defined by

$$v_3 = \frac{c_1 - p_{Def}}{1 - p_{Def}}. \tag{7.7}$$

Note that v_3 *decreases* steadily as one moves from the bottom of the region ($p_{Def} = 0$) to the top ($p_{Def} = c_1$), where it approaches 0. Thus, Soft Defenders resist less and less as their credibility grows under a Form II No-Limited-Response Equilibrium.

7.2.3.3 Form III No-Limited-Response Equilibrium

Like a Form II No-Limited-Response Equilibrium, a *Form III No-Limited-Response Equilibrium* involves certain defection by a Hard Challenger and probabilistic defection by a Soft Challenger. This defection probability is

$$u_4 = \frac{p_{\text{Ch}}(1 - d_2)}{d_2(1 - p_{\text{Ch}})}. \tag{7.8}$$

While u_4 increases from 0 to 1 as Challenger's credibility rises from $p_{\text{Ch}} = 0$ to $p_{\text{Ch}} = d_2$, u_4 increases more slowly (as p_{Ch} increases from 0) than u_3 – the probability that a Soft Challenger defects at node 1 under a Form II NLRE. In other words, at comparable credibility levels, Soft Challengers are more circumspect under a Form III No-Limited-Response Equilibrium. But this is as it should be. After all, Form III NLRE correspond to higher Defender credibility than Form II NLRE, so a Soft Challenger has better reason to hesitate at Form III than at Form II.

By contrast, a Form III No-Limited-Response Equilibrium is associated with a somewhat different behavior pattern for Defender. Under a Form III NLRE, a Soft Defender *never* resists, and a Hard Defender resists only probabilistically. When a Form III No-Limited-Response Equilibrium is in play, a Hard Defender's optimal strategy is to resist with probability

$$v_4 = \frac{c_1}{p_{\text{Def}}}. \tag{7.9}$$

Thus a Hard Defender resists less and less as its credibility increases.

Under a Form III No-Limited-Response Equilibrium, *All-Out Conflicts* occur with probability v_4 when a Hard Challenger confronts a Hard Defender; by contrast, under a Form I or II NLRE, they occur with certainty in this situation. And unlike Form II NLRE, Soft Defenders *never* provoke war by testing Challenger's resolve.[12]

7.3   Coda

In this chapter we adapt the Asymmetric Escalation Game of incomplete information to examine a strategic relationship in which one

---

[12] It is interesting to observe that throughout the regions of Forms II and III NLRE, the overall or unconditional probability that Defender will respond to a challenge always equals c_1, regardless of Defender's credibility. This "pooling" phenomenon means that, if a Form II NLRE is in play and Defender resists, or if a Form III NLRE is in play and Defender does not resist, Challenger obtains no information about Defender's type by observing its behavioral tendencies. In fact, this observation is a logical consequence of a Soft Challenger's willingness to select randomly between initiating and not initiating.

player adopts an all-or-nothing deployment policy, like the Russians in the 1990s, the British in 1914, the French in 1939, and the United States in 1954. The model centers on a Challenger who must decide whether to contest the *Status Quo* and a Defender with three distinct ways to respond to a challenge. Moreover, Defender prefers both capitulation and escalation to responding-in-kind, entering an engagement on Challenger's terms. This assumption, we believe, captures an extended deterrence defense posture that relies on a threat of escalation to deter aggression.

The dynamics of this all-or-nothing variant of the Asymmetric Escalation Game differ sharply from the complete information case (see table 6.2, games 5–8). With complete information, the outcome of a two-level escalation game in which Defender's first-stage threat lacks credibility depends only on Challenger's type. When Challenger is Soft, the *Status Quo* is stable and escalation never occurs; when Challenger is Hard, a crisis equilibrium is implied in which Challenger initiates and Defender capitulates. As is the case with all two-stage escalation games of complete information, neither escalation nor war is a rational possibility.

But with incomplete information, these statements have significant exceptions. Except under the Challenger-Soft Deterrence Equilibrium, which requires beliefs that are sometimes implausible, the only possibility of a stable *Status Quo* is accompanied by a significant risk of unwanted conflict. As in complete information games, a Hard Challenger, ready and willing to wage *All-Out Conflict*, always initiates. But under incomplete information even Soft Challengers may rationally precipitate a crisis. In fact, there are situations in which Soft Challengers initiate with certainty, and others in which Soft Challengers initiate probabilistically. More significantly, not only may escalation be rational when information is incomplete, but there are conditions when it is inevitable. *All-Out Conflict* becomes a distinct possibility when credibilities are uncertain.

Overall, the strategic position of a Defender without a credible tactical-level threat is hardly enviable. While Defender's prospects usually get better as its strategic threat becomes more and more credible, *even perfect end-game credibility may be insufficient to deter a determined Challenger* from attacking a third party. In a sense, Defender's best chance comes when Challenger itself is unable to project high credibility. This makes conflict less and less likely, though the risk of a premeditated confrontation never evaporates altogether.

Applying the model to the actual relationship of the superpowers during the 1950s provides an occasion for speculation about the underlying dynamic of that period. Assuming that the model is sufficiently representative to permit both descriptive and normative evaluations, one might begin by asking why the 1950s, characterized by such intense rivalry, never erupted into all-out thermonuclear war. The model provides no obvious answer. The most one can say for sure about the absence of a superpower war during this period is that, luckily, no Defender ever defied a Hard Challenger. For had this been the case, war would have occurred for certain. Thus crises during this period may have been initiated either by Challengers unwilling to wage all-out war, or by Hard Challengers against irresolute Defenders. Another possibility is that a Defender with an aversion to conflict may have faced down a Soft Challenger. Given the possibilities, it is likely not a coincidence that the conventional wisdom of the time characterized international crises as "competitions in risk-taking." In fact, risk-taking behavior is very much consistent with the spirit of our results, especially with a Form II No-Limited-Response Equilibrium.

One additional possibility is that, between crises, a Challenger-Soft Deterrence Equilibrium was in play. As mentioned, this equilibrium provides the most plausible explanation of the European peace during the 1950s. After all, the United States was clearly the superior military and economic power; it had twice demonstrated its willingness to wage an all-out war to protect its interests on the continent; and the Soviet Union had not as yet fully digested the spoils of World War II. Stalin's ambitions notwithstanding, the Soviet Union was very likely unwilling to wage war at this time against a superior opponent. Eisenhower's and Dulles's penchant for brinkmanship lends additional credence to this explanation.

This does not mean that we endorse Massive Retaliation. All-or-nothing defense postures remain fraught with danger. The Challenger-Soft Deterrence Equilibrium always coexists with one other, less sanguine equilibrium; so the apparent success of the Eisenhower administration's defense policy should not be misread or exaggerated (Huth and Russett, 1988: 38). There are obviously other ways to play this game. Even presuming success, there is no guarantee that similar policies will redound similarly. They certainly did not in 1914 and 1939.

On the other hand, our model does permit somewhat more detailed speculation about the context in which crises occur. Taking the issues at stake as constant, it seems reasonable to conclude that the credibility of the US extended deterrent threat was at its zenith in 1954, and in steady decline thereafter as Soviet capability grew, as a "bomber gap" and then a "missile gap" was thought to exist, and as Soviet space satellites were launched. Conversely, Soviet credibility was most likely lowest at the time of Dulles's address to the Council on Foreign Relations in 1954, increasing more-or-less steadily after that. If so, our model suggests that the most serious crises should occur toward the end of the period. As might be expected, the most intense US–Soviet crises during the Eisenhower administration centered around Berlin from 1958 to 1961.

Similarly, if credibility is considered to vary across issues, the model suggests that confrontations are least likely as issues become less salient to one side or the other. This observation is confirmed by even a cursory examination of the period. For instance, when the status quo was contested in Hungary in 1956, only token resistance was offered. From NATO's point of view, Berlin was worth defending. But Hungary clearly was not.

The Asymmetric Escalation Game model may be applicable to a number of evolving interstate relationships. One interesting case could involve a nuclear Germany with revanchist aspirations pitted against Russia defending a part of its formerly vast empire with its still considerable nuclear arsenal, but without the huge land army that so frightened Eisenhower and Dulles. Likewise, the relationship of China and Russia might also evolve in ways that match the conditions of the present model. Or one of the states of eastern Europe, or a former republic of the Soviet Union, could decide to retain or develop a nuclear force to deter possible expansionist ambitions of Germany or Russia. Eventually, Israel's strategic relationship with its more numerous Arab neighbors may come to resemble the US–USSR relationship during the 1950s. In the long run, perhaps Taiwan or Pakistan will have only an escalatory, all-or-nothing, response as a defense against invasion.

If the past is prologue and the model is a reasonable description of two-level asymmetric deterrence relationships, then events should unfold in roughly the same way again. In areas of high salience and, by implication, high credibility to a challenger, but of low importance to a defender (East Prussia or Damansky Island?), a challenger may successfully confront an uninterested defender. But in areas of more marginal importance to both sides, crises can be expected to erupt, and even escalate, as challengers or defenders, or both, take risks. And all-out conflict becomes a distinct possibility once the dice are tossed – even when Defender prefers not to fight.

From the perspective of our model, therefore, the break-up of the Soviet Union appears to have opened up possibilities for more frequent interstate crises, some of which may result in war. But contrary to the assessments of some strategic analysts (e.g., Mearsheimer, 1990), the model also suggests that a Germany (or more obviously, a Serbia) with a significant nuclear capability could actually make things worse. Nuclear weapons are no panacea. To the extent that they enhance threat capability, nuclear weapons are stabilizing. But to the extent that they undermine a defender's credibility, nuclear weapons will undermine the viability of extended deterrence.

Can this dangerous world be avoided? Can threats be fashioned in a way so as to reduce conflict possibilities? Can forces be more effectively deployed so as to eliminate the stark consequences associated with all-or-nothing postures? We continue to address these and related questions in the next two chapters.

8   Modeling Flexible Response

War is a mere continuation of policy by other means.

Carl von Clausewitz

Even a cursory examination of typical behavior patterns under an all-or-nothing defense posture reveals the weakness of a policy that forgoes a tactical-level threat. The only remotely plausible deterrence equilibrium associated with all-or-nothing deployments requires that Challenger be Soft and likely unwilling to wage a high-level conflict. This, however, is the easier case. Relying exclusively on a threat to escalate is insufficient to deter Challenger when Challenger is likely Hard and, therefore, likely to respond, tit-for-tat, to any escalation.[1]

It is no wonder, then, that the Eisenhower administration's deployment policy came under intense criticism among defense analysts almost as soon as it was announced. Critics asserted, prematurely it now appears (Gaddis, 1997), that the threat of Massive Retaliation lacked credibility (Kaufmann, 1956). And they claimed that the New Look, by stressing "more bang for the buck," placed undue reliance on strategic weapons to deter Soviet aggression in Europe and elsewhere, leaving little room for maneuver during periods of acute crisis. To avoid the stark choice of either all-out nuclear war or capitulation, they proposed that United States conventional forces be strengthened, and augmented with an arsenal of tactical nuclear weapons (Kissinger, 1957b).

When the Democrats came to power in 1961, these changes were pursued under a policy labeled *Flexible Response*. In 1967, after

[1] This chapter is based on Zagare and Kilgour (1995).

219

extensive debate and compromise, NATO formally adopted Flexible
Response (Stromseth, 1988). Today, even as it expands eastward to
include former members of the Warsaw Pact, NATO continues to
maintain both a tactical and a strategic capability.

All of which is not to suggest that Flexible Response is a well-
articulated policy. In fact, Daalder (1991: 2) argues that ever since the
early 1960s, NATO deployments have been "deliberately ambiguous"
in order to mask "differences among the allies concerning the role and
relative weight to be accorded to theater nuclear forces in support of
[its extended deterrence] strategy." Consequently, a number of competing defense postures exist, all of which claim consistency with
NATO's loosely articulated declaratory policy. Daalder (1991: 42)
describes four extended deterrence strategies (figure 8.1), but goes on
to warn that even they do not exhaust the set of logical possibilities. A
No-First-Use posture, for instance, does not fit neatly into Daalder's
typology.

In this chapter, we model the strategic relationship implied when a
state tries to safeguard the status quo by adopting a deployment
policy – such as Flexible Response – that permits a range of credible
responses to a probe or challenge. We contrast this relationship with
the consequences of all-or-nothing deployments that rely on strategic
weapons and the restricted set of response options associated with
them. Our analysis of this model allows us to provide a new and
explicit evaluation of several rival Flexible Response doctrines –
including those specified in figure 8.1 – and to ask when and how
sub-strategic deployments make limited war possible and total war
less likely. In the next chapter, we gauge the policy implications of
various "mixes" of tactical and strategic threats. For now, however,
we focus on the ideal case in which Defender's sub-strategic threat is
perfectly credible.

One might object that the demise of the Warsaw Pact, the dis-
integration of the Soviet Union, and the consequent expansion of
NATO itself has rendered our model and our investigation a historical
curiosity. We think not. As has been the case throughout this work, no
special assumption is made that limits our conclusions to nuclear
situations, nor is any restriction placed on player preferences that
confine the empirical domain to Europe. Thus our modeling effort
pertains to any situation, interstate or otherwise, in which the players
believe that certain response options are qualitatively different from

Probability of attack

	Low (Risk-averse)	High (Risk-prone)
High (Uncontrollable)	Pure Deterrence posture	Conventional Deterrence posture
Low (Controllable)	Decisive (Escalatory) Deployment posture	Warfighting Deployment posture

Probability of escalation

Fig. 8.1. Extended-deterrence deployment strategies within the strategic concept of Flexible Response. (*Source*: adapted from Daalder, 1991: 41.)

others, and that the choice of such options involves a serious escalation of the conflict.

8.1   Modeling Flexible Response: assumptions

To explore the strategic relationships implied by a Flexible Response deployment policy, we return to the *Asymmetric Escalation Game*, reproduced here with some minor modifications and additional notation as figure 8.2. In this model, Challenger can defect initially by precipitating a crisis, by launching a limited military attack, or by taking some aggressive action other than a direct strategic assault. It is precisely this broad range of sub-strategic challenges that Flexible Response options are designed to prevent.

As before, Defender's proactive response options are either to respond-in-kind or escalate.[2] We assume that a response-in-kind is commensurate with Challenger's initiation decision. Thus, at node 2, Defender may either match, in scope and intensity, the actions taken by Challenger to contest the *Status Quo*, or may "overreact" by choosing an unconstrained action, such as one associated with all-out war, which we represent by the escalation alternative (*E*). Like

---

[2] Of course, Defender can always concede.

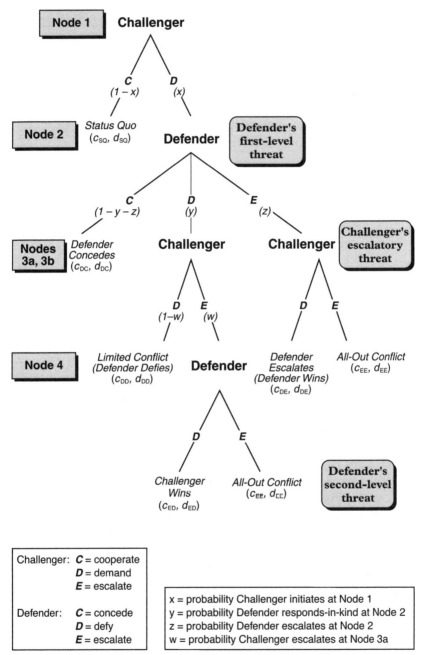

Fig. 8.2. Asymmetric Escalation Game under Flexible Response.

NATO's description and implementation of its Flexible Response declaratory policy, then, the Asymmetric Escalation Game model is "deliberately ambiguous" about the nature of Defender's response options.

One of our simplifying assumptions produces a bias that deserves special comment. As Wagner correctly points out,[3] we assume that the payoffs from *All-Out Conflict* (outcome EE) are the same no matter which player is the first to escalate. We accept the point that, in the real world, players are likely to prefer escalating first. Nonetheless, we stick with this assumption to gain mathematical tractability. Note its implications: Defender's expected payoffs at node 2 when it chooses E may be underrepresented (because Defender may prefer the mutual escalation outcome associated with this choice to the mutual escalation outcome associated with the choice of D); it follows that its expected payoff from choosing D at node 2 is overrepresented. The bias of the model, therefore, is toward *over*reporting the expected benefits of equilibria that involve the possibility that Defender responds-in-kind to a challenge. We show below, however, that even with this bias, the conditions under which such equilibria exist are quite restricted.

In exploring the strategic implications of various Flexible Response deployment policies, we continue to postulate players with incomplete information about each other's preferences between backing down after an escalatory choice or counter-escalating. We retain all previous preference assumptions except that we now assume that Defender is known to prefer *Limited Conflict* to *Defender Concedes*.[4] This distinguishing assumption is consistent with the stated rationale of Flexible Response: to provide a defender with a credible sub-strategic response to a challenge.[5] Or as Helmut Schmidt (1962: 211) put it in his argument for a strong conventional defense capability in Europe: "NATO must ... have troops and weapons on a scale ample to make non-nuclear aggression appear hopeless, and sufficient in an emergency to force

---

[3] Personal communication, April 24, 1992.

[4] Given this assumption and complete information, deterrence succeeds (1) if Challenger is Soft or (2) if Defender's second-level threat is credible. Conversely, for deterrence to fail, Challenger must be Hard and Defender's second-level threat must lack credibility. See table 6.2, Games 1–4 for details.

[5] Recall that we argued in chapter 7 that the opposite assumption is characteristic of all-or-nothing deployment policies. For the public justification of Flexible Response, see McNamara (1962).

one of two courses on the aggressor – to halt or to extend the conflict." It is precisely this choice that Challenger faces at node 3a.

Finally, we continue to assume that Defender prefers to escalate (i.e., prefers *Defender Escalates* [*Wins*] to *Limited Conflict* and, therefore, to *Defender Concedes*), *provided that Challenger does not respond by also choosing E*. To be sure, this is a strong assumption. We make it because it is an implicit premise in both Massive Retaliation and Flexible Response deployment policies: under Massive Retaliation, it is plainly required; likewise, Flexible Response presents no genuine choice of responses without it. As well, we would like to explore those situations in which the incentive to escalate is strongest. Under Flexible Response, the critical question is which response option Defender would choose in light of Challenger's capability to counter-escalate. We consider this question below.

Taken together, these assumptions restrict the players' utilities as follows:

Challenger: *Defender Concedes* $>_{Ch}$ *Status Quo* $>_{Ch}$
              Challenger Wins $>_{Ch}$ *Limited Conflict* $>_{Ch}$
              [*Defender Escalates, All-Out Conflict*]   (8.1)
Defender: *Status Quo* $>_{Def}$ *Defender Escalates* $>_{Def}$
              Limited Conflict $>_{Def}$ *Defender Concedes* $>_{Def}$
              [*Challenger Wins, All-Out Conflict*].   (8.2)

All previous restrictions and provisos apply as well.

8.2   Perfect Bayesian equilibria under Flexible Response

What are the effects of uncertainty on the escalation process when Defender's threat to respond-in-kind is inherently credible? What is the connection between the players' credibilities and stability of the status quo when a defender adopts a Flexible Response deployment policy? How credible must each player's end-game threat be to deter escalation or retaliation? Under what conditions might a sub-strategic war be waged? These are some of the specific questions we address now.

To answer them within the context of the Asymmetric Escalation Game, we begin by using backward induction to analyze Defender's choice at the last node (4). Node 4 is reached when Challenger upsets the *Status Quo* by choosing *D*, Defender responds-in-kind by also choosing *D*, and Challenger then escalates by choosing *E*. Defender's choice at node 4 is easy to analyze since Defender has complete information about its own preference between *Challenger Wins* and *All-Out Conflict*. A Hard Defender, preferring *All-Out Conflict*, always escalates, while a Soft Defender, preferring *Challenger Wins*, never does.

The same is true of Challenger's choice at node 3b, which is reached after Challenger selects *D* and Defender escalates instead of conceding or responding-in-kind. If Challenger is Hard and prefers *All-Out Conflict* to *Defender Escalates*, it always counter-escalates; if it is Soft, and prefers *Defender Escalates*, it always yields.

It follows that at any perfect Bayesian equilibrium, Challenger's and Defender's choices at nodes 3b and 4 are strictly determined by their types. Therefore, the only strategic decisions that require analysis are Challenger's choice of *C* or *D* at node 1, Challenger's choice of *D* or *E* at node 3a, and Defender's choice of *C*, *D*, or *E* at node 2. Unlike the decisions at nodes 3b and 4, the decisions at these nodes can depend on the decision-maker's beliefs about its opponent. Extending the previous notation to include the possibilities that Defender can now rationally respond-in-kind at node 2, and that Challenger can now rationally escalate at node 3a, we denote the probabilities of these choices as follows:

x_H = probability that a Hard Challenger initiates at node 1
x_S = probability that a Soft Challenger initiates at node 1
w_H = probability that a Hard Challenger escalates at node 3a
w_S = probability that a Soft Challenger escalates at node 3a
y_H = probability that a Hard Defender responds-in-kind at node 2
y_S = probability that a Soft Defender responds-in-kind at node 2
z_H = probability that a Hard Defender escalates at node 2
z_S = probability that a Soft Defender escalates at node 2.

Note that when Defender has a known preference for *Limited Conflict* over *Defender Concedes* (i.e., when its tactical-level threat is perfectly credible), its choice of *D* at node 2 cannot be automatically excluded, as it can be when Defender relies exclusively on an all-or-nothing escalatory threat (see chapter 7). The possibility that Defender might choose to respond-in-kind carries with it the occasion for Challenger to update its beliefs about Defender's type based on its observation of Defender's behavior during play of the game. For this reason, a perfect Bayesian equilibrium of the current variant of the

Asymmetric Escalation Game specifies *two* belief variables: in addition to Defender's updated probability (r) that Challenger is Hard given that Challenger demands a change in the *Status Quo* (i.e., chooses D at node 1), now a perfect Bayesian equilibrium must also specify Challenger's conditional probability (q) that Defender is Hard, given that Defender chooses D at node 2. Thus, when Defender adopts a limited-war deployment policy like Flexible Response, a perfect Bayesian equilibrium is a 10-tuple of probabilities [x_H, x_S, w_H, w_S, q; y_H, y_S, z_H, z_S, r].

Clearly the description of a perfect Bayesian equilibrium of the Asymmetric Escalation Game under limited-war deployments is considerably more complex than under an all-or-nothing stance: ten rather than five variables are involved.[6] The complexity reflects both the additional choices that become available when Defender adopts a limited-war deployment policy, and the new information about Challenger's type that Defender might acquire during play of the game.

Table 8.1 summarizes the action choices of each perfect Bayesian equilibrium of the Asymmetric Escalation Game when Defender has a completely credible first-level threat. A formal discussion with additional technical details, including restrictions on the belief variables r and q, is given in appendix 7. Table 8.2 provides an informal summary, lists the particular Flexible Response deployment posture we associate with each equilibrium form, and outlines our rationale for making the association.

For expository purposes, the equilibria are grouped into three major categories: *Escalatory Deterrence Equilibria*, *All-or-Nothing Equilibria*, and *Flexible Response Equilibria*. With the exception of one particular Escalatory Deterrence Equilibrium, equilibria of the first two categories are closely related to those equilibrium forms that exist when Defender's first-level threat lacks credibility (see chapter 7). For this reason, we discuss them briefly, highlighting only what is distinct and important. By contrast, the Flexible Response family of four equilibria is entirely new. Hence, we discuss that group in more detail.

---

[6] The description is even more complex in chapter 9 when *all* constraints are lifted on Defender's preference between *Limited Conflict* and *Defender Concedes*. As well, other equilibrium forms, and hence, other behavior patterns, become possible.

Table 8.1. *Perfect Bayesian equilibria of the Asymmetric Escalation Game when Defender's first-level threat is completely credible*

Equilibrium	Strategic Variables							
	Challenger initiates		Challenger escalates		Defender responds-in-kind		Defender escalates	
	x_H	x_S	w_H	w_S	y_H	y_S	z_H	z_S
Escalatory Deterrence Equilibria	0	0	—	—	—	—	—	—
All-or-Nothing Equilibria								
No-Response Equilibrium	1	1	—	—	0	0	0	0
Form I No-Limited-Response Equilibrium	1	1	—	—	0	0	1	0
Form II No-Limited-Response Equilibrium	1	•	—	—	0	0	1	•
Form III No-Limited-Response Equilibrium	1	•	—	—	0	0	•	0
Flexible Response Equilibria								
Form I Limited-Response Deterrence Equilibrium	0	0	0	0	1	1	0	0
Form II Limited-Response Deterrence Equilibrium	0	0	•	0	1	•	0	0
No-First-Use ELRE$_1$	1	1	•	0	1	•	0	0
Warfighting ELRE$_2$	1	•	•	0	•	•	•	0

Key: "•" = fixed value between 0 and 1
"–" = value not fixed although some restrictions may apply
ELRE = Escalatory Limited-Response Equilibrium.

8.2.1 Escalatory Deterrence Equilibria

The defining property of any deterrence equilibrium is that Challenger – whether Hard or Soft – never defects (i.e., $x_H = x_S = 0$), i.e., the *Status Quo* is never disturbed. What distinguishes an *Escalatory Deterrence Equilibrium* (EDE) from other deterrence equilibria is

Table 8.2. *Perfect Bayesian equilibria and associated deployment policies*

Equilibrium	Defining characteristics	Deployment policy	Rationale for association
Escalatory Deterrence Equilibrium EDE_1	Ubiquitous; based on implausible beliefs	Pure (Existential) Deterrence	Does not depend on Challenger's or Defender's *initial* beliefs; Challenger and Defender intend to escalate with certainty
Escalatory Deterrence Equilibrium EDE_2	Based on implausible beliefs	Warfighting Deterrence	Existence requires credible tactical-level threat; cannot be sustained existentially; Defender always intends to respond, either in-kind or by escalating
All-or-Nothing Family	Challenger generally initiates	Decisive (Escalatory) Deterrence	Existence does *not* require credible tactical-level threat; Defender either escalates or does not respond at all
Limited-Response Deterrence Equilibria	Challenger never initiates	No-First-Use	Existence requires credible tactical-level threat; Defender never intends to escalate first
No-First-Use $ELRE_1$	Challenger always initiates, and sometimes intends to escalate first	No-First-Use	Existence requires credible tactical-level threat; Defender never escalates first
Warfighting $ELRE_2$	Challenger generally initiates, and sometimes intends to escalate first	Warfighting Deterrence	Existence requires credible tactical-level threat; Defender makes use of entire range of response options

Defender's intention to escalate first should Challenger demand a change in the *Status Quo*. Under any Escalatory Deterrence Equilibrium, either z_H or z_S, or both, is *always* positive. By contrast, under a *Limited-Response Deterrence Equilibrium* (see below), Defender *never* intends to escalate first.

There are a number of Escalatory Deterrence Equilibria in the Asymmetric Escalation Game when Defender's first-level threat is completely credible. Because some Escalatory Deterrence Equilibria do not depend on Challenger's or Defender's *initial* beliefs about the other's type, at least one EDE can always exist. All but one Escalatory Deterrence Equilibrium rest *solely* on Defender's intention to escalate first (at node 2).

An important fact about Escalatory Deterrence Equilibria is that every EDE requires that Defender's updated belief that Challenger is Hard, given that Challenger initiates (i.e., r), be small.[7] In other words, for an Escalatory Deterrence Equilibrium to exist, Defender must believe that any Challenger who initiates is likely to be Soft and, hence, is unlikely to counter-escalate at node 3b. It is precisely this belief that supports Defender's intention to escalate at node 2 with sufficiently high probability to dissuade Challenger from initiating at node 1. For the very reasons noted in the discussion of the Challenger-Soft Deterrence Equilibrium (a close relative of the EDE family) in chapter 7, we find this belief to be implausible, especially when Defender initially believes Challenger to be likely Hard: *ceteris paribus*, Challengers who initiate are more likely to be Hard.

There is one form of Escalatory Deterrence Equilibrium that is ubiquitous. This form is completely independent of any *initial* beliefs that either Challenger or Defender might have about the other's type. In consequence, some might consider it difficult to justify. The irrelevance of initial beliefs, coupled with the player's implied action choices, leads us to link this particular Escalatory Deterrence Equilibria (called EDE_1 here and in appendix 7) with the Flexible Response deployment strategy that Daalder (1991: 43–48) labels *Pure Deterrence*.[8]

A Pure Deterrence policy does not require any specific deployment

---

[7] Since Challenger never initiates under any Escalatory Deterrence Equilibrium, these are beliefs "off the equilibrium path," that is, they are beliefs about events that never occur.

[8] EDE_1 is defined by the vector $[x_H, x_S, w_H, w_S, q; y_H, y_S, z_H, z_S, r] = [0, 0, 1, 1, q; 0, 0, 1, 1, r]$ (for details, see appendix 7). This configuration is a perfect Bayesian equilibrium provided that r is low enough, and q is high enough. EDE_1 exists independently of

strategy and, indeed, is inconsistent with the very notion of Flexible Response as it is commonly understood.[9] Pure Deterrence theorists (like Eisenhower) deny the existence of clear thresholds in war. In this view, any overt conflict makes immediate escalation to the highest rung of the ladder almost inevitable (i.e., w_H, w_S, z_H, and z_S are high). It is precisely the inevitability and immediacy of escalation that deters any challenger. Consequently, any effort to calibrate conventional and tactical deterrents is futile.

Pure Deterrence is one of two Flexible Response deployment policies Daalder (1991) associates with *existential deterrence*. Bundy (1983) describes this more general conception of how deterrence operates as the view that the very existence of nuclear weapons, coupled with the enormous fear that they almost surely instill in decision-makers, virtually assures a stable international system.[10] The existence of an Escalatory Deterrence Equilibrium that so closely resembles the Pure Deterrence point of view verifies the connection between the premise and the conclusion of those existential deterrence theorists who view the post-war world order as unusually stable and robust; it does not, however, verify the premise.[11] Nevertheless, the model indicates that, provided relevant decision-makers somehow acquire the set of beliefs required for this equilibrium form, an unconditionally stable deterrence relationship is possible. In fact, Challenger's belief that escalation is almost inevitable if it initiates a conflict leads to an especially benevolent self-fulfilling prophecy.

The other Flexible Response deployment stance Daalder connects with existential deterrence is *Conventional Deterrence*. Advocates of a Conventional Deterrence deployment aim to eliminate the unwanted consequences of the "stability–instability paradox," namely the

both Challenger's and Defender's initial credibilities (i.e., p_{Ch} and p_{Def}). Under EDE_1 Challenger never initiates and Defender *always* intends to escalate first at node 2.

[9] As noted in the text, Daalder (1991) argues that the formal definition of Flexible Response is intentionally vague, in part to accommodate divergent viewpoints of how deterrence operates and how forces should be structured. This is the only sense in which Pure Deterrence is compatible with Flexible Response.

[10] Some have argued that even the existence of "the *idea* of nuclear weapons – more specifically, the ability of many states to make them – is enough to create an existential deterrent effect against large-scale conflicts of all kinds" (National Academy of Sciences, 1997: 4, emphasis added).

[11] In other words, it seems reasonable (to us at least) to conclude that a Challenger expecting a highly probable escalatory response, *regardless of circumstances*, will choose not to initiate. But the ungrounded beliefs that give rise to Defender's action choices under EDE_1 are sometimes far from plausible.

increased potential for sub-strategic conflict implied by a strategic stalemate (see chapter 6 for a discussion). In this view, when strategic forces are balanced and, hence, mutually deterred (e.g., when w_H and w_S, and z_H and z_S, are low), they are unavailable for deterring lower-level conflicts. Thus, advocates of Conventional Deterrence hold that

> deterrence is enhanced by the prospects of a conventional defense capable of denying the adversary the achievement of his objectives. The conventional strategy therefore emphasizes a conventional response to attack in the hope that nuclear escalation can be avoided. Extended deterrence persists, however, by deploying some nuclear weapons in Europe to pose the existential risk that war could escalate to all-out nuclear war, thus coupling the stability of the mutual US–Soviet deterrence relationship to Europe (Daalder, 1991: 52–53).

There is no perfect Bayesian equilibrium that corresponds to this defense posture in our model.[12] There is, however, one form of Escalatory Deterrence Equilibrium (EDE$_2$ here and in appendix 7) that, like the Conventional Deterrence deployment strategy, involves a response-in-kind.[13] This (partial) reliance on a sub-strategic response at node 2 leads us to link this form of Escalatory Deterrence Equilibrium with the strategic doctrine Daalder (1991: 58–63) calls *Warfighting Deterrence*.[14]

Like Conventional Deterrence, Warfighting Deterrence does not deny the need for a potent strategic capability, but rather stresses the need for a *range* of local options, including escalatory options, to deter

---

[12] Our model may be too simple, or our assumptions too restrictive, to reflect the subtleties of a Conventional Deterrence posture.

[13] In particular, provided that Defender's initial credibility is high enough (i.e., $p_{Def} > c_q$), there is a perfect Bayesian equilibrium with $[x_H, x_S, w_H, w_S, q; y_H, y_S, z_H, z_S, r] = [0, 0, w_H, 0, c_q; y_H, 1, z_H, 0, r]$, where $0 < w_H < 1$, $0 < y_H < 1$, and $y_H + z_H = 1$ (for further details, see appendix 7). In words, Challenger never initiates (this is a Deterrence Equilibrium), but if Challenger were to initiate, a Hard Defender would either respond-in-kind or escalate first, and a Soft Defender would always respond-in-kind. After a response-in-kind, a Hard Challenger would sometimes escalate, sometimes not; a Soft Challenger would never escalate. Parenthetically, we add that this is the only Escalatory Deterrence Equilibrium for which there is positive probability that Defender will respond-in-kind at node 2.

[14] In addition to EDE$_2$, there is another equilibrium form (to be discussed below) that is consistent with a Warfighting deployment stance. It is not, however, a deterrence equilibrium.

aggression.[15] A warfighting capability, then, does not rely solely on an initial sub-strategic response, as does No-First-Use (see below), or strictly on an escalatory response, as does a Decisive Deployment policy (also see below), or on an existential link between beliefs and certain action choices, as do Pure and Conventional Deterrence policies; rather this deployment policy depends on a willingness to respond at *both* the sub-strategic and the strategic levels.

The key to Warfighting Deterrence, then, is escalation dominance, coupled with the ability to deny an adversary an advantage at every level of attack. According to Daalder (1991: 63), the strategy "relies on NATO's ability to dominate the escalation process up to the highest level of violence." Thus, Warfighting Deterrence seeks to avoid war by denying an adversary an advantage at any level of outright conflict, *even if it means escalating first.*

All of which is not to suggest that we view EDE_2 as a likely outcome of the Asymmetric Escalation Game. EDE_2 is implausible in the same way that all Escalatory Deterrence Equilibria are implausible: they place an upper bound on r, Defender's updated belief that Challenger is Hard given that Challenger has initiated. In other words, all Escalatory Deterrence Equilibria require that Defender presumes that a Challenger who initiated conflict, even one whose initial credibility was high, is very likely to be bluffing.

8.2.2   All-or-Nothing Equilibria

The *All-or-Nothing* family is comprised of variations on the four non-deterrence equilibria that arise under escalatory defense postures like Massive Retaliation: the *No-Response Equilibrium* (*NRE*) and three *No-Limited-Response Equilibria* (*NLRE*). Their overall strategic characteristics have already been discussed in detail in chapter 7. Other than the specification of a few additional action choices (see table 8.1 and appendix 7 for details), these equilibria are essentially unchanged in the Flexible Response model. Under a No-Response Equilibrium,

---

[15] Both Conventional Deterrence and Warfighting Deterrence postures require a range of response options, although, as its name implies, under a Conventional Deterrence deployment, there is a strong bias toward responding-in-kind to a challenge. By contrast, under EDE_2, there are conditions under which an escalatory response is favored. But the primary reason we associate EDE_2 with a Warfighting as opposed to a Conventional Deterrence posture is the minimum condition on Defender's *a priori* credibility (p_{Def}) required under EDE_2 – see appendix 7 and footnote 13 for details. In other words, EDE_2 cannot be sustained existentially; a sufficiently credible threat to counter-escalate at node 4 is required.

Challenger always defects at node 1 and Defender always concedes at node 2. And under any No-Limited-Response Equilibrium, Hard Challengers always initiate conflict and Soft Challengers always or sometimes initiate. Defender never responds-in-kind, but either always or sometimes escalates at node 2. As well, the existence conditions and threshold values (c_1, d_1, and d_2) separating the equilibrium regions from one another are identical to those discussed in chapter 7 and illustrated in figure 7.2. Hence, we shall not discuss these details further.

As a group, the All-or-Nothing Equilibria summarize the rational strategic consequences of the deployment stance that Daalder (1991: 53–58) terms *Escalatory Deterrence*, but which we shall refer to as *Decisive Deployment* in order to avoid unnecessary confusion between this deployment *policy* and Escalatory Deterrence *equilibria*. We have chosen this substitute label to reflect the policy's roots in Jomini's work as well as the deeply held belief of all-or-nothing advocates that military force should be used decisively – or not at all.

Proponents of Decisive Deployment hold that it is the threat of *deliberate* escalation, rather than any denial capability associated with the deployment of a potent conventional force, that is the most efficacious way of deterring aggression. According to Daalder (1991: 58), the Decisive Deployment approach, "in recognizing the reality of certain thresholds in war, seeks to deter by posing the threat of unacceptable damage through the potential use of nuclear escalation. It thus extends the deterrent threat provided by mutual assured destruction to Europe by threatening to enlarge a conflict in Europe to general nuclear war."

Like a Pure Deterrence deployment policy, then, a Decisive Deployment relies on an opponent's fear of escalation to deter aggression. Advocates of Pure Deterrence contend that this fear is inherent in any contentious nuclear relationship. Thus, deterrence in Europe can be enhanced simply by coupling European security with American security. In this view, nuclear weapons should be deployed in a way that "ensures that escalation to general nuclear war is inherent in the very use of nuclear weapons" (Daalder, 1991: 46). By contrast, proponents of a Decisive Deployment recommend a more deliberate response to a challenge. Specifically, they counsel the de-emphasis of a conventional response and the early, if not the first, use of nuclear weapons in a confrontation.

The reason we associate the No-Response Equilibrium and the three

No-Limited-Response Equilibria with a Decisive Deployment policy is that *none* of these equilibria requires that Defender's threat to respond-in-kind be credible. In other words, they can also exist even when Defender's first-level threat lacks credibility. Moreover, unlike the Escalatory Deterrence Equilibrium EDE_1, which we link to Pure Deterrence, each member of the All-or-Nothing family *does* depend on the *a priori* credibility of each player's strategic-level threat.[16]

8.2.3 Flexible Response Equilibria

The All-or-Nothing Equilibria share one important characteristic: they do not admit the possibility of Defender responding-in-kind to a challenge (i.e., $y_H + y_S = 0$). This means that, after initiation, Defender either escalates or does not respond at all. Clearly, when any member of the All-or-Nothing family is in play, limited conflict – associated with the choice of D by both players – is rationally precluded.

We know from chapter 7 that the four All-or-Nothing Equilibria, and a few implausible Escalatory Deterrence Equilibria, are the only possible perfect Bayesian equilibria when Defender's first-stage threat is known to lack credibility. But now we are assuming the opposite: that Defender prefers *Limited Conflict* to *Defender Concedes*, and that this preference is known, making Defender's first-stage deterrent threat completely credible. Thus, along with a few additional forms of Escalatory Deterrence Equilibrium, the remaining equilibria of the Asymmetric Escalation Game arise strictly as a consequence of this critical assumption about Defender's credibility. These, the *Flexible Response Equilibria*, are precisely the additional behavioral alternatives that become actual possibilities once Defender's response options become unfettered.

Putting this differently, when Defender's only credible response is to escalate, sub-strategic conflict of any kind is not rationally possible. This is the reason we associate the No-Response Equilibrium and the three No-Limited-Response Equilibria with all-or-nothing deployments like Massive Retaliation. By contrast, the remaining perfect Bayesian equilibria of the Asymmetric Escalation Game with first-level credible threats admit *some* possibility of a non-escalatory

---

[16] As discussed, EDE_1 does not depend on any particular preference relationship. Rather it exists as long as the players have the required beliefs about each other's action choices, whatever their actual preferences happen to be, and however those beliefs are formed.

response by Defender; hence, the name of this family and its association with limited-war deployment stances.

It is important to stress, however, that for any Flexible Response Equilibrium to exist, Defender's threat to respond-in-kind must not be completely incredible, that is, Defender must not be known to prefer *Defender Concedes* to *Limited Conflict*. Since the opposite preference is precisely what Flexible Response deployments are designed to signal, our model allows us to assess the immediate strategic consequences of this alternative approach to extended deterrence. The existence conditions associated with the Flexible Response Equilibria are particularly interesting since they speak directly to the possibility of a constrained conflict or a limited war, and the viability of one additional extended deterrence deployment posture – No-First-Use.

There are four members of the Flexible Response group. Two are Limited-Response Deterrence Equilibria (LRDEs) and two are Escalatory Limited-Response Equilibria (ELREs).[17] We next discuss each sub-group in turn.

8.2.3.1 Limited-Response Deterrence Equilibria: general characteristics

Limited-Response Deterrence Equilibria (LRDE) are equilibria in which there is no possibility of a challenge (i.e., $x_H + x_S = 0$); however, if there were a challenge, there would be some possibility that Defender would respond-in-kind at node 2 (i.e., $y_H > 0$ or $y_S > 0$), but no possibility that Defender would escalate first (i.e., $z_H + z_S = 0$). As with all deterrence equilibria, therefore, the *Status Quo* is secure. The important point, however, is that under any Limited-Response Deterrence Equilibrium, deterrence success requires Defender to plan to respond to a challenge in a measured way, and only in a measured way. Such an intent is the distinguishing feature of this new genus of deterrence equilibrium.

---

[17] All four equilibria are part of a larger family termed the *Limited-Response Equilibria* (LRE). In addition to Limited-Response Deterrence Equilibria and Escalatory Limited-Response Equilibria, the limited-response family includes a collection of equilibria we call *Constrained Limited-Response Equilibria* (CLRE). No Constrained Limited-Response Equilibrium is a member of the Flexible Response family (see chapter 9). Both Constrained Limited-Response Equilibria and Escalatory Limited-Response Equilibria admit the possibility that Defender may respond-in-kind at node 2. They differ with respect to Challenger's typical choice at node 3a. As we explain in the next chapter, under a CLRE, Challenger never escalates first. Under an ELRE, Challenger typically escalates first.

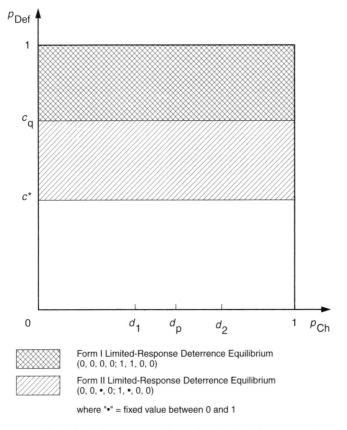

Fig. 8.3. Existence conditions for Limited-Response Deterrence
Equilibria.

This is not to say, though, that Defender's escalatory threat is
irrelevant. Indeed, both forms of Limited-Response Deterrence
Equilibria also require that Defender's strategic-level threat meet
certain credibility requirements. Figure 8.3, which locates the Limited-
Response Deterrence Equilibria in a credibility plane, shows that a
Form I LRDE exists only when Defender's escalatory threat is sufficiently credible. No Limited-Response Deterrence Equilibria can exist
when Defender's strategic-level threat is low. Form II LRDEs occur
between the two extremes.

Unlike the Escalatory Deterrence Equilibria, Limited-Response Deterrence Equilibria do not suffer from any plausibility problems. In

particular, there is no upper bound on Defender's updated belief that Challenger is Hard given that Challenger initiates. Thus, the Limited-Response Deterrence Equilibria are not so easily dismissed. They are viable alternatives under rational play.

8.2.3.2 Form I Limited-Response Deterrence Equilibria

Form I Limited-Response Deterrence Equilibria operate the way proponents of Flexible Response deployment policies might hope: Challenger *never* initiates or intends to escalate first, and Defender *always* intends to respond-in-kind. In fact, Defender's intention to always choose D at node 2 is the distinguishing feature of the Form I LRDE.

Form I Limited-Response Deterrence Equilibria require that Defender's updated belief that Challenger is Hard given that Challenger has initiated (i.e., r) be sufficiently large. It is precisely this (very plausible!) belief that deters Defender from escalating first. Similarly, Challenger's updated belief that Defender is Hard given that Defender responds-in-kind (i.e., q), must also be large for a Form I LRDE to exist. This belief, coupled with Defender's intention to respond-in-kind, supports Challenger's intention not to escalate first at node 3a.

Hard and Soft Defenders behave the same under a Form I Limited-Response Deterrence Equilibrium. Thus, should Challenger observe a response-in-kind, it will be unable to make any inference about Defender's type. This means that Challenger's initial belief about Defender's credibility (type), p_{Def}, and Challenger's updated belief about Defender's type given that Defender chooses D at node 2, q, will always be the same. The condition that $q = p_{Def}$ is unique to a Form I LRDE.

8.2.3.3 Form II Limited-Response Deterrence Equilibria

Form II Limited-Response Deterrence Equilibria occur when Defender's initial credibility is just insufficient to sustain a Form I LRDE (see figure 8.3). Since Defender is less likely to be Hard, it should not be surprising to learn that a Hard Challenger sometimes intends to escalate first (i.e., $0 < w_H < 1$). In turn, the tendency of Hard Challengers to escalate first leads Soft Defenders to compensate by sometimes intending to concede immediately (i.e., $0 < y_S + z_S < 1$). In the end, however, these intentions are never acted on. When a Form II LRDE is in play, Defender's credibility remains high enough to deter initiation completely.

In sum, the *Status Quo* is totally secure whenever either form of

Limited-Response Deterrence Equilibrium is in play. Under any LRDE, Defender's credibility is such that Challenger is generally unwilling to risk escalation. Deterrence works because Defender's concomitant commitment to respond-in-kind essentially removes the likelihood that Challenger would, on balance, gain by fomenting a crisis.

Precisely because Defender never intends to escalate first under any Limited-Response Deterrence Equilibrium, we associate this subgroup of equilibria with a *No-First-Use* declaratory policy. First proposed publicly by Robert McNamara in 1982, a No-First-Use deployment implies a commitment to a non-nuclear defense against a non-nuclear attack or, in terms of the model, a response-in-kind (Bundy *et al.*, 1982). Like a Conventional Deterrence policy, then, No-First-Use relies on a non-escalatory response to deter aggression. Still, there are significant differences between these two extended deterrence policy stances. One subtle difference was clarified in the debate about when NATO would use nuclear weapons. Advocates of Conventional Deterrence, such as former Secretary of Defense James Schlesinger, recommended that nuclear weapons be used "as late as possible" but "as early as necessary" (Daalder, 1991: 52). By contrast, under No-First-Use, nuclear weapons would be used *only* in response to a nuclear attack.

Another salient difference is rooted in the relationship between conventional and strategic options under No-First-Use. According to Daalder (1991: 50), "the assumption [of Conventional Deterrence advocates] that escalation cannot be controlled does provide a coupling mechanism, if only an existential one." By contrast, under a No-First-Use deployment, these response options are "de-coupled." Thus, proponents of No-First-Use suggest a sufficiently capable conventional defense to deny an adversary victory in a limited, non-nuclear war. In their view, the European context provided no role for tactical nuclear weapons; indeed, one of the benefits of a No-First-Use deployment policy was that NATO need deploy only survivable, second-strike nuclear weapons. Or as Stromseth (1988: 202) put it, should this policy be implemented, "the ultimate reliance on nuclear weapons to shore up a failing conventional defense would be eliminated, and conventional forces would no longer function as a 'delayed trip-wire' for nuclear war."

8.2.3.4 Escalatory Limited-Response Equilibria: general characteristics

In addition to the Limited-Response Deterrence Equilibria, the Flexible Response family includes two forms of *Escalatory Limited-Response Equilibria* (ELRE). At any Escalatory Limited-Response Equilibrium, there is some possibility of a challenge *and* of a non-escalatory response (i.e., $x_H + x_S > 0$ and $y_H + y_S > 0$). In consequence, there is always a chance of *Limited Conflict*. This small but genuine possibility, however, does not rule out higher levels of conflict – either unilateral escalation or all-out war. As well, it is possible for the *Status Quo* to survive rational play under an ELRE. Unfortunately, this chance is rather remote.

Interestingly, certain probing and bluffing activity is less likely at an Escalatory Limited-Response Equilibrium than elsewhere. To be sure, Soft Challengers may rationally initiate conflict, and Soft Defenders may rationally respond-in-kind to a challenge. Nevertheless, Soft Challengers never escalate first (i.e., $w_S = 0$) and Soft Defenders never do either.[18] This means that when Defender's first-level threat is completely credible, *All-Out Conflict* occurs only when both players are Hard. Unlike a Form II No-Limited-Response Equilibrium at which even a Soft Defender may rationally escalate, war is now impossible unless *both* sides want it.

On the other hand, Hard Challengers always intend to escalate first under an Escalatory Limited-Response Equilibrium, but only probabilistically (i.e., $0 < w_H < 1$).[19] As might be expected, therefore, limited war deployment policies that are consistent with action choices under an ELRE entail the risk of deliberate escalation. In other words, under an ELRE, limited-war deployments do not eliminate altogether the possibility of rational escalation.

Challenger's behavior under an Escalatory Limited-Response Equilibrium is the reverse of the bluffing activity associated with Form II

---

[18] This is untrue when Challenger is uncertain about Defender's preference between *Limited Conflict* and *Defender Concedes* (see chapter 9 for details). But given that Defender's first-level threat is completely credible, Soft Defenders never escalate first (i.e., $z_S = 0$).

[19] By contrast, under a Constrained Limited-Response Equilibrium, Challenger *never* escalates first. CLREs, however, do not exist when Defender has a completely credible first-level threat. Constrained Limited-Response Equilibria are discussed in detail in chapter 9.

and Form III No-Limited-Response Equilibria. Under the latter equilibria, Hard Challengers always defect, while Soft Challengers defect probabilistically. Soft Challengers, therefore, may act as if they were Hard. But under an ELRE, Soft Challengers never escalate and Hard Challengers may choose not to. In other words, Challengers may act Soft even when they are Hard!

In a sense, Challenger's probabilistic intention to escalate first, if Hard, is a protective mechanism. Since Soft Challengers never escalate, Defender would never capitulate unless there was some probability of things getting out of hand. Conversely, were this probability a certainty, Defender would never respond-in-kind (see below). Thus, this intention benefits Challenger, especially when it does not have to act on it.

To summarize, at any Escalatory Limited-Response Equilibrium, the possibility of a challenge and a non-escalatory response is real; *Limited Conflict* is possible, but not likely. *All-Out Conflict* is a realistic possibility, but only when both players prefer it to capitulation. Finally, Hard Defenders always respond under an ELRE. Nonetheless, the two forms of Escalatory Limited-Response Equilibria are not identical. We next describe their distinguishing features.

8.2.3.5 No-First-Use Escalatory Limited-Response Equilibria

Figure 8.4 superimposes on figure 7.2 the location of a typical manifestation of each form of ELRE.[20] As figure 8.4 shows, one form, the *No-First-Use Escalatory Limited-Response Equilibrium*, or ELRE$_1$, occurs at high levels of Challenger, and low levels of Defender, credibility.[21] Under this equilibrium, Defender, whatever its type, never escalates first. Defender either responds-in-kind or not at all. Thus, like both Limited-Response Deterrence Equilibria, Defender's action choices are consistent with a No-First-Use deployment.

Although the No-First-Use ELRE includes the possibility of *Limited Conflict*, the *Status Quo* is never stable. Challenger always defects (i.e., $x_H = x_S = 1$), so nothing like deterrence ever emerges under a No-First-Use ELRE. Fortunately, perhaps, Defender's equilibrium response to

---

[20] Which manifestation occurs depends on whether certain relationships among the payoff parameters hold. For details and other manifestations, see appendix 7.

[21] The No-First-Use ELRE overlaps the areas occupied by the No-Response and the Form I No-Limited-Response Equilibria. Other manifestations (see appendix 7 for details) may also overlap the existence region of the Form III NLRE. Because at least one Escalatory Deterrence Equilibrium always exists, No-First-Use ELRE always coexist with one or more EDE.

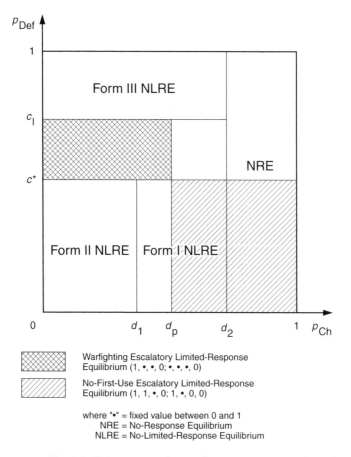

Fig. 8.4. Existence conditions for No-First-Use and Warfighting Escalatory Limited-Response Equilibria.

initiation never involves immediate escalation (i.e., $z_H = z_S = 0$). In the unlikely event that it is Hard, Defender simply responds-in-kind (i.e., $y_H = 1$). As detailed in appendix 7, Soft Defenders do likewise, but probabilistically. The higher its credibility, the higher the probability that a Soft Defender responds-in-kind rather than capitulates.

Exactly how the game unfolds after this depends on Challenger's type. If Challenger is Soft, it sticks with its prior choice and *Limited Conflict* ensues (i.e., $w_S = 0$). (But recall that Challenger is unlikely to be Soft.) *Limited Conflict* may also occur even if Challenger is Hard: when a No-First-Use ELRE is in play, a Hard Challenger may stick with its prior choice at node 3a, in which case the conflict remains constrained. However, it is more likely that a Hard Challenger will escalate; ultimately, the conflict could reach the highest level.

In sum, the modal outcome under a No-First-Use ELRE is *Defender Concedes*. The *Status Quo* never survives rational play. *Limited Conflict* is possible, but not very likely. *All-Out Conflict* is also a rational possibility, but only when both players are Hard.

8.2.3.6 Warfighting Escalatory Limited-Response Equilibria

The second major form of ELRE is called a *Warfighting Escalatory Limited-Response Equilibrium* (or ELRE$_2$). Like EDE$_2$ (see footnote 13), Defender's action choices under this equilibrium include the possibility of both a response-in-kind and escalation, which is our justification for linking both equilibria with a warfighting deployment stance. A Warfighting ELRE is the only non-deterrence equilibrium that admits the possibility of either a limited *or* an escalatory response by Defender.

As figure 8.4 indicates, the Warfighting ELRE occurs at lower levels of Challenger's, and intermediate levels of Defender's, credibility. Since the underlying conditions associated with the Warfighting ELRE differ markedly from those associated with the No-First-Use ELRE, it should come as no surprise that there are significant differences between the two forms of Escalatory Limited-Response Equilibria.

At the Warfighting ELRE, Hard Challengers initiate with certainty, and Soft Challengers initiate probabilistically. The probability of an initial probe, therefore, is lower at a Warfighting ELRE than at a No-First-Use ELRE. *Ceteris paribus*, crises can be expected to be less frequent, and the *Status Quo* somewhat more stable, when a Warfighting ELRE is in play.

A more significant difference, however, between the No-First-Use ELRE and the Warfighting ELRE concerns Defender's possible responses. Under a No-First-Use ELRE, Defender either responds-in-kind or does not respond at all. But when a Warfighting ELRE is in play, Hard Defenders may also rationally escalate first. More specifically, a Hard Defender *always* responds if challenged (i.e., $y_H + z_H = 1$), and may choose a limited or an escalatory response. Thus Defender utilizes the entire range of response options under a Warfighting ELRE.

As with the No-First-Use ELRE, *Limited Conflict* is possible under a Warfighting ELRE. Clearly, for limited conflicts to occur, Defender must respond-in-kind when Challenger initiates, and Challenger must choose not to escalate subsequently. Both of these requirements are likely to be met when both players are Soft, but they may also be satisfied when one player, or both, is Hard. In other words, at a Warfighting ELRE, *All-Out Conflict* may be avoided even when the players do not view it as the worst possible outcome.

This does not mean that *Limited Conflict* is inevitable, or even likely. The entire range of conflict outcomes, including unconstrained conflict, may evolve. As with the No-First-Use ELRE, then, the possibility of a *Limited Conflict* carries with it the risk of a more extensive conflict.

8.3 Multiple equilibria

As indicated above, at least one form of deterrence equilibrium coexists with all other perfect Bayesian equilibria of the Asymmetric Escalation Game. As well, the No-First-Use ELRE may partially overlap the region occupied by the No-Response Equilibrium and by Forms I and III No-Limited-Response Equilibria. Finally, the Warfighting ELRE may occur simultaneously with all three No-Limited-Response Equilibria.

When two equilibria coexist, it is possible that rational players will find one of them unsustainable. For example, both types of both players may prefer one to the other. As well, equilibrium refinements, which are extensions to the criteria for rationality, may eliminate one of the competing equilibria (Fudenberg and Tirole, 1991; Gibbons, 1992; van Damme, 1983).

As table 8.3 reveals, this is never the case with deterrence equilibria, either Escalatory or Limited-Response, since they always give Defender its best outcome. All other equilibria, by contrast, always involve the possibility of initiation and, therefore, the risk of a less preferred outcome; thus, both types of Defender always strictly prefer any deterrence equilibrium to any other equilibrium. The same does not hold true for Challenger, however.

In fact, a Hard Challenger *always* prefers the competing equilibrium. A Soft Challenger does also – at the three equilibria where Soft Challengers initiate for certain; Soft Challengers are indifferent among

Table 8.3. *Summary of preferences when equilibria overlap in Asymmetric Escalation Game (Flexible Response version)*

	Escalatory and Limited-Response Deterrence Equilibria	No-First-Use ELRE	Warfighting ELRE
Escalatory and Limited- Response Deterrence Equilibria	All Challengers and all Defenders are indifferent among all deterrence equilibria.	All Defenders prefer Deterrence Equilibrium. All Challengers prefer No-First-Use ELRE.	All Defenders prefer Deterrence Equilibrium. Hard Challengers prefer Warfighting ELRE. Soft Challengers are indifferent.
No-Response Equilibrium	All Defenders prefer Deterrence Equilibrium.	All Challengers and Soft Defenders prefer the No-Response Equilibrium. Hard Defenders prefer No-First-Use ELRE.	(No overlap)
Form I No-Limited-Response Equilibrium	Hard Challengers prefer the competing equilibrium.	All Challengers and Hard Defenders prefer No-First-Use ELRE. Soft Defenders are indifferent.	Hard Challengers and Hard Defenders prefer Forms I, II, and III NLRE.
Form II No-Limited-Response Equilibrium	Soft Challengers prefer the NRE and Form I NLRE.	(No overlap)	Soft Challengers prefer Forms I and III NLRE, and are indifferent between Form II NLRE and Warfighting ELRE.
Form III No-Limited-Response Equilibrium	Soft Challengers are indifferent between Forms II and III NLRE and any deterrence equilibrium.	Soft Challengers prefer No-First-Use ELRE. Hard Challengers prefer No-First-Use if p_{Def} is small. Soft Defenders prefer Form III NLRE. Hard Defenders prefer Form III NLRE if p_{Ch} is large.	Soft Defenders prefer Form III and III NLRE and are indifferent between Form I NLRE and Warfighting ELRE.

any deterrence equilibrium and the three equilibria where they initiate probabilistically. In consequence, these other equilibria simply coexist with a deterrence equilibrium – in every instance, there is no reason for the players, acting as a group, to reject either equilibrium in favor of the other.

This is a surprising and important result. Given the discovery of two plausible (Limited-Response) Deterrence Equilibria, one would hope that an unambiguous formal solution involving peace would exist. But our model suggests otherwise. Even under ideal conditions, deterrence success is not necessarily ensured, as classical deterrence theory suggests it would be. Here, as elsewhere, other rational possibilities always exist.

We admit, once again, to mild disappointment. Conflict cannot *a priori* be eliminated, and the status quo stabilized, simply by carefully calibrating threats. Unlike our equilibria, the real world is not, nor can it become, perfect, even with well-intentioned social engineering. Some political and social processes are simply beyond our control. Conflict, between and within states, appears to be among them.

Still, viewing the glass as half full, the mere existence of a new – and plausible – deterrence equilibrium leaves room for hope. With a perfectly credible sub-strategic threat, deterrence success becomes much more than just a remote possibility: peace and stability become realistic, albeit less than perfectly certain, rational alternatives to crisis and war.

Be that as it may, the status of the No-First-Use ELRE is similar to that of any deterrence equilibrium, with one important exception. When a No-First-Use ELRE coexists with the No-Response Equilibrium, Soft Defenders and both types of Challengers actually prefer the No-Response Equilibrium; only Hard Defenders prefer the No-First-Use ELRE. The net result is that either is possible.

However, both types of Challengers, and Hard Defenders as well, strictly prefer the No-First-Use ELRE to the Form I NLRE, and Soft Defenders are indifferent. We can expect, therefore, a tendency for the players, acting as a group, to switch from the Form I NLRE to the No-First-Use ELRE in the region of overlap.

Finally, under certain conditions, the No-First-Use ELRE also overlaps with the Form III NLRE. If so, Soft Challengers strictly prefer the No-First-Use ELRE, as do Hard Challengers when p_{Def} is small enough. Likewise, Soft Defenders prefer the Form III NLRE, as do

Hard Defenders when p_{Ch} is large enough. This means that neither equilibrium can be eliminated when they coexist.

The situation of the Warfighting ELRE is quite different, however. This equilibrium may coexist with any of the three No-Limited-Response Equilibria. Except for two minor exceptions, the Warfighting ELRE is strictly less preferred than the alternative. It follows that players may avoid the Warfighting Equilibrium, rejecting it in favor of the appropriate No-Limited-Response alternative.

8.4   Discussion

The preceding technical discussion of the equilibria and their characteristics raises a number of difficult empirical and theoretical questions. First, why are sub-strategic deployments and Flexible Response policies of only limited utility for stabilizing extended deterrence relationships? (Why are there other rational alternatives?) Second, given the overall tenuous stability of the status quo in the model, can we account for the "remarkably stable system that emerged in Europe in the late 1940s" (Mearsheimer, 1990: 53)? Third, in light of the theoretical improbability of limited conflicts, how can actual instances of limited wars be explained? Finally, what does the model suggest about the nature of current and future interstate conflicts now that the Cold War is over? In this section, we address each of these questions in turn.

There are at least two ways to answer the first question. We begin with the prejudices of the model. On the one hand, by crediting Defender with a perfectly capable and credible sub-strategic threat, and by assuming that there is no particular advantage to escalating first, we have weighted the model in favor of the *Status Quo* or *Limited Conflict* outcomes. But we have countered that particular prejudice by assuming also that Defender prefers unanswered escalation to limited conflict. This, we acknowledge, is a strong assumption that suggests why sub-strategic forces may not be of great value to a Defender unwilling to escalate – why, in our model, limited conflicts are rare events.

Why, then, do we make this assumption? The most important reason is its presumption by advocates of all-or-nothing policies. Jominian deployments based on the decisive application of force presuppose a preference for escalation over both limited response and (obviously) capitulation, as long as the challenger does not have the ability to counter-escalate (Kaufmann, 1956). By retaining this assumption we are able to measure directly the strategic implications of sub-strategic deployments under precisely the conditions that were taken for granted by the first wave of deterrence theorists. These conditions assume the worst – not only of Challenger, but also of Defender. In the tradition of both classical and structural realism, each state prefers unilateral advantage, and is willing to use force to gain it, unless there is a counterforce capable of preventing aggrandizement by any individual actor (Waltz, 1959: 232). In other words, our assumptions reflect the Hobbesian world feared most by strategic thinkers. To put Flexible Response to a less severe test would bias our model the other way, by presuming a Defender uninterested in winning, uninterested in individual gain.

On another level we can address, perhaps more intuitively, the lack of utility of credible sub-strategic threats by referring to the dynamics of the game. Note first that our model reflects the consensus of the wider strategic literature that all-or-nothing postures are not particularly efficacious once a challenger has a credible counter-escalatory threat. Thus, it should not be surprising that, when Challenger's threat to retaliate is credible enough, a No-Response Equilibrium exists and the *Status Quo* is never the only outcome at equilibrium.

But what if the credibility of Challenger's threat to retaliate is low? Given uncertainty about Defender's response, Challenger may still deter Defender from responding-in-kind by intending to escalate first (at node 3a). Once Defender is so deterred, Challenger can initiate with impunity. This tendency is accentuated as Defender's credibility decreases, or as Challenger's credibility increases. Of course, deterrence success becomes more likely as Challenger's credibility diminishes, *ceteris paribus*.

How, then, do we account for the persistence of the status quo in post-war Europe? There are a number of explanations. An obvious one is that by the time the Soviet Union had rendered Massive Retaliation completely obsolete by developing a nuclear capability and the means to deliver it, it had become a status quo power (if it had not been all along), content to exercise control over its own territory and those neighboring states that buffered it. Of course, this explanation, popular among revisionist historians, runs counter to standard realist assumptions, to some recent historiography (e.g.,

Gaddis, 1997), and to the logic of classical deterrence theory (see chapter 1).

It is also possible that the Escalatory Deterrence Equilibrium we associate with Pure Deterrence policy was in play, that Soviet leaders came to believe that *any* attempt to alter the post-war status quo would, inevitably, lead to an all-out nuclear conflict. While this explanation may comfort those who wish to believe that nuclear weapons have forever immunized the world from cataclysmic wars, it is not so entirely consistent with Soviet choices to reimpose control in East Germany in 1953, in Hungary in 1956, in Czechoslovakia in 1968, or in Afghanistan in 1979, or with the even more provocative decision to address a strategic imbalance by shipping medium-range and intermediate-range missiles to Cuba in 1962 (Gaddis, 1997).

A more likely explanation, one that *is* consistent with the model explored in this chapter, is that the Soviet Union, while motivated to expand, was itself unwilling to fight a costly strategic war to do so, and US leaders knew this. In the terms of the model, the Soviets were Soft and lacked a credible retaliatory threat.[22] Thus, in venues like Czechoslovakia or Afghanistan that were highly salient to the Soviet Union, but not to the United States, the Soviets could, in equilibrium, act provocatively; but otherwise they chose not to gamble, behaving like a Soft Challenger under a Form II or a Form III No-Limited-Response Equilibrium.

Next, how do we explain real-world examples of limited wars under parity? In our opinion, such events most likely occur outside the parameters of the present model. Recall again that we take Defender's sub-strategic threat to be completely capable and perfectly credible. The capability assumption implies Challenger's preference for the *Status Quo* over *Limited Conflict*, while the credibility assumption implies Defender's preference for *Limited Conflict* over *Defender Concedes*. Within the confines of the Asymmetric Escalation Game, limited conflicts are more probable when either assumption is relaxed.

Consider first the implications of the capability assumption. It is easy to demonstrate that, given complete information and mutually credible strategic level threats, *Limited Conflict* may be an equilibrium outcome if Defender's sub-strategic threat lacks capability (i.e., Chal-

---

[22] Of course, a similar argument could be used to explain why the United States never attempted to "roll back" the Iron Curtain in the 1950s, despite the rhetorical preference of some Republican leaders to do just that.

lenger actually prefers *Limited Conflict* to the *Status Quo*).[23] Under these conditions, Challenger is deterred from escalating at node 3a and Defender is deterred from escalating at node 2. Nonetheless, Challenger initiates and Defender rationally responds-in-kind. Thus, when the capability assumption is relaxed, limited conflicts are much more probable.

Prussia may have operated under these constraints in 1866. Clearly, Bismarck wanted a war with the Austrians, preferring limited bilateral conflict to an unsatisfactory status quo in which Austria played the dominant role in greater Germany. Given that the Prussian general staff was confident of a short campaign and a decisive victory, it is unlikely that there was anything that Austria could have done – unilaterally – to deter Prussia. Nonetheless, against the advice of his generals, Bismarck limited his war aims: the Prussian Minister-President feared the involvement of other powers, especially France. A war with France was a war that Bismarck was as yet unprepared to fight. Consequently, after Königgrätz (Sadowa), he convinced King William I to hold back.

Much the same could be said of US involvement in Vietnam. The North Vietnamese clearly lacked the capability to deter the United States from aiding the South. Still, the US was careful not to risk a major escalation of this conflict by threatening vital Soviet or Chinese interests.

Now consider the implications of relaxing the assumption of a perfectly credible sub-strategic threat: once this assumption is dropped, the possibility of an *unanticipated* limited response is introduced. Such a possibility may explain many crises and limited conflicts. We explore this question more formally in chapter 9, suggesting, for example, that UN forces in Korea probably would not have crossed the 38th parallel in 1950 had they correctly gauged China's intentions.

In sum, our pessimism about the possibility of limited conflict is conditional. It does not refer to the asymmetric context in which a strong state uses force merely to secure limited objectives; nor does it pertain to less-than-total conflicts that evolve when one state simply misjudges another's willingness to resist. Rather, our conclusions

---

[23] For example, given complete information, *Limited Conflict* is a (subgame-perfect) equilibrium provided Defender's first- and second-level threats are credible and Challenger's preference order is $c_{DC} > c_{ED} > c_{DD} > c_{SQ} > c_{EE} > c_{DE}$. Other outcomes can be equilibria under other conditions.

apply most directly to relations among relatively equal powers in which Defender's willingness and capability to engage Challenger at the sub-strategic level is common knowledge and, not incidentally, both sides prefer limited to total war. We believe that these are precisely the conditions against which the efficacy of Flexible Response deployments like No-First-Use and Warfighting ought to be measured. After all, the implied objective of sub-strategic deployments is to reduce the possibility of strategic wars, not to increase the probability of limited conflicts.

What are the implications of our model for present-day conflicts? One is that, under extreme conditions, restraint in warfare is unlikely. When two determined adversaries square off, chances are good that no holds will be barred. The forces of Saddam Hussein set the oilfields in Kuwait on fire; chemical weapons were used in the war between Iran and Iraq; and Sherman leveled Atlanta. Such behavior is the rule, not the exception. When it occurs, restraint is likely to evolve by accident – when Challenger is unexpectedly confronted by a resolute Defender – or by virtue of a circumspect Challenger that, nonetheless, cannot be deterred from a limited objective. NATO's 1999 attempt to secure peace in Kosovo falls into this latter category.

What is to be done? One strategy for weak states, like Belgium prior to World War I or the Baltic republics today, is to rely on their "own strength and art, for caution against all other[s]" (Hobbes, 1968 [1651]: 224). But such states, by definition, are unlikely to have threats that are sufficiently capable (not to mention credible) to deter a highly motivated Challenger; and, as we have seen, even a strong Defender with a credible threat cannot ensure a small state's integrity. Perhaps the best chance for successful extended deterrence is for a pawn to remain an unattractive prize, as Plato suggests;[24] alternately, a pawn can hope that, in a marginal case, Defender's promise to protect it is sufficiently credible that Challenger is dissuaded from attacking. Failing this, perhaps an existential fear of escalation offers the best possibility of a secure future.

8.5   Coda

The aim of this chapter is to assess the impact of credible sub-strategic deployments on a wide spectrum of extended deterrence relationships

---

[24] Part of Taiwan's problem today is that, increasingly, it is becoming an attractive target.

– to ask whether and when Flexible Response deployment stances make limited wars possible and total wars less, or more, probable.

The efficacy of sub-strategic response options is evaluated using the Asymmetric Escalation Game as a model for extended deterrence. We believe this model to be a rough approximation of the historical relationship of the United States and the Soviet Union after the implementation of NATO's Flexible Response deployment policy. It applies as well to a venue (like Korea) where a defender seeks to deter sub-strategic challenges.

The perfect Bayesian equilibria of the Asymmetric Escalation Game with credible first-level threats are identified, interpreted, and grouped into three mutually exclusive categories: Escalatory Deterrence Equilibria, All-or-Nothing Equilibria, and Flexible Response Equilibria. The Escalatory Deterrence Equilibria are the only deterrence equilibria that require that Defender intend to escalate first. At least one EDE always exists in the Asymmetric Escalation Game. The most likely form of Escalatory Deterrence Equilibrium is consistent with a Pure Deterrence deployment policy that rests on an existential fear of an escalation spiral. Another form requires a Warfighting Deterrence deployment. All of the Escalatory Deterrence Equilibria are behaviorally unlikely: they place implausible restrictions on the inferences that Defender can draw after observing Challenger initiate a conflict.

The All-or-Nothing Equilibria correspond to those non-deterrence equilibria that also exist when Defender lacks a credible first-level threat. The collective characteristics of this family clearly reflect the limitations of all-or-nothing deployments like Massive Retaliation. There is no combination of beliefs and player types that guarantees a stable status quo under any of the four equilibria in this family. When an All-or-Nothing Equilibrium is in play, Hard Challengers always initiate. There are also some situations in which Soft Challengers initiate with certainty, and none in which a Soft Challenger is completely deterred. In any case, the status quo is likely to survive only when Challenger's credibility is very low.

The inadequacy of all-or-nothing deployments helps explain NATO's migration toward Flexible Response. Flexible Response required that NATO have a capable and credible threat to respond-in-kind to a sub-strategic challenge. Accordingly, in the early 1960s, NATO's conventional and tactical nuclear forces were augmented. This build-up, it was thought, would allow decision-makers to avoid the stark choice between holocaust and humiliation, between suicide and surrender, implicit in all-or-nothing deployments.

Four additional equilibria arise when Defender's sub-strategic threat is perfectly credible. These equilibria, the Flexible Response Equilibria, capture the additional rational behavioral possibilities that a Flexible Response deployment policy provides. With the exception of one implausible Escalatory Deterrence Equilibrium, they are the only equilibria of the Asymmetric Escalation Game that involve the possibility of a limited response to a challenge and, by implication, of a constrained conflict.

The good news is that two of these equilibria are plausible deterrence equilibria under which the survival of the status quo is assured. The bad news, however, is that the two Limited-Response Deterrence Equilibria are never unique. They always coexist with some member of the All-or-Nothing family under which deterrence success is unlikely. Worse still, Challenger – whose choice determines which equilibrium form is played – never strictly prefers a Limited-Response Deterrence Equilibrium to any member of the All-or-Nothing family. In other words, even under ideal conditions, Flexible Response deployments cannot guarantee a stable status quo. Deterrence remains, at best, tenuous and fragile, and is never the only rational possibility. Thus, while necessary, non-escalatory response options are not sufficient for stabilizing extended deterrence relationships.

The other two members of the Flexible Response family are Escalatory Limited-Response Equilibria. Given that Defender's first-level threat is completely credible, ELREs are the only equilibria that even admit the *possibility* of a limited conflict. Under an Escalatory Limited-Response Equilibrium, Challenger generally initiates. In equilibrium, Defender sometimes responds-in-kind and Challenger sometimes chooses not to escalate first. When this happens, a conflict occurs – but does not escalate to the highest level.

This is not to say that limited conflicts are to be expected when Flexible Response options are deployed, or even when either ELRE is in play. Typically, under an Escalatory Limited-Response Equilibrium, Challenger initiates and Defender concedes. In the rare instances in which Defender responds-in-kind, Challenger is prone to escalate. In consequence, even under an ELRE, limited conflict is unlikely.

Like the action choices of both Limited-Response Deterrence Equilibria, the action choices associated with one Escalatory Limited-

Response Equilibrium are consistent with a No-First-Use policy. A *prima facie* case for a No-First-Use deployment exists, then, on the grounds that, under certain conditions, it is associated with successful extended deterrence.

But even when deterrence fails, as surely it must under a No-First-Use ELRE, a No-First-Use policy offers Defender certain advantages that might conceivably warrant the deployment stance associated with it. For example, in the region in which they coexist, Defender's expected payoff is greater under a No-First-Use ELRE than under a No-Response Equilibrium, provided Defender is Hard. (Soft Defenders prefer the No-Response Equilibrium.) Similarly, Hard Defenders prefer the No-First-Use ELRE to the Form I No-Limited-Response Equilibrium, and Soft Defenders are indifferent. By contrast, Soft Defenders and, under certain conditions Hard Defenders as well, actually prefer the Form III No-Limited-Response Equilibrium to the No-First-Use ELRE.

There is no question, however, about the attractiveness of the second Escalatory Limited-Response Equilibrium, the Warfighting ELRE, which, along with one form of the implausible Escalatory Deterrence Equilibrium, requires Defender to be prepared either to respond-in-kind to a challenge or to escalate. A Warfighting ELRE is never preferred by Defender or Challenger to the No-Limited-Response Equilibrium with which it coexists. Thus this deployment policy never benefits Defender unless – somehow – a Warfighting Deterrence Equilibrium (i.e., EDE_2) can be induced. In other words, a less costly all-or-nothing deployment is almost always preferable to a Warfighting stance (for Defender).[25]

In sum, our model indicates that a Flexible Response posture offers additional real opportunities for deterrence success over and above those provided by all-or-nothing deployments. These opportunities are consistent with both a Pure Deterrence and a No-First-Use deployment stance, although a Pure Deterrence policy can be sustained only by implausible beliefs. By contrast, a Warfighting stance seldom, if ever, benefits Defender. Finally, limited conflicts become distinct, albeit remote, theoretical possibilities when Defender's first-level threat is credible.

[25] Wagner's (1991: 727) conclusion that "the use of nuclear counterforce strategies is not necessarily inconsistent with rational behavior" is confirmed by the existence of the Warfighting ELRE. But as O'Neill (1992: 472) rightly points out, being consistent with rationality is not the same as being recommended by rationality.

Extended deterrence

None of which means, though, that Flexible Response deployments guarantee deterrence success. A stable status quo is most likely when Defender is able to project high credibility at both the tactical and strategic level. But other, rational, behavioral possibilities are always lurking. No amount of manipulation and control can eliminate the possibility of conflict – either limited or all-out.

9 Limited war, crisis escalation, and extended deterrence

> War is the stateman's game.
>
> Percy Bysshe Shelley

> This time I shall not chicken out.
>
> Kaiser Wilhelm II

To this point we have used the Asymmetric Escalation Game to assess the usefulness of all-or-nothing and limited-war deployment policies in extended deterrence relationships. As some might expect, we found that all-or-nothing policies are largely ineffective deterrents, unless Challenger is very likely Soft. When the odds are that Challenger is bluffing, Defender can rationally plan to move to the brink of unlimited war by escalating a crisis unilaterally, as Eisenhower and Dulles did with some success in the 1950s. Of course, Defender could plan to escalate even when Challenger is likely to be Hard. In this case, though, the beliefs that support Defender's intention to escalate first are implausible. Thus, while credible strategic-level threats may sometimes be useful for deterring direct attacks (see chapter 5), this prophylaxis is not so easily transferred to third parties.[1]

To be sure, the prospects for peace are enhanced, and the chances of extended deterrence success are increased, when highly credible strategic-level threats are buttressed with credible and capable sub-strategic threats. But even here deterrence success is no sure thing: other rational possibilities always exist. Not even the most efficacious

---

[1] This chapter draws on material in Zagare and Kilgour (1998).

Flexible Response deployment policy, No-First-Use, reliably sustains the status quo. In extended deterrence relationships, therefore, there is no quick fix, no obvious or transparent way to guarantee a third party's security. Small wonder, then, that the vast majority of major-power wars have evolved from extended deterrence failures.

Extended deterrence relationships are fragile – at best. What happens when extended deterrence fails? We know, empirically, that a wide range of possibilities exists, and our models allow for most of them: Defender could concede – in which case Challenger gets the prize; or Defender could respond-in-kind – in which case either an acute crisis (or a similar form of limited conflict) or an escalation spiral could occur; or Defender could escalate immediately, in which case an all-out conflict might break out. Yet, as presently formulated, our model can account for many of these outcomes only as remote theoretical possibilities. Thus far, both limited conflicts and escalation spirals are rare events in the Asymmetric Escalation Game. Why?

One reason – very likely the most important reason – concerns the extent of uncertainty in our model: there is simply not a great deal of it, and it is restricted to only two preference relationships. More specifically, until now we have assumed that the players know everything to be known about each other, save whether the other player prefers to execute its strategic-level threat. In other words, only end-game credibility is in doubt. Under all-or-nothing deployments, Defender's unwillingness to respond-in-kind is known to Challenger; and under limited-war deployments, Defender's sub-strategic threat has perfect credibility. Thus it is not altogether surprising that, in our model, Challenger tends to upset the status quo precisely when the chances are that Defender will not resist – either in-kind or by escalating. Indeed, *Defender Concedes* is the most likely outcome under any of the non-deterrence equilibria we have so far identified.

This should not be construed as suggesting that we believe our modeling decisions have been unsound or misleading. Rather our choices have been motivated by the questions we have addressed and the policies we have attempted to evaluate. Now, however, we adjust and broaden our perspective to a more complete examination of extended deterrence relationships. In particular, we want to know, more precisely, if and when crises and limited conflicts are likely to remain capped, and when they are prone to escalate out of control.

9.1   Theory and evidence

The theoretical literature on these questions is sharply divided. With the exception of advocates of Pure Deterrence deployments, classical deterrence theorists hold that carefully calibrated threats are usually sufficient to secure the status quo; but when they are not, lower-level conflicts can still be managed – and even won. Flexible Response deployments rest on this supposition. After all, if all disputes were destined to spiral out of control and culminate in all-out conflict, there would have been no reason for NATO to deploy conventional, or even tactical nuclear, weapons in Europe.

Yet the inevitability of unlimited war was precisely the argument that US President Eisenhower used to support his New Look policy. According to Gaddis (1997: 234), Eisenhower "never modified his conviction that *any* war was bound to escalate to the use of nuclear weapons. Not only was there no purpose in preparing for anything else, it would be *dangerous* to prepare for anything else."

Eisenhower's view on the inevitability of escalation and the dangers inherent in limited-war deployments place him squarely in the intellectual camp that Jervis (1976) calls *spiral theory*. Unlike classical deterrence theorists who contend that credible and capable threats can prevent the initiation, and help contain the escalation, of conflict, proponents of the spiral model claim that the prescriptions associated with classical deterrence theory frequently lead to vicious cycles of ever-increasing aggression. Conflicts like World War I spiral out of control when states inadvertently threaten each other's security in communicating deterrent threats or acting to shore up the credibility of their threats.[2]

---

[2] As Glaser (1997) points out, proponents of the spiral model also assume that all states are essentially satisfied with the status quo (i.e., are security seekers), while classical deterrence theorists assume the opposite (i.e., that all states are greedy). Glaser's analysis attempts to bridge the divide by considering the *extent* to which one or more states are greedy.

Glaser (pp. 184–185) develops an informal game model to explain how a rational conflict spiral might occur. Players in this game may be of one of two types, each of which prefers conflict to capitulation or, in our terminology, has a credible deterrent threat. The first type is a security-seeking (i.e., satisfied) defender; the second is a greedy, dissatisfied challenger. Glaser argues that the status quo survives when it is common knowledge that two security-seekers are playing the game, but that conflict results when at least one player is known to be greedy. Cooperation may also break down when the players are unsure of their opponent's type.

The model we first develop in chapter 5, and extend in chapters 6 through 9,

The empirical evidence on the debate between classical deterrence theorists and proponents of the spiral model appears inconclusive. As Jervis (1976: 84) writes:

> neither theory is confirmed all the time. There are lots of cases in which arms have been increased, aggression deterred, significant gains made, without setting off spirals. And there are also many instances in which the use of power and force has not only failed or even left the state worse off than it was originally ... but has led to mutual insecurity and misunderstandings that harmed both sides.

In seeking to identify the conditions associated with limited conflicts and with escalation spirals, we hope to shed light on the contradictory theoretical positions staked out by classical deterrence and spiral theorists, and to render cogent those inconsistencies in the empirical record noted by Jervis.

9.2   Assumptions

To this end we return once again to an examination of the Asymmetric Escalation Game (see figure 8.2) with incomplete information, now dropping our simplifying assumption that Defender's preference between *Limited Conflict* and *Defender Concedes* is fixed and known. Specifically, we now assume

Challenger: *Defender Concedes* $>_{Ch}$ *Status Quo* $>_{Ch}$ *Challenger*
Escalates $>_{Ch}$ *Limited Conflict* $>_{Ch}$ *[Defender Escalates,*
All-Out Conflict]   (9.1)

Defender: *Status Quo* $>_{Def}$ *Defender Escalates* $>_{Def}$ *[Defender*
Concedes, Limited Conflict] $>_{Def}$ *[Challenger*
Escalates, All-Out Conflict].   (9.2)

This more general structure proliferates Defender types. Whereas Defender was previously of one of two types – Hard or Soft – Defender may now be of one of four:

---

assumes that one player is greedy and the other is a security-seeker, and that this is common knowledge. The players in our model, however, may be uncertain about each other's preference between conflict and capitulation.

Glaser's conclusions are at odds with the models developed herein. In effect, Glaser argues that even when both players are known to have credible threats, a conflict could occur as long as one player is seen to be greedy. But in our models, the status quo has a reasonable chance of surviving when threats are credible all around. Glaser does not fully spell out the assumptions underlying his informal model. We suspect that the contradictory conclusions are due to divergent game forms.

- Type HH: Hard at both the first and second levels of play
- Type SS: Soft at both the first and second levels of play
- Type HS: Hard at the first level but Soft at the second level of play
- Type SH: Soft at the first level but Hard at the second level of play.

Of course, there is uncertainty only about Challenger's relative preference between *All-Out Conflict* and *Defender Escalates*, so there remain only two Challenger types – Hard and Soft.

We continue to assume that each player knows its own type and has probabilistic knowledge of the type of its opponent. Specifically, we assume that it is common knowledge that the utilities to Defender at outcome DD (D_{DD}) and to both players at outcome EE (C_{EE} and D_{EE}) can be described as follows:[3]

$$C_{EE} = \begin{cases} c_{EE+} \text{ with probability } p_{Ch} \\ \\ c_{EE-} \text{ with probability } 1 - p_{Ch} \end{cases}$$

$$(D_{DD}, D_{EE}) = \begin{cases} (d_{DD+}, d_{EE+}) \text{ with probability } p_{HH} \\ (d_{DD+}, d_{EE-}) \text{ with probability } p_{HS} \\ \\ (d_{DD-}, d_{EE+}) \text{ with probability } p_{SH} \\ (d_{DD-}, d_{EE-}) \text{ with probability } p_{SS} \end{cases}$$

where $d_{SQ} > d_{DE} > d_{DD+} > d_{DC} > d_{DD-} > d_{EE+} > d_{ED} > d_{EE-}$; $c_{DC} > c_{SQ} > c_{ED} > c_{DD} > c_{EE+} > c_{DE} > c_{EE-}$; $0 < p_{HH} < 1, 0 < p_{HS} < 1, 0 < p_{SH} < 1, 0 < p_{SS} < 1,$ and $p_{HH} + p_{HS} + p_{SH} + p_{SS} = 1$; and $0 < p_{Ch} < 1$.

More informally, we assume that Defender believes Challenger to be Hard with probability p_{Ch} and Soft with probability $1 - p_{Ch}$. Likewise, Challenger believes Defender to be of type HH with probability p_{HH}, of type HS with probability p_{HS}, of type SH with probability p_{SH}, and of type SS with probability p_{SS}. Each player is aware of the other's belief about its type.

The overall probability that Defender prefers conflict to capitulation at the first (or *tac*tical) level (i.e., prefers DD to DC) is the perceived credibility of Defender's first-level threat. This probability, that

---

[3] As before, these utilities are taken as binary random variables with known distributions. Challenger's utility at EE is independent of Defender's utilities at DD and EE, but Defender's utilities at DD and EE may be correlated (i.e., dependent).

Table 9.1. *Types and credibility parameters*

Variable	Probability that	Measures the perceived credibility of
p_{Ch}	Challenger is Hard	Challenger's (strategic) threat (node 3b)
$1-p_{Ch}$	Challenger is Soft	
p_{HH}	Defender is of type HH	Defender's first- *and* second-level threats
p_{HS}	Defender is of type HS	Defender's first-level (tactical) threat only
p_{SH}	Defender is of type SH	Defender's second-level (strategic) threat only
p_{SS}	Defender is of type SS	
p_{Tac}	Defender is of type HH or HS	Defender's first-level (tactical) threat (node 2)
$1-p_{Tac}$	Defender is of type SH or SS	
p_{Str}	Defender is of type HH or SH	Defender's second-level (strategic) threat (node 4)
$1-p_{Str}$	Defender is of type HS or SS	
$p_{Str\,|\,Tac}$	Defender is of type HH, Hard given it is tactically (i.e., of type HH or type	Defender's second-level (strategic) threat (node 4), given that its first-level (tactical) threat (node 2) is credible

Defender is of type HH or of type HS is denoted $p_{Tac} = p_{HH} + p_{HS}$; therefore, the overall probability that Defender prefers capitulation to conflict at the first level (i.e., DC to DD) is $1 - p_{Tac} = p_{SH} + p_{SS}$. Similarly, the perceived credibility of Defender's second-level (or *strategic*) threat is $p_{Str} = p_{HH} + p_{SH}$; so $1 - p_{Str} = p_{HS} + p_{SS}$ is the probability that Defender prefers capitulation to conflict at the second level, or ED to EE. Finally, if $p_{Tac} > 0$, Bayes' rule (or the definition of conditional probability) allows us to define the probability that Defender is strategically Hard, given that it is tactically Hard. This probability is

$$p_{Str|Tac} = \frac{p_{HH}}{p_{HH} + p_{HS}} = \frac{p_{HH}}{p_{Tac}} \tag{9.3}$$

Table 9.1 summarizes our notation for the players' types and their perceived credibilities.

9.3 Behavioral possibilities

To return to our questions about the conditions that give rise to limited conflicts and escalation spirals, we next identify the perfect Bayesian equilibria of the Asymmetric Escalation Game under the preference restrictions (9.1) and (9.2). This is the most general model we examine; it is also the most realistic. It assumes that Challenger is uncertain about (1) Defender's willingness to become involved in a limited war and (2) Defender's willingness to take on Challenger in a no-holds-barred conflict. The perfect Bayesian equilibria specify, *inter alia*, the beliefs the players must have for a conflict to remain limited or to spiral to the highest level. Thus the answers they provide to Jervis's (1976: 96) question concerning "the conditions under which one model rather than the other is appropriate" are in Jervis's terms, that is, in terms of the players' cognitive systems.

Before proceeding, however, a few caveats are in order. First, although appendix 8 is comprehensive, we restrict our analysis in the text to the special case in which Challenger is probably Hard, i.e., when its threat to counter-escalate is highly credible. There are two reasons for this focus, one technical and one theoretical. Technically, when Challenger is likely Hard, the equilibrium structure of the Asymmetric Escalation Game with incomplete information is simple and less subject to minor but complex exceptions than when Challenger is likely Soft.[4] A more important reason, however, is that this is the more interesting case. *Ceteris paribus*, deterrence is more likely, and conflict spirals less likely, when Challenger is probably Soft. Thus, the real test for proponents of deterrence occurs when Challenger is likely willing to run the risk of war. As well, this is the exact condition spiral theorists assert is most prone to deterrence failures and conflict spirals. By focusing attention on the most problematic case, then, we accentuate the theoretical distinctions between classical deterrence and spiral theorists.

---

[4] The reader will recall that under all-or-nothing deployments like Massive Retaliation (see chapter 7), there are five distinct forms of perfect Bayesian equilibria. Four additional forms, for a total of nine, may exist when Defender's response options are flexible (see chapter 8). This total expands to eighteen once Challenger is unsure whether Defender prefers *Defender Concedes* or *Limited Conflict*. Still, all equilibria not appearing in the text are variants of equilibria that are discussed. The details of the complete set of eighteen perfect Bayesian equilibria are provided in appendix 8 and summarized in table A8.1.

Second, because of the profusion of behavioral possibilities and equilibrium forms, we now refine our definition of deterrence success to include two additional, non-standard patterns of deterrence. Previously we associated successful deterrence with the survival of the status quo – an event that occurs with certainty under a deterrence equilibrium but which may also occur under other equilibrium forms. But this, the traditional notion of deterrence success, ignores the possibility that deterrence may operate even after a conflict has erupted (Snyder, 1961; Schelling, 1966: 191). For example, in a limited war, each side might choose not to escalate precisely because it fears the other will counter-escalate. Or it could be the case that one player (Defender) decides not to respond after the other (Challenger) initiates. Clearly, deterrence is working, albeit in a non-standard way, in both instances. Since we consider both *pre-war* and *intra-war* behavioral sequences to be potentially consistent with the notion of deterrence success, we henceforth associate this term with only those equilibria under which a player is *generally* dissuaded from taking an action leading to an immediately better outcome because it fears the other will retaliate – either in-kind or by escalating.[5]

Finally, we note that we do not consider conflict spirals and escalation to be equivalent. While some conflicts escalate immediately to the highest level from the very onset of hostilities, others reach an acute stage after a sequence of moves and counter-moves. The 1973 war in the Middle East, which began with a concerted surprise attack by Egypt and Syria against Israel, illustrates the former case. World War I is the prototype of the latter; what began as a minor incident in the Balkans slowly, deliberately, and perhaps inexorably, spiraled to the highest level, as ultimata were followed by mobilization plans, alerts, counter-alerts, frontal attacks and, eventually, counter-attacks. More than simply the escalation of conflicts to war, we hope to explain more fully and place in context this classic escalation spiral.

9.4   Deterrence and conflict spirals

With these stipulations in mind, we now ask: when does traditional deterrence occur? Under what conditions can the escalation process be contained? When will conflict spirals occur?

---

[5] Any instance of an immediate deterrence success, which presumes a general deterrence failure, would constitute a case in point.

To answer these questions, we consider the strategic characteristics of the three groups of perfect Bayesian equilibria that can exist when Challenger is likely Hard:

1. *Deterrence Equilibria* that depend on the threat of escalation
2. the *No-Response Equilibrium*
3. the *Spiral Group* of four equilibria that includes two additional forms of *Deterrence Equilibria*, a *Constrained Limited-Response Equilibrium*, and an *Escalatory Limited-Response Equilibrium*.

Deterrence Equilibria are associated with traditional notions of deterrence success, i.e., with the survival of the status quo; the *No-Response* and the *Constrained Limited-Response Equilibria* with *intra*-war deterrence; and the *Escalatory Limited-Response Equilibria* with conflict spirals and reciprocated levels of violence. We begin by describing the strategic properties of these equilibria (see table 9.2). Subsequently, we address their implications for classical deterrence theory and the spiral model.

9.4.1   Traditional deterrence

Traditional deterrence can arise in three very different ways in the present version of the Asymmetric Escalation Game. Regardless of the path to deterrence, however, Challenger's action choice is always the same: regardless of its type, Challenger never initiates and the outcome of the game is always the *Status Quo*. What distinguishes the various Deterrence Equilibria are Challenger's and Defender's intentions "off the equilibrium path." These intentions reflect the players' beliefs about each other's type and their planned choices at nodes (or decision points) that are not reached because deterrence is successful.

The first group of deterrence equilibria is a family of several perfect Bayesian equilibria that depend on Defender's willingness to escalate first. These equilibria are best thought of as variants or extensions of the Challenger-Soft Deterrence Equilibrium that exists when Defender adopts an all-or-nothing deployment policy. The Escalatory Deterrence Equilibria that exist when Defender's first-level threat is perfectly credible are also close relatives of this group.

Representative of this family is the most extreme member, Det_1, as shown in table 9.2. Under Det_1, all types of Defenders plan to escalate with certainty at node 2. Under any equilibrium of the Challenger-Soft

Table 9.2. *Equilibria of the Asymmetric Escalation Game when Challenger has high credibility*

| | Challenger | | | | Defender | | | | | |
| | x | | w | | q_{HH} | y | | z | | | r |
	x_H	x_S	w_H	w_S		y_{HH}	y_{HS}	z_{HH}	z_{HS}	z_{SH}	z_{SS}	
Deterrence (typical)												
Det_1	0	0	1	1	small	0	0	1	1	1	1	$\leq d_1$
No-Response												
NRE	1	1	large		small	0	0	0	0	0	0	p_{Ch}
Spiral Family												
Det_2	0	0	0	0	$p_{Str\,|\,Tac}$	1	1	0	0	0	0	$\geq d_2$
Det_3	0	0	d^*/r	0	c_q	1	v	0	0	0	0	$\geq d_2$
$CLRE_1$	1	1	0	0	$p_{Str\,|\,Tac}$	1	1	0	0	0	0	p_{Ch}
$ELRE_3$	1	1	d^*/p_{Ch}	0	c_q	1	v	0	0	0	0	p_{Ch}

Note: The table is excerpted from table A8.1 in appendix 8, which should be consulted for details of definitions and interpretations. Definitions of the strategic and belief variables appearing in this table are summarized here for convenience.

The probability that Challenger initiates at node 1 of the game of figure 8.2 is denoted x. In fact, this probability can depend on Challenger's type – if Challenger is Hard, the initiation probability is x_H; if Soft, x_S. Likewise, w_H and w_S are the probabilities that Hard and Soft Challengers, respectively, escalate at node 3a. At node 3b, Challenger always chooses E if Hard and D if Soft.

Similarly, Defender chooses D at node 2 with probability y, E with probability z, and C with probability $1-y-z$. Again, these probabilities can depend on Defender's type, so they are denoted y_{HH}, z_{HS}, etc. It can be proven that $y_{SH} = y_{SS} = 0$ at any perfect Bayesian equilibrium. At node 4, Defender chooses E if strategically Hard (type HH or SH), and chooses D otherwise.

Finally, players revise their initial probabilities about their opponent's type as they observe the opponent's actions. Of these revised probabilities, the only two that are important to the equilibria are shown in this table. Defender's revised probability that Challenger is Hard, given that Challenger initiates, is denoted r. Challenger's revised probability that Defender is of type HH, given that Defender chooses D (response-in-kind) at node 2, is denoted q_{HH}.

Deterrence Equilibrium family, at least some types of Defender intend to escalate by choosing E at node 2.[6]

For a member of the Challenger-Soft Deterrence Equilibrium family to exist, Defender must believe that any demand for a change in the status quo would be a mistake made by a genuinely Soft Challenger. In other words, for a Challenger-Soft Deterrence Equilibrium to come into play, Defender must believe that Challenger is unlikely to be Hard, *even should Challenger initiate a conflict*. For reasons previously discussed, we find this particular belief to be implausible. It is especially so given the current assumption that, initially, Challenger is likely Hard. Consequently, we are prepared to dismiss the entire family as behaviorally unrealistic.[7]

By contrast, the *Defender-Hard Deterrence Equilibrium* (Det$_2$) *is* plausible. Unlike variants of the Challenger-Soft Deterrence Equilibrium, the Defender-Hard Deterrence Equilibrium does *not* require Defender to escalate first. In fact, the form of traditional deterrence that emerges under Det$_2$ rests *entirely* on the more limited threat of responding-in-kind at node 2.[8]

The existence of a Defender-Hard Deterrence Equilibrium depends solely on Challenger's beliefs about Defender's type. (Defender's *a priori* beliefs are immaterial to the existence of Det$_2$.) Specifically, for Det$_2$ to exist, *both* Defender's first- and second-level threats must be highly credible: Challenger must believe it quite likely that Defender is tactically Hard, and given that Defender is tactically Hard, Challenger must place a fairly high probability on Defender being strategically Hard also.

Given these beliefs, Challenger intends not to escalate at node 3a because it believes that Defender will likely counter-escalate at node 4;

---

[6] Det$_1$ is represented by $[x_H, x_S, w_H, w_S, q_{HH}; y_{HH}, y_{HS}, z_{HH}, z_{HS}, z_{SH}, z_{SS}, r] = [0, 0, 1, 1, q_{HH}; 0, 0, 1, 1, 1, 1, r]$ where $q_{HH} \leq c_r$ and $r \leq d_1$. Det$_1$ exists for *all* values of Challenger and Defender credibilities. The Challenger-Soft Deterrence Equilibrium family is defined as deterrence equilibria ($x_H = x_S = 0$) for which Defender never plans a limited response ($y_{HH} = y_{HS} = 0$). See appendix 8 for another example. The family of Hybrid Deterrence Equilibria is related to this family.

[7] As shown in appendix 8, $r > d_2$ is inconsistent with all perfect Bayesian equilibria of the Challenger-Soft Deterrence Equilibrium family.

[8] Det$_2$ is an extension of the Form I Limited-Response Deterrence Equilibrium that exists when Defender's deployment policy includes limited-war capabilities. Det$_2$ is defined by $[x_H, x_S, w_H, w_S, q_{HH}; y_{HH}, y_{HS}, z_{HH}, z_{HS}, z_{SH}, z_{SS}, r] = [0, 0, 0, 0, p_{Str|Tac}; 1, 1, 0, 0, 0, 0, r]$ where $r \geq d_2$. As shown in appendix 8, Det$_2$ exists iff $p_{Tac} \geq c_3$ and $p_{Str|Tac} \geq c_q$.

and because Challenger believes that Defender will almost certainly respond-in-kind at node 2 – thereby subjecting Challenger to a *Limited Conflict* at node 3a – Challenger decides not to initiate at node 1.

Although the final Deterrence Equilibrium, Det$_3$, is also a plausible outcome of the Asymmetric Escalation Game, it is not likely.[9] As explained in the next section, the conditions under which Det$_3$ exists are quite restricted. Nonetheless, because it is closely linked to Det$_2$, and is an integral component of the Spiral Group, Det$_3$ remains a theoretical possibility worth describing.

Det$_2$ and Det$_3$ are the only deterrence equilibria that depend completely on Defender's threat to respond-in-kind to deter Challenger. Both are related to the probability that Defender is Hard at the second level, given it is Hard at the first level of play. The maximum value for this conditional probability under Det$_3$ equals its minimum value under Det$_2$.

The action choices at Det$_3$ are interesting. Defender plans to respond-in-kind with certainty if it is of type HH, and probabilistically if it is of type HS; otherwise Defender will not respond at all (i.e., it will capitulate at node 2). Since the conditional probability that Defender is Hard at the second level, given that it is Hard at the first, is lower under Det$_3$ than under Det$_2$, a Hard Challenger will intend to escalate probabilistically at node 3a. It is the willingness of a Defender of type HS to respond-in-kind sometimes that permits a Hard Challenger to risk escalating sometimes, and contrariwise. In the end, Challenger is deterred. Keep in mind that for this delicate balancing act to take place, both of Defender's threats must be fairly credible, that is, Defender must be likely to be both tactically Hard and strategically Hard.

9.4.2 Non-traditional deterrence

As already noted, deterrence can still operate even after the status quo has been violated. Crises that do not erupt into open hostilities, cold wars that do not turn hot, unilateral acts of aggression and limited conflicts that do not escalate illustrate that traditional deterrence can break down in a way that respects some limits. True – general deterrence fails. But on another level, the absence of all-out conflict

---

[9] Det$_3$ roughly corresponds to the Form II Limited-Response Deterrence Equilibrium discussed in chapter 8. Det$_3$ is defined by [x_H, x_S, w_H, w_S, q_{HH}; y_{HH}, y_{HS}, z_{HH}, z_{HS}, z_{SH}, z_{SS}, r] = [0, 0, d^*/r, 0, c_q; 1, v, 0, 0, 0, 0, r] where $r \geq d_2$ and v is as given in appendix 8. Det$_3$ exists if $p_{Str \mid Tac} \leq c_q$ and $p_{HH} \geq c^*$.

signals both a modicum of restraint and deployment success – albeit circumscribed: in each situation at least one player eschews an action leading to an immediately better outcome precisely because it fears the other's response.

When Challenger is likely Hard, non-traditional deterrence can occur in two distinct ways. In each case, the status quo is upset: Challenger, whether Hard or Soft, simply initiates. Defender's action choices, however, depend on its type and on which of two perfect Bayesian equilibria is in play.

Under the No-Response Equilibrium, Defender simply capitulates – as the British and French did after Hitler seized what remained of Czechoslovakia in 1939. *Defender* gives in (i.e., is deterred from either responding-in-kind or escalating) because Challenger is very likely Hard and, therefore, prone to escalate at node 3a or to counter-escalate at node 3b. To support its choice at node 3a, however, Challenger must believe that a Defender who unexpectedly *responds-in-kind* at node 2 is more likely to be of type HS than of type HH. We find this to be a plausible belief since, *ceteris paribus*, type HH Defenders would seem more likely to *escalate* than type HS Defenders.[10]

By contrast, Defender's action choices under $CLRE_1$ – the only form of Constrained Limited-Response Equilibrium that exists when Challenger is likely Hard – involve a response-in-kind for certain, but only when Defender is of type HH or HS. Otherwise, Defender capitulates. In fact, *Defender Concedes* is the most likely outcome of play under $CLRE_1$ since this member of the Spiral Group of perfect Bayesian equilibria exists when Defender is likely Soft at the first level, i.e., when p_{Tac} is low and p_{HS} is not too large. Thus, when Challenger chooses D at node 1, it does so with the expectation that its demands will almost certainly be met.[11]

Put in another way, a response-in-kind will surprise Challenger under $CLRE_1$. In this unlikely event, Challenger will be forced to update its beliefs about Defender's type. Clearly, Challenger will conclude that Defender is of type HH or HS, since only Defenders of

---

[10] The No-Response Equilibrium is defined by $[x_H, x_S, w_H, w_S, q_{HH}, y_{HH}, y_{HS}, z_{HH}, z_{HS}, z_{SH}, z_{SS}, r] = [1, 1, 1, 1, q_{HH}; 0, 0, 0, 0, 0, 0, p_{Ch}]$, where $q_{HH} \leq c_q$. As shown in appendix 8, it exists if and only if $p_{Ch} \geq d_2$. Truncated forms of the No-Response Equilibrium exist under both all-or-nothing and limited-war deployments.

[11] $CLRE_1$ is defined by $[x_H, x_S, w_H, w_S, q_{HH}; y_{HH}, y_{HS}, z_{HH}, z_{HS}, z_{SH}, z_{SS}, r] = [1, 1, 0, 0, p_{Str|Tac}; 1, 1, 0, 0, 0, 0, p_{Ch}]$. As shown in appendix 8, $CLRE_1$ exists if and only if $p_{Ch} \geq d_2, p_{Tac} \leq c_3$, and $p_{Str|Tac} \geq c_q$.

these two types can rationally choose *D* at node 2. Moreover, under any Constrained Limited-Response Equilibrium, *if* Defender is Hard at the first level, then it is likely Hard at the second level as well, i.e., more likely to be of type HH than of type HS. Fearing this possibility, Challenger is, understandably, deterred from escalating at node 3a; instead, it always chooses *D* at node 3a, settling for a *Limited Conflict*.

As indicated, CLRE$_1$ is a member of the Constrained Limited-Response Equilibrium family.[12] As such, it is the only perfect Bayesian equilibrium of the Asymmetric Escalation Game that has not previously been encountered in any form. The Constrained Limited-Response Equilibrium family, then, is unique to the environment in which Challenger is uncertain about Defender's relative preference between *Defender Concedes* and *Limited Conflict*, and where both players are uncertain about the other's willingness to endure an *All-Out Conflict*.

The Constrained Limited-Response Equilibrium family of perfect Bayesian equilibria is strategically significant, if only because members of this family are most likely to give rise to limited conflicts.[13] In the next section, we pay particular attention to the conditions under which CLRE$_1$ exists. For now, we simply observe that the existence of a Constrained Limited-Response Equilibrium may help to explain why, at times, states abruptly shift gears and adjust their behavior in mid-crisis, an explanation, we submit, that is fully consistent with Snyder and Diesing's (1977: 397) observation that "strategy revision is initiated when a massive input of new information breaks through the barrier of the image and makes a decision-maker realize that his diagnosis and expectations were somehow radically wrong and must be corrected."

As an example of the sudden reassessment of an opponent's level of resolve, consider the Soviet Union's change of heart during the Berlin crisis of 1948. Reacting to attempts to unify the US, British, and French zones of occupied Berlin and the rest of Germany, the Soviets blockaded the occupied city. The Soviet hope and expectation was that Western decision-makers would back down and drop their plans

---

[12] There are five distinct forms of Constrained Limited-Response Equilibria defined by perfect Bayesian equilibria where $x_H > 0$ or $x_S > 0$, $y_{HH} > 0$ or $y_{HS} > 0$, and $w_H = w_S = 0$. The remaining four forms exist only when Challenger is likely Soft. For details, see appendix 8.

[13] As noted below, limited conflicts are remote theoretical possibilities under Escalatory Limited-Response Equilibria.

for a West German state. But the response of airlifting supplies to the city demonstrated that the Allies placed a higher priority on holding their ground in Berlin than the Soviets expected. The Soviets dropped their blockade rather than risk open conflict, and the crisis faded.[14]

While it is always dangerous to associate particular real-world events with specific equilibrium forms, Soviet behavior during the Berlin crisis is, certainly, consistent with behavior under a Constrained Limited-Response Equilibrium.[15] At the height of the crisis, for example, the United States decided to send several B-29s, aircraft known to be capable of delivering atomic bombs, to British and German bases to augment the signal that the Allies were prepared to risk all-out war (Young, 1968: 183, 315). In terms of our model, by responding at the tactical level, the Allies signaled that they were strategically Hard. In retrospect, it seems safe to suggest that the signal worked.[16]

Much the same pattern can be discerned in those instances of general deterrence failure in Huth and Russett's (1988) data set for which the short-term balance of forces favors Defender. As Fearon (1994a: 252) points out, the vast majority of these cases are limited probes by weaker Challengers who are likely to be highly uncertain, *ex ante*, of Defender's willingness to resist. Immediate deterrence failed (i.e., a war occurred) in only two of the nineteen cases. The strategic characteristics of the Constrained Limited-Response Equilibrium family help explain why: Challenger's estimate of Defender's preference to hold firm, updated in light of an unanticipated response, was high enough, *ex post*, to deter escalation.

It is worth mentioning that $CLRE_1$ is the only form of Constrained Limited-Response Equilibrium under which *All-Out Conflict* is totally precluded. When $CLRE_1$ is in play and Challenger contests the status

---

[14] Gaddis (1997: 31) characterizes the Berlin crisis and the Korean War as two Cold War "situations in which the Soviet Union would show great caution after provoking an unexpectedly strong American response."

[15] As will be seen, it is also consistent with the existence of an Escalatory Limited-Response Equilibrium.

[16] Other examples include the Fashoda crisis of 1898, the Agadir crisis of 1911, and the Cuban missile crisis of 1962. In 1898, France was compelled to back down in the face of Britain's unanticipated resistance to its plan to take control of the Upper Nile. In 1911, Britain's unforeseen support of France persuaded Germany to accept limited compensation for ceding control of Morocco to France. And in 1962, the Soviet Union withdrew its missiles from Cuba when the United States unexpectedly blockaded the island.

quo, Defenders of types SH and SS always capitulate, while Defenders of types HH and HS always respond-in-kind. (In the latter instance, a limited conflict occurs.) Under all other CLREs, however, even a Defender who strictly prefers to capitulate rather than fight at the final level of the game might still find itself engaged in conflict at the highest rung of the escalation ladder. This occurs because after initiation, Defender's updated belief that Challenger is Hard is low enough that some Defenders will risk escalating (see appendix 8 for details).

In sum, while the status quo does not survive under either a No-Response Equilibrium or under $CLRE_1$, deterrence still plays an important role in the Asymmetric Escalation Game with incomplete information when either of these non-traditional deterrence equilibria is in play. In the first instance, deterrence is asymmetric: precisely because Defender is deterred, Challenger is able to initiate with impunity. In the second instance, deterrence is more uniform: each player is able to deter not initiation, but escalation. As a consequence, limited conflicts may evolve under $CLRE_1$; and when they do, they *always* remain limited.

9.4.3 Conflict spirals

Such is not the case, however, under $ELRE_3$, the only form of Escalatory Limited-Response Equilibrium that exists when Challenger is likely Hard. While it is *possible* for a *Limited Conflict* (outcome DD) to occur under $ELRE_3$, such a denouement is, at best, a remote possibility. In fact, the most likely outcome of a game played under this "spiral" equilibrium is, once again, DC, *Defender Concedes*.

As with the No-Response Equilibrium and $CLRE_1$, Challenger, whatever its type, always chooses D at node 1, thereby upsetting the status quo. What happens next depends on Defender's type. Under $ELRE_3$, Defender is likely to be of either type SS or SH. Such Defenders always concede at node 2, which is why *Defender Concedes* is the most likely outcome under any Escalatory Limited-Response Equilibrium. In the less likely event that Defender is Hard at the first level, it would respond-in-kind, with certainty if it is also Hard at the second level (i.e., of type HH) and probabilistically if it is Soft at the second level (i.e., of type HS). Given the probabilities, however, a response-in-kind would once again surprise Challenger.

Up to this point of surprise, behavior and expectations are similar under $ELRE_3$ and $CLRE_1$. What separates these two equilibria are

Challenger's expectations should Defender unexpectedly choose D at node 2. Recall that under $CLRE_1$, Defender responds-in-kind only if Hard at the first level; and that if Defender is Hard at the first level, then it is likely Hard at the second level as well. This is why Challengers never escalate first under a Constrained Limited-Response Equilibrium.

Under $ELRE_3$, though, a Defender that responds-in-kind is much more likely to be of type HS than of type HH. For this reason, a Hard Challenger, the focus of our attention, simply escalates at node 3a. If it so happens that Defender is actually Hard, the heretofore limited conflict then spirals to the highest level.[17]

According to Smoke (1977: 137), "one of the general paradoxes embedded in the escalation problem is that as the perceived hazard of uncontrolled escalation declines, belligerents feel more free to take some deliberate escalatory step." Smoke's observation is illustrated by Prussian Chancellor Otto von Bismarck's behavior following the Battle of Sedan in 1870. After Emperor Napoleon III surrendered himself and the main remnant of the French army to Prussia at Sedan, the probability that Austria would intervene on the French side dropped substantially. Sensing this, Prussia promptly elevated its war aims. Previously Bismarck had sought only to defeat the French, but now he demanded Alsace-Lorraine as his price for terminating the conflict.

The behavioral pattern associated with $ELRE_3$ and the other Escalatory Limited-Response Equilibria helps to explain both the escalation paradox and the change in Bismarck's strategy. In the Asymmetric Escalation Game with incomplete information, this pattern is unique to the family of Escalatory Limited-Response Equilibria, so the existence conditions for this family also delimit the circumstances to which Smoke's maxim applies.

To understand why, note that these two sub-families of Limited-Response Equilibria (Constrained and Escalatory) are distinguished by Challenger's possible responses should it be faced with an unexpected choice at node 3a. Under a Constrained Limited-Response Equilibrium, Challenger never escalates first at node 3a. But under an Escalatory Limited-Response Equilibrium, a Hard Challenger *is*

---

[17] An Escalatory Limited-Response Equilibrium is any perfect Bayesian equilibrium with $x_H > 0$ or $x_S > 0$, $y_{HH} > 0$ or $y_{HS} > 0$ and $w_H > 0$ or $w_S > 0$. $ELRE_3$ is defined by $[x_H, x_S, w_H, w_S, q_{HH}; y_{HH}, y_{HS}, z_{HH}, z_{HS}, z_{SH}, z_{SS}, r] = [1, 1, d^*/p_{Ch}, 0, c_q; 1, v, 0, 0, 0, 0, p_{Ch}]$, where v is as given in appendix 8. $ELRE_3$ exists iff $p_{Ch} \geq d_2$, $p_{HH} \leq c^*$, and $p_{Str \mid Tac} \leq c_q$.

willing to escalate first at node 3a, precisely because it believes Defender is unlikely to counter-escalate at node 4 – even if Defender has already chosen D at node 2. Put another way, under an Escalatory Limited-Response Equilibrium, a Challenger such as Bismarck may escalate simply because it has come to believe that Defender will no longer resist.

9.5 Discussion

We now return to our original questions: when does deterrence work? Under what conditions are limited conflicts possible? When will conflicts take on a life of their own, escalating out of control? Our model is, of course, too simple to be definitive, but it does suggest answers.

Given our fixed assumption that Challenger is likely to prefer to escalate at node 3b, it should not be surprising that our answers are in terms of the main parameters of the model: *Defender's* perceived credibilities. In fact, another way to pose these questions is: what kind of commitment must Defender be seen to have to deter conflict altogether, or to prevent low-level conflicts from escalating, given the likelihood that Challenger considers the stakes worth fighting for?

To answer this question, we next consider the existence conditions associated with each possible perfect Bayesian equilibrium of the Asymmetric Escalation Game with incomplete information. We begin by noting that perfect Bayesian equilibria of the Challenger-Soft family, and the No-Response Equilibrium, *always* exist no matter what Defender's credibilities. But since Det_1 and other members of the Challenger-Soft Deterrence Equilibrium family are based on beliefs that are implausible, particularly so given our presumption about Challenger's credibility, we do not consider them compelling solutions to the Asymmetric Escalation Game. The No-Response Equilibrium, however, is more viable. As long as Challenger is likely Hard, it will always exist as a logical possibility along with *precisely one* of the Spiral Family of perfect Bayesian equilibria: Det_2, Det_3, $CLRE_1$, and $ELRE_3$. Which of these four equilibria will exist is determined by the perceived credibilities of Defender's first- and second-level threats.

Defender's credibilities determine which Spiral Family equilibrium exists as depicted in three-dimensional space in figure 9.1. Every possible combination of Defender's credibilities is represented as a point in the tetrahedron shown in the center of this figure. The right horizontal axis represents the probability that Defender is of type HH, the lower-left (horizontal) axis the probability that Defender is of type SH, and the vertical axis the probability that Defender is of type HS. Thus, any point in the three-dimensional triangle, or simplex, has a combination of non-negative coordinates (p_{HH}, p_{HS}, p_{SH}), with a sum less than or equal to 1. The fourth credibility p_{SS}, equals the difference between this sum and 1; this amount is also the (perpendicular) distance between the point (p_{HH}, p_{HS}, p_{SH}) and the front face of the tetrahedron. For example, the point (0,0,0) represents the combination $p_{HH} = p_{SH} = p_{HS} = 0$, $p_{SS} = 1$.

Speaking more informally, figure 9.1 can be visualized as a corner of a room with two walls and a floor, all at right angles – the fourth face of the simplex is the downward-sloping plane. The side wall is light gray, the back wall is medium gray, and the floor is dark gray. Of course, to enable us to peer into this corner, the front face must remain transparent.

As figure 9.1 suggests, for traditional deterrence to have a chance, *both* of Defender's threats must be fairly credible. Thus, the two closely related Defender-Hard Deterrence Equilibria, Det_2 and Det_3, occupy a small region in the right-hand side of the tetrahedron, where p_{HH} is large, p_{HS} is not too large, and p_{SH} and p_{SS} are small. Defender is likely tactically Hard; this explains its propensity under either Det_2 or Det_3 to respond-in-kind at node 2, whatever its actual type. But this tendency alone is not sufficient to deter Challenger. Defender's willingness to respond-in-kind also rests on its ability to dissuade Challenger from escalating at node 3a. For this to occur, Defender's second-level threat must be highly credible as well; in other words, for deterrence to succeed under either Det_2 or Det_3, Defender must likely be both strategically and tactically Hard – i.e., p_{HH} must be large.

A somewhat different behavioral pattern emerges, however, when the credibility of Defender's first-level threat is too small to sustain either Defender-Hard Deterrence Equilibrium. This is the region of $CLRE_1$, a forward-leaning wedge running from the left side wall to the front face of the tetrahedron (highlighted at the lower right of figure 9.1).

A small reduction in the credibility of Defender's first-level threat can provide even a Soft Challenger with an incentive to initiate at node 1. After all, under Det_2 or Det_3, Defender believes that Challenger is likely Hard and, therefore, is deterred from escalating first,

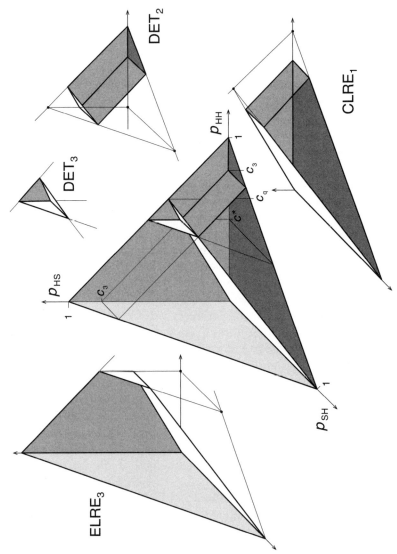

Fig. 9.1. Existence regions for equilibria of the Spiral Family.

274

even when it is of type HH. Under $CLRE_1$, Challenger banks on Defender preferring *Defender Concedes* over *Limited Conflict* and takes decisive action. Often, Challenger's gamble pays off and Defender capitulates. From time to time, however, Challenger guesses wrong and Defender reacts.

Defender's response-in-kind is Challenger's first clue that Defender is prepared to fight, since only a Defender who is tactically Hard, i.e., prefers *Limited Conflict* over *Defender Concedes*, would rationally choose D at node 2. But it is the conclusion that Challenger draws from Defender's unexpected response that is the distinguishing feature of $CLRE_1$.

Notice from figure 9.1 that the upper face of the $CLRE_1$ region slopes upward away from the bottom edge of the left side wall. At $CLRE_1$, the probability that Defender is of type HH is never very large (maximum c_2). However this sloping "ceiling" means that the probability that Defender is of type HS is always small *relative to the probability that it is of type HH*. In consequence, given that Defender has already demonstrated that it is tactically Hard (HH or HS) by responding-in-kind, there is a relatively high probability that it is in fact strategically Hard (HH rather than HS), and would prefer to counter-escalate at node 4. This probability is high enough to convince Challenger, whatever its type, *never* to escalate at node 3a.

Conflict spirals occur precisely when these conditions are not satisfied. Notice from figure 9.1 that under $ELRE_3$, Defender is less likely to be of type HH than under $CLRE_1$, and much more likely to be of type HS than of type HH. With this greater confidence that Defender will not escalate, both types of Challenger initiate, again with the expectation that their demands will probably be met. Usually they are not disappointed.

As under $CLRE_1$, however, over time Challenger may face measured resistance from a Defender with a preference for *Limited Conflict* over *Defender Concedes* (i.e., a Defender of type HS or HH). In the unlikely event that Challenger is Soft, it will choose not to escalate and a limited conflict will ensue. But in the more likely event that Challenger is Hard, it *may* escalate precisely because Defender is unlikely to counter-escalate at node 4. As figure 9.1 shows, under $ELRE_3$, a tactically Hard Defender is *less* likely to be of type HH than of type HS.

At this point, Defender will back off – provided Challenger has guessed correctly. A Defender of type HH simply counter-escalates at node 4. If so, the spiral will be complete, the result tragic. This, the lone path to *All-Out Conflict* in our model, succinctly describes the conditions under which deterrence completely breaks down and unlimited violence takes place. In our model, as in the real world, the unthinkable can occur when both words and deeds fail, when a truly determined Defender is unable to convince an equally determined Challenger it intends to resist every step of the way. Both world wars, unfortunately, are harsh testimony that this dire possibility can indeed occur.

9.6   Coda

It is easy to see classical deterrence theory and the spiral model as polar opposites. Deterrence theorists argue that carefully calibrated threats, judiciously applied, can stabilize a status quo and prevent deadly conflicts from developing or intensifying. Spiral theorists, on the other hand, worry that an elaborate plan for deterrence is really a prescription for disaster. Making much of the analogy with the sequence of events prior to World War I, they claim that threats lead only to counter-threats, and that threats are inevitably reciprocated and escalated to the point that violence is unavoidable.

To evaluate the conflicting claims of classical deterrence and spiral theory we again analyze the Asymmetric Escalation Game. In particular, we try to associate particular perfect Bayesian equilibria, and the specific circumstances that give rise to them, to successful deterrence, to limited conflicts, and to escalation spirals. In so doing we assume that Challenger would likely prefer to counter-escalate, rather than give in, should Defender escalate first, but make no assumptions about Defender's preferences about giving in – either between *Defender Concedes* and *Limited Conflict* at the first level, or between *Challenger Wins* and *All-Out Conflict* at the second level. We believe that this is the most appropriate context for a comparison of deterrence and spiral theory. *Ceteris paribus*, the status quo is more stable, and conflict spirals less probable, when Challenger is likely Soft, i.e., unwilling to enter a high-level conflict.[18]

---

[18] Kydd (1997) develops an alternative incomplete information game model of conflict spirals. There are two rounds in his model. In the first, the players decide whether to attack. Like most classical deterrence theorists, Kydd assumes that an attack choice by either side *always* leads to war. If the players choose not to attack, they then decide whether to build weapons. In the second round, the players decide once more whether to attack. Again, war follows if either side attacks.

As it turns out, one of the three families of perfect Bayesian equilibria consistent with this context requires that the players hold beliefs that are implausible, particularly when Challenger is likely Hard. We dismiss this family, which leaves just five possible equilibria. Furthermore, only two of these can exist at once, and one of them is always the No-Response Equilibrium.

Rational play under the No-Response Equilibrium is easy to describe. Without regard to credibilities or beliefs about them, Challenger always initiates and Defender always capitulates. Deterrence fails – in the traditional sense – but there is never any escalation. This behavior pattern lies outside the purview of both classical deterrence and spiral theory, except insofar as it shows Defender's response being deterred by Challenger. In the Asymmetric Escalation Game with incomplete information, a No-Response Equilibrium is always a rational possibility, but it throws no light at all on either deterrence or escalation spirals.

We call the remaining four perfect Bayesian equilibria the Spiral Family. Exactly one member of this family always exists and, therefore, always coexists with the No-Response Equilibrium. Which Spiral Family equilibrium is possible is determined by Defender's credibility parameters. Within the Spiral Family, two equilibria are easy to identify with successful deterrence, one with limited conflict, and one with a

---

The players in this model may be of one of four types: greedy and fearful, greedy and trusting, security seeking and fearful, and security seeking and trusting. Security seeking players are satisfied with the status quo; greedy players are motivated to upset it. Fearful players believe it is more likely that its opponent is greedy than do trustful players.

Kydd focuses on two of the model's many equilibria: the *spiral equilibrium*, under which two fearful security seeking types build weapons and then attack one another, and the *downward spiral equilibrium*, under which all security seeking players choose not to build and not to attack. Thus Kydd is able to separate those situations under which an arms competition does not occur from those where an arms race ends in war. For a downward spiral equilibrium to occur, greedy players must not be so greedy that they attack in the first round, but are greedy enough that security seeking players can signal their type by not building in the first round. Note, however, that only security seekers refrain from attacking.

By contrast, the Asymmetric Escalation Game model assumes, to use Kydd's terminology, that one player is greedy and that the other is a security seeker. The various deterrence equilibria of this model specify the conditions under which a *greedy* player will choose not to upset the status quo. Other equilibrium forms delineate the conditions under which limited and all-out conflicts occur. Since all attack choices automatically lead to war, Kydd's model is unable to explain why crises occur, or why some conflicts remain limited and others escalate.

conflict spiral. These equilibria are mutually exclusive, so knowing when they occur in the model enables us to formulate a prediction of when each of these behavior patterns is likely to be observed.

Traditional deterrence – which we associate with the certain preservation of the status quo – is definitely possible in our model, provided that *both* of Defender's threats are credible enough to dissuade Challenger from issuing a demand. For deterrence to succeed, Defender must convince Challenger that it is likely prepared to endure an all-out (strategic) conflict, and also that it is likely willing to respond at the lower (tactical) level.

This requirement explains why all-or-nothing deployment policies like Massive Retaliation are not well suited to deterring Challengers who would likely prefer a strategic conflict to capitulation. In part, the explanation is straightforward: because Challenger's threat to counter-escalate is highly credible, Defender tends to be deterred from escalating first. It is hardly surprising, therefore, that Defender's threat to respond-in-kind is also critical, not only for establishing traditional deterrence, but also for distinguishing between the remaining two Spiral Family equilibria.

When the credibilities of Defender's first- and second-level threats fall too low, Challenger initiates. If Defender is unwilling to endure a fight (which must often be true, as Defender's credibilities are low), then it capitulates and the game ends, no matter which of the remaining two equilibria happens to be in play. But other behavior patterns are possible when Defender is willing to fight at one or both levels. After Defender responds, deterrence might be re-established, and conflict contained, at the tactical level; another possibility, though, is escalation to the strategic level.

Once again, Defender's credibilities are the key determinants. After it observes an unexpected response-in-kind, Challenger revises its original estimates of Defender's type. For a conflict to be limited, Challenger must conclude, having observed Defender to be tactically Hard, that it is likely strategically Hard as well. In other words, our model indicates that the crucial variable is the conditional probability ($p_{Str \mid Tac}$ in table 9.2) that Defender is strategically Hard, given that it is tactically Hard. If Challenger finds it sufficiently probable that a Defender who appears to be tactically Hard is also strategically Hard, then conflict is capped at the tactical level. If not, there is an escalation spiral.

In one sense, then, our model indicates that both limited conflicts and conflict spirals depend on unanticipated events. It thus provides an answer to Israeli Prime Minister Menachem Begin's query: "If both sides don't want war, how can war break out?"[19] Under parity, acute crises and limited conflicts are largely unforeseen byproducts of interstate competition. Further, confirming the suspicions of most spiral theorists, many all-out conflicts are situations that states blunder into, each anticipating that it will out-escalate the other. When compared to the status quo, these are truly wars that no one wants.

The Korean War is a clear example of a conflict that was capped when a second-level threat suddenly gained high credibility. According to de Rivera (1968: 53), after UN forces crossed the 38th parallel in 1950, "the Assistant Secretary of State for Far Eastern Affairs [like other senior US officials] did not expect [a Chinese] invasion and, hence, failed to detect it even when he was confronted with a rather strong signal."[20] (For a similar assessment, see Lampton [1973: 28].) But soon after this unexpected event occurred, the UN command adjusted its actions. Fearing a wider war with China and perhaps the Soviet Union, US Secretary of Defense George Marshall decided to "use all available political, economic and psychological action to limit the war" (quoted in Gacek [1994: 57]).[21]

Both world wars illustrate the second behavioral pattern: conflicts that spiral to the highest level after unanticipated resistance. The difference is that in this case Challenger incorrectly believes that any resistance by Defender will be token. Escalation, therefore, is seen as a way to coerce Defender into submission.

In the years prior to World War I, for instance, Great Britain chose not to conscript and therefore not to maintain a large standing army, limiting its ability to defend its continental allies. Rather, the British relied primarily on an escalatory threat (i.e., its fleet) to deter war.

---

[19] The question, of course, is ambiguous. "Not wanting war" compared to what, the status quo or capitulation? In our models, *Conflict* never occurs unless at least one state prefers war to capitulation.

[20] A similar explanation has been given as to why in 1998 the CIA failed to predict India's tests of nuclear weapons, despite all indications to the contrary.

[21] Much the same can be said about Soviet behavior in 1950 immediately after the United States intervened on South Korea's behalf. As Gaddis (1997: 104) observes, "Stalin had indeed been imprudent in allowing Kim Il-Sung to attack South Korea, but he was prudent to the point of hyper-cautiousness once it became clear that his actions had provoked an unexpected American military response."

Germany knew all this, but found the escalatory threat alone to be insufficiently credible:[22]

> Up to the last prewar days [British Foreign Minister Sir Edward] Grey was discussing with the Germans what it would take to keep Britain neutral; the majority of the Cabinet regarded it as possible not to come to the aid of the French; many thought that Britain need not go to war if Belgium was invaded; and even after the idea of war was accepted, many thought Britain should not send an army to the Continent. Not only could Britain's friends and enemies not be sure what the British would do until the last minute, the British themselves did not know. In those circumstances it may not be surprising that even so cautious and conservative a man as [German Chancellor] Bethmann [Hollweg] was willing to take the great risk that brought on the war (Kagan, 1995: 211).

Much the same could be said about the backdrop to World War II. In attempting to appease Germany, Britain and France simply encouraged aggression. In the end, Hitler came to believe that events like the invasion of Poland would not provoke Britain into fighting. But like Bethmann Hollweg before him, he was wrong.

Deterrence theorists and proponents of the spiral model have drawn different lessons from these and similar events, leading Jervis (1976: 84) to remark that these two conceptual models "contradict each other at every point." Classical deterrence theorists like Kagan claim that war follows when real or intended threats are not convincingly communicated. Spiral theorists argue that wars are rooted in the threats implied by an accelerating arms race, by a military alliance, or by a standing army.

Our analysis helps to explain why "neither theory is confirmed all the time" (Jervis, 1976: 84), or why deterrence sometimes succeeds and why conflicts sometimes escalate out of control.[23] Successful deterrence and conflict spirals are events that take place under different circumstances. Deterrence theory and the spiral model are complements rather than substitutes. Each is inspired by a distinct theoretical and empirical dynamic. Although a number of strong qualifications are required, it seems safe to suggest that classical

---

[22] As noted in chapter 3, in 1906 von Schlieffen thought the British *would* intervene in a continental war. For von Schlieffen, then, Britain's first-level threat *was* indeed credible. Unfortunately, while credible to some, the British threat may not have been capable. Both von Schlieffen and his successors discounted the military impact of Britain's small expeditionary force (Kagan, 1995: 212).

[23] And why, sometimes, limited conflicts occur.

deterrence theorists are correct in asserting that capable and credible threats have the *potential* to avert disaster and prevent conflict. And spiral theorists are equally correct in pointing out that misjudgments and unrealistic expectations are but a prelude to catastrophe. Our conclusion is that empirical attempts to validate either theoretical framework at the expense of the other are doomed to failure. The dichotomy posed by Jervis is false. The real world is more complex and more varied than either classical deterrence or spiral theorists admit. We believe that our model and our analysis have captured fundamental features of the complexity and the variety of real-world interstate interactions.

Part IV
Implications

10   Perfect Deterrence Theory

Striving to better, oft we mar what's well.

William Shakespeare

The indefatigable pursuit of an unattainable perfection ... is what alone gives a meaning to our life on this unavailing star.

Logan Pearsall Smith

For some, the mere idea of deterrence conjures up stark images of the bipolar world that existed before the Soviet Union splintered apart, an unwelcome vestige of the superpower rivalry that dominated most of the latter half of the twentieth century. Now that the Cold War is over, some analysts have concluded that deterrence, and all its attendant concepts, are no longer relevant. Regional and ethnic conflicts seem sure to dominate the new millennium, so the argument goes, and therefore deterrence theory can be safely relegated to the dustbin of history, or sent to a home for outdated or decrepit theories. Notwithstanding the recent accession of India and Pakistan to the nuclear club, the interstate war between NATO and Serbia, and the all-but-inevitable proliferation of weapons of mass destruction, other theories and other concepts are required to explain conflict and cooperation, and to guide policy, in the postmodern era.

Admittedly, the world is different from what it was during the heyday of the Cold War, and the international system will undoubtedly continue to change in the twenty-first century. But this does not mean that deterrence is dead, either as an objective, as a policy, or as a theory. News of deterrence's death is most assuredly premature, if only because deterrence remains the cornerstone of the defense policy of the United States and many other countries.

For example, the *Report of the Quadrennial Defense Review* (US

Department of Defense, 1997) boldly asserted that "the primary purpose of US forces is to deter and defeat the threat of organized violence against the United States and its interests." Similarly, the National Academy of Sciences (1997: 3) released a well-publicized report in June 1997 that recognized the short-term utility of nuclear weapons in their *"core function* of deterring nuclear attack." And a 1997 Presidential Decision Directive, based on the *Quadrennial Defense Review,* made deterrence (not warfighting) the primary mission of US nuclear forces.[1]

Of course, this proves nothing except that deterrence remains a primary policy objective, at least in the United States, and therefore has some conceptual importance. Still, not much has changed since the Roman strategist Vegetius' time. To be sure, the international system has evolved, states have grown more powerful, and technology has marched on. Nonetheless, some countries now have, as some empires then had, a strong interest in avoiding war and conflict. And when they do, the goal they are pursuing, whatever it is called and however it is packaged, is deterrence.

In our opinion, those who see deterrence as an anachronism do so because they define the term too narrowly, restricting it unnecessarily, usually to the US–USSR nuclear competition during the Cold War. But deterrence is a universal concept, relevant across time and space. It operates across a wide variety of contexts and environments (Naroll, Bullough, and Naroll, 1974; Cioffi-Revilla, 2000). In principle, the dynamics of deterrence are the same whether the relationship is interpersonal, intergroup, or interstate. A theory that explains one type of deterrent relationship, then, should suffice to explain others.

Unfortunately, classical deterrence theory, born in the 1950s and developed fully in the 1960s, was articulated within the narrow confines of the dominant interstate relationship of that era, and was unduly influenced by the menacing specter of thermonuclear weapons. In consequence of this narrow focus, both theoretical and empirical research has been distorted, leading not only to an incorrectly specified theory, but also to some ill-conceived empirical research.[2] Perfect Deterrence Theory was developed to overcome the

---

[1] This directive represented the first major change in US policy for deploying nuclear weapons since 1981, and thus marked officially the shift of US policy goals away from winning a nuclear war toward preventing one.

[2] See Zagare (1987) for the former position, and Huth and Russett (1990) for the latter.

limitations of classical deterrence theory. Our purpose was to specify a theory of deterrence that is not only logically consistent, but also empirically plausible. In our opinion, classical deterrence theory is neither.

To recapitulate our reasons for this negative view, we highlight once again the major propositions and deficiencies of the two major strands of classical deterrence theory. Recall that structural deterrence theory focuses on the impact of interstate power relationships in the deterrence equation. By contrast, decision-theoretic deterrence theory highlights the interplay of outcomes, preferences, and rational choice in determining deterrence success and failure.

Structural deterrence theorists argue that deterrence is most likely to prevail when the costs of war are high and belligerent states are "in balance." Thus, the absence of a superpower war during the Cold War period comes as no surprise to structural deterrence theorists. In their view, the bipolar structure of the post-war period, coupled with the existence of weapons of mass destruction, practically guaranteed peace. Indeed, many structural deterrence theorists continue to believe that the probability of nuclear war between two states with invulnerable second-strike capabilities is negligible.

By extension, structural deterrence theorists hold that the probability of war is much higher either when power is out of balance, or when war costs are low. This is why they argue that quantitative arms races help prevent war (additional weapons increase the cost of war), why they contend that qualitative arms races and defensive weapons are destabilizing (certain weapons may reduce costs for one or both sides), and why some structural deterrence theorists are in favor of managed nuclear proliferation (again, nuclear weapons make war more costly). Given the low probability of war between nuclear equals, structural deterrence theorists conclude that the gravest threat to peace is an accident or a mishap.

Although structural deterrence theory is consistent with the absence of a superpower war since 1945 (or at least since the late 1960s), it is not consistent with the fact that most major-power wars have been waged under parity conditions, or with the observation that power imbalances are poor predictors of interstate conflict. Structural deterrence theory is also inconsistent with a wealth of empirical research suggesting that, in crisis, nuclear states do not behave differently than non-nuclear states. The absence of war between the United States and the Soviet Union until the latter achieved nuclear parity with the former toward the end of the 1960s, and between the Soviet Union and China after the break-up of their alliance in the late 1950s, simply cannot be explained by structural deterrence theory without resorting to *ad hoc* arguments. The fact that most states eschew proliferation policies also calls into question the theoretical underpinnings of structural deterrence theory.[3]

Much the same can be said of decision-theoretic deterrence theory. Starting where structural deterrence theorists leave off, decision-theoretic deterrence theorists presume that nuclear war is irrational. Consequently, the key to successful policy in the nuclear age lies in crisis management. The critical task is then to manipulate optimally an adversary's behavior and, at the same time, to avoid mistakes.

Like structural deterrence theorists, decision-theoretic deterrence theorists are hard put to explain the absence of a superpower conflict during the Cold War. The status quo in Chicken – the game form most decision-theoretic deterrence theorists use to model conflict in the nuclear age – is never a (subgame-perfect) equilibrium, that is, it is never consistent with rational contingent decision-making. Again, the behavior prescribed by decision-theoretic deterrence theorists is rarely observed in practice. Rather than being implacable, irrational, or manipulative, states appear to be cautious, flexible, and generally loath to take precipitous action during intense crises.[4]

As mentioned, Perfect Deterrence Theory was developed to overcome the empirical and logical deficiencies of classical deterrence theory. But Perfect Deterrence Theory should not be thought of as a substitute theory of Cold War interactions. Its domain includes, but is not limited to, the US–USSR nuclear relationship. By design, the logical framework of the theory can be used to explore deterrence relationships of almost any ilk. This is why, in constructing the theory, we avoided fixed or specific assumptions about the nature or impact of atomic, nuclear, chemical, biological, or other weapons of mass

---

[3] It is interesting to observe that most Western nations condemned India's and Pakistan's decisions in 1998 to test nuclear weapons. One leading Indian official, by contrast, claimed that *Pakistan's* tests were good for India. Another asserted that both sides' tests would secure the status quo in Kashmir (Burns, 1998). And a third (Singh, 1998: 43) asked, rhetorically, "If deterrence works in the West . . . by what reasoning will it not work in India?"

[4] Saddam Hussein would appear to be a recent prominent exception. Tellingly, Iraq found itself at war with Iran throughout most of the 1980s, and again with a United States-led coalition in 1991.

destruction. In Perfect Deterrence Theory, the costs of conflict (as reflected in utilities and preferences) are variables. Because costs are not set, Perfect Deterrence Theory is able to explore the full range of deterrence relationships, including those satisfying the particular assumptions that delineate the decision-making strand of classical deterrence theory. In this sense, Perfect Deterrence Theory subsumes classical deterrence theory.

Perfect Deterrence Theory begins with the argument that mutual deterrence works best when both players have capable and credible threats. Capability means that a threat hurts. Credibility means that a threat can rationally be believed. Believability is linked to rationality in that threats can be believed only when it would be rational to carry them out. Thus, only rational threats can be credible. More than anything else, it is the connection between rationality and credibility that distinguishes Perfect Deterrence Theory from the decision-theoretic strand of classical deterrence theory.

We do not claim that the linkage we make between credibility and rationality is new. Indeed, the two terms are normally treated as one in the rational choice literature. For instance, the concept of a subgame-perfect equilibrium,[5] which can be thought of as a credibility check on players' choices, requires that all players make rational choices at every opportunity in a game. This is precisely the credibility requirement in Perfect Deterrence Theory – hence its name.[6]

As a general theory, Perfect Deterrence Theory is well placed to explore deterrence relationships in a wide variety of contexts. Nonetheless, in this book we have concentrated on contentious interstate relations. In addition, we have tended to focus on rough parity relationships in which each side's retaliatory threat is capable of inflicting unacceptable damage on the other side. "Unacceptable" means worse than what a state would get by not initiating conflict. We pay special attention to parity relationships because they are the most

---

[5] And its many refinements, including perfect Bayesian equilibrium.
[6] There is an alarming gap, however, between this notion of credibility and its treatment in most empirical studies. In the empirical literature, credibility typically gets dissected into a number of constituent parts but, like Humpty Dumpty, never gets put back together again. Huth's (1988a) and Harvey's (1998: 686–687) works are examples of this tendency. Nonetheless, both Huth's and Harvey's empirical results provide powerful empirical support for the central conclusions of Perfect Deterrence Theory (see below).

interesting. They are also the most dangerous: a balance of power is the best structural predictor of major interstate war.

In exploring contentious parity relationships, we focus on a number of specific questions and address them in an assortment of deterrence *milieux*. Specifically, we examine direct deterrence situations in which either one or both players is dissatisfied with the status quo. We also analyze the dynamics of extended deterrence relationships under a variety of informational and credibility constraints. When appropriate, we have tried to provide answers to the following general questions:

- When is deterrence most likely to succeed?
- What is the most important determinant of deterrence success?
- When is deterrence most likely to break down?
- If deterrence breaks down, how will it unravel?
- Which extended deterrence defense postures are most efficacious, and under what circumstances?
- Are limited conflicts possible and, if so, under what conditions?
- When do escalation spirals occur?

Where the answers to these questions have important policy implications we have tried to lay them out. And whenever possible, we have attempted to give necessary and sufficient answers to these questions.

10.1 Capability: a necessary condition

As it turns out, there is only one condition that is absolutely necessary for deterrence success – threat capability.[7] As already noted, capability is defined as the ability to hurt. Our conception of capability has two dimensions, one physical and one psychological. The physical aspect concerns the capability to execute a threat. A threat to do what is known to be impossible will obviously be ineffective.

---

[7] This necessary condition helps explain why a show of force is such an important signaling tactic in international politics. In addition to augmenting credibility, a demonstration of power may help establish threat capability, real or not. Surely such was the intention behind the now famous "fly-by" of long-range Bison bombers during the June 1955 Aviation Day show in Moscow.

Threats that can be nullified by an opponent's preemptive strike also lack capability. Consequently, deterrence is unlikely to succeed if a challenger has a first-strike capability. Or, to state this differently, a second-strike capability remains necessary for deterrence success (Zagare, 1987). Huth, Gelpi, and Bennett's (1993: 618) finding that a "defender's possession of a second-strike capability has a powerful deterrent effect on the escalatory behavior of the challenger" lends systematic empirical support to our conclusion. Mearsheimer's generalization that *blitzkrieg* (1983: 64) is the military strategy "most likely to lead to a deterrence failure" reinforces it.

The psychological aspect of capability concerns a potential challenger's cost assessment. If a challenger calculates that bearing the cost of conflict is *less* onerous than suffering the costs of doing nothing, deterrence will *always* fail. As Harvey (1998: 700), echoing others, notes: "even clear and credible threats from resolute defenders will fail if the challenger believes that the challenge is worth costs incurred by triggering the threatened response." Jervis's (1976: 79) example is even more to the point: "the problem with the United States' strategy of putting pressure on North Vietnam was not that the threats were not believed, but rather that the North preferred to take the punishment rather than stop supporting the war in the South."[8]

The absence of a capable threat was almost certainly the reason why deterrence failed when Germany invaded Poland in 1939, when Prussia attacked Austria in 1866, when Japan occupied Manchuria in 1931, when the Soviet Union marched into Afghanistan in 1979, when Ethiopia struck Eritrea in 1998, when the United States declared war on Mexico in 1848, on Spain in 1898, and when it intervened in Grenada in 1983 and Panama in 1989, or whenever a large powerful state moves against a smaller opponent, including non-state forces.[9] Thus, Bueno de Mesquita's (1981: 155–156) finding that conflict

---

[8] NATO's threatened airstrike of Serbia in March 1999 is a more recent example. In a last-ditch effort to avoid conflict, US special envoy Richard C. Holbrooke met with Yugoslav President Slobodan Milosevic and asked him: "Are you absolutely clear in your own mind what will happen when I get up and walk out of this palace?" Holbrooke reported that Milosevic replied: "You're going to bomb us" (McManus, 1999).

[9] In another context, a state may fail to deter a potential opponent from increasing its armaments simply because its threat to engage the opponent in an arms competition is insufficiently capable. For example, Germany in the 1930s and the Soviet Union during the 1950s were likely undeterrable (Downs and Rocke, 1990: 5).

initiators are generally stronger than their opponents should come as no surprise. Weak states, by definition, lack the wherewithal to impose costs sufficient to deter aggression. Hence, we take Bueno de Mesquita's empirical finding as confirmatory evidence for Perfect Deterrence Theory. And, as Harvey (1998: 691) notes, the results of his recent empirical analysis "indirectly support [Perfect Deterrence Theory's] claim about the crucial role of capabilities" in deterrence relationships.

One way to think about capability is in terms of a continuum of costs. The point at which a threat becomes capable corresponds to the point of minimum cost necessary for deterrence to succeed. If a threat is not capable, it does not hurt enough to deter. By contrast, a capable threat makes deterrence *possible* simply because it exceeds this minimum threshold.

As one might expect, in Perfect Deterrence Theory, an increase in conflict costs past this lower threshold generally increases the probability of deterrence success. Thus, to the extent that nuclear and other weapons of mass destruction have an impact on these costs, as they most certainly do, they can be expected to contribute to a stable order, *ceteris paribus*.[10]

Significantly, however, our models also reveal a *maximum* threshold past which further increases in the cost of conflict do not contribute to the probability of deterrence success. Contrary to those classical deterrence theorists like Quester (1998) who argue for an overkill capability, then, Perfect Deterrence Theory suggests a more circumspect approach to defense procurement, and provides a compelling theoretical rationale for arms control. A minimum deterrence deployment posture, for example, is consistent with the deductions of Perfect Deterrence Theory, and makes perfect sense to us. A maximum deterrence deployment or overkill capability is wasteful through redundancy.

It is reassuring that in Perfect Deterrence Theory capability emerges as the only absolutely necessary condition for deterrence success, if only because there seems to be almost universal agreement on this point in the literature (Huth, 1999: 71).[11] Nonetheless, a capable

---

[10] The *ceteris paribus* condition is, of course, a major qualification. Things are hardly ever equal in politics. Below we consider other factors that lead us to temper this conclusion.

[11] This is one reason why we concentrate on parity relationships where, *ceteris paribus*, deterrent threats are more likely to be capable.

retaliatory threat is not a sufficient condition for deterrence success. Unlike classical deterrence theory, then, Perfect Deterrence Theory is entirely consistent with the lack of empirical support for the so-called *para bellum* hypothesis (Levy, 1988: 489–495). Moreover, the absence of a capable threat is not a necessary condition for general deterrence *failure*. Deterrence can break down in many other ways.

It is quite difficult, however, to summarize these conditions precisely. The reason is that, under parity, deterrence success is almost always less than certain. More technically, deterrence equilibria – or equilibria under which the status quo is never upset – almost always coexist with other less attractive equilibria, under which either a crisis, a limited conflict, or an all-out war is a distinct possibility. Conversely, it is even possible for the status quo to persist when a non-deterrence equilibrium is in play.

Putting this in another way, under almost any state of any of the models we developed, almost anything can happen, ranging from no attack to an escalation spiral. In other words, the conditions of war and peace generally exist simultaneously. From this we conclude that deterrence is, at best, a tenuous and fragile relationship: conflict is almost always possible. At worst, deterrence is a patently unstable relationship: at times, conflict may be inevitable.

10.2   Deterrence and the status quo

That said, it remains to specify the conditions that make peaceful cooperation most likely. One clear condition, consistent across all our modeling efforts, that, *ceteris paribus*, enhances the prospects of deterrence success is a relatively positive evaluation of the status quo. Recent empirical work lends strong support for this intuitively satisfying observation. Both Reed (1998) and Rousseau *et al.* (1996) find that satisfaction with the international status quo has a significant dampening effect on conflict initiation. Again, we take these important empirical results as confirmatory evidence for Perfect Deterrence Theory.[12] They do not, however, surprise us at all. In our opinion they should be patently obvious.

What is surprising, however, is the comparative slighting of this aspect of major-power relationships in both the theoretical and

---

[12] For a summary of the empirical literature on the impact of status quo orientations, see Geller and Singer (1998: 64–65, 89–92).

empirical literature of deterrence – especially since an increase in the costs associated with conflict will have absolutely no bearing on the probability of deterrence success under certain conditions and, under other conditions, may actually lead to a deterrence failure. Generally speaking, studies in the mainstream deterrence literature have focused on what George (1993) calls *forceful persuasion*, much to the neglect of tactics designed to enhance the prospects of peace by addressing a common root cause of conflict: dissatisfaction with the existing order (Huth, 1999: 76). As Van Gelder (1989: 163) observes, "it is too often forgotten that [successful deterrence] requires not only that the expected utility of acting be relatively low, but that the expected utility of refraining be acceptably high."

It is likely that the theoretical primitives of their paradigm have blinded some classical deterrence theorists to the impact of status quo evaluations on war and peace decisions. If "all other states are potential threats," as Mearsheimer (1990: 12) asserts, dissatisfaction with the status quo can only be a constant. In Perfect Deterrence Theory, by contrast, satisfaction and dissatisfaction are variables and, hence, subject to theoretical investigation. In general, our analysis suggests that Downs and Rocke's (1995: 17) observation that "the strategy of deterrence gets an extra boost from the fact that both states are often operating from a reference point that is defined by the status quo" is slightly misleading. When dissatisfaction is relatively high, deterrence stability becomes increasingly tenuous.

The scant attention paid to the status quo by classical deterrence theorists has had important theoretical consequences, sometimes leading to a distorted and overly pessimistic evaluation of the prospects of deterrence success. For example, consider the position of Lebow and Stein (1990: 347), who contend that inferences about the dynamics of immediate deterrence should be drawn by examining only those crises in which a potential challenger *seriously* considered an attack, presumably because a strong incentive to initiate conflict exists. Putting aside the fact that intensity of intentions is extremely difficult to get at empirically (Danilovic, 1998), Lebow and Stein's criterion creates a selection bias problem: those situations in which deterrence succeeded because the incentive to attack was somewhat weaker are ignored, as Huth and Russett (1990: 478) correctly point out.

Huth and Russett attempt to avoid case selection bias by requiring only that the use of force be *considered*. Their criterion alleviates the problem, but does not eliminate it (Levy, 1988).[13] In our view deterrence remains relevant even when it is *least* likely to fail, that is, when *no consideration* is given to using force. Such could be the case when a potential challenger is extremely satisfied with the status quo, but it could also be the case when a serious capability asymmetry exists. Thus, the United States today might not consider an attack on Canada because it has no compelling reason to do so (i.e., it is relatively content), and Canada might not consider an attack on the United States, even if it had a motive to do so, because its chance of success is nonexistent. In both cases deterrence can be said to be operative. Should, in the future, the United States become sufficiently dissatisfied, or should a dissatisfied Canada become sufficiently capable, the stability of this relatively tranquil relationship could be eroded.

It is at this point in the development of deterrence theory that we start to see the very important impact, and the theoretical conse-quences, of how deterrence is defined and delimited. Huth and Russett's (1990: 470) position is that rational deterrence theory

> should not be viewed as a general theory of the causes of inter-national conflict and war. It is limited in scope to how sanctions and rewards can be used to affect the cost benefit estimates of the attacker's two policy choices. Economic and political considerations beyond the defender's influence may also shape the attacker's estimate of the costs and benefits of using or not using force. In principle, these conditions can be incorporated into a rational choice model, but they are outside the scope of deterrence theory per se.

We disagree. Our view – which motivated many of our modeling decisions in developing Perfect Deterrence Theory – is that factors strictly outside a defender's control may contribute, and perhaps contribute substantially, to a potential attacker's evaluation of the status quo. To exclude them, by definition, not only severely and unnecessarily limits the scope of the theory, but also makes more problematic the specification of a necessary and sufficient causal model. In Most and Starr's (1989) terms, Huth and Russett's restricted definition of deterrence implies an exclusive focus on the willingness variables at the expense of those environmental elements (i.e., oppor-tunity constraints) responsible for creating attack incentives. As Most and Starr rightly point out, the specification of a necessary and

---

[13] See also Fink (1965).

sufficient theory requires that all aspects of a security relationship be accounted for.[14]

10.3   Credibility and deterrence

All of which is not to suggest that elements of the opportunity matrix are the only variables that matter. While a highly valued status quo is an important though neglected determinant of peace, it is not the deciding piece of the puzzle. In Perfect Deterrence Theory, threat credibility emerges as the quintessential determinant of deterrence success.

The centrality of credibility in the deterrence equation lies beneath a fundamental and persistent political regularity: the norm of reciprocity. For some time now, empirical researchers have been accumulating compelling evidence that political actors, including states, tend to respond-in-kind to one another, tit-for-tat, trading amity for friendship and enmity for hostility. It seems safe to say that the biblical injunction "an eye for an eye, a tooth for a tooth" is more descriptive of the interaction of great powers than is the biblical plea to "turn the other cheek." Leng and Wheeler (1979: 659) note the "universality of the norm of reciprocity." The available empirical evidence suggests that this norm holds across time, across regions, across systems, and across cultures.

Consider, for example, Sullivan's (1976) comprehensive review of the first wave of behavioral research in international politics that included, *inter alia*, Holsti, Brody, and North's (1964, 1968) analyses of World War I and the Cuban missile crisis, Wilkenfeld, Lussier, and Tahtinen's (1972) study of the Middle East from 1949 to 1967, and Gamson and Modigliani's (1971) examination of the Cold War. Sullivan (1976: 294, 63) found the strongest empirical support for a stimulus – response model, leading him to conclude that it is "very likely . . . that other states react in kind to our own actions."

---

[14] There is growing sensitivity to this point in the literature. For example, in their seminal study of interstate war, Bueno de Mesquita and Lalman (1992) included a representative sample of non-events in their data set; in a more recent analysis of border disputes, Huth (1996) includes a random sample of neighboring states not involved in a territorial conflict. Failure to include non-conflict situations in studies of deterrence introduces the same potential problems for inference that Fearon (1994a) uncovers in Huth and Russett's (1984) work on extended deterrence and that Smith (1995, 1996) finds in alliance reliability studies.

Since Sullivan's early review, there have been a number of confirmatory studies. For example, Wilkenfeld (1991: 143) finds "a very high degree of matching behavior" for states involved in an intense crisis. Brecher's (1993: 82) examination of ten international crises between 1938 and 1982 finds that "eight of the ten target states responded either tit-for-tat ... or with a more intense act." In a descriptive analysis of the pattern of triangular relations among the United States, the People's Republic of China, and the Soviet Union during the Cold War period, Goldstein and Freeman (1990: 78) discover "a strong convergence toward the conclusion that bilateral reciprocity is the behavioral norm on all three sides of the triangle." And Jensen (1984: 535–536) notes that "no proposition related to bargaining behavior has been better documented in both experimental studies and real life situations than the one suggesting that concessions tend to be reciprocated." Numerous other studies detect the same pattern (e.g., Ward, 1982; Downs, Rocke, and Siverson, 1985; Leng, 1993; or Kroll, 1995). Summarizing this now extensive literature, Cashman (1993: 184) concludes that "a large array of scientific studies provide evidence to support a stimulus–response theory of international conflict ... Nations seem to respond to others in the same manner as they are treated. Cooperation begets cooperation; hostility begets hostility."

From the vantage point of Perfect Deterrence Theory, reciprocity is perfectly natural and easy to explain. Establishing reciprocity, or tit-for-tat expectations, is tantamount to bolstering credibility, which in turn leads to an increase in the probability of cooperative behavior in others. Thus, it is hardly remarkable that in Huth's (1988a) statistical analysis of extended deterrence relationships, firm-but-flexible negotiating styles and tit-for-tat deployments are highly correlated with extended deterrence success. Huth defines a firm-but-flexible diplomatic stance as a signal that the defender is willing to compromise, but not capitulate. And a tit-for-tat policy involves an actual response-in-kind during a crisis or mobilization. Thus, the essence of both a firm-but-flexible bargaining approach and a tit-for-tat response to an actual provocation is reciprocity, the norm that signals credibility when promised or threatened, and demonstrates it when practiced.

All this might seem perfectly obvious – and from the vantage point of Perfect Deterrence Theory it is. Still, the widespread norm of reciprocal behavior is difficult, if not impossible, for classical deterrence theory to explain. Recall that classical deterrence theorists start with the presumption that all end-game threats are irrational to execute. This assumption underlies the use of Chicken as a metaphor for crises and related major-power disputes. But in games based on Chicken, mutual cooperation and mutual defection are never subgame-perfect equilibria. Indeed, in Chicken, each player's optimal strategy is always the *reverse* of the other player's, which is why models derived from Chicken tend to speak to the question of which side can expect to win or lose in a crisis (see, for instance, Powell, 1987). Ties, however, which involve reciprocity, are extremely rare events in these models. In other words, *both* war and peace are unfathomable. Clearly, the pertinent theoretical puzzle for classical deterrence theory is reconciling the absence of war with the persistence of peace.

By contrast, mutual cooperation *and* mutual defection (or peace and war) are readily understood when the axioms that set off Perfect Deterrence Theory from other approaches are used to analyze deterrence. To be sure, Axelrod's (1984) seminal study sheds important light on the conditions that lead to cooperation in iterated Prisoners' Dilemma games, but only Perfect Deterrence Theory can explain why decision-makers might act to modify a game's underlying structure so as to create a new game with a preference structure similar to Prisoners' Dilemma, or why a successful negotiator like Henry Kissinger would have an operational code that "approximates game theory's 'prisoner's dilemma' description of politics" (Walker, 1977: 129).

In even the simplest sequential games that combine the salient structural characteristics of Prisoners' Dilemma with strategies that permit retaliation, there are at least two subgame-perfect equilibria. Both involve *reciprocity*: one is associated with mutual cooperation and the other with reciprocated conflict. Clearly, it is the prospect of peace that provides the incentive to manipulate a game's preference structure. But to induce the change, players must convince each other that they actually prefer, or are likely to prefer, resistance to capitulation, that is, each must demonstrate or establish that its retaliatory threat is credible.

We emphasize that we see structure the same way that Snyder and Diesing (1977: 480) do: as the players' ordinal rankings of a game's gross outcomes: win, lose, compromise, and conflict. It is probably no accident, then, that our modeling efforts provide a natural explanation for the heretofore unexplained pattern Snyder and Diesing find between crisis "structures" and outcomes (see table 10.1).

Table 10.1. *Crisis structures and outcomes*

Structures	Cases	Typical outcome
Symmetrical		
1. Prisoner's Dilemma	Agadir, 1911 Berlin, 1958–1962 Yom Kippur, 1973	Compromise
2. Chicken	Munich, 1938 (late phase) Berlin, 1948 Lebanon, 1958 Iran, 1946 (late phase)	One side capitulates
3. Leader	Bosnia, 1908 (early phase) Germany–Austria, 1914 Ruhr, 1923 Iran, 1946 (early stage)	One partner leads, the other follows; or alliance or détente breaks up
4. Deadlock	US–Japan, 1940–1941	War
Asymmetrical		
5. Called Bluff (one party in Prisoner's Dilemma; other in Chicken)	Morocco, 1905 Quemoy, 1958 Cuba, 1962	Capitulation by Chicken party or unequal compromise
6. Bully (Bully–Chicken)	Fashoda, 1898 Bosnia, 1909 (later phase)	Capitulation by Chicken party
7. Bully–Prisoner's Dilemma	Germany–Austria vs. Russia–France, 1914	War
8. Big Bully (Big Bully–Chicken)	Munich, 1938 (early phase)	War (avoided in this case by shift of German structure to Chicken or Bully)
9. Protector (Bully–Leader)	Suez, 1956 (US–Great Britain) Quemoy, 1958 (US–Taiwan)	Dominant ally protects and restrains client

Source: Snyder and Diesing, 1977: 482.

From the vantage point of Perfect Deterrence Theory, Snyder and Diesing's findings make perfect sense: compromise occurs if and only if the "structure" is Prisoners' Dilemma; war is typical of those structures in which both players have credible threats but at least one lacks a capable retaliatory threat (i.e., Deadlock, Bully–Prisoner's Dilemma, and Big Bully). And capitulation is associated with those structures in which at least one player's threat lacks credibility (i.e., Chicken, Called Bluff, and Bully–Chicken).[15] Thus, the expectations of Perfect Deterrence Theory are in perfect correspondence with Snyder and Diesing's case analysis. We take this correspondence as an additional indicator of Perfect Deterrence Theory's explanatory power: no other formal study we know of can explain these observations. In other words, without Perfect Deterrence Theory, the empirical results summarized in table 10.1 are simply inexplicable.

To say that structure is the key to explicating Snyder and Diesing's case studies is simply another way of highlighting the critical role that credibility plays in the deterrence equation, for threat credibility is the main determinant of structure. Nonetheless, we must be careful not to overstate our argument. Although credibility is an important determinant of deterrence dynamics, it is not absolutely necessary for deterrence success. Indeed, in some circumstances, the absence of credibility can help stabilize a status quo, while its presence can precipitate deterrence failure!

Of course, we are now speaking of a potential challenger's threat, not a defender's. For instance, in an extended deterrence relationship where the challenger's escalatory threat lacks credibility, deterrence should prevail, regardless of the nature of the defender's tactical-level or strategic-level threat – demonstrating that credibility need not be present for deterrence to succeed. Those who find this observation perfectly obvious should question why this aspect of deterrence has received so little attention in the empirical literature. Traditionally, empirical studies have focused solely on the defender's threat: whether it has been communicated, whether it is clear and understood, whether it is real, and whether it would hurt.[16]

One additional theoretical contribution of Perfect Deterrence Theory, then, is that it brings to the fore the critical role of the challenger's threat in the deterrence equation. A challenger may be deterred, even when a defender's threat lacks credibility, if the challenger is unable to deter the defender from resisting. Empirical studies that attempt to explain deterrence success, yet focus only on

---

[15] See Snyder and Diesing (1977) for detailed definitions of these 2×2 games. "Leader" and "Protector" are alliance games that do not directly pertain to adversarial deterrence relationships.

[16] One reason for the focus on the defender's threat characteristics is the mania for explaining deterrence failure and the comparative lack of interest in explaining deterrence success.

the characteristics of a defender's threat, miss this essential dimension of extended deterrence.[17]

To recapitulate briefly: the probability of deterrence success depends directly on the players' evaluation of the status quo, their threat capabilities, and the interaction effects of their threat credibilities. Deterrence will always fail when capability is absent. It is more likely to succeed when the status quo is highly valued, or when all threats are credible all-around, or when the challenger's threat lacks credibility. In direct deterrence games in which the challenger and the defender are clearly identifiable, deterrence is certain, provided the defender's retaliatory threat is highly credible.

10.4 Deterrence breakdowns, limited conflicts, and escalation spirals

All of which raises questions about the likely consequences of a breakdown of deterrence. In our models, deterrence failure is generally associated with an asymmetric distribution of credibility, that is, with an imbalance of resolve. As one might expect, therefore, one-sided victories constitute the modal outcome category when deterrence fails. One player initiates conflict, and the other simply concedes defeat. Thus, we are not surprised by the fact that this same pattern is evident in Snyder and Diesing's (1977) extensive case analysis which is summarized in table 10.1, or by the finding that "do nothing" or "take no military action" is also the modal category of all defenders involved in militarized interstate disputes (Hart and Ray, 1996).[18] Huth and Russett's (1988: 29) observation that "most international conflicts are resolved far short of war" is also consistent with the "gestalt" of Perfect Deterrence Theory.

But there are other behavioral possibilities, and although they are relatively rare events in our models, the specification of the circumstances under which they occur constitutes still another theoretical contribution of Perfect Deterrence Theory. Specifically, the preconditions for limited conflicts and escalation spirals are similar, yet

---

[17] We do not mean to imply that Perfect Deterrence Theory is the only theoretical framework that highlights the importance of a challenger's threat, only that it does so explicitly. Models that find that conflict initiation depends on a challenger's positive expected utility (e.g., Bueno de Mesquita, 1981; Wu, 1990) are also suggestive of the interactive nature of threat characteristics.

[18] We are indebted to Douglas Lemke for this observation.

distinct. Both require that an initiator be surprised when its demands are not satisfied immediately, something that happens all the time in international politics (Huth and Russett, 1988: 43). Thus, both patterns depend critically on strategic uncertainty and an unanticipated response, and both may be broadly construed as mistakes traceable to an intelligence failure, bureaucratic bungling, miscalculation, or some other cognitive or information-gathering deficiency. Such behavioral sequences can be explained within a rational choice framework: given that players find themselves in situations they would have thought unlikely, their action choices leading to these two distinct classes of conflict may nonetheless be consistent with their goals.

For an unforeseen conflict to remain limited, however, one additional requirement must be satisfied. A challenger must conclude, after observing an unexpected response, that further escalation will lead to an even worse outcome: all-out conflict. For example, consider the May 1995 US–Japan trade dispute touched off when the United States announced punitive tariffs on thirteen Japanese luxury automobiles. Apparently taken aback by President Clinton's steadfastness,[19] Japan agreed in June to open its market to American automobiles and automobile parts. Japan thereby avoided not only the immediate imposition of stiff trade sanctions, but also the possibility of a dramatic rupture of the underlying economic and strategic relationship. For its part, the United States made subtle but clear reference to the risks of noncompliance. Significantly, White House press secretary Michael McCurry at once reassured Japan that the United States was trying "to keep our disagreements on trade isolated" but warned that, if such disputes were allowed to fester, they could "have an impact on some other aspects of cooperation" (Sanger, 1995). The end result was that "the United States and Japan reached a last minute agreement, ... [and averted] a fight that could have escalated into a nasty and dangerous trade war" (Stein, 1995).[20]

In a sense, then, limited conflicts remain limited because informational discrepancies are resolved in a defender's favor. By contrast, an escalation spiral occurs precisely when they are not. As is generally

[19] The actual imposition of sanctions is anomalous in US–Japan trade disputes.

[20] As is generally the case, real-world interactions are sometimes difficult to categorize. In the US–Japan trade dispute, tariff sanctions were in fact imposed on May 19, leading us to judge it a limited conflict. The tariffs were to be collected retroactively after June 28, when they were to take effect. But the final-hour agreement rendered the tariff null and void.

the case, a challenger will initiate a conflict with the expectation that its demands will be met, that resistance will be minimal. Conflicts spiral to the highest level when there is unexpected resistance *and* when a challenger incorrectly estimates that the unforeseen response is merely the prelude to eventual capitulation. Thus, conflict spirals are the result of choices that have unanticipated consequences. World War I and the US involvement in Vietnam are good examples. In the former case, the belligerents expected a short and decisive conflict. Had the carnage resulting from the stalemate on the Western Front been foreseen, the decisions of Germany and Austria-Hungary that set off the crucial chain reaction of moves and counter-moves would surely have been more circumspect. Similarly, the US commitment to South Vietnam would likely have been different had American decision-makers known in advance that the war would escalate as it did.

Perfect Deterrence Theory, then, can help to explain wars, like World War I and the Vietnam War, that, in retrospect, no one wanted. It can also help to account for the prevalence of analyses that explain the occurrence of war using human emotion, perception, or miscalculation. That a large number of conflicts can be traced to human error is no surprise to us. Under parity, the most common path to all-out war can be traversed only when the players are uncertain about each other's preferences. Some theorists attribute this uncertainty to psychological dynamics; others to cognitive deficiencies or to intelligence failures. Because they can be so diverse, we prefer not to attempt any characterization of the root causes of human uncertainty. Rather, we have restricted ourselves to an exploration of its rational implications.

10.5   Nuclear weapons and deterrence

Turning now to the role of nuclear weapons in the deterrence equation, we ask whether nuclear weapons are a stabilizing force in international politics, or whether they are terrible inventions likely to turn the next great war into the last great war. Our answer is that they can be both. Clearly, one major difference between nuclear and more conventional weapons is the impact that nuclear weapons have on the cost of conflict. Thus, one way to gain insight into these questions is to ask how increased conflict costs affect the probability of deterrence success.

When the costs that one side associates with conflict are such that the opponent's retaliatory threat would not hurt, increasing these costs past the point at which they become unacceptable can only make deterrence success more likely, *ceteris paribus*. In other words, nuclear weapons help to stabilize a status quo precisely when they render threats capable.

Of course, depending on the locale, the circumstances, and the values of the parties, conventional weapons may already be sufficient for this purpose. If so, nuclear weapons may well be irrelevant. As already noted, further increases in the cost of conflict beyond a certain point will have no impact on deterrence stability, which is why we oppose an overkill capability and support minimum deterrence postures (see section 10.1).

In other words, when costs alone are considered, the stabilizing properties of nuclear weapons have distinct limits. Moreover, even when they render threats capable, nuclear weapons may be insufficient to guarantee peace. As already discussed, capability is necessary but not sufficient for deterrence success. Thus, a more complete response to the question hinges on the presumed connection between nuclear weapons and the credibility of threats to use them. We claim no special expertise on this matter, so our answer is contingent, not only on the assumption of threat credibility, but also on the context of deterrence, that is, whether it is direct or extended. We consider direct deterrence relationships first.

If one assumes, as do classical deterrence theorists, that nuclear war is inherently irrational, and therefore that retaliatory threats are of dubious credibility (or lack it altogether), then nuclear weapons are obviously destabilizing agents: under these conditions deterrence is unlikely and extremely tenuous. To be sure, some classical deterrence theorists have constructed models that suggest otherwise, but these models depend on special assumptions, or on violations of the canons of rationality, underscoring the instability that characterizes deterrence relationships when the irrationality of threats is taken as a given.

How reasonable is this assumption? On its face it would seem unassailable. What could be worse than an all-out nuclear war? Nothing – except perhaps bearing the costs of a nuclear attack with no ability to respond. Indeed, most strategic thinkers, including some who construct models of deterrence that posit players with irrational threats, argue (at times, inconsistently) that in direct deterrence relationships retaliatory threats are anything but irrational. Schelling

(1966: 36), in particular, notes that "the difference between the national homeland and everything 'abroad' is the difference between threats that are inherently credible, even if unspoken, and the threats that have to be made credible." Similarly, Howard (1983: 96) submits that "there is little reason to question the credibility of a governmental decision to retaliate after its territory has been subjected to nuclear attack." In the same vein, Quester (1989) asserts, matter-of-factly, that "there is no doubt in anyone's mind that the Soviet Union will suffer terrible retaliation if it attacks the United States itself and that the United States will suffer similar retaliation if it attacks the Soviet Union." Finally, Cioffi-Revilla and Starr (1995: 448) observe that in the historical case of "US–Soviet homeland deterrence, willingness is a minor issue and is assumed to exist if the other side initiates a nuclear strike."

If these assertions are embraced, Perfect Deterrence Theory suggests a different answer. Deterrence is certain in unilateral or one-sided deterrence situations when capable end-game threats are also credible. The story is slightly different in mutual deterrence games: all-out war is always a rational possibility; but so is the status quo. Thus, provided both sides have a second-strike capability, nuclear weapons may help secure the status quo. Of course, these stabilizing properties must be weighed against the risk of a deterrence breakdown, which is the principal reason we do not support the selective proliferation of nuclear weapons.

Interestingly, and perhaps fortuitously, our conclusions run in the opposite direction when attention is restricted to extended deterrence relationships. Accept for a moment the dubious assumption that end-game threats are as credible in an extended deterrence situation as they would be in a direct deterrence relationship. Given such acceptance, deterrence stability depends on the credibility of the defender's tactical or lower-level threat. In situations of very high salience to the defender, as for instance when a close ally or a vital strategic issue is at stake, chances are good that deterrence will succeed. But in more peripheral areas, extended deterrence is likely to break down.

If anything, however, extended deterrent threats based on nuclear weapons tend to be less credible, as de Gaulle was fond of pointing out. Perfect Deterrence Theory suggests that the more this tendency is accentuated, the better. *Ceteris paribus*, the less credible a potential challenger's strategic-level threat, the *more* likely extended deterrence success, and conversely.

The association we draw between threat credibility and the stability of direct and extended deterrence relationships also has implications for the optimal deployment of military force. To wit, all-or-nothing deployments like Massive Retaliation can be effective in exactly two situations: (1) when a potential challenger lacks a capable strategic threat, as for example the Soviet Union did throughout the 1950s, or (2) when a potential challenger's strategic threat is simply not credible. Generally, under parity, even when the first condition holds, it does not hold for very long. Witness the history of the US–USSR strategic relationship and Pakistan's tit-for-tat response to India's tests of nuclear weapons in 1998 and of ballistic missiles in 1999. Israel appears to be an exception to this statement, although several of Israel's potential opponents, including Iran, Iraq, and Libya, may acquire a nuclear capability at some time in the future, perhaps soon. When this happens, the key to Israel's security may well be its ability to fend off a conventional attack, which justifies Israel's avoidance of all-or-nothing approaches to defense.

By contrast, less rigid deployments offer additional opportunities for deterrence, even of a determined challenger.[21] Clearly, flexible response deployments work best when a defender's threats – whether tactical or strategic – are highly credible. A case in point, again, is Israel. But note one consequence of Israel's unique position: by effectively deterring all-out war since 1973, Israel has left its enemies with little choice but to wage conflict at the sub-tactical (i.e., terrorist) level.

The most efficacious flexible response deployment is no-first-use. A no-first-use deployment can lead to deterrence success, even when a defender's threat to respond-in-kind is only moderately credible. But other rational possibilities always exist under these same conditions, so there is never a guarantee that the status quo will persist. Deterrence is most likely to unravel when the challenger is prepared to wage a strategic war. Pure deterrence deployments are also consistent with successful deterrence. But the existential beliefs that support this conclusion are implausible, leading us to discount the effectiveness of this "policy." Much the same could be said about a warfighting

---

[21] Current US deployment policy is in accord with this conclusion, as is the reason given to support it. As Secretary of Defense William S. Cohen described US policy in his 1998 *Annual Report to the President and the Congress* (US Department of Defense, 1998), "a wide range of nuclear options will continue to be planned to ensure the United States is not left with an all-or-nothing response."

posture which rarely, if ever, offers a benefit to a defender of the status quo relative to an all-or-nothing stance.

10.6 Coda

To conclude, we would like it known that we are well aware that the theory we have constructed is far from perfect. In Perfect Deterrence Theory, *perfect* modifies *deterrence*, not *theory*. Still, it is legitimate to ask what, if anything, Perfect Deterrence Theory adds to our understanding of contentious dyadic relationships.

The contribution of Perfect Deterrence Theory does not necessarily rest on the development of countless novel propositions or counter-intuitive policy recommendations; one reason is that it is a daunting task to make policy pronouncements about deterrence that have not already been made. There are, for instance, proponents and opponents of proliferation, overkill capabilities, flexible response deployments, all-or-nothing strategies, and arms control, to name just a few of the issues we have addressed. Many of the strategic recommendations we have made, then, already exist in the policy literature. There is nothing necessarily new or novel here.

Nonetheless, we do claim to offer a consistent perspective in which to view the dynamics of deterrence, and a clear logic supporting our prescriptions. We are quite comfortable admitting that most of our conclusions are manifest, even though many of them run counter to the conventional wisdom, i.e., to classical deterrence theory. In fact, we would have it no other way. It is our hope that Perfect Deterrence Theory explains why much of the conventional wisdom is misguided, and justifies many propositions that in fact seem undeniable.

The virtues of Perfect Deterrence Theory, we believe, are many. On its face, Perfect Deterrence Theory is consistent with the best empirical work in the field. The theory helps to explain why policy-makers avoid proliferation. It speaks to the efficacy of deployment strategies like Massive Retaliation and Flexible Response. It offers a consistent perspective for evaluating the impact of force reductions.[22] It is consistent with arms reduction initiatives and no-first-use deployments. It demonstrates the importance of escalation dominance. It illustrates the counter-intuitive destabilizing impact that credible

---

[22] For an explicit discussion of the impact of force reductions on deterrence stability, see Kilgour and Zagare (1997).

threats may have (e.g., the stability-instability paradox) and the stabilizing impact of threats that are not credible (e.g., Challenger-Soft Equilibria). And it helps explain a range of real-world outcomes, including limited conflicts and escalation spirals. It is our hope that all of this makes perfect sense to the reader as well.

Appendices

Appendix 1   **Deterrence models**

Four deterrence models are developed in the text and analyzed in appendices 3–8. The purpose of this appendix is to collect information about these models for easy reference and comparison. Appendix 2 collects the definitions and basic properties of quantities used in the analyses. The four deterrence models are listed in table A1.1.

As suggested in table A1.1, several versions of the Asymmetric Escalation Game are considered. The complete-information version of this game is discussed in chapter 6. Before the general incomplete-information model is analyzed in appendix 8 and discussed in chapter 9, two special cases are addressed: the "Massive Retaliation" version, introduced in chapter 7 and analyzed in appendix 6, and the "Flexible Response" version, introduced in chapter 8 and analyzed in appendix 7.

The four deterrence models of table A1.1 have many common features. All are discrete game models with two players, who are called A and B, or Challenger (abbreviated Ch) and Defender (abbreviated Def). Each model has only a few outcomes, including one called *Status Quo* (SQ). In the first three models, there is one outcome, DD, representing *Conflict*. In these models, strategies are denoted C and D; generally, C strategies represent acceptance of the *Status Quo* (or willingness to accept it), and D strategies represent willingness (or threats) to fight to overturn the *Status Quo*. In the fourth model, the Asymmetric Escalation Game, there are three strategic levels, C, D, and E; C and D are as before, and E represents escalation of a conflict that has already begun. Thus this model has two conflict outcomes, DD and EE; the latter represents a higher (or "strategic") level of conflict, called *All-Out Conflict*, and the former a lower (or "tactical") level of conflict, called *Limited Conflict*.

Table A1.1. *Four deterrence models*

Appendix 1 section	Model	Game-tree figure	Text chapter	Analyzed in appendix
A1.1	Rudimentary Asymmetric Deterrence Game	A1.1 A3.1	3	3
A1.2	Generalized Mutual Deterrence Game	A1.3 A4.1	4	4
A1.3	Unilateral Deterrence Game	A1.5 A5.1	5	5
A1.4	Asymmetric Escalation Game	A1.7	6	
	"Massive Retaliation" version	A6.1	7	6
	"Flexible Response" version	A7.1	8	7
	General version	A8.1	9	8

Each of the deterrence models consists of an extensive game form – a game tree, or extensive game, specified using (physical) outcomes, rather than utilities – plus a standard preference ordering over the outcomes. This preference ordering is incomplete, but only in that it leaves ambiguous the position of the conflict outcome(s). Players' preferences are expressed by their von Neumann–Morgenstern utilities. Notation for these utilities is simple: an outcome denoted K gives player A utility a_K and player B utility b_K; a player called Challenger receives utility c_K and a player named Defender receives utility d_K.

The von Neumann–Morgenstern utilities that are incorporated into each model include two possible utilities for each *Conflict* outcome over which there is ambiguity of value. A player who places the higher value on *Conflict* is of type Hard, and one who places the lower value on *Conflict* is of type Soft. A Hard player's utility is indicated by a "+" (for example, b_{DD+}), a Soft player's utility by "−" (for example, b_{DD-}). The complete set of utility values for a model are its *payoff parameters*.

A consequence of this system is that each model can be analyzed as a game of complete information or a game of incomplete information. To construct a game of complete information, specific assumptions are required about the types, Hard or Soft, of the players. To construct a game of incomplete information, the probabilities of each type must

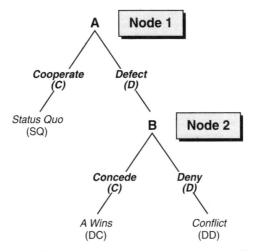

Fig. A1.1. Rudimentary Asymmetric Deterrence Game.

be fixed. These type probabilities are called *credibilities*, or *credibility parameters*.

In appendices 3–8, incomplete information games based on the four models are analyzed. These analyses are based on the assumption that the payoff parameters and credibility parameters are fixed and known.

A1.1 Rudimentary Asymmetric Deterrence Game

The Rudimentary Asymmetric Deterrence Game, introduced in section 3.4, is shown in figure A1.1 (see also figure A3.1). The two players are called A and B. The three outcomes are called *Status Quo* (SQ), *A Wins* (DC), and *Conflict* (DD). Following the convention described above, the players' utilities for these outcomes are given by

$$\text{For } A: \quad a_{DC} > a_{SQ} > a_{DD}$$
$$\text{For } B: \quad b_{SQ} > b_{DD+} > b_{DC} > b_{DD-}.$$

These utilities are shown schematically in figure A1.2. Note that the Rudimentary Asymmetric Deterrence Game is a very simple model, and includes ambiguity about B's preferences for *Conflict*, but not about A's.

In the Rudimentary Asymmetric Deterrence Game with incomplete

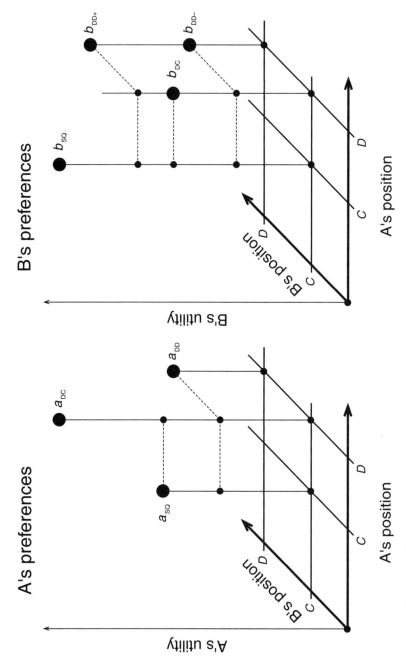

Fig. A1.2. Utilities in the Rudimentary Asymmetric Deterrence Game.

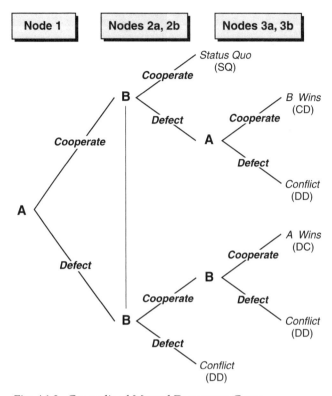

Fig. A1.3. Generalized Mutual Deterrence Game.

information, the probability that B is Hard, i.e., that B's utility for DD is b_{DD+}, is denoted p_B; consequently, the probability that B is Soft, and therefore has utility b_{DD-} for DD, is $1-p_B$. Parenthetically, it is noted in appendix 3 that this model is overdetermined in the sense that the analysis of the incomplete-information game does not require all of the specific assumptions above concerning payoff parameters.

A1.2 Generalized Mutual Deterrence Game

The Generalized Mutual Deterrence Game, introduced in section 4.2, is shown in figure A1.3 (see also figure A4.1). The two players are called A and B. Note that the game begins with effectively simultaneous moves by A and B; in figure A1.3, the two decision nodes in B's information set are joined by a solid line.

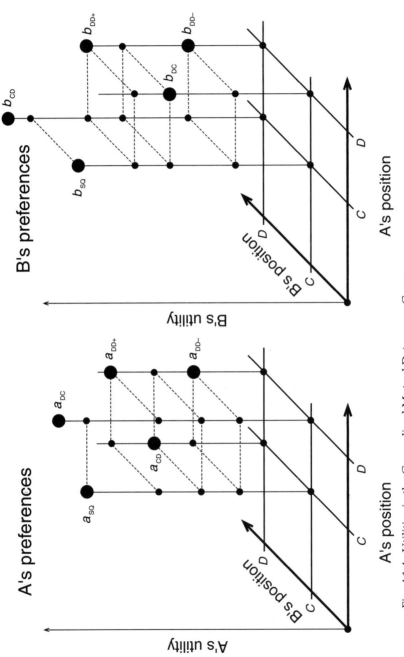

Fig. A1.4. Utilities in the Generalized Mutual Deterrence Game.

The four outcomes of the Generalized Mutual Deterrence Game are called *Status Quo* (SQ), *A Wins* (DC), *B Wins* (CD), and *Conflict* (DD). Following the convention described above, the players' utilities for these outcomes are given by

For A: $\quad a_{DC} > a_{SQ} > a_{DD+} > a_{CD} > a_{DD-}$
For B: $\quad b_{CD} > b_{SQ} > b_{DD+} > b_{DC} > b_{DD-}$.

These utilities are shown schematically in figure A1.4. In the Generalized Mutual Deterrence Game with incomplete information, the probability that A is Hard, i.e., that A's utility for DD is a_{DD+}, is denoted p_A; likewise, the probability that B is Hard, i.e., that B's utility for DD is b_{DD+}, is denoted p_B.

A1.3 Unilateral Deterrence Game

The Unilateral Deterrence Game, introduced in section 5.1, is shown in figure A1.5 (see also figure A5.1). The two players are called Challenger and Defender. The four outcomes are called *Status Quo* (SQ), *Defender Concedes* (DC), *Challenger Defeated* (CD), and *Conflict* (DD). Following the convention described above, the players' utilities for these outcomes are given by

For Challenger: $\quad c_{DC} > c_{SQ} > c_{DD+} > c_{CD} > c_{DD-}$
For Defender: $\quad d_{CD} > d_{SQ} > d_{DD+} > d_{DC} > d_{DD-}$.

These utilities are shown schematically in figure A1.6. It is noteworthy (compare figures A1.4 and A1.6) that the preference orderings for corresponding outcomes in the Unilateral Deterrence Game and the Generalized Mutual Deterrence Game are identical. Parenthetically, it is observed in appendix 5 that the solution would be unchanged if Defender's utilities were instead to satisfy

$$d_{SQ} \geq d_{CD} > d_{DD+} > d_{DC} > d_{DD-}.$$

In the Unilateral Deterrence Game with incomplete information, the probability that Challenger is Hard, i.e., that Challenger's utility for DD is c_{DD+}, is denoted p_{Ch}; likewise, the probability that Defender is Hard, i.e., that Defender's utility for DD is d_{DD+}, is denoted p_{Def}.

A1.4 Asymmetric Escalation Game

The Asymmetric Escalation Game, introduced as figure 6.3 in section 6.2, is shown in figure A1.7. The two players are called Challenger

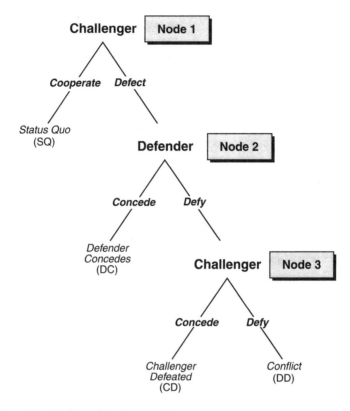

Fig. A1.5. Unilateral Deterrence Game.

and Defender. The six outcomes are called *Status Quo* (SQ), *Defender Concedes* (DC), *Limited Conflict* (or *Defender Defies*) (DD), *Challenger Wins* (ED), *Defender Escalates* (DE), and *All-Out Conflict* (EE). Following the convention described above, the players' utilities for these outcomes are given by

For Challenger: $c_{DC} > c_{SQ} > c_{ED} > c_{DD} > c_{EE+} > c_{DE} > c_{EE-}$
For Defender: $d_{SQ} > d_{DE} > d_{DD+} > d_{DC} > d_{DD-} > d_{EE+} > d_{ED} > d_{EE-}$.

These utilities are shown schematically in figure A1.8. Note that there is ambiguity about Challenger's value for *All-Out Conflict* (EE), and about Defender's values for both *Limited Conflict* (DD) and *All-Out Conflict* (EE).

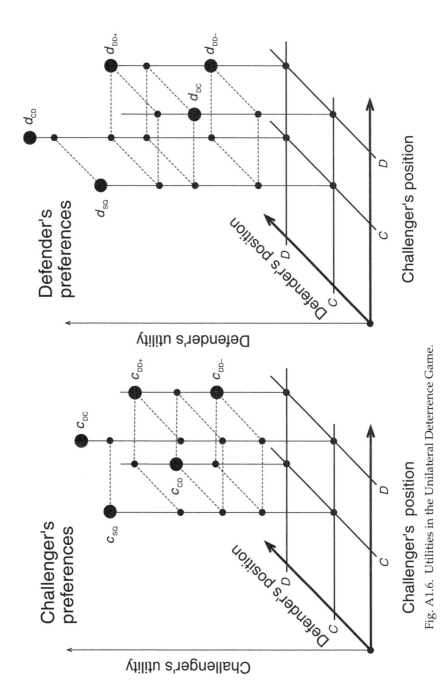

Fig. A1.6. Utilities in the Unilateral Deterrence Game.

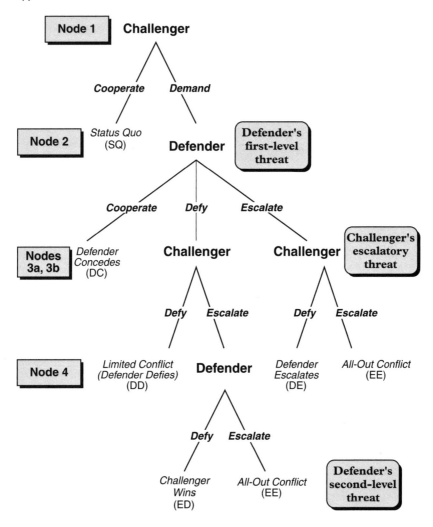

Fig. A1.7. Asymmetric Escalation Game.

In the Asymmetric Escalation Game with incomplete information, the probability that Challenger is Hard, i.e., that Challenger's utility for DD is c_{DD+}, is, as usual, denoted p_{Ch}. Defender's conflict preferences are more complex, however. As noted in table 9.1, Defender is tactically Hard if its value for *Limited Conflict* is d_{DD+}, and tactically Soft if this value is d_{DD-}. Similarly, Defender is strategically Hard if

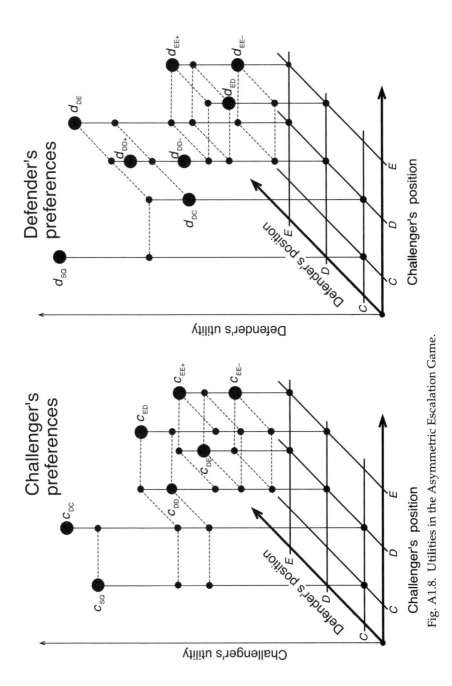

Fig. A1.8. Utilities in the Asymmetric Escalation Game.

its value for *All-Out Conflict* is d_{EE+}, and strategically Soft if this value is d_{EE-}.

Defender's credibility parameters are probabilities, p_{HH}, p_{HS}, p_{SH}, and p_{SS}, satisfying

$$p_{HH} + p_{HS} + p_{SH} + p_{SS} = 1.$$

Defender is interpreted to be both tactically and strategically Hard with probability p_{HH}, tactically Hard but strategically Soft with probability p_{HS}, tactically Soft but strategically Hard with probability p_{SH}, and both tactically and strategically Soft with probability p_{SS}.

The "Massive Retaliation" version of the Asymmetric Escalation Game, analyzed in appendix 6, corresponds to credibility parameters satisfying

$$p_{HH} = 0, p_{HS} = 0, p_{SH} = p_{Def}, p_{SS} = 1 - p_{Def}$$

where $0 < p_{Def} < 1$ (see figure A6.1). The "Flexible Response" version of the Asymmetric Escalation Game, analyzed in appendix 7, corresponds to credibility parameters satisfying

$$p_{HH} = p_{Def}, p_{HS} = 1 - p_{Def}, p_{SH} = 0, p_{SS} = 0$$

where $0 < p_{Def} < 1$ (see figure A7.1). In the general version of the Asymmetric Escalation Game analyzed in appendix 8 (see figure A8.1), the credibility parameters satisfy

$$p_{HH} > 0, p_{HS} > 0, p_{SH} > 0, p_{SS} > 0, p_{HH} + p_{HS} + p_{SH} + p_{SS} = 1.$$

Appendix 2 **Useful definitions**

The four deterrence games developed in the text are summarized in appendix 1 and analyzed in appendices 3–8. Each deterrence model includes payoff parameters and credibility parameters. The analyses often turn on the magnitude of a credibility parameter relative to a function of the payoff parameters; such a function is called a *threshold*. Also relevant to the analyses are certain quantities involving both payoff and credibility parameters; these are called *strategy functions*, and will usually be expressed as functions of the credibility parameters.

  The purpose of this appendix is to collect the definitions and basic properties of the thresholds and strategy functions for easy reference and comparison. Each of the models described in appendix 1 corresponds to a section of this appendix. Strategy functions appearing frequently in the analysis are given special symbols; these functions, and their properties, are described in section A2.5.

A2.1 Rudimentary Asymmetric Deterrence Game

The analysis (see appendix 3) of the Rudimentary Asymmetric Deterrence Game (see section A1.1) refers to only one threshold,

$$a_{\mathrm{m}} = \frac{a_{\mathrm{DC}} - a_{\mathrm{SQ}}}{a_{\mathrm{DC}} - a_{\mathrm{DD}}}.$$

Note that $0 < a_{\mathrm{m}} < 1$. No strategy functions are required for the analysis of this simple model.

A2.2 Generalized Mutual Deterrence Game

The analysis (see appendix 4) of the Generalized Mutual Deterrence Game (see section A1.2) refers to the following thresholds:

$$a_1 = \frac{a_{DC} - a_{SQ}}{a_{DC} - a_{DD-}}, \quad a_u = \frac{a_{DC} - a_{SQ}}{a_{DC} - a_{SQ} + a_{CD} - a_{DD-}}, \quad a_2 = \frac{a_{DC} - a_{SQ}}{a_{DC} - a_{DD+}},$$

$$b_1 = \frac{b_{CD} - b_{SQ}}{b_{CD} - b_{DD-}}, \quad b_u = \frac{b_{CD} - b_{SQ}}{b_{CD} - b_{SQ} + b_{DC} - b_{DD-}}, \quad b_2 = \frac{b_{CD} - b_{SQ}}{b_{CD} - b_{DD+}}.$$

Note that $0 < a_1 < \min\{a_u, a_2\} \le \max\{a_u, a_2\} < 1$, and $a_2 > a_u$ iff $a_{CD} - a_{DD-} > a_{SQ} - a_{DD+}$. Analogously, $0 < b_1 < \min\{b_u, b_2\} \le \max\{b_u, b_2\} < 1$, and $b_2 > b_u$ iff $b_{DC} - b_{DD-} > b_{SQ} - b_{DD+}$.

The analysis of the Generalized Mutual Deterrence Game also makes reference to the following strategy functions:

$$k(p_A; b_2), g(p_A; b_u), u_{1G}(p_A) = \frac{p_A(b_{CD} - b_{DD-}) - (b_{CD} - b_{SQ})}{p_A(b_{SQ} - b_{DC})},$$

$$k(p_B; a_2), g(p_B; a_u), v_{1G}(p_B) = \frac{p_B(a_{DC} - a_{DD-}) - (a_{DC} - a_{SQ})}{p_B(a_{SQ} - a_{CD})}.$$

It can be shown that $0 < u_{1G}(p_A) < 1$ iff $b_1 < p_A < b_u$ and $0 < v_{1G}(p_B) < 1$ iff $a_1 < p_B < a_u$. For definitions and properties of strategy functions, including $k(p; e)$ and $g(p; e)$, see section A2.5.

A2.3 Unilateral Deterrence Game

The analysis (see appendix 5) of the Unilateral Deterrence Game (see section A1.3) refers to the following thresholds:

$$c_s = \frac{c_{DC} - c_{SQ}}{c_{DC} - c_{CD}}, \quad c_t = \frac{c_{DC} - c_{SQ}}{c_{DC} - c_{DD+}},$$

$$d_n = \frac{d_{CD} - d_{DC}}{d_{CD} - d_{DD-}}, \quad d_{del} = \frac{d_{CD} - d_{SQ}}{d_{DC} - d_{DD+}}.$$

It is easy to verify that $0 < c_s < c_t < 1$, $0 < d_n < 1$, and $d_{del} > 0$ iff $d_{CD} > d_{SQ}$.

The analysis of the Unilateral Deterrence Game also makes reference to the strategy functions

$$g(p_{Def}; c_t), \quad g(p_{Def}; c_s), \quad f(p_{Ch}; d_n).$$

Definitions and fundamental properties of these functions are given in section A2.5.

A2.4 Asymmetric Escalation Game

The analysis (see appendices 6–8) of the Asymmetric Escalation Game (see section A1.4) makes use of a number of thresholds that are listed here for convenience. The thresholds based on Challenger's payoff parameters are:

$$c_1 = \frac{c_{DC} - c_{SQ}}{c_{DC} - c_{DE}}, \quad c_2 = \frac{c_{DC} - c_{SQ}}{c_{DC} - c_{EE+}}, \quad c_3 = \frac{c_{DC} - c_{SQ}}{c_{DC} - c_{DD}},$$

$$c_r = \frac{c_{ED} - c_{DD}}{c_{ED} - c_{EE-}}, \quad c_q = \frac{c_{ED} - c_{DD}}{c_{ED} - c_{EE+}}, \quad c^* = c_3 c_q.$$

Note that $0 < c_1 < c_2 < c_3 < 1$, $0 < c_r < c_q < 1$, and $c^* < \min\{c_3, c_q\}$. In addition, define

$$C_{ind} = (c_{DC} - c_{ED})(c_{DD} - c_{EE+}) - (c_{ED} - c_{DD})(c_{EE+} - c_{DE})$$

$$c_m = \frac{(c_{ED} - c_{DD})(c_{EE+} - c_{DE}) - (c_{SQ} - c_{ED})(c_{DD} - c_{EE+})}{(c_{ED} - c_{EE+})(c_{DD} - c_{DE})}.$$

The indicator C_{ind} may be positive, negative, or zero. If $C_{ind} > 0$, then $c_m < c^* < c_1$; if $C_{ind} < 0$, then $c_1 < c^* < c_m$; and if $C_{ind} = 0$, then $c_m = c^* = c_1$.

The thresholds based on Defender's payoff parameters are:

$$d_1 = \frac{d_{DE} - d_{DC}}{d_{DE} - d_{EE-}}, \quad d_2 = \frac{d_{DE} - d_{DC}}{d_{DE} - d_{EE+}}, \quad d_q = \frac{d_{DE} - d_{DD}}{d_{DE} - d_{EE+}},$$

$$d_p = \frac{d_{DE} - d_{DD+}}{d_{DE} - d_{EE-}}, \quad d_r = \frac{d_{DD+} - d_{DC}}{d_{DD+} - d_{ED}}, \quad d_s = \frac{d_{DD+} - d_{DC}}{d_{DD+} - d_{EE+}},$$

$$d_t = \frac{(d_{DE} - d_{DD+})(d_{DD+} - d_{ED}) + (d_{DD+} - d_{EE+})(d_{DD+} - d_{DC})}{(d_{DE} - d_{EE+})(d_{DD+} - d_{ED})}.$$

and $d^* = \max\{d_1, d_t\}$. It is easy to verify that $0 < d_r < d_s < 1$; $0 < d_p < \min\{d_q, d_1\} \leq \max\{d_q, d_1\} < d_2 < 1$; $\max\{d_q, d_r\} < d_t < d_2$. Note that d_q and d_t appear in appendix 7, where $d = d_{DD-}$, and in appendix 8, where d_{DD+} is meaningful. All relevant inequalities remain true.

The following strategy functions appear in the three appendices where the Asymmetric Escalation Game is analyzed:

$$f(p_{Ch}; d_2), \ f(p_{Ch}; d_1), \ g(p_{Def}; c_1). \tag{App. 6}$$

$$f(p_{Ch}; d_2), \ f(p_{Ch}; d_1), \ f(p_{Ch}; d_t), \ k(r; d_q),$$
$$f(p_{Def}; c_q), \ g(p_{Def}; c_1), \ h(p_{Def}; c_1), \tag{App. 7}$$
$$y_{HL}(p_{Def}) = \frac{c_{ED} - c_{DD}}{p_{Def}} \left[\frac{(c_{DC} - c_{SQ}) - p_{Def}(c_{DC} - c_{DE})}{c_{ind}} \right]$$

$$f(p_{Ch}; d_2), \ f(p_{Ch}; d_1), \ f(p_{Ch}; d_q), \ f(p_{Ch}; d_t), \ h(p_{Ch}; d_r), \ h(r; d_r),$$
$$h(d_2; d_r), h(d_t; d_r), h(p_{Ch}; d_q), k(p_{Ch}; d_q), k(d_1; d_q), \alpha = \frac{p_{HH}(1 - c_q)}{p_{HS}c_q},$$
$$z_{E2} = \frac{1 - p_{HH}/c^*}{p_{SH}/c_1}, \quad z_{C2} = \frac{1 - p_{HH}/c_3 - p_{HS}/c_3}{p_{SH}/c_1}, \tag{App. 8}$$
$$z_{C4} = \frac{1 - p_{HH}/c_3 - p_{HS}/c_3 - p_{SH}/c_1}{p_{SS}/c_1},$$
$$y_{C5} = \frac{p_{HH}/c_1 - p_{HS}/c_3 - p_{SH}/c_1 - 1}{p_{HH}(1/c_1 - 1/c_3)},$$
$$z_{E5} = \frac{1 - p_{HH}/c_1 - p_{HS}(1/c^* - 1/c_1)c_q/(1 - c_q) - p_{SH}/c_1}{p_{SS}/c_1},$$
$$y_{E6} = \frac{1 - p_{HH}/c_1 - p_{SH}/c_1}{p_{HH}/(1/c^* - 1/c_1)}.$$

For definitions and properties of the standard strategy functions f, g, h, j, and k, see section A2.5.

A2.5 Standard strategy functions

Let e be a payoff parameter (for example, e might represent a_{SQ} or d_{EE+}) and let p be a credibility (p might represent a credibility parameter, such as p_B or p_{Ch}, or a conditional probability, such as r). Define

$$f(p; e) = \frac{p(1 - e)}{e(1 - p)}, \quad g(p; e) = \frac{e - p}{1 - p},$$

$$h(p; e) = \frac{e}{p}, \quad j(p; e) = \frac{p - e}{p}, \quad k(p; e) = \frac{p - e}{p(1 - e)}.$$

Because $0 < p < 1$ and $0 < e < 1$, the values of $f(p; e)$, $g(p; e)$, $h(p; e)$, $j(p; e)$, and $k(p; e)$ all lie between 0 and 1 under certain conditions, as follows:

$f(p; e) > 0$ always, and $f(p; e) < 1$ iff $p < e$;
$g(p; e) > 0$ iff $p < e$, and $g(p; e) < 1$ always;
$h(p; e) > 0$ always, and $h(p; e) < 1$ iff $p > e$;
$j(p; e) > 0$ iff $p > e$, and $j(p; e) < 1$ always;
and $k(p; e) > 0$ iff $p > e$, and $k(p; e) < 1$ always.

Appendix 3 **Rudimentary Asymmetric Deterrence Game**

This appendix contains the detailed analysis of the *Rudimentary Asymmetric Deterrence Game with incomplete information* introduced in section 3.4 and specified in detail in section A1.1. (See also figure 3.7 and figure A1.1.)

Recall that the eight parameter values satisfy $0 < p_B < 1$, $a_{DD} < a_{SQ} < a_{DC}$, and $b_{DD-} < b_{DC} < b_{DD+} < b_{SQ}$. Moreover, player B is Hard, i.e. B's utility for outcome DD is b_{DD+}, with probability p_B, and B is Soft, i.e. B's utility for outcome DD is b_{DD-}, with probability $1 - p_B$. Observe that there is one-sided incomplete information in this game – there are two types of B, but only one type of A.

Our primary objective is to identify the Bayesian equilibria of the Rudimentary Asymmetric Deterrence Game. For details on Bayesian equilibria and perfect Bayesian equilibria, see Fudenberg and Tirole (1991). We take A's only strategic variable to be x, and B's strategic variables to be y_H and y_S, as follows:

$$x \ = \Pr\{A \text{ chooses } D\}$$
$$y_H = \Pr\{B \text{ chooses } D \mid B \text{ is Hard}\}$$
$$y_S = \Pr\{B \text{ chooses } D \mid B \text{ is Soft}\}$$

This produces the game shown in figure A3.1. Bayesian equilibria will be denoted $[x\,;y_H, y_S]$.

First, $y_H = 1$ and $y_S = 0$ at any Bayesian equilibrium. This is easy to verify (see figure A3.1): at node 2, B must choose D ($y = 1$), yielding outcome DD, or C ($y = 0$), yielding outcome DC. When B is Hard, B's utility for outcome DD is b_{DD+}, which by assumption exceeds B's utility for DC, b_{DC}. Thus, a Hard B must choose D at node 2, i.e., $y_H = 1$. Similarly, when B is Soft, B's utility for DD is $b_{DD-} < b_{DC}$, so B must choose C at node 2, i.e., $y_S = 0$.

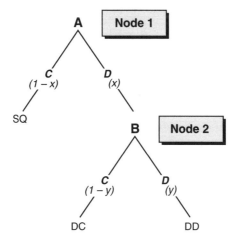

Fig. A3.1. Rudimentary Asymmetric Deterrence Game.

Now consider node 1, at which A must choose either C ($x = 0$) or D ($x = 1$). If A chooses C, outcome SQ follows, yielding utility $E_A(C) = a_{SQ}$ to A. If A chooses D, then B must choose at node 2. Because B is Hard with probability p_B and Soft with probability $1 - p_B$, it follows that A's expected utility should it choose D at node 1 is

$$E_A(D) = p_B a_{DD} + (1 - p_B) a_{DC}.$$

Thus, a Bayesian equilibrium requires that A choose D iff $E_A(D) > a_{SQ}$. Because $a_{DD} > a_{SQ} > a_{DC}$, this condition is equivalent to

$$p_B < \frac{a_{DC} - a_{SQ}}{a_{DC} - a_{DD}} = a_m.$$

The unique Bayesian equilibrium of the game is therefore $[x; y_H, y_S] = [1; 1, 0]$ if $p_B < a_m$. It is easy to verify directly that if $p_B > a_m$ the unique Bayesian equilibrium is $[x; y_H, y_S] = [0; 1, 0]$. (Any value of x is consistent with Bayesian equilibrium if $p_B = a_m$. However, equilibria that can occur only on a "set of measure zero" in parameter space – i.e., that occur only when the parameter values satisfy a functional equation that is not identically true – will not be emphasized here.)

In summary, the Rudimentary Asymmetric Deterrence Game has a unique Bayesian equilibrium $[x; y_H, y_S] = [0; 1, 0]$ if $p_B > a_m$. The outcome at this equilibrium, called the *Deterrence Equilibrium*, is SQ for certain. A's expected utility is a_{SQ} and B's is b_{SQ}, whether B is Hard or

Soft. If $p_B < a_m$, the unique Bayesian equilibrium is $[x; y_H, y_S] = [1; 1, 0]$ and is called the *Attack Equilibrium*. The outcome at the Attack Equilibrium is DD with probability p_B and DC with complementary probability $1 - p_B$. A's expected utility is $p_B a_{DD} + (1 - p_B) a_{DC}$, and B's is b_{DD+} if B is Hard and b_{DC} if B is Soft.

Finally, note that not all of the assumptions about the Rudimentary Asymmetric Deterrence Game detailed in section A1.1 are necessary to the analysis. The analysis of strategic choices depends only on the ordering $b_{DD+} > b_{DC} > b_{DD-}$, and not on the specific values, nor on the absolute or relative value of B's utility for outcome SQ, b_{SQ}. Of course, B's expected utilities at the equilibrium depend on b_{SQ}, b_{DD+}, and b_{DC}.

Appendix 4 Generalized Mutual Deterrence Game

This appendix contains the detailed analysis of the *Generalized Mutual Deterrence Game with incomplete information*, introduced in chapter 4 and specified in section A1.2. (See also figures 4.1 and A1.3.) Recall that the twelve parameter values satisfy $0 < p_A < 1$, $0 < p_B < 1$, $a_{DD-} < a_{CD} < a_{DD+} < a_{SQ} < a_{DC}$, and $b_{DD-} < b_{DC} < b_{DD+} < b_{SQ} < b_{CD}$. Moreover, player A is Hard, i.e., A's utility for outcome DD is a_{DD+}, with probability p_A, and A is Soft, i.e., A's utility for outcome DD is a_{DD-}, with probability $1 - p_A$. Similarly, B is Hard (utility b_{DD+} for DD) with probability p_B, and Soft (utility b_{DD-} for DD) with probability $1 - p_B$.

We are interested only in subgame-perfect equilibria, so we can assume that choices at nodes 3a and 3b are made optimally, according to type. Thus we take A's only strategic variables to be x_H and x_S for the probabilities that A chooses D at node 1 when Hard and when Soft, respectively. Likewise, B's strategic variables, representing the probability that B chooses D at nodes 2a and 2b, are y_H if B is Hard and y_S if B is Soft. This produces the game shown in figure A4.1. A's expected utilities are

$$
\begin{aligned}
E_{A|H}(x_H; y_H, y_S) &= p_B\Big[(1 - x_H)(1 - y_H)a_{SQ} + (x_H + y_H - x_H y_H)a_{DD+}\Big] \\
&\quad + (1 - p_B)\Big[(1 - x_H)(1 - y_S)a_{SQ} + x_H(1 - y_S)a_{DC} + y_S a_{DD+}\Big] \\
E_{A|S}(x_S; y_H, y_S) &= p_B\Big[(1 - x_S)(1 - y_H)a_{SQ} + (1 - x_S)y_H a_{CD} + x_S a_{DD-}\Big] \\
&\quad + (1 - p_B)\Big[(1 - x_S)(1 - y_S)a_{SQ} + x_S(1 - y_S)a_{DC} \\
&\quad + (1 - x_S)y_S a_{CD} + x_S y_S a_{DD-}\Big]
\end{aligned}
\tag{A4.1}
$$

given that A is Hard or Soft, respectively. B's expected payoffs are analogous.

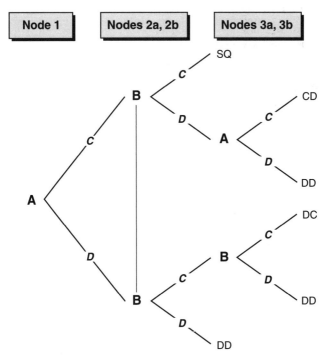

Fig. A4.1. Generalized Mutual Deterrence Game.

Taking the parameter values as fixed, we will find all subgame-perfect Bayesian equilibria of this game. Our search is greatly aided by four lemmas.

Lemma A4.1

(a) $\dfrac{\partial E_{A|H}}{\partial x_H} \geq 0$ iff $X_H = -p_B(1 - y_H)(a_{SQ} - a_{DD+})$

$$+ (1 - p_B)(1 - y_S)(a_{DC} - a_{SQ}) \geq 0$$

with equality iff $X_H = 0$;

(b) $\dfrac{\partial E_{A|S}}{\partial x_S} \geq 0$ iff $X_S = -p_B\Big[(a_{SQ} - a_{DD-}) - y_H(a_{SQ} - a_{CD})\Big]$

$$+ (1 - p_B)\Big[(1 - y_S)(a_{DC} - a_{SQ})$$

$$- y_S(a_{CD} - a_{DD-})\Big] \geq 0$$

with equality iff $X_S = 0$.

Proof Differentiate (A4.1) and combine terms. ∎

To illustrate the usefulness of lemma A4.1, suppose that a specific strategy combination $[x_H, x_S; y_H, y_S]$ is an equilibrium. Notice that the value of X_H depends only on B's strategic variables, not on A's. If it happens that $X_H > 0$, then $x_H = 1$ is necessary. Also $X_H < 0$ implies $x_H = 0$, whereas $X_H = 0$ is consistent with any value of x_H. Similar inferences can be drawn about the relations of X_S with x_S, Y_H with y_H, and Y_S with y_S, where Y_H and Y_S are defined analogously to X_H and X_S.

Some direct consequences of lemma A4.1 give important information about the structure of equilibria.

Lemma A4.2 Suppose that $[x_H, x_S; y_H, y_S]$ is an equilibrium.

If $x_S > 0$, then $x_H = 1$. If $x_H < 1$, then $x_S = 0$.
If $y_S > 0$, then $y_H = 1$. If $y_H < 1$, then $y_S = 0$.

Proof All of the conclusions will follow from lemma A4.1 if it can be shown that

$$X_H > X_S \text{ and } Y_H > Y_S. \tag{A4.2}$$

But $X_H - X_S = p_B(1 - y_H)(a_{DD+} - a_{CD}) + (p_B + y_S - p_B y_S)(a_{CD} - a_{DD-})$
> 0, and analogously for $Y_H - Y_S$. ∎

Lemma A4.3 Suppose that $[x_H, x_S; y_H, y_S]$ is an equilibrium. If $y_H = 1$ and $y_S < 1$, then $x_H = 1$. If $x_H = 1$ and $x_S < 1$, then $y_H = 1$.

Proof If $y_H = 1$ and $y_S < 1$, then $X_H > 0$, so $x_H = 1$ follows from lemma A4.1. The proof of the second assertion is analogous. ∎

Lemma A4.4 Suppose that $[x_H, x_S; y_H, y_S]$ is an equilibrium. If $y_S = 1$, then $x_S = 0$. If $x_S = 1$, then $y_S = 0$.

Proof If $y_S = 1$, $X_S = -p_B(1 - y_H)(a_{SQ} - a_{CD}) - (a_{CD} - a_{DD-}) < 0$. Therefore $x_S = 0$ follows from lemma A4.1. The second assertion is proven analogously. ∎

It is a consequence of lemmas A4.2, A4.3, and A4.4 that the only possible equilibria are the fourteen combinations shown in the "stra-

Table A4.1. *Subgame-perfect Bayesian equilibria of the Generalized Mutual Deterrence Game*

Class	Symbol	Strategic variables				Existence conditions	
		x_H	x_S	y_H	y_S	on p_A	on p_B
1	STDE	0	0	0	0	$p_A \geq b_2$ and	$p_B \geq a_2$
	HE	$k(p_A; b_2)$	0	$k(p_B; a_2)$	0	$p_A > b_2$ and	$p_B > a_2$
	SE	1	0	1	0	$p_A \geq b_u$ and	$p_B \geq a_u$
2A	AE_{1A}	1	1	0	0		$p_B \leq a_1$
	AE_{2A}	1	1	$\geq v_{1G}(p_B)$	0		$p_B < a_u$
	AE_{3A}	1	1	1	0		$p_B \leq a_u$
2B	AE_{1B}	0	0	1	1	$p_A \leq b_1$	
	AE_{2B}	$\geq u_{1G}(p_A)$	0	1	1	$p_A < b_u$	
	AE_{3B}	1	0	1	1	$p_A \leq b_u$	
3	BE	1	$g(p_A; b_u)$	1	$g(p_B; a_u)$	$p_A < b_u$ and $p_B < a_u$	
T	TE_1	$\leq k(p_A; b_2)$	0	0	0	$p_A \geq b_2$ and	$p_B = a_2$
	TE_2	0	0	$\leq k(p_B; a_2)$	0	$p_A = b_2$ and	$p_B \geq a_2$
	TE_3	1	$\geq g(p_A; b_u)$	1	0	$p_A < b_u$ and	$p_B = a_u$
	TE_4	1	0	1	$\geq g(p_B; a_u)$	$p_A = b_u$ and	$p_B < a_u$

tegic variables" columns of table A4.1. (In table A4.1, and throughout this appendix, u denotes a value of a strategic variable of A satisfying $0 < u < 1$, and v denotes a value of a strategic variable of B satisfying $0 < v < 1$.) Other symbols appearing in table A4.1 are defined in the text, or below.

In terms of the game model described in chapter 4 and figure 4.1, the interpretation of lemma A4.2 is simple: at equilibrium, a player is at least as aggressive when Hard as when Soft. This is hardly surprising, because a Hard player is not so averse to the conflict outcome that aggressiveness might bring about. Lemma A4.3 indicates that if your opponent is always aggressive when Hard but not always when Soft, then you should always be aggressive if you are Hard (because you may be able to take advantage of a Soft opponent "chickening out"). Lemma A4.4 says that a player whose opponent is always aggressive when Soft should never be aggressive when Soft – a conclusion that is easy to accept on the basis of the complete information game.

The thresholds for the Generalized Mutual Deterrence Game (see appendix 2) are as follows:

$$a_1 = \frac{a_{DC} - a_{SQ}}{a_{DC} - a_{DD-}}, \quad a_u = \frac{a_{DC} - a_{SQ}}{a_{DC} - a_{SQ} + a_{CD} - a_{DD-}}, \quad a_2 = \frac{a_{DC} - a_{SQ}}{a_{DC} - a_{DD+}},$$

$$b_1 = \frac{b_{CD} - b_{SQ}}{b_{CD} - b_{DD-}}, \quad b_u = \frac{b_{CD} - b_{SQ}}{b_{CD} - b_{SQ} + b_{DC} - b_{DD-}}, \quad b_2 = \frac{b_{CD} - b_{SQ}}{b_{CD} - b_{DD+}}.$$

Note that $0 < a_1 < a_u < 1$, $a_1 < a_2 < 1$, and $a_2 \geq a_u$ iff $a_{SQ} - a_{DD+} \leq a_{CD} - a_{DD-}$ with equality iff $a_{SQ} - a_{DD+} = a_{CD} - a_{DD-}$; similarly for b_1, b_u, and b_2.

We now begin a systematic process to determine existence conditions for each possible equilibrium. First suppose that $y_H = y_S = 0$. It is easy to check that $X_H \leq 0$ iff $p_B \geq a_2$. By (A4.2), $p_B \geq a_2$ implies $X_S < 0$, and now lemma A4.1 shows that A's best response is $x_H = 0$ and $x_S = 0$. Carrying out an analogous calculation for B completes the justification of STDE of table A4.1; the combination [0, 0; 0, 0] is an equilibrium iff $p_B \geq a_2$ and $p_A \geq b_2$.

Again assuming that $y_H = y_S = 0$, it is easy to verify that $X_S \geq 0$ iff $p_B \leq a_1$. By (A4.2), $X_S \geq 0$ implies $X_H > 0$, and lemma A4.1 now shows that A's best response is $x_H = 1$ and $x_S = 1$. Now assume that $x_H = x_S = 1$ and consider B's best response. It is easy to verify that $Y_H = 0$ and $Y_S < 0$, so lemma A4.1 shows that B can do no better than to choose $y_H = 0$ and $y_S = 0$. Thus [1, 1; 0, 0] is an equilibrium iff $p_B \leq a_1$; this equilibrium is denoted AE_{1A} in table A4.1; the analysis for AE_{1B} is analogous.

The calculations supporting the other assertions about pure strategy equilibria in table A4.1 are similar. In particular,

SE: [1, 0; 1, 0] is an equilibrium iff $p_B \geq a_u$ and $p_A \geq b_u$
AE_{3A}: [1, 1; 1, 0] is an equilibrium iff $p_B \leq a_u$
AE_{3B}: [1, 0; 1, 1] is an equilibrium iff $p_A \leq b_u$.

There are no pure strategy equilibria other than STDE, AE_{1A}, AE_{1B}, SE, AE_{3A}, and AE_{3B}.

To begin the analysis of equilibria involving exactly one mixed strategy, assume again that $y_H = y_S = 0$. It is easy to verify that $X_H = 0$ iff $p_B = a_2$. Therefore, A's best response can be $x_H = u$ (for some u satisfying $0 < u < 1$) only if $p_B = a_2$. By lemma A4.2, $x_S = 0$. Now, if $x_H = u$ and $x_S = 0$, $Y_H = -p_A(1-u)(b_{SQ} - b_{DD+}) + (1-p_A)(b_{CD} - b_{SQ})$, so that $Y_H \leq 0$ iff

$$u \leq \frac{p_A(b_{CD} - b_{DD+}) - (b_{CD} - b_{SQ})}{p_A(b_{SQ} - b_{DD+})} = k(p_A; b_2), \tag{A4.3}$$

which implies $Y_S < 0$ by (A4.2). Furthermore $k(p_A; b_2) \geq 0$ iff $p_A \geq b_2$, as noted in section A2.5. Thus necessary conditions for TE_1 of table A4.1, $[u, 0; 0, 0]$, are $p_B = a_2$, $p_A \geq b_2$, and (A4.3). It can be verified that these conditions are also sufficient. Existence conditions for TE_2 are analogous. Observe that TE_1 and TE_2 are Transitional Equilibria, because they exist only when $p_B = a_2$ (for TE_1) and $p_A = b_2$ (for TE_2).

Now suppose that $y_H = y_S = 1$. Because $X_H = 0$ and $X_S = -(a_{CD} - a_{DD-})$, a best response for A is $x_H = u$ (where $0 < u < 1$) and $x_S = 0$. Now assume that $x_H = u$, $x_S = 0$. By (A4.2), $y_H = 1$ and $y_S = 1$ will be a best response for B iff $Y_S \geq 0$. But $Y_S = -p_A[(b_{SQ} - b_{DD-}) - u(b_{SQ} - b_{DC})] + (1 - p_A)(b_{CD} - b_{SQ}) \leq 0$ iff

$$u \geq \frac{p_A(b_{CD} - b_{DD-}) - (b_{CD} - b_{SQ})}{p_A(b_{SQ} - b_{DC})} = u_{1G}(p_A). \tag{A4.4}$$

Furthermore $u_{1G}(p_A) < 1$ iff $p_A < b_u$, as noted in section A2.5. This shows that AE_{2B} of table A4.1, $[u, 0; 1, 1]$, is an equilibrium iff $p_A < b_u$ and (A4.4) holds. The analysis for AE_{2A} is parallel.

If $y_H = 1$ and $y_S = 0$, then $X_H > 0$. Also, $X_S = 0$ iff $p_B = a_u$. By lemma A4.1, a best response for A is $x_H = 1$ and $x_S = u$, where $0 < u < 1$. Now if $x_H = 1$ and $x_S = u$, $Y_H > 0$ and $Y_S = -p_A (b_{DC} - b_{DD-}) + (1 - p_A) [(b_{CD} - b_{SQ}) - u (b_{CD} - b_{SQ} + b_{DC} - b_{DD-})] \leq 0$ iff

$$u \geq 1 - \frac{b_{DC} - b_{DD-}}{(1 - p_A)(b_{CD} - b_{SQ} + b_{DC} - b_{DD-})} = g(p_A; b_u). \tag{A4.5}$$

As noted in section A2.5, $g(p_A; b_u) > 0$ iff $p_A < b_u$. Thus TE_3 of table A4.1, $[1, u; 1, 0]$, is an equilibrium iff $p_A < b_u$, $p_B = a_u$, and (A4.5) holds. TE_4 is similar. Note that TE_3 and TE_4 are transitional. This completes the analysis of equilibria involving exactly one mixed strategy.

To analyze HE of table A4.1, assume that $y_H = v$ and $y_S = 0$, for some v satisfying $0 < v < 1$. In order that $x_H = u$ and $x_S = 0$ be A's best response, it is necessary and sufficient that $X_H = 0$, by (A4.2). But $X_H = -p_B (1 - v) (a_{SQ} - a_{DD+}) + (1 - p_B) (a_{DC} - a_{SQ}) = 0$ iff

$$v = \frac{p_B(a_{DC} - a_{DD+}) - (a_{DC} - a_{SQ})}{p_B(a_{SQ} - a_{DD+})} = k(p_B; a_2). \tag{A4.6}$$

(Compare with (A4.3).) It now follows that equilibrium HE, $[u, 0; v, 0]$, occurs iff $p_A > b_2$, $p_B > a_2$, $u = k(p_A; b_2)$, and $v = k(p_B; a_2)$.

A similar argument can be used to prove that BE, $[1, u; 1, v]$, occurs iff $p_A < b_u$, $p_B < a_u$, $u = g(p_A; b_u)$, and $v = g(p_B; a_u)$. This completes the justification of the necessary and sufficient conditions for existence of all equilibria of the Generalized Mutual Deterrence Game with incomplete information, and table A4.1.

It is evident from inspection of table A4.1 that there is generally a multiplicity of equilibria corresponding to any particular set of parameter values. Fortunately some of these equilibria can be interpreted as unlikely to occur because others are preferred, often strictly preferred, by both players, and these preferences are independent of type. We now carry out expected utility comparisons for concurrent equilibria.

If $p_A > b_2$ and $p_B > a_2$, both STDE and HE exist. It is easy to verify that the players' expected utilities at STDE are $E_{A|H}(\text{STDE}) = E_{A|S}(\text{STDE}) = a_{SQ}$, and $E_{B|H}(\text{STDE}) = E_{B|S}(\text{STDE}) = b_{SQ}$.

To calculate A's payoffs at HE, note that the first equation of (A4.1) can be rewritten in the form $E_{A|H} = X_H x_H + W$. Because $0 < x_H < 1$ at HE, and it follows from lemma A4.1 that $X_H = 0$. This fact, combined with $y_H = k(p_B; a_2)$ and $y_S = 0$, yields

$$E_{A|H}(\text{HE}) = p_B a_{DD+} + (1 - p_B)a_{DC}. \tag{A4.7}$$

It follows easily that

$$E_{A|H}(\text{STDE}) - E_{A|H}(\text{HE}) = (a_{DC} - a_{DD+})(p_B - a_2) > 0. \tag{A4.8}$$

Analogously, the second equation of (A4.1) can be used to obtain

$$E_{A|S}(\text{HE}) = a_{SQ} - p_B k(p_B; a_2)(a_{SQ} - a_{CD})$$

which implies that $E_{A|S}(\text{STDE}) - E_{A|S}(\text{HE}) = p_B k(p_B; a_2)(a_{SQ} - a_{CD}) > 0$. In summary, both types of A strictly prefer STDE to HE whenever they coexist. Analogous conclusions can be drawn for B, leading to the conclusion that both types of both players strictly prefer STDE to HE whenever $p_B > a_2$ and $p_A > b_2$.

As is clear from table A4.1, STDE and HE are not the only equilibria when p_A and p_B are large. These two equilibria can coincide with SE = $[1, 0; 1, 0]$. It is easy to verify from (A4.1) that

$$E_{A|H}(\text{SE}) = p_B \, a_{DD+} + (1 - p_B)a_{DC}$$

so $E_{A|H}(\text{STDE}) \geq E_{A|H}(\text{SE})$ when $p_B \geq a_2$, with equality iff $p_B = a_2$. Similarly

$$E_{A|S}(\text{SE}) = p_B \, a_{CD} + (1 - p_B)a_{SQ}$$

which implies that $E_{A|S}(\text{STDE}) > E_{A|S}(\text{SE})$ for all $p_B \geq a_2$. Analogous results can be obtained for B, confirming that STDE is Pareto-superior to SE when these equilibria coexist. In particular, when both p_A and p_B are close to 1, the unique Pareto-optimal equilibrium is STDE.

When p_B is small, Class 2A equilibria $[1, 1; y_H, 0]$ arise – specifically AE_{1A}, AE_{2A}, and AE_{3A} (see table A4.1). It is easy to check that neither player's expected payoff ever depends on y_H in this circumstance. (In fact, the path through the extensive game tree [see figure A4.1] does not actually depend on y_H.) Therefore both types of both players are indifferent among all equilibria of the form $[0, 0; y_H, 1]$. The situation is similar for all equilibria of Class 2B, specifically AE_{1B}, AE_{2B}, and AE_{3B}, which exist when p_A is small.

When $p_A \leq b_u$ and $p_B \leq a_u$, three groups of equilibria coexist: Class 2A; Class 2B; and Class 3, which contains only BE. With lengthy calculation it can be shown that

$$E_{A|H}(2B) < E_{A|H}(\text{BE}) < E_{A|H}(2A)$$
$$E_{A|S}(2B) < E_{A|S}(\text{BE}) < E_{A|S}(2A)$$

and, analogously,

$$E_{B|H}(2A) < E_{B|H}(\text{BE}) < E_{B|H}(2B)$$
$$E_{B|S}(2A) < E_{B|S}(\text{BE}) < E_{B|S}(2B).$$

Thus, the players' preferences over these equilibria are always exactly opposite, and all three equilibria are always Pareto-optimal.

Finally, it is possible for STDE to coexist with equilibria of Class 2A, when $a_1 < a_2 \leq a_u$, and with equilibria of Class 2B, when $b_1 < b_2 \leq b_u$. It is easy to verify that both types of A always prefer STDE to equilibria of Class 2B when they coexist, and that if A is of type S, then A prefers STDE to equilibria of Class 2A. If A is of type H, A prefers STDE to equilibria of Class 2A if $p_B > a_2$, and has the reverse preference if $p_B < a_2$.

Appendix 5   Unilateral Deterrence Game

This appendix contains the detailed analysis of the *Asymmetric Deterrence Game with incomplete information* introduced in chapter 5 and specified in section A1.3. (See also figures 5.1 and A1.5.) In the base case, the twelve parameter values satisfy $0 < p_{Ch} < 1$, $0 < p_{Def} < 1$, $c_{DD-} < c_{CD} < c_{DD+} < c_{SQ} < c_{DC}$ and $d_{DD-} < d_{DC} < d_{DD+} < d_{SQ} < d_{DC}$. Moreover, player Challenger is Hard, i.e., Challenger's utility for outcome DD is c_{DD+}, with probability p_{Ch}, and Challenger is Soft, i.e., Challenger's utility for outcome DD is c_{DD-}, with probability $1 - p_{Ch}$. Analogously, player Defender is Hard, i.e., Defender's utility for outcome DD is d_{DD+}, with probability p_{Def}, and Defender is Soft, i.e., Defender's utility for outcome DD is d_{DD-}, with probability $1 - p_{Def}$.

Taking parameter values as fixed, we will find all perfect Bayesian equilibria (PBE) of the Unilateral Deterrence Game. These equilibria are expressed in terms of the following thresholds (see section A2.3):

$$c_s = \frac{c_{DC} - c_{SQ}}{c_{DC} - c_{CD}}, \quad c_t = \frac{c_{DC} - c_{SQ}}{c_{DC} - c_{DD+}}$$

$$d_n = \frac{d_{CD} - d_{DC}}{d_{CD} - d_{DD-}}, \quad d_{del} = \frac{d_{CD} - d_{SQ}}{d_{DC} - d_{DD+}}.$$

It is easy to verify that $0 < c_s < c_t < 1$ and $0 < d_n < 1$. Also, $d_{del} > 0$; but if $d_{CD} \leq d_{SQ}$, a possibility discussed in the text, $d_{del} \leq 0$.

First we note that, at node 3 of the game (see figure A1.5), optimal behavior for Challenger must depend only on Challenger's type; a Hard Challenger chooses D because choosing D leads to utility c_{DD+} whereas choosing C leads to utility $c_{CD} < c_{DD+}$; a Soft Challenger chooses C because choosing C leads to c_{CD} whereas choosing D leads to $c_{DD-} < c_{CD}$. Thus, at any equilibrium, a Hard Challenger chooses D at node 3, and a Soft Challenger chooses C.

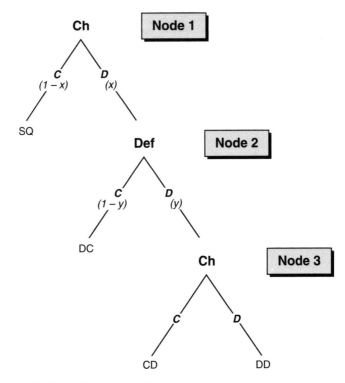

Fig. A5.1. Unilateral Deterrence Game.

Therefore Challenger's strategic variables to be determined at equilibrium are x_H, the probability that Challenger chooses D at node 1 given that it is Hard, and x_S, the probability that Challenger chooses D at node 1 given that it is Soft. Defender's strategic variables are y_H, the probability that Defender chooses D at node 2 given that Defender is Hard, and y_S, the probability that Defender chooses D at node 2 given that Defender is Soft. This produces the game shown in figure A5.1.

At node 1, players' beliefs about each other's types are the credibility parameters, p_{Ch} and p_{Def}. At node 2, Defender's beliefs about Challenger's type are to be updated based on Defender's observation of Challenger's behavior at node 1. In fact, Defender's choice at node 2 can rationally depend on Defender's updated beliefs about Challenger's type, because, as already noted, Challenger's equilibrium choice at node 3 depends explicitly on its type. Let p be a probability representing Defender's beliefs about Challenger's type given that the game reaches node 2; in other words, p is the conditional probability that Challenger is Hard given that Challenger chose D at node 1. We will denote an equilibrium by $[x_H, x_S; y_H, y_S, p]$.

We now develop necessary and sufficient conditions on x_H, x_S, y_H, y_S, and p in order that $[x_H, x_S; y_H, y_S, p]$ be an equilibrium. First, note that a Hard Defender's optimal choice at node 2 does not in fact depend on its beliefs about Challenger's type. If Defender is Hard, then Defender rationally chooses D for certain at node 2, because the two utility values it might receive by choosing D, d_{CD} and d_{DD+}, both exceed the utility value it would receive by choosing C, d_{DC}. Thus, at any equilibrium, $y_H = 1$.

Observe next that the Bayesian updating condition is

$$\text{if } x_H + x_S > 0, \ p = \frac{p_{Ch}x_H}{p_{Ch}x_H + (1 - p_{Ch})x_S}. \tag{A5.1}$$

Of course, (A5.1) is void if $x_H = x_S = 0$.

A Soft Defender's expected utility at node 2 is

$$E_{Def|S} = y_S\left[pd_{DD-} + (1-p)d_{CD}\right] + (1 - y_S)d_{DC},$$

from which it follows that

$$\frac{dE_{Def|S}}{dy_S} = pd_{DD-} + (1-p)d_{CD} - d_{DC}.$$

This derivative must be non-negative if y_S is to equal 1 at equilibrium and non-positive if y_S is to equal 0. It is easy to verify that the sign of the derivative is the same as the sign of $d_n - p$, where d_n is defined above. Thus the condition that a Soft Defender maximize its expected utility at equilibrium is equivalent to

$$\begin{array}{ll} \text{either} & y_S = 1 \text{ and } p \le d_n \\ \text{or} & y_S = 0 \text{ and } p \ge d_n \\ \text{or} & p = d_n. \end{array} \tag{A5.2}$$

We turn now to the analysis of Challenger's decision at node 1. Challenger's expected utility if Hard is

$$E_{Ch|H} = (1 - x_H)c_{SQ} + x_H\left[(1 - p_{Def})(1 - y_S)c_{DC} + (p_{Def} + y_S - p_{Def}\,y_S)c_{DD+}\right],$$

from which it follows that

$$\frac{dE_{Ch|H}}{dx_H} = -c_{SQ} + c_{DD+} - (1 - p_{Def})(1 - y_S)(c_{DD+} - c_{DC}).$$

This derivative must be non-negative if x_H is to equal 1 at equilibrium and non-positive if x_H is to equal 0. It is easy to verify that the sign of the derivative is the same as the sign of $(1 - p_{Def})(1 - y_S) - (1 - c_t)$, where c_t is as defined above. Thus the condition that a Hard Challenger choose so as to maximize its expected utility at node 1 is equivalent to

$$
\begin{array}{lll}
\text{either} & x_H = 1 \text{ and } (1 - p_{Def})(1 - y_S) \geq 1 - c_t & \\
\text{or} & x_H = 0 \text{ and } (1 - p_{Def})(1 - y_S) \leq 1 - c_t & \text{(A5.3)} \\
\text{or} & (1 - p_{Def})(1 - y_S) = 1 - c_t. &
\end{array}
$$

Analogously, for a Soft Challenger at node 1,

$$E_{Ch|S} = (1 - x_S)c_{SQ} + x_S\left[(1 - p_{Def})(1 - y_S)c_{DC} + (p_{Def} + y_S - p_{Def}\, y_S)c_{CD}\right].$$

Similar calculations now show that the condition that a Soft Challenger's choice at node 1 maximize its expected utility is equivalent to

$$
\begin{array}{lll}
\text{either} & x_S = 1 \text{ and } (1 - p_{Def})(1 - y_S) \geq 1 - c_s & \\
\text{or} & x_S = 0 \text{ and } (1 - p_{Def})(1 - y_S) \leq 1 - c_s & \text{(A5.4)} \\
\text{or} & (1 - p_{Def})(1 - y_S) = 1 - c_s, &
\end{array}
$$

where c_s is as defined above.

Our calculations have shown that an equilibrium is a 5-tuple of probabilities, $[x_H, x_S; y_H, y_S, p]$, satisfying $y_H = 1$ and (A5.1)–(A5.4). The following lemma makes the search for equilibria easier:

> **Lemma A5.1** Suppose x_H and x_S are probabilities satisfying (A5.3) and (A5.4). Then
>
> (i) if $x_S > 0$, $x_H = 1$;
> (ii) if $x_H < 1$, $x_S = 0$.
>
> **Proof** Both (i) and (ii) follow immediately from the fact that $1 - c_s > 1 - c_t$, which follows from the relation $c_s < c_t$, noted above. ∎

The equilibria are most conveniently classified using the values of x_H and x_S; the lemma is helpful because it reduces the number of classes.

Deterrence Equilibria ($x_H = x_S = 0$)

Any equilibrium with $x_H = x_S = 0$ is called a Deterrence Equilibrium, as it always results in the *Status Quo*. For such an equilibrium, the Bayesian updating condition (A5.1) does not apply because node 2 is off the equilibrium path.

For a Deterrence Equilibrium with $y_S = 1$, (A5.2) requires that $p \leq d_n$. Because $(1 - p_{Def})(1 - y_S) = 0 < 1 - c_t < 1 - c_s$, (A5.3) and (A5.4) are satisfied automatically. For a Deterrence Equilibrium with $y_S = 0$, (A5.2) implies $p \geq d^*$, and (A5.3) is satisfied iff

$$p_{Def} \geq \frac{c_{DC} - c_{SQ}}{c_{DC} - c_{DD+}} = c_t.$$

Of course, if (A5.3) holds, (A5.4) does also. Finally, for a Deterrence Equilibrium with $0 < y_S < 1$, conditions (A5.2) and (A5.3) yield $p = d_n$ and $y_S \geq u^* = g(p_{Def}; c_t)$.

In summary, there is a *Deterrence Equilibrium* for any values of p_{Ch} and p_{Def}. If $p_{Def} \geq c_t$, the Deterrence Equilibria are described by $y_S = 0$ and $p \geq d_n$, or $0 < y_S < 1$ and $p = d_n$, or $y_S = 1$ and $p \leq d_n$. If $p_{Def} < c_t$, the Deterrence Equilibria are given by $g(p_{Def}; c_t) \leq y_S < 1$ and $p = d_n$, or $y_S = 1$ and $p \leq d_n$.

Separating Equilibria ($x_H = 1$, $x_S = 0$)

From (A5.1), $p = 1$ at any Separating Equilibrium, so $y_S = 0$ is the only possibility consistent with (A5.2). But now (A5.3) shows that $x_H = 1$ can occur only if $p_{Def} \leq c_t$. Similarly, (A5.4) shows that $x_S = 0$ can occur only if $p_{Def} \geq c_s$.

In summary, there is a *Separating Equilibrium* iff $c_s \leq p_{Def} \leq c_t$. In this case, the unique Separating Equilibrium has $y_S = 0$ and $p = 1$.

Attack Equilibria ($x_H = x_S = 1$)

Condition (A5.1) implies that $p = p_{Ch}$ at any Attack Equilibrium. It is clear that $y_S \neq 1$, because $y_S = 1$ is inconsistent with $x_S = 1$, by (A5.4). Suppose that $y_S = 0$. Then $p_{Ch} \geq d_n$, by (A5.2). Also $x_S = 1$ only if $p_{Def} \leq c_s$, by (A5.4). Lemma A5.1 shows that $x_H = 1$ if $x_S = 1$, so (A5.3) need not be considered.

Now suppose that $0 < y_S < 1$. Then (A5.2) shows that $p_{Ch} = d_n$, and (A5.4) permits $x_S = 1$ iff $(1 - p_{Def})(1 - y_S) \geq 1 - c_s$, which is equivalent to $y_S \leq u = g(p_{Def}; c_s)$. Clearly the latter condition can be met iff $g(p_{Def}; c_s) > 0$, which is true iff $p_{Def} < c_s$.

In summary, there is an *Attack Equilibrium* iff $p_{Ch} \geq d_n$ and $p_{Def} \leq c_s$. Either $y_S = 0$ and $p = p_{Ch}$ or $p_{Ch} = d_n$, $p_{Def} < c_s$, $0 < y_S \leq g(p_{Def}; c_s)$ and $p = d_n$.

Transitional Equilibria ($0 < x_H < 1$, $x_S = 0$)

By (A5.1), $p = 1$ at any Transitional Equilibrium, so $y_S = 0$ by (A5.2). Lemma A5.1 and (A5.3) show that the only remaining condition is $p_{Def} = c_t$.

In summary, there is a *Transitional Equilibrium* iff $p_{Def} = c_t$. In this case, the value of x_H is unrestricted, but $y_S = 0$ and $p = 1$.

Bluff Equilibria ($x_H = 1$, $0 < x_S < 1$)

Note first that, at a Bluff Equilibrium,

$$p = \frac{p_{Ch}}{p_{Ch} + (1 - p_{Ch})x_S},$$

by (A5.1). Now (A5.4) shows that $(1 - p_{Ch})(1 - y_S) = 1 - c_s$ is required for $0 < x_S < 1$; this condition is equivalent to $y_S = g(p_{Def}; c_s)$. Clearly $g(p_{Def}; c_s) \geq 0$, which is equivalent to $p_{Def} \leq c_s$, is necessary. By lemma A5.1, the only remaining condition to be applied is (A5.2).

Because $g(p_{Def}; c_s) < 1$, $y_S = 1$ is impossible. In order that $y_S = 0$, $p_{Def} = c_s$ is required. Furthermore, (A5.2) implies that $p \geq d_n$, which is equivalent to $x_S \leq f(p_{Ch}; d_n)$. Similarly for $0 < y_S < 1$, $p = d_n$ and $p_{Def} < c_s$ are required. Therefore, $x_S = f(p_{Ch}; d_n)$ from (A5.2).

In summary, there is a *Bluff Equilibrium* iff $p_{Def} \leq c_s$ and, if $p_{Def} < c_s$, $p_{Ch} \leq d_n$. If $p_{Def} = c_s$, these equilibria satisfy $y_S = 0$, $p \geq d_n$, and $x_S \leq f(p_{Ch}; d_n)$. (The latter condition actually restricts x_S iff $p_{Ch} < d_n$.) If $p_{Def} < c_s$, the Bluff Equilibria satisfy $y_S = u = g(p_{Def}; c_s)$, $p = d_n$, and $x_S = v = f(p_{Ch}; d_n)$. (This group of equilibria exists only when $p_{Ch} < d_n$.)

Parenthetically, it is worth noting that, where $p_{Def} < c_s$ and $p_{Ch} < d_n$, the Bluff Equilibrium is pooling for Defender, in that the *a priori* probability that Defender will defend is $p_{Def} \cdot 1 + (1 - p_{Def}) \cdot g(p_{Def}; c_s) = c_t$, independent of p_{Def}. But the *a priori* probability of initiation is $p_{Ch} \cdot 1 + (1 - p_{Ch}) \cdot f(p_{Ch}; d_n) = p_{Ch}/d_n$, so an analogous property does not hold for Challenger. In fact, the frequency of initiation is proportional to Challenger's credibility in this region.

This completes the determination of all the perfect Bayesian equilibria of the Unilateral Deterrence Game with incomplete information. The non-transitional equilibria (those that exist on sets of positive measure

Table A5.1. *Perfect Bayesian equilibria of Unilateral Deterrence Game with incomplete information*

Name	Existence conditions	Strategies*	$E_{Ch|H}$	$E_{Ch|S}$	$E_{Def|H}$	$E_{Def|S}$
(Certain)	$p_{Def} \geq c_t$	$x_H = 0, x_S = 0$ y_S unrestricted				
Deterrence (Steadfast)	$p_{Def} < c_t$	$x_H = 0, x_S = 0$ $y_S \geq g(p_{Def}; c_t)$	c_{SQ}	c_{SQ}	d_{SQ}	d_{SQ}
Separating	$c_s \leq p_{Def} \leq c_t$	$x_H = 1$ $x_S = 0$ $y_S = 0$	$c_{DC} - p_{Def}(c_{DC} - c_{DD+})$	c_{SQ}	$d_{SQ} - p_{Ch}(d_{SQ} - d_{DD+})$	$d_{SQ} - p_{Ch}(d_{SQ} - d_{DC})$
Attack	$p_{Def} \leq c_s$ and $p_{Ch} \geq d_n$	$x_H = 1$ $x_S = 1$ $y_S = 0$	$c_{DC} - p_{Def}(c_{DC} - c_{DD+})$	$c_{DC} - p_{Def}(c_{DC} - c_{CD})$	$d_{DC} - p_{Ch}(d_{DC} - d_{DD+})$	d_{DC}
Bluff	$p_{Def} \leq c_s$ and $p_{Ch} \leq d_n$	$x_H = 1$ $x_S = f(p_{Ch}; d_n)$ $y_S = g(p_{Def}; c_s)$	$c_{DD+} + c_3(c_{DC} - c_{DD+})$	c_{SQ}	$d_{SQ} + p_{Ch}\left[(d_{CD} - d_{SQ})\left(\dfrac{1 - d_n}{d_n}\right) - d_{SQ} - d_{DD+}\right]$	$d_{DC} + (d_{SQ} - d_{DC})\left(\dfrac{d_n - p_{Ch}}{d_n}\right)$

Note: $y_H = 1$ always.

in the (p_{Ch}, p_{Def})-square) are indicated in figure 5.4. Note that the only Deterrence Equilibria shown in figure 5.4 are those with $y_S = 0$. In fact, a Deterrence Equilibrium can always be constructed at any point of the (p_{Ch}, p_{Def})-square by making p small enough and y_S large enough. All equilibria are summarized and the corresponding payoffs – to both types of each player – are shown in table A5.1.

We now consider the players' preferences for coexisting equilibria. Such coexistence can occur in essentially one way – if $p_{Def} < c_t$, there is always a Deterrence Equilibrium along with one other equilibrium which may be Separating, Attack, or Bluff. (In this discussion, sets of measure zero in the (p_{Ch}, p_{Def})-square will be ignored.) Using table A5.1, it is possible to assess the players' relative preferences between the competing equilibria as a function of their types.

If $c_s \leq p_{Def} \leq c_t$, a Deterrence Equilibrium and a Separating Equilibrium coexist. In this case, a Soft Challenger is indifferent between the two equilibria, a Hard Challenger prefers the Separating Equilibrium, and a Defender, whether Hard or Soft, prefers the Deterrence Equilibrium.

If $p_{Def} \leq c_s$ and $p_{Ch} \geq d_n$, a Deterrence Equilibrium and an Attack Equilibrium coexist. In this case, both types of Challenger strictly prefer the Attack Equilibrium, and a Soft Defender strictly prefers the Deterrence Equilibrium. A Hard Defender prefers the Deterrence Equilibrium if p_{Ch} is high enough ($p_{Ch} > d_{del}$), but prefers the Attack Equilibrium otherwise.

Finally, a Deterrence Equilibrium coexists with a Bluff Equilibrium if $p_{Def} \leq c_s$ and $p_{Ch} \leq d_n$. A Soft Challenger is indifferent between the two equilibria, whereas a Hard Challenger strictly prefers the Bluff Equilibrium. A Soft Defender prefers the Deterrence Equilibrium, as does a Hard Defender provided $d_n > d_{del}$ (which can always be arranged by taking d_{SQ} large enough). But if $d_n < d_{del}$, a Hard Defender prefers the Bluff Equilibrium.

Appendix 6 Asymmetric Escalation Game: "Massive Retaliation" version

This appendix contains the detailed analysis of the "Massive Retaliation" version of the *Asymmetric Escalation Game with incomplete information*, introduced in chapter 6 and section 7.1, and specified in section A1.4. (See also figures 6.3, 7.1, and A1.7.) Recall that the twelve parameter values satisfy $0 < p_{Ch} < 1$, $0 < p_{Def} < 1$, $c_{EE-} < c_{CD} < c_{EE+} < c_{SQ} < c_{DC}$, and $d_{EE-} < d_{EE+} < d_{DC} < d_{DE} < d_{SQ}$. Moreover, player Challenger is (strategically) Hard, i.e., Challenger's utility for outcome EE is c_{EE+}, with probability p_{Ch}; otherwise, Challenger is (strategically) Soft, i.e., Challenger's utility for outcome EE is c_{EE-}, with probability $1 - p_{Ch}$. Similarly, player Defender is (strategically) Hard, with utility d_{EE+} for outcome EE, with probability p_{Def}, and (strategically) Soft, with utility d_{EE-}, for outcome EE, with probability $1 - p_{Def}$. For convenience, we repeat here the definitions of the thresholds:

$$c_1 = \frac{c_{DC} - c_{SQ}}{c_{DC} - c_{DE}}, \quad c_2 = \frac{c_{DC} - c_{SQ}}{c_{DC} - c_{EE+}}, \quad d_1 = \frac{d_{DE} - d_{DC}}{d_{DE} - d_{EE-}}, \quad d_2 = \frac{d_{DE} - d_{DC}}{d_{DE} - d_{EE+}}.$$

See section A2.4 for more details about these thresholds.

We are interested only in perfect Bayesian equilibria (PBE), so we make use of the fact (explained in section 7.1) that no PBE can possibly involve Defender choosing response-in-kind (D) at node 2 in figure 6.3. As well, at any PBE, Challenger must choose according to type at node 3; Challenger chooses E if Hard and D if Soft. Thus the game has two strategic decisions to be analyzed: Challenger's choice of C or D at node 1, and Defender's choice of C or E at node 2. Let Challenger's strategic variables be x_H and x_S, representing the probabilities that Challenger chooses D at node 1 when Hard and when Soft, respectively. Likewise, let Defender's strategic variables, representing the probability that Defender chooses E at node 2, be z_H (if Defender is

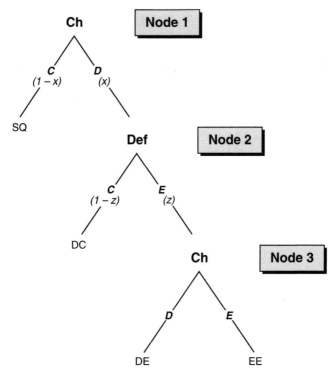

Fig. A6.1. Asymmetric Escalation Game: "Massive Retaliation" version.

Hard) and z_S (if Defender is Soft). This produces the game shown in figure A6.1.

Perfect Bayesian equilibria of the game of figure A6.1 will be denoted $[x_H, x_S; z_H, z_S, r]$. The strategic variables, x_H, x_S, z_H, and z_S are as given above. The belief variable, r, is the conditional probability that Defender places on Challenger being Hard, given that Defender must take action (i.e., that the game reaches node 2 in figure A6.1).

Suppose that there exists an equilibrium with $x_H + x_S > 0$, so that there is a positive probability of reaching node 2. As usual,

$$r = \frac{p_{Ch}x_H}{p_{Ch}x_H + (1 - p_{Ch})x_S}.$$

If the game continues to node 3, Challenger will choose E if Hard and

D if Soft. Therefore, if Defender is Hard, its expected value at node 2 is

$$E_{\text{Def}|H}(z_H) = (1 - z_H)d_{DC} + z_H\left[rd_{EE+} + (1 - r)d_{DE}\right].$$

At equilibrium, z_H must be chosen to maximize this expected value; in other words,

$$z_H = \underset{0 \leq z \leq 1}{\arg\max}\left\{z\left[rd_{EE+} + (1 - r)d_{DE} - d_{DC}\right]\right\}.$$

This requirement is easily seen to be equivalent to

$$z_H = \underset{0 \leq z \leq 1}{\arg\max}\left\{z(d_{DE} - d_{EE+})(d_2 - r)\right\},$$

where d_2 is as in section A2.4. By a similar argument, another equilibrium condition is

$$z_S = \underset{0 \leq z \leq 1}{\arg\max}\left\{z(d_{DE} - d_{EE-})(d_1 - r)\right\}$$

where d_1 is also given in section A2.4.

Now suppose that Challenger is Hard, and consider Challenger's choice at node 1. It is easy to verify directly that Challenger's expected value is

$$E_{\text{Ch}|H}(x_H) = (1 - x_H)c_{SQ} + x_H\, p_{\text{Def}}\left[(1 - z_H)c_{DC} + z_H\, c_{EE+}\right] +$$
$$x_H(1 - p_{\text{Def}})\left[(1 - z_S)c_{DC} + z_S\, c_{EE+}\right].$$

At equilibrium, x_H must be chosen to maximize this expected value; this equilibrium condition is equivalent to

$$x_H = \underset{0 \leq x \leq 1}{\arg\max}\left\{x\left[\left(p_{\text{Def}}(1 - z_H) + (1 - p_{\text{Def}})(1 - z_S)\right)c_{DC}\right.\right.$$
$$\left.\left. + \left(p_{\text{Def}}\, z_H + (1 - p_{\text{Def}})z_S\right)c_{EE+} - c_{SQ}\right]\right\}$$

which can be expressed as

$$x_H = \underset{0 \leq x \leq 1}{\arg\max}\left\{x(c_{DC} - c_{EE+})(c_2 - z_p)\right\}$$

where c_2 is given in section A2.4, and

$$z_p = p_{Def} z_H + (1 - p_{Def}) z_S.$$

The analogous equilibrium condition applicable when Challenger is Soft is

$$x_S = \underset{0 \le x \le 1}{\arg\max} \left\{ x(c_{DC} - c_{DE})(c_1 - z_p) \right\},$$

where c_1 is as in section A2.4.

In summary, any five probabilities x_H, x_S, z_H, z_S, and r define a perfect Bayesian equilibrium $[x_H, x_S; z_H, z_S, r]$ iff

$$x_H = \underset{0 \le x \le 1}{\arg\max} \left\{ x \left(c_2 - z_p \right) \right\}, \tag{A6.1}$$

$$x_S = \underset{0 \le x \le 1}{\arg\max} \left\{ x \left(c_1 - z_p \right) \right\}, \tag{A6.2}$$

$$z_H = \underset{0 \le z \le 1}{\arg\max} \left\{ z \left(d_2 - r \right) \right\}, \tag{A6.3}$$

$$z_S = \underset{0 \le z \le 1}{\arg\max} \left\{ z \left(d_1 - r \right) \right\}, \tag{A6.4}$$

and, if $x_H + x_S > 0$,

$$r = \frac{p_{Ch} x_H}{p_{Ch} x_H + (1 - p_{Ch}) x_S}. \tag{A6.5}$$

(In conditions (A6.1)–(A6.4), strictly positive factors have been dropped from the argmax specification.)

> **Lemma A6.1** At any perfect Bayesian equilibrium $[x_H, x_S; z_H, z_S, r]$, either $x_H = 1$ or $x_S = 0$.
>
> **Proof** From A2.4, $c_1 < c_2$. The lemma then follows immediately from (A6.1) and (A6.2). ∎
>
> **Lemma A6.2** At any perfect Bayesian equilibrium $[x_H, x_S; z_H, z_S, r]$, either $z_H = 1$ or $z_S = 0$.
>
> **Proof** From A2.4, $d_1 < d_2$. The lemma then follows immediately from (A6.3) and (A6.4). ∎

A Deterrence Equilibrium is defined to be any equilibrium with $x_H = x_S = 0$. By lemma A6.1 and (A6.1), this occurs iff

$$z_p = p_{Def} z_H + \left(1 - p_{Def}\right) z_S \geq c_2. \tag{A6.6}$$

Because condition (A6.5) is void, (A6.6) can always be arranged by choosing r small enough. For example, $CSDE_1 = [0, 0; 1, 1, r]$ is always an equilibrium provided $r \leq d_1$, for in this case $z_p = 1$ regardless of the values of the parameters. There are other Deterrence Equilibria, but they occur only if appropriate conditions on the parameters are met. For example, $CSDE_3 = [0, 0; 1, 0, r]$, where $d_1 \leq r \leq d_2$, is easily seen to be an equilibrium iff $p_{Def} \geq c_2$. Note that $r > d_2$ implies that $z_H = z_S = 0$ by lemma A6.2 and (A6.3), so (A6.6) must fail. This observation demonstrates that for any equilibrium in the Deterrence Equilibrium family, $r \leq d_2$. (This conclusion explains the name Challenger-Soft Deterrence Equilibria, as discussed in the text.)

We now show that at any equilibrium other than Deterrence, $x_H = 1$ and $x_S > 0$. By lemma A6.1 we need only show that there can be no equilibrium with $x_H > 0$ and $x_S = 0$. Assume otherwise. Then (A6.5) gives $r = 1$, so (A6.3) and (A6.4) imply $z_H = z_S = 0$. But now $c_1 - z_p = c_1 > 0$ so (A6.2) shows that $x_S = 1$. This contradiction proves that any equilibrium with $x_H + x_S > 0$ has $x_H = 1$ and $x_S > 0$. We call any equilibrium with $x_H = x_S = 1$ an *Initiate Regardless Equilibrium*, and any equilibrium with $x_H = 1$ and $0 < x_S < 1$ a *Probing Equilibrium*.

We now organize our search for equilibria according to the equilibrium values of z_H and z_S. By lemma A6.2 and (A6.4), any equilibrium with $z_H = z_S = 0$ must have $r \geq d_2$. But if $z_H = z_S = 0$, (A6.1) and (A6.2) show that $x_H = x_S = 1$, so (A6.5) gives $r = p_{Ch}$. It is easy to verify that the condition $p_{Ch} \geq d_2$ is sufficient as well as necessary, so that the *No-Response Equilibrium* (NRE) $[1, 1; 0, 0, p_{Ch}]$ exists iff $p_{Ch} \geq d_2$.

Now we look for an equilibrium with $0 < z_H < 1$, $z_S = 0$. By (A6.3), $r = d_2$. By lemma A6.1 and (A6.2), $z_p = p_{Def} z_H \leq c_1$. First suppose $z_H \leq h(p_{Def}; c_1) = c_1/p_{Def}$ and $x_S = 1$. Then $r = p_{Ch} = d_2$ and we have found an equilibrium $(1, 1; z_H, 0, p_{Ch})$ for $z_H \leq h(p_{Def}; c_1)$ that exists iff $p_{Ch} = d_2$. This equilibrium is transitional because it exists only on a set of measure zero in (p_{Ch}, p_{Def})-space. Now suppose that $z_H = v_4 = h(p_{Def}; c_1)$ and $x_S < 1$. Clearly $p_{Def} > c_1$ is necessary. Also

$$r = \frac{p_{Ch}}{p_{Ch} + (1 - p_{Ch}) x_S} = d_2,$$

by (A6.5), which is equivalent to

$$x_S = u_4 = f(p_{Ch}; d_2) = \frac{p_{Ch}(1 - d_2)}{d_2(1 - p_{Ch})}.$$

Moreover $x_S < 1$ only if $p_{Ch} < d_2$. It can be verified directly that these necessary conditions are also sufficient, so that the (Form III) *No-Limited-Response Equilibrium* (NLRE$_3$) $[1, f(p_{Ch}; d_2); h(p_{Def}; c_1), 0, d_2]$ exists iff $p_{Def} > c_1$ and $p_{Ch} < d_2$.

Now we identify equilibria with $z_H = 1$, $z_S = 0$. By (A6.3) and (A6.4) we must have $d_1 \leq r \leq d_2$. For an equilibrium with $0 < x_S < 1$ we need $c_1 = z_p = p_{Def}$. The condition $d_1 \leq r \leq d_2$ is satisfied iff $d_1 \leq p_{Ch} \leq d_2$ and

$$f(p_{Ch}; d_2) \leq x_S \leq f(p_{Ch}; d_1).$$

Thus a transitional equilibrium $[1, x_S; 1, 0, r]$ exists iff $p_{Def} = c_1$ and $d_1 \leq p_{Ch} \leq d_2$. Any other equilibrium with $z_H = 1$, $z_S = 0$ must have $x_S = 1$, so $p_{Def} \leq c_1$ by (A6.2). But now $r = p_{Ch}$, and the condition $d_1 \leq p_{Ch} \leq d_2$ follows. Consequently, it is easy to verify that the (Form I) *No-Limited-Response Equilibrium* (NLRE$_1$) $[1, 1; 1, 0, p_{Ch}]$ exists iff $p_{Def} \leq c_1$ and $d_1 \leq p_{Ch} \leq d_2$.

Now consider the possibility of equilibria with $z_H = 1$, $0 < z_S < 1$. By (A6.4), $r = d_1$. Suppose first that $z_p = p_{Def} + (1 - p_{Def}) z_S \leq c_1$, and $x_S = 1$. Then $z_S \leq g(p_{Def}; c_1) = (c_1 - p_{Def})/(1 - p_{Def})$, which can be arranged only if $p_{Def} < c_1$ and $r = p_{Ch} = d_1$. We have identified the transitional equilibrium $[1, 1; 1, z_S, r]$, which exists iff $p_{Ch} = d_1$ and $p_{Def} < c_1$. Otherwise $z_p = p_{Def} + (1 - p_{Def})z_S = c_1$ and $0 < x_S < 1$. Thus $z_S = v_3 = g(p_{Def}; c_1)$ which is possible only when $p_{Def} < c_1$ and

$$r = \frac{p_{Ch}}{p_{Ch} + (1 - p_{Ch})x_S} = d_1.$$

This latter equation is equivalent to

$$x_S = u_3 = \frac{p_{Ch}(1 - d_1)}{d_1(1 - p_{Ch})} = f(p_{Ch}; d_1),$$

and can be satisfied iff $p_{Ch} < d_1$. It can be verified directly that these necessary conditions are also sufficient, so that the (Form II) *No-Limited-Response Equilibrium* (NLRE$_2$) $[1, f(p_{Ch}; d_1); 1, g(p_{Def}; c_1), d_1]$ exists iff $p_{Ch} < d_1$ and $p_{Def} < c_1$.

Under the assumption that $x_H + x_S > 0$, we have identified all equilibria with $z_H = 0$, $z_S = 0$; $0 < z_H < 1$, $z_S = 0$; $z_H = 1$, $z_S = 0$; and $z_H = 1$, $0 < z_S < 1$. By (A6.6) and lemma A6.2, no other equilibria are possible unless $z_S = z_H = 1$. But if so, $z_p = 1$, (A6.1) and (A6.2) then imply $x_H = x_S = 0$, and the equilibrium is a Deterrence Equilibrium. Therefore we have already identified all perfect Bayesian equilibria.

Finally, the unconditional (*a priori*) probability that Defender will respond to a challenge is referred to in chapter 7. This quantity is $z_p = p_{Def} z_H + (1 - p_{Def}) z_S$; it is easy to verify that $z_p = c_1$ at any (Form II or III) No-Limited-Response Equilibrium.

Appendix 7: Asymmetric Escalation Game: "Flexible Response" version

This appendix contains the detailed analysis of the "Flexible Response" version of the *Asymmetric Escalation Game with incomplete information*, introduced in chapter 6 and section 8.1, and specified in section A1.4. (See also figures 6.3, 8.2, and A1.7.) Recall that the sixteen relevant parameter values satisfy $0 < p_{Ch} < 1$, $0 < p_{Def} < 1$, $c_{EE-} < c_{DE} < c_{EE+} < c_{DD} < c_{ED} < c_{SQ} < c_{DC}$, and $d_{EE-} < d_{ED} < d_{EE+} < d_{DC} < d_{DD} < d_{DE} < d_{SQ}$. Moreover, player Challenger is (strategically) Hard, i.e., Challenger's utility for outcome EE is c_{EE+}, with probability p_{Ch}; otherwise, Challenger is (strategically) Soft, i.e., Challenger's utility for outcome EE is c_{EE-}, with probability $1 - p_{Ch}$. Similarly, player Defender is (strategically) Hard, with utility d_{EE+} for outcome EE, with probability p_{Def}, and (strategically) Soft, with utility d_{EE-} for outcome EE, with probability $1 - p_{Def}$. For convenience, we repeat here the definitions of the thresholds

$$c_1 = \frac{c_{DC} - c_{SQ}}{c_{DC} - c_{DE}}, \quad c_r = \frac{c_{ED} - c_{DD}}{c_{ED} - c_{EE-}}, \quad c_q = \frac{c_{ED} - c_{DD}}{c_{ED} - c_{EE+}}, \quad c_3 = \frac{c_{DC} - c_{SQ}}{c_{DC} - c_{DD}},$$

$$C_{ind} = (c_{DC} - c_{ED})(c_{DD} - c_{EE+}) - (c_{ED} - c_{DD})(c_{EE+} - c_{DE}),$$

$$c_m = \frac{(c_{ED} - c_{DD})(c_{EE+} - c_{DE}) - (c_{SQ} - c_{ED})(c_{DD} - c_{EE+})}{(c_{ED} - c_{EE+})(c_{DD} - c_{DE})},$$

$$d_1 = \frac{d_{DE} - d_{DC}}{d_{DE} - d_{EE-}}, \quad d_2 = \frac{d_{DE} - d_{DC}}{d_{DE} - d_{EE+}}, \quad d_q = \frac{d_{DE} - d_{DD}}{d_{DE} - d_{EE+}},$$

$$d_t = \frac{(d_{DE} - d_{DD})(d_{DD} - d_{ED}) + (d_{DD} - d_{EE+})(d_{DD} - d_{DC})}{(d_{DE} - d_{EE+})(d_{DD} - d_{ED})},$$

$c^* = c_3 c_q$, and $d^* = \max\{d_1, d_t\}$. It is easy to verify that $0 < c_1 < c_2 < 1$, $0 < c^* < c_q < 1$, $0 < c_r < c_q$, $0 < d_1 < d_2 < 1$, $0 < d_q < d_t < d_2$, and

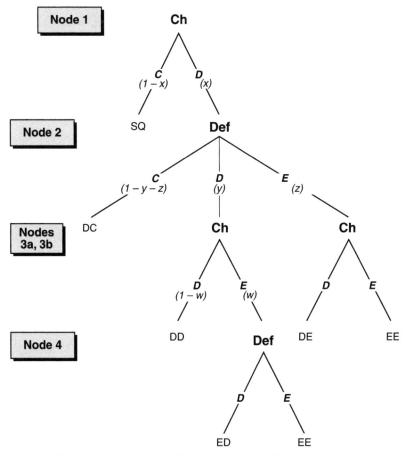

Fig. A7.1. Asymmetric Escalation Game: "Flexible Response" version.

$d^* < d_2$. If $C_{ind} > 0$, then $c_m < c^* < c_1$, and if $C_{ind} < 0$, then $c_1 < c^* < c_m$.

Perfect Bayesian equilibria (PBE) of the game of figure 8.2 will be denoted $[x_H, x_S, w_H, w_S, q; z_H, z_S, y_H, y_S, r]$. The interpretations of the strategic variables, $x_H, x_S, w_H, w_S, z_H, z_S, y_H,$ and y_S, are as given in section 8.2 and shown in figure A7.1. The belief variable r is Defender's conditional probability that Challenger is Hard given that the game reaches node 2 in figure A7.1, and the belief variable q is Challenger's conditional probability that Defender is Hard given that the game reaches node 3a in figure A7.1.

It can be shown that a 10-tuple of probabilities, $[x_H, x_S, w_H, w_S, q; z_H, z_S, y_H, y_S, r]$, constitutes a perfect Bayesian equilibrium if and only if the following conditions are met:

$$x_H = \underset{0 \le x \le 1}{\arg\max}\{x[(c_{DC} - c_{SQ}) - y_p[(c_{DC} - c_{DD}) - w_H(c_{ED} - c_{DD})$$
$$+ w_H q(c_{ED} - c_{EE+})] - z_p(c_{DC} - c_{EE+})]\} \tag{A7.1}$$

$$x_S = \underset{0 \le x \le 1}{\arg\max}\{x[(c_{DC} - c_{SQ}) - y_p[(c_{DC} - c_{DD}) - w_S(c_{ED} - c_{DD})$$
$$+ w_S q(c_{ED} - c_{EE-})] - z_p(c_{DC} - c_{DE})]\}. \tag{A7.2}$$

If $x_H + x_S > 0$,

$$r = p_{Ch}x_H / (p_{Ch}x_H + (1 - p_{Ch})x_S) \tag{A7.3}$$

$$(y_H, z_H) = \underset{\substack{0 \le y \le 1 \\ 0 \le z \le 1}}{\arg\max}\{y[(d_{DD} - d_{DC}) - w_r[(d_{DD} - d_{EE+})]$$
$$+ z[(d_{DE} - d_{DC}) - r(d_{DE} - d_{EE+})]\} \tag{A7.4}$$

$$(y_S, z_S) = \underset{\substack{0 \le y \le 1 \\ 0 \le z \le 1}}{\arg\max}\{y[(d_{DD} - d_{DC}) - w_r[(d_{DD} - d_{ED})]$$
$$+ z[(d_{DE} - d_{DC}) - r(d_{DE} - d_{EE-})]\}. \tag{A7.5}$$

If $y_H + y_S > 0$,

$$q = p_{Def}y_H / y_p \tag{A7.6}$$

$$w_H = \underset{0 \le w \le 1}{\arg\max}\{w[(c_{ED} - c_{DD}) - q(c_{ED} - c_{EE+})]\} \tag{A7.7}$$

$$w_S = \underset{0 \le w \le 1}{\arg\max}\{w[(c_{ED} - c_{DD}) - q(c_{ED} - c_{EE-})]\} \tag{A7.8}$$

where $y_p = p_{Def}y_H + (1 - p_{Def})y_S$, $z_p = p_{Def}z_H + (1 - p_{Def})z_S$, $w_r = rw_H + (1 - r)w_S$.

For convenience, we define $C_y^H = (d_{DD} - d_{DC}) - w_r(d_{DD} - d_{EE+})$, $C_z^H = (d_{DE} - d_{DC}) - r(d_{DE} - d_{EE+})$, $C_y^S = (d_{DD} - d_{DC}) - w_r(d_{DD} - d_{ED})$, $C_z^S = (d_{DE} - d_{DC}) - r(d_{DE} - d_{EE-})$. Then (A7.4) and (A7.5) can be rewritten

$$(y_H, \ z_H) = \underset{\substack{0 \le y \le 1 \\ 0 \le z \le 1}}{\arg\max} \{y \ C_y^H + z \ C_z^H\} \tag{A7.9}$$

$$(y_S, \ z_S) = \underset{\substack{0 \le y \le 1 \\ 0 \le z \le 1}}{\arg\max} \{y \ C_y^S + z \ C_z^S\}. \tag{A7.10}$$

Lemma A7.1 At any perfect Bayesian equilibrium $[x_H, x_S, w_H, w_S, q;$ $z_H, z_S, y_H, y_S, r]$,

$$\text{either} \quad q > c_q \text{ and } w_H = w_S = 0$$
$$\text{or} \quad q = c_q \text{ and } w_S = 0$$
$$\text{or} \quad q < c_q \text{ and } w_H = 1.$$

Proof From (A7.7) and (A7.8), it follows that the value of w_H is unrestricted iff $q = c_q$, and that $w_H \ge w_S$. ∎

Lemma A7.2 At any perfect Bayesian equilibrium $[x_H, x_S, w_H, w_S, q;$ $z_H, z_S, y_H, y_S, r]$ with $w_H = 1$, $y_H = y_S = 0$.

Proof Assume $w_H = 1$. Then $w_r = r + (1 - r)w_S$, from which it can be shown that

$$C_y^H - C_z^H = (1 - r)[-(d_{DE} - d_{DD}) - w_S(d_{DD} - d_{EE+})] \le 0$$

with equality iff $r = 1$. From (A7.9), a necessary condition for $y_H > 0$ at equilibrium is $C_y^H - C_z^H \ge 0$. It follows that either $y_H = 0$ or $r = 1$. But $r = 1$ forces $w_r = 1$, and now direct substitution produces $C_y^H = -d_{DC} + d_{EE+} < 0$. Again using (A7.9), $y_H = 0$ at equilibrium.

Now suppose that $w_H = 1$, $y_H = 0$, and $y_S > 0$. By (A7.6), $q = 0$, and (A7.8) now implies that $w_S = 1$. It follows that, for any value of r, $w_r = 1$. Thus $C_y^S = -d_{DC} + d_{ED} < 0$, which contradicts the assumption that $y_S > 0$ by (A7.5). The lemma follows. ∎

Deterrence Equilibria $(x_p = 0)$

A *Deterrence Equilibrium* is a perfect Bayesian equilibrium with $x_p = 0$, i.e., $x_H = x_S = 0$. Consideration of (A7.1) and (A7.2) shows that either $y_p > 0$ or $z_p > 0$ is necessary for $x_p = 0$. A Deterrence Equilibrium with $z_p = 0$ (i.e., $z_H = z_S = 0$) is called a *Limited Response Deterrence Equilibrium* (LRDE). Any other Deterrence Equilibrium, which must have $z_H > 0$ or $z_S > 0$, is an *Escalatory Deterrence Equilibrium* (EDE).

We now identify all LRDEs. It follows from the above that, at any

LRDE, $y_p > 0$, i.e., $y_H > 0$ or $y_S > 0$. An LRDE with $y_H = 0$ and $y_S > 0$ would have $q = 0$ by (A7.10), from which $w_H = 1$ follows by (A7.7). Lemma A7.2 now shows that $y_S = 0$, a contradiction. Similarly, an LRDE with $y_H > 0$ and $y_S = 0$ would have $q = 1$, which would imply $w_H = 0$ by (A7.7), and $w_S = 0$ by (A7.8). But then $w_r = 0$, so $C_y^S > 0$, so either $y_S > 0$ or $z_S > 0$ by (A7.10). Neither of these possibilities is consistent with an LRDE with $y_S = 0$. We conclude that, at any LRDE, $y_H > 0$ and $y_S > 0$.

Lemma A7.2 now implies that any LRDE has $w_H < 1$. By lemma A7.1, either $q = c_q$, $0 \le w_H < 1$, and $w_S = 0$, or $q > c_q$ and $w_H = w_S = 0$. It can be shown that there is an LRDE with $w_H = 0$ iff $p_{Def} \ge c_q$. This PBE, called LRDE$_1$ is $[x_H, x_S, w_H, w_S, q; z_H, z_S, y_H, y_S, r] = [0, 0, 0, 0, p_{Def}; 0, 0, 1, 1, r]$, where $r \ge d_q$. The second possibility, an LRDE with $w_H > 0$, can occur iff $c^* \le p_{Def} \le c_q$. This PBE, called LRDE$_2$ has the form $[x_H, x_S, w_H, w_S, q; z_H, z_S, y_H, y_S, r] = [0, 0, w_H, 0, c_q; 0, 0, 1, y_S, r]$, where $r \ge d^*$,

$$w_H = \frac{1}{r}\frac{d_{DD} - d_{DC}}{d_{DD} - d_{ED}}, \text{ and } y_S = f(p_{Def}; c_q) = \frac{p_{Def}(1 - c_q)}{c_q(1 - p_{Def})}.$$

There are many Escalatory Deterrence Equilibria. EDE$_1$, which exists for all values of p_{Def} and p_{Ch}, is $[x_H, x_S, w_H, w_S, q; z_H, z_S, y_H, y_S, r] = [0, 0, 1, 1, q; 1, 1, 0, 0, r]$, where $r \ge d_2$ and $q < c_r$. It is easy to verify that EDE$_1$ satisfies (A7.1)–(A7.8). Another Escalatory Deterrence Equilibrium, one that depends in part on threats to respond-in-kind rather than to escalate, is EDE$_2$, defined by $[x_H, x_S, w_H, w_S, q; z_H, z_S, y_H, y_S, r] = [0, 0, w_H, 0, c_q; z_H, 0, f(p_{Def}; c_q), 1, r]$, where $z_H = 1 - y_H$, $d_q \le r \le d_2$, and $w_H = k(r; d_q)$. (See section A2.4.) It can be shown that EDE$_2$, as defined above, satisfies (A7.1)–(A7.8) iff $p_{Def} \ge c_q$.

At any EDE, either $z_H > 0$ or $z_S > 0$. From (A7.9) and (A7.10), the corresponding necessary conditions are $C_z^H \ge 0$ and $C_z^S \ge 0$. Neither possibility is consistent with $r > d_2$. In other words, $r \le d_2$ at any EDE.

No-Response Equilibria $(x_p > 0, \ y_p = z_p = 0)$

A *No-Response Equilibrium* (NRE) is any equilibrium with $x_H + x_S > 0$, but $y_H = y_S = z_H = z_S = 0$. To identify all NRE, first observe from (A7.1) and (A7.2) that $y_p = z_p = 0$ implies $x_H = x_S = 1$. Then, from (A7.3), $r = p_{Ch}$. The next requirement for an NRE is that all of C_y^H, C_z^H, C_y^S, and C_z^S be non-positive. Because

$$C_y^H - C_y^S = w_r(d_{EE+} - d_{ED}) \geq 0$$
$$C_z^H - C_z^S = r(d_{EE+} - d_{EE-}) > 0,$$

this requirement is equivalent to

$$w_r = p_{Ch}w_H + (1 - p_{Ch})w_S \geq \frac{d_{DD} - d_{DC}}{d_{DD} - d_{EE+}},$$

and $r = p_{Def} \geq d_2$. Because q is not restricted by (A7.6), it is always possible to arrange that w_r satisfy the above inequality. A necessary condition is that q be small enough. For example, $q < c_r$ forces $w_H = w_S = 1$ by (A7.7) and (A7.8), so $w_r = 1$.

In summary, there is an NRE $[x_H, x_S, w_H, w_S, q; z_H, z_S, y_H, y_S, r] = [1, 1, w_H, w_S, q; 0, 0, 0, 0, p_{Ch}]$, whenever q is small enough, provided $p_{Ch} \geq d_2$.

No-Limited-Response Equilibria ($x_p > 0$, $y_p = 0$, $z_p > 0$)

A *No-Limited-Response Equilibrium* (NLRE) is any equilibrium with $x_H + x_S > 0$, $z_H + z_S > 0$, and $y_H = y_S = 0$. First we show that, at any NLRE, $x_S > 0$ and $x_H = 1$. From (A7.1) and (A7.2), note that at any NLRE,

$$x_H = \arg\max_{0 \leq x \leq 1}\{x[(c_{DC} - c_{SQ}) - z_p(c_{DC} - c_{EE+})]\}$$
$$x_S = \arg\max_{0 \leq x \leq 1}\{x[(c_{DC} - c_{SQ}) - z_p(c_{DC} - c_{DE})]\}$$

The difference between the right-side coefficients of x is

$$[(c_{DC}-c_{SQ})-z_p(c_{DC}-c_{EE+})]-[(c_{DC}-c_{SQ})-z_p(c_{DC}-c_{DE})]=z_p(c_{EE+}-c_{DE})>0.$$

which proves that if $x_S > 0$, then $x_H = 1$. To complete the proof, note that if $x_S = 0$, then $x_H > 0$ (for an NLRE) so that $r = 1$ by (A7.3). But now $C_z^H = (d_{DE} - d_{DC}) - (d_{DE} - d_{EE+}) = d_{EE+} - d_{DC} < 0$, implying that $z_H = 0$. Similarly, $C_z^S < 0$, so $z_S = 0$, contradicting the definition of an NLRE.

Thus, at any NLRE, either $x_H = x_S = 1$ or $x_H = 1$ and $0 < x_S < 1$. (The first case occurs only when $z_p \leq c_1$, and the second when $z_p = c_1$.) Because $r > 0$ always,

$$C_z^H - C_z^S = r(d_{EE+} - d_{EE-}) > 0,$$

which implies that, at any NLRE, $z_S > 0$ only if $z_H = 1$. Furthermore, $z_H > 0$ only if $r \leq d_2$ from (A7.4), and $z_S > 0$ only if $r \leq d_1$ from (A7.5). Clearly, $r \leq d_2$ at any NLRE.

We now identify necessary conditions for an NLRE with $x_H = x_S = 1$, called a Form I NLRE, or NLRE$_1$. Note that $r = p_{Ch}$ for NLRE$_1$, so $p_{Ch} \leq d_2$ is required. Moreover, if $p_{Ch} = r < d_1$, (A7.10) shows that $z_H = z_S = 1$, so $z_p = 1$, contradicting the fundamental requirement that $z_p \leq c_1$. Thus, any NLRE$_1$ has $d_1 \leq p_{Ch} \leq d_2$. Except for transitional variants ($0 < z_H < 1$, $z_S = 0$ at $p_{Ch} = d_1$, and $z_H = 1$, $0 < z_S < 1$ at $p_{Ch} = d_2$), the only NLRE$_1$ has $z_H = 1$ and $z_S = 0$, and exists for $d_1 \leq p_{Ch} \leq d_2$.

Now we turn to NLRE with $x_H = 1$, $0 < x_S < 1$. For such an equilibrium, we have already shown that $z_p = c_1$ and

$$r = \frac{p_{Ch}}{p_{Ch} + (1 - p_{Ch})x_S}.$$

A Form II NLRE, or NLRE$_2$, occurs when $r = d_2$. For this equilibrium,

$$x_S = f(p_{Ch}; d_2) = \frac{p_{Ch}(1 - d_2)}{d_2(1 - p_{Ch})},$$

$z_S = 0$, and $z_H = h(p_{Def}; c_1) = c_1/p_{Def}$. Note that $p_{Ch} \leq d_2$ and $p_{Def} \geq c_1$ are both necessary for this equilibrium. A Form III NLRE, or NLRE$_3$, occurs when $r = d_1$. For this equilibrium,

$$x_S = f(p_{Ch}; d_1) = \frac{p_{Ch}(1 - d_1)}{d_1(1 - p_{Ch})},$$

$z_H = 1$, and $z_S = g(p_{Def}; c_1) = (c_1 - p_{Def})/(1 - p_{Def})$. Note that $p_{Ch} \leq d_1$ and $p_{Def} \leq c_1$ are both necessary for this equilibrium. There is another NLRE with $x_H = 1$ and $0 < x_S < 1$ and $d_1 < r < d_2$, but it is transitional. As previously, no NLRE corresponds to $r < d_1$.

There are additional requirements for the three forms of non-transitional NLRE. Because the equilibria have $z_H > 0$, (A7.9) shows that $y_H = 0$ only if $C_y^H \leq C_z^H$, or

$$(d_{DE} - d_{DD}) + w_r(d_{DD} - d_{ED}) \geq r(d_{DE} - d_{EE+}) \tag{A7.11}$$

Because $r \leq d_2 < 1$, this inequality is true whenever w_r is large enough. To increase w_r, it is necessary to increase the values of w_H and/or w_S, which, by (A7.7) and (A7.8), can always be accomplished by taking q small enough. By (A7.6) and $y_H = y_S = 0$, q is arbitrary, so this choice is always feasible. For example, $q < c_r$ implies that $w_H = w_S = 1$, so $w_r = 1$, making (A7.11) true.

In summary, we have identified three forms of NLRE, as follows:

NLRE$_1$ $[x_H, x_S, w_H, w_S, q; z_H, z_S, y_H, y_S, r] = [1, 1, w_H, w_S, q; 1, 0, 0, 0, p_{Ch}]$, where q is sufficiently small that w_H and w_S satisfy (A7.7), (A7.8), and (A7.11). This equilibrium exists iff $d_1 \leq p_{Ch} \leq d_2$ and $p_{Def} \leq c_1$.

NLRE$_2$ $[x_H, x_S, w_H, w_S, q; z_H, z_S, y_H, y_S, r] = [1, f(p_{Ch}; d_2), w_H, w_S, q; h(p_{Def}; c_1), 0, 0, 0, d_2]$ where q is sufficiently small that w_H and w_S satisfy (A7.7), (A7.8), and (A7.11). This equilibrium exists iff $p_{Ch} \leq d_2$ and $p_{Def} \geq c_1$.

NLRE$_3$ $[x_H, x_S, w_H, w_S, q; z_H, z_S, y_H, y_S, r] = [1, f(p_{Ch}; d_1), w_H, w_S, q; 1, g(p_{Def}; c_1), 0, 0, d_1]$, where q is sufficiently small that w_H and w_S satisfy (A7.7), (A7.8), and (A7.11). This equilibrium exists iff $p_{Ch} \leq d_1$ and $p_{Def} \leq c_1$.

Limited-Response Equilibria ($x_p > 0$, $y_p > 0$)

A *Limited-Response Equilibrium* (LRE) is any equilibrium with $x_H + x_S > 0$ and $y_H + y_S > 0$. We begin by showing that any LRE has $w_S = 0$ and $0 < w_H < 1$. First we show that there are no LRE with $w_S = w_H = 0$. This would imply $w_r = 0$, so that C_y^H and C_y^S would be strictly positive, yielding $y_H + z_H = 1$ and $y_S + z_S = 1$. The coefficient of x in (A7.1) is then

$$(c_{DC} - c_{SQ}) - y_p(c_{DC} - c_{DD}) - z_p(c_{DC} - c_{EE+}) < (1 - y_p - z_p)(c_{DD} - c_{SQ}) = 0$$

because $y_p + z_p = 1$. It follows that $x_H = 0$, and, by an analogous calculation using (A7.2), $x_S = 0$. Thus an equilibrium with $w_S = w_H = 0$ cannot be an LRE.

Now note that lemma A7.1 implies that, if $w_S > 0$, then $w_H = 1$. For an LRE with $w_H = 1$,

$$C_z^H - C_y^H = (1 - r)[(d_{DE} - d_{DD}) + w_S(d_{DD} - d_{EE+})],$$

which is positive unless $r = 1$. Clearly $y_H = 0$ if $r < 1$. If $r = 1$, direct substitution in (A7.4) shows $y_H = z_H = 0$ at equilibrium. But if $y_H = 0$ at an LRE, then $y_S > 0$, $q = 0$, and $w_S = 1$ all follow. But now $w_r = 1$, and (A7.10) fails unless $y_S = 0$. This contradiction shows that, at any LRE, $w_H = 1$ is impossible. The proof that $w_S = 0$ and $0 < w_H < 1$ at any LRE is now complete. A further requirement, from lemma A7.1, is $q = c_q$. Observe that $0 < q < 1$, which in turn implies that $y_H > 0$ and $y_S > 0$.

Comparison of C_y^H and C_y^S shows that if $y_S > 0$ at equilibrium, then $y_H + z_H = 1$. Furthermore, it must be the case that $y_S + z_S < 1$, because, as proven above, the equalities $y_H + z_H = 1$ and $y_S + z_S = 1$ are inconsistent with any equilibrium in which $x_H + x_S > 0$. We now show that, at any LRE, $z_S = 0$.

First note that we have already proven that at any LRE $C_y^S = 0$, $C_y^H > C_{y'}^S$, $C_z^H \leq C_y^H$, and $C_z^S \leq C_y^S = 0$. We now show that $C_z^S < 0$. In order that $C_y^S = 0$, $w_r = (d_{DD} - d_{DC})/(d_{DD} - d_{ED})$ is required. Next, $C_y^H - C_z^H = (d_{DD} - d_{DC}) - w_r(d_{DD} - d_{EE+}) - (d_{DE} - d_{DC}) + r(d_{DE} - d_{EE+})$, whence $C_y^H \geq C_z^H$ iff

$$r \geq \frac{(d_{DE} - d_{DD}) + w_r(d_{DD} - d_{EE+})}{d_{DE} - d_{EE+}},$$

which means that

$$C_z^S \leq (d_{DE} - d_{DC}) - \left[\frac{(d_{DE} - d_{DD}) + w_r(d_{DD} - d_{EE+})}{d_{DE} - d_{EE+}} \right] (d_{DE} - d_{EE-}).$$

After substitution and manipulation, the right side of this inequality can be shown to be strictly negative, so that $C_z^S < 0$ as claimed.

Note that, coincidentally, we have demonstrated that $r \geq d_t$ at any LRE. In fact, $r = d_t$ if $C_z^H = C_y^H$ (necessary for $z_H > 0$), and $r \geq d_t$ if $z_H = 0$ (when $C_z^H \leq C_y^H$).

We now identify all LRE with $z_H = 0$. Clearly $y_H = 1$, and y_S is determined by the condition $q = c_q$. Application of (A7.6) gives

$$y_S = f(p_{Def}; c_q) = \frac{p_{Def}(1 - c_q)}{c_q(1 - p_{Def})}.$$

Recall that $p_{Def} \leq c_q$ is necessary in order that $y_S \leq 1$.

It is easy to verify that $z_p = 0$ and that $w(c_{ED} - c_{DD}) - wq(c_{ED} - c_{EE+}) = 0$, because $q = c_q$. Define $C_x = (c_{DC} - c_{SQ}) - y_p(c_{DC} - c_{DD})$. Now (A7.1) and (A7.2) reduce to

$$x_H = \arg\max\{xC_x\}, \quad x_S = \arg\max\{xC_x\}.$$

By definition there is no LRE with $x_H = x_S = 0$. There is an LRE with $0 < x_H < 1$ or $0 < x_S < 1$ when $C_x = 0$, but this equilibrium is transitional, because it occurs only when

$$y_p = \frac{p_{Def}}{c_q} = c_3,$$

which is true only on a set of measure zero in (p_{Ch}, p_{Def})-space.

Thus an LRE with $z_H = 0$ must satisfy $x_H = x_S = 1$, so that $C_x \geq 0$, which occurs exactly when $p_{Def} \leq c^*$. Note that $p_{Def} \leq c^*$ implies $p_{Def} < c_q$, and that $r \geq d_t$ can be satisfied only when $p_{Ch} \geq d_t$. There is one more necessary condition for this equilibrium: $C_z^S \leq 0$, which is true iff $p_{Ch} \geq d_1$.

It can be verified directly that the preceding necessary conditions are also sufficient. They yield LRE_1, $[x_H, x_S, w_H, w_S, q; z_H, z_S, y_H, y_S, r] = [1, 1, (d_{DD} - d_{DC})/(p_{Ch}(d_{DD} - d_{ED})), 0, c_q; 0, 0, 1, f(p_{Def}; c_q), p_{Ch}]$. LRE_1 exists iff $p_{Ch} \geq d^*$ and $p_{Def} \leq c^*$. The parameter c^* could be greater than, less than, or equal to the parameter c_1, according as C_{ind} is negative, positive, or zero, respectively.

We turn now to the identification of LRE with $z_H > 0$. Clearly $z_H = 1 - y_H$. The conditions (A7.1) and (A7.2) reduce to

$$x_H = \arg\max\{x[(c_{DC} - c_{SQ}) - y_p(c_{DC} - c_{DD}) - z_p(c_{DC} - c_{EE+})]\} \quad \text{(A7.12)}$$
$$x_S = \arg\max\{x[(c_{DC} - c_{SQ}) - y_p(c_{DC} - c_{DD}) - z_p(c_{DC} - c_{DE})]\}. \quad \text{(A7.13)}$$

Because $z_p > 0$, the coefficient of x in (A7.12) exceeds the corresponding coefficient in (A7.13). The requirement $r = d_t$ can therefore be met only by $x_H = 1$ and $x_S > 0$, because $0 < d_t < 1$. In fact,

$$x_S = f(p_{Ch}; d_t) = \frac{p_{Ch}(1 - d_t)}{d_t(1 - p_{Ch})}$$

in order that $r = d_t$; it follows that $p_{Ch} \leq d_t$ is necessary for an LRE of this form.

The requirement that $q = c_q$ implies that $y_S = f(p_{Def}; c_q)y_H$. Along with $z_H = 1 - y_H$, this equation can be substituted into the coefficient of x in (A7.13). This coefficient must vanish, which implies an equation that can be solved for y_H to yield

$$y_H = y_{HL}(p_{Def}) = \frac{c_{ED} - c_{DD}}{p_{Def}}\left[\frac{(c_{DC} - c_{SQ}) - p_{Def}(c_{DC} - c_{DE})}{C_{ind}}\right].$$

The only remaining conditions concern $0 \leq y_H \leq 1$ and $0 \leq y_S \leq 1$. It is straightforward to show that, if $C_{ind} > 0$, then $y_H \geq 0$ iff $p_{Def} \leq c_1$, $y_S \geq 0$ iff $y_H \geq 0$, $y_H \leq 1$ iff $p_{Def} \geq c^*$, and $y_S \leq 1$ iff

$$p_{Def} \geq c_m = \frac{(c_{ED} - c_{DD})(c_{EE+} - c_{DE}) - (c_{SQ} - c_{ED})(c_{DD} - c_{EE+})}{(c_{ED} - c_{EE+})(c_{DD} - c_{DE})}.$$

Likewise, if $C_{ind} < 0$, $y_H \geq 0$ iff $p_{Def} \geq c_1$, $y_S \geq 0$ iff $y_H \geq 0$, $y_H \leq 1$ iff $p_{Def} \leq c^*$, and $y_S \leq 1$ iff $p_{Def} \leq c_m$. As noted in (A7.4), $c^* > c_m$ when $C_{ind} > 0$, and $c^* < c_m$ when $C_{ind} < 0$.

It can now be demonstrated that the preceding necessary conditions are also sufficient, yielding LRE$_2$, $[x_H, x_S, w_H, w_S, q; z_H, z_S, y_H, y_S, r] = [1, f(p_{Ch}; d_t), (d_{DD} - d_{DC})/(d_t(d_{DD} - d_{ED})), 0, c_q; z_H, 0, y_{HL}(p_{Def}), y_S, d_t]$ where $z_H = 1 - y_{HL}(p_{Def})$ and $y_S = f(p_{Def}; c_q)y_{HL}(p_{Def})$. LRE$_2$ exists iff $p_{Ch} \leq d_t$ and $c^* \leq p_{Def} \leq c_1$ if $C_{ind} > 0$, or $c_1 \leq p_{Def} \leq c^*$ if $C_{ind} < 0$.

Appendix 8 Asymmetric Escalation Game: general version

This appendix contains the analysis of the general version of the *Asymmetric Escalation Game with incomplete information*, introduced in chapter 6 and section 9.2, and specified in section A1.4. (See also figures 6.3 and A1.7.) Recall that the twenty relevant parameter values satisfy $0 < p_{Ch} < 1$, $0 < p_{HH}$, $0 < p_{HS}$, $0 < p_{SH}$, $0 < p_{SS}$, $p_{HH} + p_{HS} + p_{SH} + p_{SS} = 1$, $c_{EE-} < c_{DE} < c_{EE+} < c_{DD} < c_{ED} < c_{SQ} < c_{DC}$, and $d_{EE-} < d_{ED} < d_{EE+} < d_{DD-} < d_{DC} < d_{DD+} < d_{DE} < d_{SQ}$.

As usual, player Challenger is strategically Hard, i.e., Challenger's utility for outcome EE is c_{EE+}, with probability p_{Ch}; otherwise, Challenger is strategically Soft, i.e., Challenger's utility for outcome EE is c_{EE-}, with probability $1 - p_{Ch}$. Player Defender is said to be strategically Hard when its utility for outcome EE is d_{EE+}; otherwise Defender is strategically Soft and has utility d_{EE-} for outcome EE. As well, Defender is either tactically Hard, with utility d_{DD+} for outcome DD, or tactically Soft, with utility d_{DD-} for DD. Defender's credibility parameters are interpreted as follows: with probability p_{HH}, Defender is both tactically and strategically Hard; with probability p_{HS}, Defender is tactically Hard but strategically Soft; with probability p_{SH}, Defender is tactically Soft but strategically Hard; and with probability p_{SS}, Defender is both tactically and strategically Soft.

For convenience, we repeat here the definitions of the thresholds (see section A2.4 for more details). The thresholds based on Challenger's payoff parameters are

$$c_1 = \frac{c_{DC} - c_{SQ}}{c_{DC} - c_{DE}}, \quad c_2 = \frac{c_{DC} - c_{SQ}}{c_{DC} - c_{EE+}}, \quad c_3 = \frac{c_{DC} - c_{SQ}}{c_{DC} - c_{DD}},$$

$$c_r = \frac{c_{ED} - c_{DD}}{c_{ED} - c_{EE-}}, \quad c_q = \frac{c_{ED} - c_{DD}}{c_{ED} - c_{EE+}}, \quad c^* = c_3 c_q.$$

Note that $0 < c_1 < c_2 < c_3 < 1$, $0 < c_r < c_q < 1$, and $c^* < \min\{c_3, c_q\}$. The thresholds based on Defender's payoff parameters are

$$d_1 = \frac{d_{DE} - d_{DC}}{d_{DE} - d_{EE-}}, \quad d_2 = \frac{d_{DE} - d_{DC}}{d_{DE} - d_{EE+}}, \quad d_q = \frac{d_{DE} - d_{DD+}}{d_{DE} - d_{EE+}},$$

$$d_p = \frac{d_{DE} - d_{DD+}}{d_{DE} - d_{EE-}}, \quad d_r = \frac{d_{DD+} - d_{DC}}{d_{DD+} - d_{ED}}, \quad d_s = \frac{d_{DD} - d_{DC}}{d_{DD+} - d_{EE+}},$$

$$d_t = \frac{(d_{DE} - d_{DD+})(d_{DD+} - d_{ED}) + (d_{DD+} - d_{EE+})(d_{DD+} - d_{DC}),}{(d_{DE} - d_{EE+})(d_{DD+} - d_{ED})}$$

and $d^* = \max\{d_1, d_t\}$. It is easy to verify that $0 < d_r < d_s < 1$; $0 < d_p < \min\{d_q, d_1\} \le \max\{d_q, d_1\} < d_2 < 1$; $\max\{d_q, d_r\} < d_t < d_2$.

The object of this appendix is to describe all non-transitional perfect Bayesian equilibria (PBE) of the general version of the Asymmetric Escalation Game with incomplete information, as given in figures 6.3, A1.7, and A8.1. The notation for strategic variables (see also sections 9.3 and 9.4) is as follows: Challenger chooses D at node 1 with probability x, and chooses C with the complementary probability, $1 - x$; Challenger chooses E at node 3a with probability w, and D with probability $1 - w$; and Defender chooses C, D, and E at node 2 with probabilities $1 - y - z$, y, and z, respectively. Of course, a player's strategy may depend on its type, so a PBE must be specified in terms of x_H, x_S, w_H, w_S, y_{HH}, y_{HS}, y_{SH}, y_{SS}, z_{HH}, z_{HS}, z_{SH}, and z_{SS}. Figure A8.1 shows these strategies on the extensive-form Asymmetric Escalation Game. Note that any PBE must require Challenger to choose according to type at node 3b (a Hard Challenger chooses E, and a Soft Challenger chooses D). Similarly, Defender's choice at node 4 must be E if Defender is strategically Hard (i.e., of type HH or SH), and D if Defender is strategically Soft (i.e., of type HS or SS). Therefore, figure A8.1 does not show strategic variables for these two nodes.

As usual, specification of a PBE requires specification of both strategic choices and beliefs. The strategic variables defined above serve to specify the strategic choices at a PBE. Beliefs are probabilities over the opponent's type; initially they are the credibility parameters. Subsequent beliefs relevant to PBE are r, Defender's conditional probability that Challenger is Hard given that Defender must take action (i.e. that the game reaches node 2 in figure A8.1), and q_T, Challenger's conditional probability that Defender is of type T ($T = $ HH, HS, SH, or SS), given that Challenger must respond to Defender's D response (i.e., that the game reaches node 3a in figure A8.1).

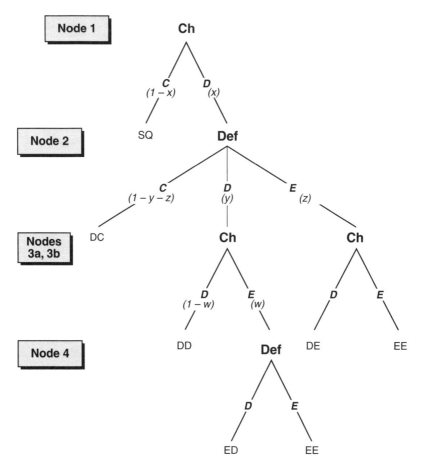

Fig. A8.1. Asymmetric Escalation Game: general version.

At any PBE, $y_{SH} = y_{SS} = 0$. To see why, observe in figure A8.1 that Defender's node 2 alternative D is dominated by alternative C when Defender is of type SH or SS. In consequence, $q_{SH} = q_{SS} = 0$, and $q_{HS} = 1 - q_{HH}$, at any PBE. Therefore, a PBE is completely specified by a 12-tuple

$$[x_H, \ x_S, \ w_H, \ w_S, \ q_{HH}; \ y_{HH}, \ y_{HS}, \ z_{HH}, \ z_{HS}, \ z_{SH}, \ z_{SS}, \ r]$$

of probabilities. There are no *a priori* conditions on these twelve probabilities, except that $y_{HH} + z_{HH} \leq 1$ and $y_{HS} + z_{HS} \leq 1$.

Following Fudenberg and Tirole (1991: ch. 8), such a 12-tuple constitutes a PBE if and only if the following conditions are met:

$$x_H = \arg\max_{0 \leq x \leq 1}\{x \cdot CXH\} \tag{A8.1}$$

where $CXH = (c_{DC} - c_{SQ}) - y_p[(c_{DC} - c_{DD}) - w_H(c_{ED} - c_{DD})$
$+ w_H q_{HH}(c_{ED} - c_{EE+})] - z_p(c_{DC} - c_{EE+})$

$y_p \equiv p_{HH}y_{HH} + p_{HS}y_{HS}$

$z_p \equiv p_{HH}z_{HH} + p_{HS}z_{HS} + p_{SH}z_{SH} + p_{SS}z_{SS}$

$$x_S = \arg\max_{0 \leq x \leq 1}\{x \cdot CXS\} \tag{A8.2}$$

where $CXS = (c_{DC} - c_{SQ}) - y_p[(c_{DC} - c_{DD}) - w_S(c_{ED} - c_{DD})$
$+ w_S q_{HH}(c_{ED} - c_{EE-})] - z_p(c_{DC} - c_{DE})$.

If $x_H + x_S > 0$, $r = p_{Ch}x_H/x_p$ (A8.3)
where $x_p \equiv p_{Ch}z_H + (1 - p_{Ch})x_S$

$$(y_{HH}, z_{HH}) = \arg\max_{\substack{0 \leq y \leq 1 \\ 0 \leq z \leq 1}}\{y \cdot CYHH + z \cdot CZHH\} \tag{A8.4}$$

where $CYHH = (d_{DD+} - d_{DC}) - w_r(d_{DD+} - d_{EE+})$
$CZHH = (d_{DE} - d_{DC}) - r(d_{DE} - d_{EE+})$
$w_r \equiv rw_H + (1 - r)w_S$

$$(y_{HS}, z_{HS}) = \arg\max_{\substack{0 \leq y \leq 1 \\ 0 \leq z \leq 1}}\{y \cdot CYHS + z \cdot CZHS\} \tag{A8.5}$$

where $CYHS = (d_{DD+} - d_{DC}) - w_r(d_{DD+} - d_{ED})$
$CZHS = (d_{DE} - d_{DC}) - r(d_{DE} - d_{EE-})$

$$z_{SH} = \arg\max_{0 \leq z \leq 1}\{z \cdot CSH\} \tag{A8.6}$$

where $CSH = CZHH$

$$z_{SS} = \arg\max_{0 \leq z \leq 1}\{z \cdot CSS\} \tag{A8.7}$$

where $CSS = CZHS$

If $y_{HH} + y_{HS} > 0$, $q_{HH} = p_{HH} \, y_{HH}/y_p$ (A8.8)

$$w_H = \arg\max_{0 \le w \le 1}\{w \cdot CWH\} \qquad\qquad (A8.9)$$

where $CWH = (c_{ED} - c_{DD}) - q_{HH}(c_{ED} - c_{EE+})$

$$w_S = \arg\max_{0 \le w \le 1}\{w \cdot CWS\} \qquad\qquad (A8.10)$$

where $CWS = (c_{ED} - c_{DD}) - q_{HH}(c_{ED} - c_{EE-})$

Deterrence Equilibria ($x_p = 0$)

A *Deterrence Equilibrium* is any PBE with $x_p = 0$, i.e., $x_H = x_S = 0$. At any Deterrence Equilibrium, the outcome is SQ. Inspection of (A8.1) and (A8.2) shows that $CXH \le 0$ and $CXS \le 0$ are required for any Deterrence Equilibrium; this can occur if and only if either $z_p > 0$, or $y_p > 0$, or both. Deterrence Equilibria can be usefully partitioned into two classes, Limited-Response Deterrence ($y_p > 0$, $z_p = 0$) and Escalatory Deterrence ($z_p > 0$).

First, we examine in detail one particular Escalatory Deterrence Equilibrium. This equilibrium, called DET$_1$, is characterized by $z_p = 1$, i.e., $z_{HH} = z_{HS} = z_{SH} = z_{SS} = 1$. Of course, $x_H = x_S = 0$ and $y_{HH} = y_{HS} = 0$. To specify Det$_1$ in detail, note first that (A8.1) and (A8.2) are immediate. Furthermore $CZHH > 0$ and $CZHS > 0$ provided

$$r \le \frac{d_{DE} - d_{DC}}{d_{DE} - d_{EE-}} \equiv d_1,$$

which can always be arranged because condition (A8.3) presents no restriction on the choice of r. Thus (A8.6) and (A8.7) are satisfied; as well, (A8.4) and (A8.5) hold provided w_r is large enough that $CYHH \le CZHH$ and $CYHS \le CZHS$. To see that these inequalities can also be arranged, observe first that (A8.8) places no restriction on q_{HH}. Therefore, $q_{HH} \le c_r$ can be chosen so that $w_H = w_S = 1$ by (A8.9) and (A8.10). In turn, this implies $w_r = rw_H + (1-r)w_S = 1$, so that (A8.4) and (A8.5) hold. We have now verified that Det$_1$, [x_H, x_S, w_H, w_S, q_{HH}; y_{HH}, y_{HS}, z_{HH}, z_{HS}, z_{SH}, z_{SS}, r] = [0, 0, 1, 1, q_{HH}; 0, 0, 1, 1, 1, 1, r], is an equilibrium whenever $r \le d_1$ and $q_{HH} \le c_r$. Notice that Det$_1$ exists no matter what the values of the payoff parameters and the credibility parameters.

There are other Escalatory Deterrence Equilibria besides Det$_1$, but

Table A8.1. *Perfect Bayesian equilibria of Asymmetric Escalation Game with incomplete information*

	Challenger					Defender						
	x		w			y		z				
	x_H	x_S	w_H	w_S	q_{HH}	y_{HH}	y_{HS}	z_{HH}	z_{HS}	z_{SH}	z_{SS}	r
Det$_1$	0	0	1	1	$\leq c_r$	0	0	1	1	1	1	$\leq d_1$
Det$_2$	0	0	0	0	$p_{Str\,|\,Tac}$	1	1	0	0	0	0	$\geq d_2$
Det$_3$	0	0	$h(r; d_r)$	0	c_q	1	α	0	0	0	0	$\geq d_2$
NRE	1	1	Large	Large	Small	0	0	0	0	0	0	p_{Ch}
NLRE$_1$	1	1	Large	Large	Small	0	0	1	1	0	0	p_{Ch}
NLRE$_2$	1	$f(p_{Ch}; d_2)$	Large	Large	Small	0	0	Large	0	Large	0	d_2
NLRE$_3$	1	$f(p_{Ch}; d_1)$	Large	Large	Small	0	0	1	Large	1	Large	d_1
CLRE$_1$	1	1	0	0	$p_{Str\,|\,Tac}$	1	1	0	0	0	0	p_{Ch}
CLRE$_2$	1	$f(p_{Ch}; d_2)$	0	0	$p_{Str\,|\,Tac}$	1	1	0	0	z_{C2}	0	d_2
CLRE$_3$	1	1	0	0	$p_{Str\,|\,Tac}$	1	1	0	0	1	0	p_{Ch}
CLRE$_4$	1	$f(p_{Ch}; d_1)$	0	0	$p_{Str\,|\,Tac}$	1	1	0	0	1	z_{C4}	d_1
CLRE$_5$	1	$f(p_{Ch}; d_q)$	0	0	$\dfrac{p_{HH}y_{C5}}{y_P}$	y_{C5}	1	$1-y_{C5}$	0	0	0	d_q
ELRE$_1$	1	1	$h(p_{Ch}; d_r)$	0	c_q	1	α	0	0	1	0	p_{Ch}
ELRE$_2$	1	$f(p_{Ch}; d_2)$	$h(d_2; d_r)$	0	c_q	1	α	0	0	z_{E2}	0	d_2
ELRE$_3$	1	1	$h(p_{Ch}; d_r)$	0	c_q	1	α	0	0	0	0	p_{Ch}
ELRE$_4$	1	$f(p_{Ch}; d_q)$	$k(p_{Ch}; d_q)$	0	c_q	$1/\alpha$	1	$1-1/\alpha$	0	1	0	p_{Ch}
ELRE$_5$	1	$f(p_{Ch}; d_1)$	$k(d_1; d_q)$	0	c_q	$1/\alpha$	1	$1-1/\alpha$	0	1	z_{E5}	d_1
ELRE$_6$	1	$f(p_{Ch}; d_t)$	$h(d_t; d_r)$	0	c_q	y_{E6}	αy_{E6}	$1-y_{E6}$	0	1	0	d_t

they exist only when the parameters satisfy certain conditions. For instance, there is a Deterrence Equilibrium with $z_{HH} = z_{SH} = 1$, $z_{HS} = z_{SS} = 0$, provided

$$p_{Str} \equiv p_{HH} + p_{HS} \geq \frac{c_{DC} - c_{SQ}}{c_{DC} - c_{EE+}} \equiv c_2.$$

All Escalatory Deterrence Equilibria place a maximum on r. For instance, Det_1 requires $r \leq d_1$, while the example described above requires $d_1 \leq r \leq d_2$ where

$$d_2 \equiv \frac{d_{DE} - d_{DC}}{d_{DE} - d_{EE+}}$$

By (A8.3), such conditions can always be met at any Deterrence Equilibrium, because $x_H = x_S = 0$. However, it is noteworthy that $r > d_2$ is impossible at any Escalatory Deterrence Equilibrium.

There are two Limited-Response Deterrence Equilibria, and both exist only when the parameters satisfy certain conditions. It can be shown that an equilibrium with $y_p > 0$ and $z_p = 0$ must have $y_{HH} = 1$ and $y_{HS} > 0$. We first construct Det_2, the Limited-Response Deterrence Equilibrium with $y_{HH} = y_{HS} = 1$. Of course $x_H = x_S = 0$ and $z_{HH} = z_{HS} = z_{SH} = z_{SS} = 0$. Note that, by (A8.8),

$$q_{HH} = \frac{p_{HH}}{p_{HH} + p_{HS}} \equiv p_{Str|Tac}.$$

From (A8.9) and (A8.10) it follows that $w_H = w_S = 0$ provided that

$$q_{HH} > \frac{c_{ED} - c_{DD}}{c_{ED} + c_{EE+}} \equiv c_q.$$

Thus, one requirement for Det_2 is $p_{Str|Tac} \geq c_q$. It is now easy to apply (A8.1) and (A8.2) to identify another condition:

$$p_{Tac} \equiv p_{HH} + p_{HS} \geq c_3 = \frac{c_{DC} - c_{SQ}}{c_{DC} - c_{DD}}.$$

We have now verified all conditions except (A8.4)–(A8.7). Because $w_r = 0$, it is easily seen that these four conditions hold provided $r \geq d_2$. To summarize, Det_2, $[x_H, x_S, w_H, w_S, q_{HH}; y_{HH}, y_{HS}, z_{HH}, z_{HS}, z_{SH}, z_{SS}, r] = [0, 0, 0, 0, p_{Str|Tac}; 1, 1, 0, 0, 0, 0, r]$, is an equilibrium whenever $r \leq d_2$ provided $p_{Tac} \geq c_3$ and $p_{Str|Tac} \geq c_q$.

In a similar way, it can be verified that the other Limited-Response Deterrence Equilibrium is Det_3, defined by $[x_H, x_S, w_H, w_S, q_{HH};$ $y_{HH}, y_{HS}, z_{HH}, z_{HS}, z_{SH}, z_{SS}, r] = [0, 0, h(r; d_r), 0, c_q; 1, \alpha, 0, 0, 0, 0, r]$. Here $r \leq d_2$ is required, as is

$$y_{HS} = v = \alpha \equiv \frac{p_{HH}(1 - c_q)}{p_{HS}c_q}, w_H = h(r; d_r) = \frac{d_r}{r}.$$

Det_3 exists whenever $p_{\text{Str}|\text{Tac}} \leq c_q$ and $p_{HH} \geq c^* \equiv c_3 c_q$.

Finally, we mention the existence of Escalatory Deterrence Equilibria at which both $y_p > 0$ and $z_p = 0$. For instance, there is an equilibrium $[x_H, x_S, w_H, w_S, q_{HH}; y_{HH}, y_{HS}, z_{HH}, z_{HS}, z_{SH}, z_{SS}, r] = [0, 0,$ $0, 0, p_{\text{Str}|\text{Tac}}; 1, 1, 0, 0, 1, 0, r]$. Here, $\max\{d_1, d_q\} \leq r \leq d_2$ is required. This equilibrium exists iff $p_{\text{Str}|\text{Tac}} \geq c_q$ and

$$(c_{DC} - c_{SQ}) - p_{\text{Tac}}(c_{DC} - c_{DD}) - p_{SH}(c_{DC} - c_{ED}) \leq 0,$$

a condition slightly weaker than $p_{\text{Tac}} \geq c_3$.

No-Response Equilibria $(x_p > 0, \ y_p = z_p = 0)$

A *No-Response Equilibrium* (NRE) is any PBE with $x_p > 0$, but $y_p = z_p = 0$. In other words, either x_H or x_S is positive but $z_{HH} = z_{HS} = z_{SH} = z_{SS} = y_{HH} = y_{HS} = 0$. Inspection of (A8.1) and (A8.2) shows that, at any NRE, $x_H = x_S = 1$. Furthermore, $r = p_{Ch}$, from (A8.3). As well, all of the coefficients of y and z in (A8.4)–(A8.7) must be non-positive. Because $CYHS \leq CYHH$ and $CSS = CZHS \leq CSH = CZHH$, this requirement is met if and only if

$$w_r \geq \frac{d_{DD+} - d_{DC}}{d_{DD+} - d_{EE+}} \equiv d_s,$$

which is true provided w_H and w_S are large. It follows that an NRE exists if and only if $p_{Ch} \geq d_2$, and w_r is large enough. (Since (A8.8) has no bite, the latter condition can be arranged by taking q_{HH} small, thereby making w_H, and if necessary also w_S, large. For example, $q_{HH} < c_r$ implies $w_H = w_S = 1$, so $w_r = 1$.) At any NRE, the outcome is DC, and the players' utilities are c_{DC} and d_{DC}.

No-Limited-Response Equilibria $(x_p > 0, \ y_p = 0, \ z_p > 0)$

A *No-Limited-Response Equilibrium* (NLRE) is any PBE with $x_p > 0$ and $z_p > 0$ but $y_p = 0$. (In other words, $y_{HH} = y_{HS} = 0$, while at least one of z_{HH}, z_{HS}, z_{SH}, and z_{SS} is positive, as is either x_H or x_S.) We show first that, at any NLRE, $x_H = 1$ and $x_S > 0$. Because $y_p = 0$,

$$CXH - CXS = z_p(c_{EE+} - c_{DE}) > 0,$$

which proves that if $x_S > 0$, then $x_H = 1$. Now suppose that $x_S = 0$. Clearly $x_H > 0$ is required, for otherwise $x_p = 0$. By (A8.3), $r = 1$. But it is now easy to verify that $CZHS < CZHH < 0$, which implies by (A8.4)–(A8.7) that $z_{HH} = z_{HS} = z_{SH} = z_{SS} = 0$. This contradiction demonstrates that $x_S > 0$ and $x_H = 1$ at any NLRE. Note that, necessarily, $r > 0$.

Observe that $CZHH - CZHS = r(d_{EE+} - d_{EE-}) > 0$, so that if either $z_{HS} > 0$ or $z_{SS} > 0$ at an NLRE, then $z_{HH} = z_{SH} = 1$. Furthermore $z_{HS} > 0$ or $z_{SS} > 0$ at equilibrium if and only if $CZHS \geq 0$, which is equivalent to $r \leq d_1$; also $z_{HH} > 0$ or $z_{SH} > 0$ at equilibrium if and only if $CZHH \geq 0$, which is equivalent to $r \leq d_2$.

We now identify necessary conditions for the NLRE with $x_H = x_S = 1$, or NLRE$_1$. Note that $r = p_{Ch}$ and, because $CXS \geq 0$ is required,

$$z_p \leq \frac{c_{DC} - c_{SQ}}{c_{DC} - c_{DE}} \equiv c_1.$$

An NLRE$_1$ with either $0 < z_{HS} < 1$ or $0 < z_{SS} < 1$ cannot exist unless $p_{Ch} = d_1$; such a PBE is clearly transitional. An NLRE$_1$ with $0 < z_{HH} < 1$ or $0 < z_{SH} < 1$ is likewise transitional, corresponding to $p_{Ch} = d_2$. As already demonstrated, NLRE$_1$ cannot have $p_{Ch} = r > d_2$. Furthermore, there are no NLRE$_1$ with $z_{HH} = z_{SH} = z_{HS} = z_{SS} = 1$, for this would imply $z_p = 1$, contradicting the requirement that $z_p \leq c_1$. The only remaining possibility is $z_{HH} = z_{SH} = 1$, $z_{HS} = z_{SS} = 0$, which is consistent with equilibrium iff $d_1 \leq p_{Ch} \leq d_2$. Clearly $z_p = p_{HH} + p_{SH} = p_{Str} \leq c_1$ is also necessary, as are sufficiently large values of w_H and w_S that $CYHH \leq CZHH$ and $CYHS \leq 0$. As usual, $q_{HH} < c_r$ will suffice.

Any NLRE other than NLRE$_1$ must have $x_H = 1$, $0 < x_S < 1$, and $z_p = c_1$. As noted above, there can be no such PBE with $r > d_2$, nor is $r < d_1$ possible, for that would imply $z_p = 0$. Suppose now that $d_1 < r < d_2$. Then $z_{HH} = z_{SH} = 1$ and $z_{HS} = z_{SS} = 0$, so that $z_p = p_{HH} + p_{SH} = c_1$, which shows that any such NLRE is transitional. Thus any NLRE other than NLRE$_1$ must have either $r = d_1$ or $r = d_2$.

NLRE$_2$ is the NLRE with $x_H = 1$, $0 < x_S < 1$, and $r = d_2$. Condition (A8.3) implies that, at equilibrium

$$x_S = \frac{p_{Ch}(1 - d_2)}{d_2(1 - p_{Ch})} = f(p_{Ch}; d_2).$$

Note that $x_S \leq 1$ iff $p_{Ch} \leq d_2$. Because $r = d_2 > d_1$, $z_{HS} = z_{SS} = 0$. But by (A8.2), $z_p = c_1$, so that

$$p_{HH} z_{HH} + p_{SH} z_{SH} = c_1.$$

It is possible to find values of z_{HH} and z_{SH} large enough to satisfy this relationship if and only if $p_{Str} = p_{HH} + p_{SH} \geq c_1$. In addition, values of w_H and w_S sufficiently large that $CYHH \leq 0$ are required, as usual.

NLRE$_3$ is the NLRE with $x_H = 1$, $0 < x_S < 1$ and $r = d_1$. Condition (A8.3) now implies that

$$x_S = \frac{p_{Ch}(1 - d_1)}{d_1(1 - p_{Ch})} = f(p_{Ch}; d_1).$$

Note that $x_S \leq 1$ iff $p_{Ch} \leq d_1$. Because $r = d_1 < d_2$, $z_{HH} = z_{SH} = 1$. But (A8.2) now implies $z_p = c_1$, i.e.,

$$z_p = p_{HH} + p_{SH} + p_{HS} z_{HS} + p_{SS} z_{SS} = c_1.$$

Non-negative values of z_{HS} and z_{SS} satisfying this equation can be found if and only if $p_{Str} = p_{HH} + p_{SH} \leq c_1$. As before, values of w_H and w_S large enough that $CYHH \leq CZHH$ and $CYHS \leq CZHS = 0$ are also required.

See table A8.1 for summaries of the values of the strategic and belief variables at NLRE$_1$. There are three outcomes that could occur at any NLRE: DC (if Defender does not respond); DE (if Defender escalates and Challenger then backs down); and EE (if Defender escalates and Challenger does too). In addition, a fourth outcome, SQ, can occur under NLRE$_2$ or NLRE$_3$, when a Soft Challenger chooses not to initiate.

Limited-Response Equilibria ($x_p > 0$, $y_p > 0$)

A *Limited-Response Equilibrium* (LRE) is any PBE with $x_p > 0$ and $y_p > 0$. In other words, at least one of y_{HH} and y_{HS} is positive, as is at least one of x_H and x_S. Note that there is no restriction on z_p.

To begin with, our objective is to show that, at any LRE, $y_{HH} > 0$,

$w_S = 0$, and $0 \leq w_H < 1$. First suppose that $q_{HH} = 0$. Then $w_H = w_S = 1$ by (A8.9) and (A8.10). But now $CYHH < 0$ and $CYHS < 0$, so (A8.4) and (A8.5) imply that $y_{HH} = 0$ and $y_{HS} = 0$, contradicting the requirement that $y_p > 0$ at any LRE. Thus $q_{HH} > 0$, and now $y_{HH} > 0$ follows from (A8.8). Also

$$CWH - CWS = q_{HH}(c_{EE+} - c_{EE-}) > 0;$$

from (A8.9) and (A8.10) it follows that if $w_S > 0$, then $w_H = 1$.

Now suppose that $w_H = 1$. Because $w_r = r + (1-r)w_S$, $CZHH - CYHH = (1-r)[(d_{DE} - d_{DD+}) + w_S(d_{DD+} - d_{EE+})] \geq 0$, with equality iff $r = 1$. But when $r = 1$, $CYHH = CZHH < 0$. Because neither $r = 1$ nor $r < 1$ is compatible with the $y_{HH} > 0$ requirement, it follows that $w_H < 1$, and therefore $w_S = 0$, at any LRE.

A Limited-Response Equilibrium with $w_H = w_S = 0$ is called a *Constrained Limited-Response Equilibrium*, or CLRE. We now identify all CLRE. From the assumption that $w_H = w_S = 0$, it follows that

$$
\left.
\begin{aligned}
CYHH &\geq CZHH \text{ iff } r \geq d_q \equiv \frac{d_{DE} - d_{DD+}}{d_{DE} - d_{EE+}} \\
CYHS &\geq CZHS \text{ iff } r \geq d_p \equiv \frac{d_{DE} - d_{DD+}}{d_{DE} - d_{EE-}} \\
CSH &= CZHH \geq 0 \text{ iff } r \leq d_2 \\
CSS &= CZHS \geq 0 \text{ iff } r \leq d_1
\end{aligned}
\right\}
\tag{A8.11}
$$

Furthermore, each left-hand inequality in (A8.11) is strict iff the corresponding right-hand inequality is strict. Recall that $0 < d_p < \min \{d_q, d_1\} \leq \max \{d_q, d_1\} < d_2 < 1$.

Note first that all CLRE have $r \geq d_q$, for (A8.11) shows that $r < d_q$ implies $CYHH < CZHH$, which, by (A8.4), implies $y_{HH} = 0$. Now suppose that $r < d_1$ at some CLRE. Then (A8.11), in combination with (A8.4)–(A8.7), implies that $y_{HH} + z_{HH} = 1$, $y_{HS} + z_{HS} = 1$, $z_{SH} = 1$, and $z_{SS} = 1$. But now $z_p > 0$ and $y_p + z_p = 1$, so

$$CXS < CXH < (c_{DC} - c_{SQ}) - (y_p + z_p)(c_{DC} - c_{DD}) = c_{DD} - c_{SQ} < 0,$$

because $w_H = w_S = 0$. By (A8.1) and (A8.2), $x_H = x_S = 0$, contradicting the requirement that $x_p > 0$ for an LRE. We conclude that, at any CLRE, $r \geq d_q$ and $r \geq d_1$.

We now identify all non-transitional CLRE with $y_{HH} = 1$. By (A8.11),

$r \geq d_q$, which implies $r > d_p$, which by (A8.11) and (A8.5) implies $y_{HS} = 1$ and $y_p = p_{HH} + p_{HS} = p_{Tac}$. By (A8.8)–(A8.10)

$$q_{HH} = p_{Str|Tac} \geq c_q = \frac{c_{ED} - c_{DD}}{c_{ED} - c_{EE+}}$$

is necessary.

First suppose that there is a CLRE with $y_{HH} = 1$ and $z_p = 0$. By (A8.11), $r \geq d_2$ is required. Also

$$CXH = CXS = (c_{DC} - c_{SQ}) - y_p(c_{DC} - c_{DD}),$$

so a non-transitional CLRE occurs only if $p_{Tac} \leq c_3$ and $x_H = x_S = 1$. Because $r = p_{Ch}$ by (A8.3), an additional requirement is $p_{Ch} \geq d_2$. These necessary conditions are also sufficient: a CLRE called $CLRE_1$, with $y_{HH} = 1$ and $z_p = 0$, occurs iff $p_{Ch} \geq d_2$, $p_{Tac} \leq c_3$, and $p_{Str|Tac} \geq c_q$. At $CLRE_1$, $x_H = x_S = 1$, $q_{HH} = p_{Str|Tac}$, $w_H = w_S = 0$; $r = p_{Ch}$, $y_{HH} = y_{HS} = 1$, and $z_{HH} = z_{HS} = z_{SH} = z_{SS} = 0$. Note that the outcome is always DD if Defender is of type HH or HS, and always DC otherwise.

Now we search for a CLRE with $y_{HH} = 1$ and $0 < z_{SH} < 1$. By (A8.11), $z_{SS} = 0$, $z_p = p_{SH}z_{SH}$, and $r = d_2$. Now $CXS < CXH$, so for a non-transitional equilibrium, $x_H = 1$, $0 < x_S \leq 1$, and $CXS = 0$ are required. The requirement that $r = d_2$ can then be met if and only if $p_{Ch} \leq d_2$ and $x_S = f(p_{Ch}; d_2)$. The equality $CXS = 0$ is satisfied iff

$$(c_{DC} - c_{SQ}) - (p_{HH} + p_{HS})(c_{DC} - c_{DD}) - p_{SH}(c_{DC} - c_{DE}) \leq 0,$$
$$0 \leq (c_{DC} - c_{SQ}) - (p_{HH} + p_{HS})(c_{DC} - c_{DD}),$$

and

$$z_{SH} = z_{C2} \equiv \frac{1 - p_{HH}/c_3 - p_{HS}/c_3}{p_{SH}/c_1}.$$

Note that the second inequality is equivalent to $p_{Tac} \leq c_3$, and the first to

$$\frac{p_{HH}}{c_3} + \frac{p_{HS}}{c_3} + \frac{p_{SH}}{c_1} \geq 1. \tag{A8.12}$$

In summary, a CLRE with $y_{HH} = 1$ and $0 < z_{SH} < 1$, or $CLRE_2$, occurs iff $p_{Ch} \leq d_2$, $p_{Tac} \leq c_2$, $p_{Str|Tac} \geq c_q$, and (A8.12) holds. At $CLRE_2$, $x_H = 1$, $x_S = f(p_{Ch}; d_2)$, $q = p_{Str|Tac}$, $w_H = w_S = 0$; $r = d_2$, $y_{HH} = y_{HS} = 1$, $z_{HH} =$

$z_{HS} = z_{SS} = 0$, and $z_{SH} = z_{C2}$. The possible outcomes are SQ, DC, DD, DE, and EE.

We next identify the CLRE with $y_{HH} = 1$, $z_{SH} = 1$, and $z_{SS} = 0$. Clearly $z_p = p_{SH}$ and max $\{d_1, d_q\} \leq r \leq d_2$. Consideration of (A8.1) and (A8.2) now shows that a non-transitional equilibrium occurs iff $x_H = x_S = 1$ and $CXS \geq 0$, i.e.,

$$\frac{p_{HH}}{c_3} + \frac{p_{HS}}{c_3} + \frac{p_{SH}}{c_1} \leq 1 \tag{A8.12^r}$$

(Note that (A8.12)^r refers to inequality (A8.12) with the direction of inequality reversed.) Because $r = p_{Ch}$, a further requirement is max $\{d_1, d_q\} \leq p_{Ch} \leq d_2$. Again, a necessary condition for (A8.12)^r is $p_{Tac} \leq c_2$. We name this equilibrium CLRE$_3$; it occurs iff max $\{d_1, d_q\} \leq p_{Ch} \leq d_2$, $p_{Str \mid Tac} \geq c_q$, and (A8.12)^r holds. At CLRE$_3$, $x_H = x_S = 1$, $q_{HH} = p_{Str \mid Tac}$, $w_H = w_S = 0$; $r = p_{Ch}$, $y_{HH} = y_{HS} = 1$, $z_{HH} = z_{HS} = z_{SS} = 0$, and $z_{SH} = 1$. The possible outcomes are DC, DD, DE, and EE.

Finally, a CLRE with $y_{HH} = 1$, $z_{SH} = 1$, and $0 < z_{SS} < 1$ can occur iff $r = d_1 \geq d_q$. For a non-transitional equilibrium, $x_H = 1$, $0 < x_S < 1$, and $x_S = f(p_{Ch}; d_1)$ are required. Clearly, $p_{Ch} \leq d_1$ and (A8.12)^r are required, as is

$$z_{SS} = z_{C4} \equiv \frac{1 - p_{HH}/c_3 - p_{HS}/c_3 - p_{SH}/c_1}{p_{SS}/c_1}.$$

For this equilibrium, called CLRE$_4$, to occur, not only must (A8.12)^r hold, but also

$$\frac{p_{HH}}{c_3} + \frac{p_{HS}}{c_3} + \frac{p_{SH}}{c_1} + \frac{p_{SS}}{c_1} \geq 1 \tag{A8.13}$$

But, after substitution for p_{SS}, it can be shown that (A8.12)^r implies (A8.13). Thus CLRE$_4$ exists iff $d_1 \geq d_q$, $p_{Ch} \leq d_1$, $p_{Str \mid Tac} \geq c_q$, and (A8.12)^r holds. At CLRE$_4$, $x_H = 1$, $x_S = f(p_{Ch}; d_1)$, $q_{HH} = p_{Str \mid Tac}$, $w_H = w_S = 0$; $r = d_1$, $y_{HH} = y_{HS} = 1$, $z_{HH} = z_{HS} = 0$, $z_{SH} = 1$, and $z_{SS} = z_{C4}$. Possible outcomes are SQ, DC, DD, DE, and EE.

There is no non-transitional CLRE with $y_{HH} = 1$ and $z_{SS} = 1$, for such a CLRE would require $r < d_1$. Since every LRE has $y_{HH} > 0$, the only remaining possibility is $0 < y_{HH} < 1$, $r = d_q > d_1$, $y_{HS} = 1$, and $q_{HH} = p_{HH}y_{HH}/y_p \geq c_q$; the latter inequality is equivalent to

$$y_{HH} \geq \frac{c_q p_{HS}}{(1 - c_q)p_{HH}} = \frac{1}{\alpha}$$

which can be satisfied iff $p_{Str|Tac} \geq c_q$. A CLRE with $y_{HH} < 1$ must have $z_{HH} = 1 - y_{HH}$ and $z_{SH} = 1$, for $CHS = CZHH = CYHH > 0$ is required. Also $z_{SS} > 0$ cannot occur unless $r \leq d_1$, so, for a non-transitional equilibrium, $z_{SS} = 0$. Another necessary condition is $x_H = 1$ and

$$x_S = f(p_{Ch}; d_q) \equiv \frac{p_{Ch}(1 - d_q)}{d_q(1 - p_{Ch})},$$

for which $p_{Ch} \leq d_q$ is necessary. The final requirement is $CXS = 0$, which is equivalent to (A8.12)^r,

$$\frac{p_{HH}}{c_1} + \frac{p_{HS}}{c_3} + \frac{p_{SH}}{c_1} \geq 1 \tag{A8.14}$$

and

$$y_{HH} = y_{C5} \equiv \frac{p_{HH}/c_1 + p_{HS}/c_3 + p_{SH}/c_1 - 1}{p_{HH}(1/c_1 - 1/c_3)}$$

The final requirement for CLRE$_5$, is $y_{C5} \geq 1/\alpha$ which is equivalent to

$$\frac{p_{HH}}{c_1} + p_{HS} \left(\frac{1}{c^*} - \frac{1}{c_1} \right) \frac{c_q}{1 - c_q} + \frac{p_{SH}}{c_1} \geq 1, \tag{A8.15}$$

where $c^* \equiv c_3 c_q$. Because (A8.14) is easily seen to be a consequence of (A8.15), it follows that CLRE$_5$ occurs iff $d_1 \leq d_q$, $p_{Ch} \leq d_q$, $p_{Str|Tac} \geq c_q$, and (A8.12)^r and (A8.15) both hold. At CLRE$_5$, $x_H = 1$, $x_S = f(p_{Ch}; d_q)$, $q_{HH} = p_{HH} y_{C5}/(p_{HH} y_{C5} + p_{HS})$, $w_H = w_S = 0$; $r = d_q$, $y_{HH} = y_{C5}$, $y_{HS} = 1$, $z_{HH} = 1 - y_{HH}$, $z_{HS} = 0$, $z_{SH} = 1$, and $z_{SS} = 0$. Possible outcomes are SQ, DC, DD, DE, and EE.

A Limited-Response Equilibrium that is not a Constrained Limited-Response Equilibrium must have $w_S = 0$ and $0 < w_H < 1$. Such a PBE is called an *Escalating Limited-Response Equilibrium* (ELRE). We now identify all ELRE.

First (A8.9) shows that $q_{HH} = c_q$ is required for an ELRE. Because $0 < c_q < 1$, (A8.8) implies that both $y_{HH} > 0$ and $y_{HS} > 0$ at any ELRE. Also, substitution of $q_{HH} = c_q$ and $w_S = 0$ yields

$$CXH - CXS = z_p(c_{EE+} - c_{DE}) \geq 0,$$

with equality iff $z_p = 0$. It follows that $r = 0$ is possible only if $z_p = 0$. But substitution in (A8.4) shows that, if $r = 0$, $z_{HH} = 1$ and, therefore $z_p > 0$. We conclude that, at any ELRE, $r > 0$.

Because $w_r = rw_H > 0$,

$$CYHH - CYHS = rw_H(d_{EE+} - d_{ED}) > 0$$

so that, if $y_{HS} > 0$ at an ELRE, then $y_{HH} + z_{HH} = 1$. Of course, $CZHH \leq CYHH$ and $CZHS \leq CYHS$ because neither y_{HH} nor y_{HS} can vanish. Also $CZHH = CSH > CZHS = CSS$.

Suppose that $CZHH > 0$ at an ELRE. Then $y_{HH} + z_{HH} = 1$, $y_{HS} + z_{HS} = 1$, $z_{SH} = z_{SS} = 1$, so $y_p + z_p = 1$. But now it is easy to show that

$$CXS < CXH < (c_{DC} - c_{SQ}) - (y_p + z_p)(c_{DC} - c_{DD}) < 0,$$

so $x_H = x_S = 0$, contradicting the requirement that $x_p > 0$ at any LRE. It follows that $CZHS \leq 0$ at any ELRE.

Now suppose that there is an ELRE with $CZHS = CYHS$. From the foregoing, $CYHS = 0$, which implies

$$w_r = \frac{d_{DD+} - d_{DC}}{d_{DD+} - d_{ED}} = d_r.$$

Now $CYHH \geq CZHH$ is required, which is equivalent to

$$r \geq \frac{d_{DE} - d_{DD+} + d_r(d_{DD+} - d_{EE+})}{d_{DE} - d_{EE+}} \equiv d_t,$$

which in turn implies that

$$CZHS \leq d_{DE} - d_{DC} - d_t(d_{DE} - d_{EE-}).$$

After substitution and manipulation, the right side of this inequality can be shown to be strictly negative. We conclude that $CZHS < CYHS$, and therefore $z_{HS} = 0$, at any ELRE.

An ELRE with $y_{HH} = y_{HS} = 1$ would be transitional, because of the requirement that

$$q_{HH} = p_{Str|Tac} = c_q.$$

It follows that all non-transitional ELRE belong to one of two disjoint groups:

(a) $y_{HH} = 1$; $0 < y_{HS} < 1$; $z_{HH} = z_{HS} = z_{SS} = 0$;
(b) $y_{HS} > 0$; $0 < y_{HH}, z_{HH} < 1$; $y_{HH} + z_{HH} = 1$; $z_{SH} = 1$; $z_{HS} = 0$.

We first search for all ELRE in group (a). Clearly $CYHS = 0$ is required. Thus $w_r = d_r$. Also $q_{HH} = c_q$, so

$$y_{HS} = \frac{p_{HH}(1 - c_q)}{p_{HS}c_q} = \frac{p_{HH}(c_{DD} - c_{EE+})}{p_{HS}(c_{ED} - c_{DD})} = \alpha,$$

which can be satisfied iff $p_{Str \mid Tac} \leq c_q$. Because $w_r = d_r$, the condition $CYHH \geq CZHH$ can be met iff

$$r \geq d_t = \frac{(d_{DE} - d_{DD+})(d_{DD+} - d_{ED}) + (d_{DD+} - d_{DC})(d_{DD+} - d_{EE+})}{(d_{DE} - d_{EE+})(d_{DD+} - d_{ED})}.$$

Note that $d_t < d_2$. There are now three possibilities:

$d_t \leq r \leq d_2$ and $z_{SH} = 1$
$r = d_2$ and $0 < z_{SH} < 1$
$d_2 \leq r$ and $z_{SH} = 0$

which will be analyzed in turn.

The first of these possibilities is $ELRE_1$, where $y_p = p_{HH} + p_{HS}\,\alpha$ and $z_p = p_{SH} > 0$. It is easy to verify that $CXH > CXS$, and this, combined with the requirement that $0 < r < 1$, implies that $x_S > 0$ and $x_H = 1$. Furthermore, an equilibrium with $0 < x_S < 1$ is transitional, because of the requirement that $CXS = 0$. Thus the non-transitional $ELRE_1$ has $x_H = x_S = 1$ and $r = p_{Ch}$. Of course, $d_t \leq p_{Ch} \leq d_2$ is necessary, as is $p_{Str \mid Tac} \leq c_q$ and $CXS \geq 0$, which is equivalent to

$$\frac{p_{HH}}{c^*} + \frac{p_{SH}}{c_1} \leq 1. \tag{A8.16}$$

At $ELRE_1$, $w_H = h(p_{Ch}; d_r) = d_r/p_{Ch}$, $w_S = 0$, and $q_{HH} = c_q$.

The second possibility is $ELRE_2$, which requires $w_H = h(d_2; d_r) = d_r/d_2$ in addition to $w_S = 0$, $w_r = d_r$, and $q_{HH} = c_q$. At $ELRE_2$, $y_{HH} = 1$, $y_{HS} = \alpha$, $z_{HH} = z_{HS} = z_{SS} = 0$, and $0 < z_{SH} < 1$. Because $CXH > CXS$ and $0 < r < 1$, this implies $x_H = 1$ and $0 < x_S < 1$, which in turn implies $CXS = 0$. The latter condition can be fulfilled iff $(A8.16)^r$, the inequality reverse to (A8.16), holds, as well as $p_{HH} \leq c^*$ and

$$z_{SH} \equiv z_{E2} = \frac{1 - p_{HH}/c^*}{p_{SH}/c_1}.$$

Also, the condition $r = d_2$ can be met only if $x_S = f(p_{Ch}; d_2)$, which requires $p_{Ch} \leq d_2$. In summary, $ELRE_2$ occurs iff $(A8.16)^r$ holds, $p_{HH} \leq c^*$, $p_{Str \mid Tac} \leq c_q$, and $p_{Ch} \leq d_2$. At $ELRE_2$, $x_H = 1$, $x_S = f(p_{Ch}; d_2)$, $w_H = h(d_2; d_r)$, $w_S = 0$, $q_{HH} = c_q$, $y_{HH} = 1$, $y_{HS} = \alpha$, $z_{HH} = z_{HS} = z_{SS} = 0$, $z_{SH} = z_{E2}$, and $r = d_2$.

The third possibility is ELRE$_3$, where $y_p = p_{HH} + p_{HS}\alpha$ and $z_p = 0$. Now $r > 0$ and

$$CXH = CXS = (c_{DC} - c_{SQ}) - p_{HH}(c_{DC} - c_{DD})/c_q;$$

it follows that any non-transitional ELRE$_3$ has $x_H = x_S = 1$, and therefore $r = p_{Ch}$. Thus $p_{Ch} \geq d_2$ is necessary, as are $p_{Str \mid Tac} \leq c_q$ and $CXS \geq 0$, which is equivalent to $p_{HH} \leq c^*$. At ELRE$_3$, $x_H = x_S = 1$, $q_{HH} = c_q$, $w_H = h(p_{Ch}; d_r)$, $w_S = 0$; $y_{HH} = 1$, $y_{HS} = \alpha$, $z_{HH} = z_{HS} = z_{SH} = z_{SS} = 0$, and $r = p_{Ch}$.

Any non-transitional ELRE not yet identified must belong to group (b), where $y_{HS} > 0$, $y_{HH} > 0$, $z_{HH} = 1 - y_{HH}$, and $z_{SH} = 1$. Of course $z_{HS} = 0$ and $z_{SS} < 1$. First we identify those ELRE in group (b) with $y_{HS} = 1$. The requirement that $q_{HH} = c_q$ now implies $y_{HH} = 1/\alpha$, which can be satisfied iff $p_{Str \mid Tac} \geq c_q$. Because $y_p + z_p < 1$ is required (otherwise the contradiction $x_H = x_S = 0$ follows, as above), it is necessary that $z_{SS} < 1$. By (A8.7), this occurs only if $CSS = CZHS \leq 0$, or $r \geq d_1$.

As usual, $x_H = 1$ and $x_S > 0$ are required at equilibrium, so $CXS \geq 0$ is necessary. First suppose that $z_{SS} = 0$. Then $CXS \geq 0$ is equivalent to (A8.15). Clearly $x_S = 1$ for a non-transitional equilibrium. Also $r = p_{Ch}$, so additional necessary conditions are $p_{Ch} \geq d_1$ and (A8.14). At this equilibrium, called ELRE$_4$, the requirement $CYHH = CZHH$ forces

$$w_H = \frac{p_{Ch} - d_q}{p_{Ch}(1 - d_q)} = k(p_{Ch}; d_q).$$

There are two remaining conditions: $CZHH \geq 0$ (to produce $z_{SH} = 1$ and $z_{HH} > 0$) and $CYHS \geq 0$ (to produce $y_{HS} = 1$). Using $w_r = p_{Ch}k(p_{Ch}; d_q)$, it can be shown that both of these conditions hold iff $p_{Ch} \leq d_t$. In summary, ELRE$_4$ has $x_H = x_S = 1$, $q_{HH} = c_q$, $w_H = k(p_{Ch}; d_q)$, $w_S = 0$; $y_{HH} = 1/\alpha$, $y_{HS} = 1$; $z_{HH} = 1 - 1/\alpha$, $z_{HS} = 0$, $z_{SH} = 1$, $z_{SS} = 0$, and $r = p_{Ch}$. It exists whenever $p_{Str \mid Tac} \geq c_q$, max $\{d_1, d_q\} \leq p_{Ch} \leq d_t$, and (A8.15) holds.

A related equilibrium is ELRE$_5$, which occurs when $y_{HH} = 1/\alpha$, $z_{HH} = 1 - 1/\alpha$, $y_{HS} = 1$, $z_{SH} = 1$, and $0 < z_{SS} < 1$. For ELRE$_5$, $q_{HH} = c_q$ and $r = d_1$ are required. Note that $p_{Str \mid Tac} \geq c_q$; also, $0 < x_S < 1$ and $CXS = 0$ are necessary for a non-transitional equilibrium. The latter conditions can be met iff (A8.15)^r and (A8.17) hold and $z_{SS} = z_{E5}$, where

$$\frac{p_{HH}}{c_1} + p_{HS}\left(\frac{1}{c^*}-\frac{1}{c_1}\right)\frac{c_q}{1-c_q}+\frac{p_{SH}}{c_1}+\frac{p_{SS}}{c_1} \geq 1 \qquad\qquad (A8.17)$$

$$z_{E5} \equiv \frac{1-p_{HH}/c_1-p_{HS}\left(\frac{1}{c^*}-\frac{1}{c_1}\right)\frac{c_q}{1-c_q}-p_{SH}/c_1}{p_{SS}/c_1}.$$

But, by substituting for p_{SS} and using $c^* = c_3 c_q$, it can be shown that (A8.17) is equivalent to

$$p_{HS} \leq \frac{(1-c_1)c_3(1-c_q)}{c_3-c_1}.$$

Now $p_{Str \mid Tac} \geq c_q$ and $(A8.15)^r$ together imply that $p_{HS} \leq c_3 (1-c_q)$, from which (A8.17) therefore follows. Furthermore, $x_S = f(p_{Ch}; d_1)$ is required for $ELRE_5$, and this is possible iff $p_{Ch} \leq d_1$. Finally, the condition $CYHH = CZHH$ can be met only if

$$w_H = \frac{d_1-d_q}{d_1(1-d_q)} = k(d_1; d_q).$$

In summary, $ELRE_5$ has $x_H = 1$, $x_S = f(p_{Ch}; d_1)$, $q_{HH} = c_q$, $w_H = k(d_1; d_q)$, $w_S = 0$; $y_{HH} = 1/\alpha$, $z_{HH} = 1-1/\alpha$, $y_{HS} = 1$, $z_{HS} = 0$, $z_{SH} = 1$, $z_{SS} = z_{E5}$, and $r = d_1$. It exists iff $p_{Str \mid Tac} \geq c_q$, $p_{Ch} \leq d_1$, $d_1 \geq d_q$, and $(A8.15)^r$ holds.

Any remaining $ELRE$ must satisfy $0 < y_{HH} < 1$, $z_{HH} = 1-y_{HH}$, $0 < y_{HS} < 1$, $z_{HS} = 0$, $z_{SH} = 1$ and $z_{SS} = 0$. By (A8.5) $w_r = d_r$ is required, and (A8.4) now shows that $r = d_t$ is also necessary. Because y_p and z_p are both positive, consideration of (A8.1) and (A8.2) now shows that no equilibrium is possible unless $x_H = 1$, $x_S = f(p_{Ch}; d_t)$, and

$$CXS = (c_{DC}-c_{SQ})-y_p(c_{DC}-c_{DD})-z_p(c_{DC}-c_{DE}) = 0.$$

Clearly, $p_{Ch} \leq d_t$ is required. Also, the condition that $q_{HH} = c_q$ implies $y_{HS} = \alpha y_{HH}$, $y_p = p_{HH}y_{HH}/c_q$, and $z_p = p_{HH}(1-y_{HH}) + p_{SH}$. Substitution and manipulation now shows that $CXS = 0$ iff

$$y_{HH} = y_{E6} \equiv \frac{1-\frac{p_{HH}}{c_1}-\frac{p_{SH}}{c_1}}{p_{HH}\left(\frac{1}{c^*}-\frac{1}{c_1}\right)}.$$

(Because we are interested only in non-transitional equilibria, we can ignore the possibility that $c^* = c_1$.)

Suppose that $c_1 > c^*$. Clearly, $y_{HH} \geq 0$ iff $p_{Str} \equiv p_{HH} + p_{SH} \leq c_1$, and

$y_{HS} \geq 0$ iff $y_{HH} \geq 0$. Substitution shows that $y_{HH} \leq 1$ iff (A8.16)^r holds, and $y_{HS} \leq 1$ iff (A8.15) holds. In summary, if $c_1 > c^*$, the equilibrium ELRE$_6$ exists iff $p_{Str} \leq c_1$, $p_{Ch} \leq d_t$, and (A8.15) and (A8.16)^r hold. At ELRE$_6$, $x_H = 1$, $x_S = f(p_{Ch}; d_t)$, $q_{HH} = c_q$, $w_H = h(d_t; d_r)$, $w_S = 0$; $r = d_t$, $y_{HH} = y_{E6}$, $y_{HS} = \alpha y_{E6}$, $z_{HH} = 1 - y_{E6}$, $z_{HS} = 0$, $z_{SH} = 1$, and $z_{SS} = 0$. Likewise it can be verified that exactly the same values result in an LRE, also called ELRE$_6$, when $c_1 < c^*$, provided $p_{Ch} \leq d_t$, $p_{Str} \geq c_1$, and (A8.15)^r and (A8.16) both hold.

References

Abrams, Herbert L. (1988). "Inescapable Risk: Human Disability and 'Accidental' Nuclear War." *Current Research on Peace and Violence*, 11: 48–60.

Achen, Christopher H. (1987). "A Darwinian View of Deterrence." In Jacek Kugler and Frank C. Zagare (eds.), *Exploring the Stability of Deterrence*. Boulder, CO: Lynne Rienner Publishers.

Achen, Christopher H. and Duncan Snidal (1989). "Rational Deterrence Theory and Comparative Case Studies." *World Politics*, 41: 143–169.

Allan, Pierre and Cédric Dupont (1999). "International Relations Theory and Game Theory: Baroque Modeling Choices and Empirical Robustness." *International Political Science Review*, 20: 23–47.

Allison, Graham T. (1971). *Essence of Decision: Explaining the Cuban Missile Crisis*. Boston: Little, Brown.

Alsharabati, Carole (1997). "Dynamics of War Initiation." Ph.D. thesis, Claremont Graduate School, Claremont, CA.

Alt, James E., Randall L. Calvert, and Brian Humes (1988). "Reputation and Hegemonic Stability: A Game-Theoretic Analysis." *American Political Science Review*, 82: 445–466.

Altfeld, Michael F. (1985). "Uncertainty as a Deterrence Strategy: A Critical Assessment." *Comparative Strategy*, 5: 1–26.

Anderton, Charles H. and Thomas Fogarty (1990). "Consequential Damage and Nuclear Deterrence." *Conflict Management and Peace Science*, 11: 1–15.

Angell, Norman (1910). *The Great Illusion: A Study of the Relation of Military Power to National Advantage*. New York: Putnam's.

Art, Robert J. (1985). "Between Assured Destruction and Nuclear Victory: The Case for the 'MAD-Plus' Posture." *Ethics*, 95: 497–516.

Aspin, Les (1986). "Midgetman: Why We Need a Small Missile." *Issues in Science and Technology*, 2: 38–48.

Aumann, Robert (1976). "Agreeing to Disagree." *Annals of Statistics*, 4: 1236–1239.

Axelrod, Robert (1984). *The Evolution of Cooperation*. New York: Basic Books.

Bacharach, Michael (1977). *Economics and the Theory of Games*. Boulder, CO: Westview Press.

Bailer, Seweryn and Joan Afferica (1982/83). "Russia and Reagan." *Foreign Affairs*, 61: 249–271.

Banks, Jeffrey S. (1990). "Equilibrium Behavior in Crisis Bargaining Games." *American Journal of Political Science*, 34: 599–614.

Baugh, William H. (1984). *The Politics of Nuclear Balance*. New York: Longman.

Bennett, Peter G. (1995). "Modeling Decisions in International Relations: Game Theory and Beyond." *Mershon International Studies Review*, 39: 19–52.

Berkowitz, Bruce D. (1985). "Proliferation, Deterrence, and the Likelihood of Nuclear War." *Journal of Conflict Resolution*, 29: 112–136.

Betts, Richard K. (1987). *Nuclear Blackmail and Nuclear Balance*. Washington, DC: Brookings Institution.

Blair, Bruce G. (1993). *The Logic of Accidental Nuclear War*. Washington, DC: Brookings Institution.

Blechman, Barry M. and Stephen S. Kaplan (1978). *Force Without War: US Armed Forces as a Political Instrument*. Washington, DC: Brookings Institution.

Bracken, Paul (1983). *The Command and Control of Nuclear Forces*. New Haven: Yale University Press.

Brams, Steven J. (1975). *Game Theory and Politics*. New York: Free Press.

(1985). *Superpower Games: Applying Game Theory to Superpower Conflict*. New Haven: Yale University Press.

(1994). *Theory of Moves*. New York: Cambridge University Press.

Brams, Steven J. and D. Marc Kilgour (1988). *Game Theory and National Security*. New York: Basil Blackwell.

Brands, H.W., Jr. (1988). "Testing Massive Retaliation: Credibility and Crisis Management in the Taiwan Strait." *International Security*, 12: 124–151.

Brecher, Michael (1993). *Crises in World Politics: Theory and Reality*. New York: Pergamon.

Bremer, Stuart A. (1992). "Dangerous Dyads: Conditions Affecting the Likelihood of Interstate War, 1816–1965." *Journal of Conflict Resolution*, 36: 309–341.

Brito, Dagobert L. and Michael Intriligator (1996). "Proliferation and the Probability of War." *Journal of Conflict Resolution*, 40: 206–214.

Brodie, Bernard, ed. (1946). *The Absolute Weapon: Atomic Power and World Order*. New York: Harcourt Brace.

(1954). "Unlimited Weapons and Limited War." *The Reporter*, November 18.

(1959). "The Anatomy of Deterrence." *World Politics*, 11: 173–179.

(1973). *War and Politics*. New York: Macmillan.

(1978). "The Development of Nuclear Strategy." *International Security*, 2: 65–83.

Bueno de Mesquita, Bruce (1981). *The War Trap*. New Haven: Yale University Press.

References

(1985a). "The War Trap Revisited." *American Political Science Review,* 79: 156–177.

(1985b). "Toward a Scientific Understanding of International Conflict: A Personal View." *International Studies Quarterly,* 29: 121–136.

(1990). "Pride of Place: The Origins of German Hegemony." *World Politics,* 43: 28–52.

(1996). "Counterfactuals and International Affairs: Some Insights from Game Theory." In Philip E. Tetlock and Aaron Belkin (eds.), *Counterfactual Thought Experiments in World Politics.* Princeton: Princeton University Press.

Bueno de Mesquita, Bruce and David Lalman (1988). "Arms Races and the Opportunity for Peace." *Synthese,* 76: 263–283.

(1992). *War and Reason: Domestic and International Imperatives.* New Haven: Yale University Press.

Bueno de Mesquita, Bruce, James D. Morrow, and Ethan R. Zorick (1997). "Capabilities, Perception and Escalation." *American Political Science Review,* 91: 15–27.

Bueno de Mesquita, Bruce and William H. Riker (1982). "An Assessment of the Merits of Selective Nuclear Proliferation." *Journal of Conflict Resolution,* 26: 283–306.

Bundy, McGeorge (1983). "The Bishops and the Bomb." *New York Review of Books,* June 16.

Bundy, McGeorge, George F. Kennan, Robert S. McNamara, and Gerald Smith (1982). "Nuclear Weapons and the Atlantic Alliance." *Foreign Affairs,* 60: 753–768.

(1984/85). "The President's Choice: Star Wars or Arms Control." *Foreign Affairs,* 63: 264–278.

Burns, John F. (1998). "Nuclear Fear Helps Enforce the Calm in Kashmir." *New York Times,* June 14.

Buzan, Barry, Charles Jones, and Richard Little (1993). *The Logic of Anarchy.* New York: Columbia University Press.

Carlson, Lisa J. (1995). "A Theory of Escalation and International Conflict." *Journal of Conflict Resolution,* 39: 511–534.

(1998). "Crisis Escalation: An Empirical Test in the Context of Extended Deterrence." *International Interactions,* 24: 225–253.

Cashman, Greg (1993). *What Causes War? An Introduction to Theories of International Conflict.* New York: Lexington Books.

Cioffi-Revilla, Claudio (1983). "A Probability Model of Credibility." *Journal of Conflict Resolution,* 27: 73–108.

(1998). *Politics and Uncertainty: Theory, Models, and Applications.* New York: Cambridge University Press.

(2000). "Ancient Warfare: Origins and Systems." In Manus I. Midlarsky (ed.), *Handbook of War Studies II.* Ann Arbor: University of Michigan Press.

Cioffi-Revilla, Claudio and Harvey Starr (1995). "Opportunity, Willingness and Political Uncertainty." *Journal of Theoretical Politics,* 7: 447–476.

Clairborne, William (1992). "What Would US Do If Quebec Cuts Canada Tie?" *Buffalo News*, March 8.

Claude, Inis L., Jr. (1962). *Power and International Relations*. New York: Random House.

Craig, Gordon A. and Alexander L. George (1995). *Force and Statecraft: Diplomatic Problems of Our Time*, 3rd edn. New York: Oxford University Press.

Daalder, Ivo H. (1991). *The Nature and Practice of Flexible Response: NATO Strategy and Theater Nuclear Forces Since 1967*. New York: Columbia University Press.

Danilovic, Vesna (1995). "Major Powers, Crisis Escalation, and War." Ph.D. thesis, University at Buffalo, State University of New York.

(1998). "A Quantitative Analysis of Deterrence Encounters: Conceptual Refinements and New Findings." Paper delivered at the 32nd Annual Meeting of the Peace Science Society (International), New Brunswick, NJ, October 16–18.

(n.d.). "Conflict Escalation: Conceptual and Methodological Issues." Department of Political Science, Texas A&M University.

Deibel, Terry L. (1980). *Commitment in American Foreign Policy: A Theoretical Examination for the Post-Vietnam Era*. National Security Affairs Monograph Series 80–4. Washington, DC: National Defense University Press.

DeNardo, James (1995). *The Amateur Strategist: Intuitive Deterrence Theories and the Politics of the Nuclear Arms Race*. New York: Cambridge University Press.

de Rivera, Joseph (1968). *The Psychological Dimension of Foreign Policy*. Columbus, OH: Merrill.

de Soysa, Indra, John R. Oneal, and Yong-Hee Park (1997). "Testing Power Transition Theory Using Alternative Measures of National Capabilities." *Journal of Conflict Resolution*, 41: 509–528.

Deutsch, Karl W. (1988). *The Analysis of International Relations*. Englewood Cliffs, NJ: Prentice-Hall.

Dixit, Avinish and Barry Nalebuff (1991). *Thinking Strategically: The Competitive Edge in Business, Politics, and Everyday Life*. New York: Norton.

Doran, Charles F. (1989a). "Power Cycle Theory of System Structure and Stability: Commonalties and Complementarities." In Manus I. Midlarsky (ed.), *Handbook of War Studies*. Boston: Unwin Hyman.

(1989b). "Systemic Disequilibrium, Foreign Policy Role, and the Power Cycle." *Journal of Conflict Resolution*, 33: 371–401.

Downs, George W. (1989). "The Rational Deterrence Debate." *World Politics*, 41: 225–237.

(1991). "Arms Races and War." In Philip E. Tetlock, Jo L. Husbands, Robert Jervis, Paul Stern, and Charles Tilly (eds.), *Behavior, Society, and Nuclear War*, vol. II. New York: Oxford University Press.

Downs, George W. and David M. Rocke (1990). *Tacit Bargaining, Arms Races, and Arms Control*. Ann Arbor: University of Michigan Press.

(1994). "Conflict, Agency, and Gambling for Resurrection: The Principal–Agent Problem Goes to War." *American Journal of Political Science*, 38: 362–380.

(1995). *Optimal Imperfection? Domestic Uncertainty and Institutions in International Relations*. Princeton: Princeton University Press.

Downs, George W., David M. Rocke, and Randolph M. Siverson (1985). "Arms Races and Cooperation." *World Politics*, 38: 118–146.

Eden, Lynn and Steven E. Miller, eds. (1989). *Nuclear Arguments: Understanding the Strategic Nuclear Arms and Arms Control Debates*. Ithaca: Cornell University Press.

Ellsberg, Daniel (1959). "The Theory and Practice of Blackmail." Lecture at the Lowell Institute, Boston, March 10. Reprinted in Oran R. Young (ed.), *Bargaining: Formal Theories of Negotiation*. Urbana: University of Illinois Press (1975).

(1961). "The Crude Analysis of Strategic Choice." *American Economic Review*, 51: 472–478.

Elman, Colin (1996). "Horses for Courses: Why *Not* Neorealist Theories of Foreign Policy?" *Security Studies*, 6: 7–53.

Engleberg, Stephen (1995). "US Took a Calculated Risk In Not Curbing Croat Attack." *New York Times*, August 13.

Erlanger, Steven (1996). "'Ambiguity' on Taiwan? Will the US Fight a Chinese Attack?" *New York Times*, March 12.

Fang, Liping, Keith W. Hipel, and D. Marc Kilgour (1993). *Interactive Decision Making: The Graph Model for Conflict Resolution*. New York: Wiley.

Fearon, James D. (1990). "Deterrence and the Spiral Model: The Role of Costly Signals in Crisis Bargaining." Presented at the Annual Meeting of the American Political Science Association, San Francisco, August 30–September 2.

(1994a). "Signaling Versus the Balance of Power and Interests: An Empirical Test of a Crisis Bargaining Model." *Journal of Conflict Resolution*, 38: 236–269.

(1994b). "Domestic Political Audiences and the Escalation of International Disputes." *American Political Science Review*, 88: 577–592.

(1997). "Signaling Foreign Policy Interests." *Journal of Conflict Resolution*, 41: 68–90.

Fink, Clinton F. (1965). "More Calculations About Deterrence." *Journal of Conflict Resolution*, 9: 54–65.

Fink, Evelyn C., Scott Gates, and Brian Humes (1998). *Game Theory Topics: Incomplete Information, Repeated Games, and N-Player Games*. Thousand Oaks, CA: Sage.

Fraser, Niall M. and Keith W. Hipel (1979). "Solving Complex Conflicts." *IEEE Transactions on Systems, Man, and Cybernetics*, SMC-9, 12: 805–816.

(1984). *Conflict Analysis: Models and Resolution*. New York: North-Holland.

Freedman, Lawrence (1987). "On the Tiger's Back: The Development of the Concept of Escalation." In Roman Kolkowitz (ed.), *The Logic of Nuclear Terror*. Boston: Allen & Unwin.

(1989). *The Evolution of Nuclear Strategy*, 2nd edn. New York: St. Martin's Press.

Friedman, James W. (1986). *Game Theory with Applications to Economics*. New York: Oxford University Press.

Friedman, Milton (1953). *Essays in Positive Economics*. Chicago: University of Chicago Press.

Fudenberg, Drew and Jean Tirole (1991). *Game Theory*. Cambridge, MA: MIT Press.

Fukuyama, Francis (1992). *The End of History and the Last Man*. New York: Free Press.

Gacek, Christopher M. (1994). *The Logic of Force: The Dilemma of Limited War in American Foreign Policy*. New York: Columbia University Press.

Gaddis, John Lewis (1982). *Strategies of Containment: A Critical Appraisal of Postwar American National Security Policy*. New York: Oxford University Press.

(1986). "The Long Peace: Elements of Stability in the Postwar International System." *International Security*, 10: 99–142.

(1987). *The Long Peace: Inquiries Into the History of the Cold War*. New York: Oxford University Press.

(1997). *We Now Know: Rethinking Cold War History*. New York: Oxford University Press.

Gallois, Pierre (1961). *The Balance of Terror*. Boston: Houghton-Mifflin.

Gamson, William and André Modigliani (1971). *Untangling the Cold War: A Strategy for Testing Rival Theories*. Boston: Little, Brown.

Garnett, John (1975). "Limited War." In John Baylis, Ken Booth, John Garnett, and Phil Williams (eds.), *Contemporary Strategy: Theories and Policies*. New York: Holmes & Meier.

Garnham, David (1976). "Power Parity and Lethal International Violence, 1969–1973." *Journal of Conflict Resolution*, 26: 379–394.

Gauthier, David (1984). "Deterrence, Maximization, and Rationality." *Ethics*, 94: 474–495.

Geller, Daniel S. (1990). "Nuclear Weapons, Deterrence, and Crisis Escalation." *Journal of Conflict Resolution*, 34: 291–310.

(1993). "Power Differentials and War in Rival Dyads." *International Studies Quarterly*, 37: 173–193.

Geller, Daniel S. and J. David Singer (1998). *Nations at War: A Scientific Study of International Conflict*. Cambridge: Cambridge University Press.

George, Alexander L. (1993). *Forceful Persuasion: Coercive Diplomacy as an Alternative to War*. Washington, DC: United States Institute of Peace Press.

George, Alexander L. and Richard Smoke (1974). *Deterrence in American Foreign Policy: Theory and Practice*. New York: Columbia University Press.

(1989). "Deterrence and Foreign Policy." *World Politics*, 41: 170–182.

Gibbons, Robert (1992). *Game Theory for Applied Economists*. Princeton: Princeton University Press.

References

Gilpin, Robert (1975). *US Power and the Multinational Corporation*. New York: Basic Books.

(1981). *War and Change in World Politics*. New York: Cambridge University Press.

Glaser, Charles (1989). "Why Do Strategists Disagree about the Requirements of Strategic Nuclear Deterrence?" In Lynn Eden and Steven E. Miller (eds.), *Nuclear Arguments: Understanding the Strategic Nuclear Arms and Arms Control Debates*. Ithaca: Cornell University Press.

(1990). *Analyzing Strategic Nuclear Policy*. Princeton: Princeton University Press.

(1997). "The Security Dilemma Revisited." *World Politics*, 50: 171–201.

Gochman, Charles S. (1990). "Capability Driven Disputes." In Charles S. Gochman and Alan Ned Sabrosky (eds.), *Prisoners of War: Nation-States in the Modern Era*. Lexington, MA: Lexington Books.

Goldstein, Joshua S. and John R. Freeman (1990). *Three-Way Street: Strategic Reciprocity in World Politics*. Chicago: University of Chicago Press.

Gray, A.M. (1989). *Warfighting*. FMFM1. Washington, DC: Department of the Navy.

Gray, Colin S. (1974). "The Urge to Compete: Rationales for Arms Racing." *World Politics*, 26: 207–233.

(1979). "Nuclear Strategy: The Case for a Theory of Victory." *International Security*, 4: 54–87.

Green, Philip (1966). *Deadly Logic*. New York: Schocken Books.

Haig, Alexander M. (1984). *Caveat: Realism, Reagan and Foreign Policy*. New York: Macmillan.

Hardin, Russell, John J. Mearsheimer, Gerald Dworkin, and Robert E. Goodwin, eds. (1985). *Nuclear Deterrence: Ethics and Strategy*. Chicago: University of Chicago Press.

Hargreaves Heap, Shaun P. and Yanis Varoufakis (1995). *Game Theory: A Critical Introduction*. New York: Routledge.

Harsanyi, John C. (1967–68). "Games with Incomplete Information Played by 'Bayesian' Players," 3 pts. *Management Science* 14 (Series A): 159–182, 320–334, 486–502.

(1973). "Review of *Paradoxes of Rationality*." *American Political Science Review*, 67: 599–600.

(1974a). "Communications." *American Political Science Review*, 68: 731–732.

(1974b). "Communications." *American Political Science Review*, 68: 1694–1695.

(1977). "Advances in Understanding Rational Behavior." In Robert E. Butts and Jaakko Hintikka (eds.), *Foundational Problems in the Special Sciences*. Dordrecht, The Netherlands: D. Reidel.

Hart, Robert A. and James Lee Ray (1996). "Democracy and the Escalation of Militarized Interstate Disputes." Paper delivered at the Annual Meeting of the American Political Science Association, San Francisco, August 29– September 1.

Harvey, Frank P. (1998). "Rigor Mortis, or Rigor, More Tests: Necessity,

Sufficiency, and Deterrence Logic." *International Studies Quarterly*, 42: 675–707.

Harvey, Frank P. and Patrick James (1992). "Nuclear Deterrence Theory: The Record of Aggregate Testing and an Alternative Research Agenda." *Conflict Management and Peace Science*, 12: 17–45.

Haywood, O.J., Jr. (1954). "Military Decision and Game Theory." *Operations Research*, 2: 365–385.

Hermann, Charles F. (1969). "International Crisis as a Situational Variable." In James N. Rosenau (ed.), *International Politics and Foreign Policy*. New York: Free Press.

Hobbes, Thomas (1968 [1651]). *Leviathan*, edited by C.B. Macpherson. Harmondsworth: Penguin.

Hoffman, Stanley (1965). *The State of War: Essays on the Theory and Practice of International Politics*. New York: Praeger.

Holler, Manfred J. (1988). "Three Characteristic Functions and Tentative Remarks on Credible Threats." Memo 1988–1, Institute of Economics, University of Aarhus.

Holsti, Ole R., Richard A. Brody, and Robert C. North (1964). "Measuring Affect and Action in International Relations Models: Empirical Materials from the 1962 Cuban Crisis." *Journal of Peace Research*, 1: 170–189.

Holsti, Ole R., Robert C. North, and Richard A. Brody (1968). "Perception and Action in the 1914 Crisis." In J. David Singer (ed.), *Quantitative International Politics: Insights and Evidence*. New York: Free Press.

Hopkins, Raymond F. and Richard W. Mansbach (1973). *Structure and Process in International Politics*. New York: Harper and Row.

Houwelling, Henk and Jan G. Siccama (1988a). *Studies of War*. Dordrecht, The Netherlands: Martinus Nijhoff.

(1988b). "Power Transitions as a Cause of War." *Journal of Conflict Resolution*, 32: 87–102.

Howard, Michael (1983). *The Causes of War*, 2nd edn. Cambridge, MA: Harvard University Press.

Howard, Nigel (1971). *Paradoxes of Rationality: Theory of Metagames and Political Behavior*. Cambridge, MA: MIT Press.

(1973). "Comment on a Mathematical Error in a Review by Harsanyi." *International Journal of Game Theory*, 2: 251–252.

(1974a). "Communications." *American Political Science Review*, 68: 729–730.

(1974b). "Communications." *American Political Science Review*, 68: 1692–1693.

Huntington, Samuel P. (1958). "Arms Races: Prerequisites and Results." Reprinted in Robert J. Art and Kenneth N. Waltz (eds.), *The Use of Force: International Politics and Foreign Policy*. Boston: Little, Brown (1971).

(1989). "No Exit – The Errors of Endism." *The National Interest*, 17: 3–11.

Huth, Paul K. (1988a). *Extended Deterrence and the Prevention of War*. New Haven: Yale University Press.

(1988b). "Extended Deterrence and the Outbreak of War." *American Political Science Review*, 82: 423–443.

References

(1990). "The Extended Deterrent Value of Nuclear Weapons." *Journal of Conflict Resolution*, 34: 270–290.

(1996). *Standing Your Ground: Territorial Disputes and International Conflict.* Ann Arbor: University of Michigan Press.

(1999). "Deterrence and International Conflict: Empirical Findings and Theoretical Debates." *Annual Review of Political Science*, 2: 61–84.

Huth, Paul K., D. Scott Bennett, and Christopher Gelpi (1992). "System Uncertainty, Risk Propensity, and International Conflict." *Journal of Conflict Resolution*, 36: 478–517.

Huth, Paul K., Christopher Gelpi, and D. Scott Bennett (1993). "The Escalation of Great Power Disputes: Testing Rational Deterrence Theory and Structural Realism." *American Political Science Review*, 87: 609–623.

Huth, Paul K. and Bruce M. Russett (1984). "What Makes Deterrence Work? Cases from 1900–1980." *World Politics*, 36: 496–526.

(1988). "Deterrence Failure and Crisis Escalation." *International Studies Quarterly*, 32: 29–45.

(1990). "Testing Deterrence Theory: Rigor Makes a Difference." *World Politics*, 42: 466–501.

Intriligator, Michael D. and Dagobert L. Brito (1981). "Nuclear Proliferation and the Probability of Nuclear War." *Public Choice*, 37: 247–260.

(1984). "Can Arms Races Lead to the Outbreak of War?" *Journal of Conflict Resolution*, 28: 63–84.

(1987). "The Stability of Mutual Deterrence." In Jacek Kugler and Frank C. Zagare (eds.), *Exploring the Stability of Deterrence*. Boulder, CO: Lynne Rienner Publishers.

(1988). "Accidental Nuclear War: A Significant Issue for Arms Control." *Current Research on Peace and Violence*, 11: 14–23.

Intriligator, Michael D. and Urs Luterbacher, eds. (1994). *Cooperative Models in International Relations Research*. Boston: Kluwer.

Janis, Irving L. and Leon Mann (1977). *Decision Making: A Psychological Analysis of Conflict, Choice, and Commitment*. New York: Free Press.

Jensen, Lloyd (1984). "Negotiating Strategic Arms Control, 1969–1979." *Journal of Conflict Resolution*, 28: 535–559.

Jervis, Robert (1968). "Hypotheses on Misperception." *World Politics*, 20: 454–479.

(1970). *The Logic of Images in International Relations*. Princeton: Princeton University Press.

(1972). "Bargaining and Bargaining Tactics." In J. Roland Pennock and John W. Chapman (eds.), *Coercion. Nomos XIV: Yearbook of the American Society for Political and Legal Philosophy*. Chicago: Aldine.

(1976). *Perception and Misperception in International Politics*. Princeton: Princeton University Press.

(1978). "Cooperation under the Security Dilemma." *World Politics*, 30: 167–214.

(1979). "Deterrence Theory Revisited." *World Politics*, 31: 289–324.

(1984). *The Illogic of American Nuclear Strategy*. Ithaca: Cornell University Press.

(1985). "Introduction." In Robert Jervis, Richard Ned Lebow, and Janice Gross Stein (eds.), *Psychology and Deterrence*. Baltimore: Johns Hopkins University Press.

(1988a). "Realism, Game Theory, and Cooperation." *World Politics*, 40: 317–349.

(1988b). "The Utility of Nuclear Weapons." *International Security*, 13: 80–90.

(1989). "Rational Deterrence: Theory and Evidence." *World Politics*, 41: 183–207.

Johnson, Robert H. (1983). "Periods of Peril: The Window of Vulnerability and Other Myths." *Foreign Affairs*, 61: 950–970.

Jones, T.K. and W. Scott Thompson (1978). "Central War and Civil Defense." *Orbis*, 22: 681–712.

Joynt, Carey B. and Percy E. Corbett (1978). *Theory and Reality in World Politics*. Pittsburgh: University of Pittsburgh Press.

Kagan, Donald (1995). *On the Origins of War and the Preservation of Peace*. New York: Doubleday.

Kahan, Jerome H. (1975). *Security in the Nuclear Age*. Washington, DC: Brookings Institution.

Kahn, Herman (1960). *On Thermonuclear War*. Princeton: Princeton University Press.

(1962). *Thinking About the Unthinkable*. New York: Horizon Press.

(1965). *On Escalation*. New York: Praeger.

Kahneman, Daniel and Amos Tversky (1979). "Prospect Theory: An Analysis of Decision under Risk." *Econometrica*, 47: 263–291.

Kaplan, Fred (1983). *The Wizards of Armageddon*. New York: Simon and Schuster.

Kaplan, Morton (1957). *System and Process in International Politics*. New York: Wiley.

Kaufmann, Chaim D. (1994). "Out of the Lab and into the Archives: A Method for Testing Psychological Explanations of Political Decision Making." *International Studies Quarterly*, 38: 557–586.

Kaufmann, William (1956). "The Requirements of Deterrence." In William Kaufmann (ed.), *Military Policy and National Security*. Princeton: Princeton University Press.

Kegley, Charles W., Jr. and Gregory Raymond (1994). *A Multipolar Peace? Great Power Politics in the Twenty-First Century*. New York: St. Martin's Press.

Kegley, Charles W., Jr. and Eugene Wittkopf, eds. (1989). *The Nuclear Reader: Strategy, Weapons, War*, 2nd edn. New York: St. Martin's Press.

Kenny, Anthony (1985). *The Logic of Deterrence*. Chicago: University of Chicago Press.

Keylor, William R. (1984). *The Twentieth-Century World*. New York: Oxford University Press.

Kilgour, D. Marc (1991). "Domestic Political Structure and War Behavior." *Journal of Conflict Resolution*, 35: 266–284.

References

Kilgour, D. Marc and Frank C. Zagare (1991). "Credibility, Uncertainty, and Deterrence." *American Journal of Political Science*, 35: 303–334.

(1994). "Uncertainty and the Role of the Pawn in Extended Deterrence." *Synthese*, 100: 379–417.

(1997). "Can Deterrence Be Effective When Forces Are Small?" Paper delivered at the Annual Meeting of the American Political Science Association, Washington, DC, August 28–31.

Kim, Woosang (1989). "Power, Alliance, and Major Wars, 1816–1975." *Journal of Conflict Resolution*, 33: 255–273.

(1991). "Alliance Transitions and Great Power War." *American Journal of Political Science*, 35: 833–849.

Kim, Woosang and Bruce Bueno de Mesquita (1995). "How Perceptions Influence the Risk of War." *International Studies Quarterly*, 39: 51–65.

Kim, Woosang and James D. Morrow (1992). "When Do Power Shifts Lead to War?" *American Journal of Political Science*, 36: 896–922.

Kindleberger, Charles P. (1974). *The World in Depression, 1929–1939*. Berkeley: University of California Press.

(1976). "Systems of International Economic Organization." In David P. Calleo (ed.), *Money and the Coming World Order*. New York: New York University Press.

Kissinger, Henry A. (1957a). *A World Restored: Metternich, Castlereagh and the Problems of Peace 1812–1822*. Boston: Houghton-Mifflin.

(1957b). *Nuclear Weapons and Foreign Policy*. New York: Harper.

(1979). *White House Years*. Boston: Little, Brown.

(1994). *Diplomacy*. New York: Simon and Schuster.

Kraig, Michael R. (1999). "Nuclear Deterrence in the Developing World: A Game-Theoretic Treatment." *Journal of Peace Research*, 36: 141–167.

Krasner, Stephen D. (1976). "State Power and the Structure of International Trade." *World Politics*, 28: 317–347.

Krauthammer, Charles (1991). "The Unipolar Moment." *Foreign Affairs*, 70: 23–33.

Kreps, David M. (1990). *A Course in Microeconomic Theory*. Princeton: Princeton University Press.

Kreps, David M. and Robert Wilson (1982a). "Reputation and Imperfect Information." *Journal of Economic Theory*, 27: 253–279.

(1982b). "Sequential Equilibria." *Econometrica*, 50: 863–894.

Kroll, John A. (1995). *Closure in International Politics: The Impact of Strategy, Blocs, and Empire*. Boulder, CO: Westview Press.

Kugler, Jacek (1984). "Terror Without Deterrence." *Journal of Conflict Resolution*, 28: 470–506.

Kugler, Jacek and Douglas Lemke, eds. (1996). *Parity and War: Evaluations and Extensions of "The War Ledger."* Ann Arbor: University of Michigan Press.

Kugler, Jacek and Susanne Werner (1993). "Conditional Anarchy: The Constraining Power of the Status Quo." Paper delivered at the Annual Meeting of the Midwest Political Science Association, Chicago, April 15–17.

Kugler, Jacek and Frank C. Zagare, eds. (1987a). *Exploring the Stability of Deterrence*. Boulder, CO: Lynne Rienner Publishers.

(1987b). "Risk, Deterrence, and War." In Jacek Kugler and Frank C. Zagare (eds.), *Exploring the Stability of Deterrence*. Boulder, CO: Lynne Rienner Publishers.

(1990). "The Long-term Stability of Deterrence." *International Interactions*, 15: 255–278.

Kuhn, Harold W. (1950). "Extensive Games." *Proceedings of the National Academy of Sciences of the United States*, 36: 570–576.

(1953). "Extensive Games and the Problem of Information." In Harold W. Kuhn and Albert W. Tucker (eds.), *Contributions to the Theory of Games*, vol. II. Princeton: Princeton University Press.

Kydd, Andrew (1997). "Game Theory and the Spiral Model." *World Politics*, 49: 371–400.

Lampton, David M. (1973). "The US Image of Peking in Three International Crises." *Western Political Quarterly*, 26: 28–50.

Langlois, Jean-Pierre P. (1989). "Modeling Deterrence and International Crises." *Journal of Conflict Resolution*, 33: 67–83.

(1991). "Rational Deterrence and Crisis Stability." *American Journal of Political Science*, 35: 801–832.

Lebow, Richard Ned (1981). *Between Peace and War: The Nature of International Crisis*. Baltimore: Johns Hopkins University Press.

(1984). "Windows of Opportunity: Do States Jump Through Them?" *International Security*, 9: 147–186.

(1989). "Deterrence: A Political and Psychological Critique." In Paul C. Stern *et al.* (eds.), *Perspectives on Deterrence*. New York: Oxford University Press.

Lebow, Richard Ned and Janice Gross Stein (1989). "Rational Deterrence Theory: I Think, Therefore I Deter." *World Politics*, 41: 208–224.

(1990). "Deterrence: The Elusive Dependent Variable." *World Politics*, 42: 336–369.

Lemke, Douglas (1996). "Small States and War: An Expansion of Power Transition Theory." In Jacek Kugler and Douglas Lemke (eds.), *Parity and War: Evaluations and Extensions of "The War Ledger."* Ann Arbor: University of Michigan Press.

Leng, Russell J. (1993). *Interstate Crisis Behavior, 1816–1990: Realism Versus Reciprocity*. New York: Cambridge University Press.

Leng, Russell J. and Hugh G. Wheeler (1979). "Influences, Strategies, Success, and War." *Journal of Conflict Resolution*, 23: 655–684.

Levy, Jack S. (1983). *War in the Modern Great Power System, 1495–1975*. Lexington: University of Kentucky Press.

(1985). "The Polarity of the System and International Stability: An Empirical Analysis." In Alan Ned Sabrosky (ed.), *Polarity and War*. Boulder, CO: Westview Press.

(1987). "Declining Power and the Preventive Motivation for War." *World Politics*, 40: 82–107.

(1988). "When Do Deterrent Threats Work?" *British Journal of Political Science*, 18: 485–512.

(1992a). "An Introduction to Prospect Theory." *Political Psychology*, 13: 171–186.

(1992b). "Prospect Theory and International Relations: Theoretical Applications and Analytical Problems." *Political Psychology*, 13: 283–310.

(1997). "Prospect Theory, Rational Choice, and International Relations." *International Studies Quarterly*, 41: 87–112.

Luce, R. Duncan and Howard Raiffa (1957). *Games and Decisions: Introduction and Critical Survey*. New York: Wiley.

McDonald, John (1950). *Strategy in Poker, Business and War*. New York: Norton.

McDonald, John and John W. Tukey (1949). "Colonel Blotto: A Problem of Military Strategy." *Fortune*, June.

MacIntyre, Alastair (1973). "The Essential Contestability of Some Social Concepts." *Ethics*, 84: 1–9.

McManus, Doyle (1999). "Debate Turns to Finger Pointing on Kosovo." *Los Angeles Times*, April 11.

McNamara, Robert S. (1962). Address at the Commencement Exercises, University of Michigan. Ann Arbor, June 16.

Mansbach, Richard W. (1997). *The Global Puzzle: Issues and Actors in World Politics*. New York: Houghton-Mifflin.

Massie, Robert K. (1991). *Dreadnought: Britain, Germany, and the Coming of the Great War*. New York: Ballantine Books.

Maxwell, Stephen (1968). "Rationality in Deterrence." *Adelphi Paper*, no. 50. London: Institute for Strategic Studies.

Mayer, Thomas F. (1986). "Arms Races and War Initiation: Some Alternatives to the Intriligator–Brito Model." *Journal of Conflict Resolution*, 30: 3–28.

Mearsheimer, John J. (1983). *Conventional Deterrence*. Ithaca: Cornell University Press.

(1990). "Back to the Future: Instability in Europe After the Cold War." *International Security*, 15: 5–56.

(1993). "The Case for a Ukrainian Nuclear Deterrent." *Foreign Affairs*, 72: 50–66.

Midlarsky, Manus I. (1988). *The Onset of War*. Boston: Unwin Hyman.

Miller, Steven E. (1993). "The Case against a Ukrainian Nuclear Deterrent." *Foreign Affairs*, 72: 67–80.

Milner, Helen (1991). "The Assumption of Anarchy in International Relations Theory: A Critique." *Review of International Studies*, 17: 67–85.

(1997). *Interests, Institutions, and Information: Domestic Politics and International Relations*. Princeton: Princeton University Press.

Modelski, George (1983). "Long Cycles of World Leadership." In William R. Thompson (ed.), *Contending Approaches to World Systems Analysis*. Beverly Hills, CA: Sage.

Modelski, George and William R. Thompson (1989). "Long Cycles and Global War." In Manus I. Midlarsky (ed.), *Handbook of War Studies*. Boston: Unwin Hyman.

Mor, Ben D. (1991). "Nasser's Decision-making in the 1967 Middle East Crisis: A Rational Choice Explanation." *Journal of Peace Research*, 28: 359–376.

Morgan, Patrick M. (1977). *Deterrence: A Conceptual Analysis*. Beverly Hills, CA: Sage.

Morgan, T. Clifton (1994). *Untying the Knot of War: A Bargaining Theory of International Crisis*. Ann Arbor: University of Michigan Press.

Morgan, T. Clifton and Peter M. Dawson (1990). "Bargaining Tough: Commitment Strategy in International Conflict." Paper presented at the Annual Meeting of the American Political Science Association, San Francisco, August 30–September 2.

Morgenstern, Oskar (1959). *The Question of National Defense*. New York: Random House.

(1961a). "The Cold War is Cold Poker." *New York Times Magazine*, February 5.

(1961b). "Review of *The Strategy of Conflict*." *Southern Economic Journal*, 28: 105.

Morgenthau, Hans J. (1948). *Politics Among Nations*. New York: Knopf.

Morrow, James D. (1989a). "Capabilities, Uncertainty, and Resolve: A Limited Information Model of Crisis Bargaining." *American Journal of Political Science*, 33: 941–972.

(1989b). "Bargaining in Repeated Crises: A Limited Information Model." In Peter C. Ordeshook (ed.), *Models of Strategic Choice in Politics*. Ann Arbor: University of Michigan Press.

(1994a). *Game Theory for Political Scientists*. Princeton: Princeton University Press.

(1994b). "Alliances, Credibility, and Peacetime Costs." *Journal of Conflict Resolution*, 38: 270–297.

(2000). "The Ongoing Game-Theoretic Revolution." In Manus I. Midlarsky (ed.), *Handbook of War Studies II*. Ann Arbor: University of Michigan Press.

Most, Benjamin A. and Harvey Starr (1989). *Inquiry, Logic and International Politics*. Columbia: University of South Carolina Press.

Mueller, John (1988). "The Essential Irrelevance of Nuclear Weapons: Stability in the Postwar World." *International Security*, 13: 55–79.

(1995). *Quiet Cataclysm: Reflections on the Recent Transformation of World Politics*. New York: Harper Collins.

Nalebuff, Barry (1986). "Brinkmanship and Nuclear Deterrence: The Neutrality of Escalation." *Conflict Management and Peace Science*, 9: 19–30.

(1991). "Rational Deterrence in an Imperfect World." *World Politics*, 43: 313–335.

Naroll, Raoul, Vern L. Bullough, and Frada Naroll (1974). *Military Deterrence in History: A Pilot Cross-Historical Survey*. Albany: State University of New York Press.

References

Nash, John (1951). "Non-cooperative Games." *Annals of Mathematics*, 54: 286–295.

National Academy of Sciences (1997). *The Future of US Nuclear Weapons Policy.* Washington, DC: National Academy Press.

Nicholson, Michael (1989). *Formal Theories in International Relations.* Cambridge: Cambridge University Press.

(1992). *Rationality and the Analysis of International Conflict.* Cambridge: Cambridge University Press.

Nitze, Paul H. (1976/1977). "Deterring Our Deterrent." *Foreign Policy*, 25: 195–210.

O'Neill, Barry (1986). "International Escalation and the Dollar Auction." *Journal of Conflict Resolution*, 30: 33–50.

(1989). "Game Theory and the Study of Deterrence of War." In Paul C. Stern, Robert Axelrod, Robert Jervis, and Roy Radner (eds.), *Perspectives on Deterrence.* New York: Oxford University Press.

(1992). "Are Game Models of Deterrence Biassed Towards Arms-Building? Wagner on Rationality and Misperception." *Journal of Theoretical Politics*, 4: 459–477.

(1994). "Game Theory Models of Peace and War." In Robert J. Aumann and Sergui Hart (eds.), *Handbook of Game Theory with Economic Applications*, vol. II. Amsterdam: Elsevier.

Ordeshook, Peter C., ed. (1989). *Models of Strategic Choice in Politics.* Ann Arbor: University of Michigan Press.

Organski, A.F.K. (1958). *World Politics.* New York: Knopf.

Organski, A.F.K. and Jacek Kugler (1980). *The War Ledger.* Chicago: University of Chicago Press.

Osgood, Robert E. (1957). *Limited War: The Challenge to American Strategy.* Chicago: University of Chicago Press.

(1979). *Limited War Revisited.* Boulder, CO: Westview Press.

Paul, T.V., Richard J. Harknett, and James J. Wirtz, eds. (1998). *The Absolute Weapon Revisited.* Ann Arbor: University of Michigan Press.

Payne, James L. (1981). *The American Threat: National Security and Foreign Policy.* College Station, TX: Lytton.

Posen, Barry R. (1991). *Inadvertent Escalation: Conventional War and Nuclear Risks.* Ithaca: Cornell University Press.

(1993). "The Security Dilemma and Ethnic Conflict." *Survival*, 35: 27–47.

Powell, Robert (1987). "Crisis Bargaining, Escalation, and MAD." *American Political Science Review*, 81: 717–735.

(1988). "Nuclear Brinkmanship with Two-sided Incomplete Information." *American Political Science Review*, 82: 155–178.

(1989). "Nuclear Deterrence and the Strategy of Limited Retaliation." *American Political Science Review*, 83: 503–519.

(1990). *Nuclear Deterrence Theory: The Search for Credibility.* New York: Cambridge University Press.

(1993). "Guns, Butter, and Anarchy." *American Political Science Review*, 87: 115–132.

(1996a). "Uncertainty, Shifting Power, and Appeasement." *American Political Science Review*, 90: 749–764.

(1996b). "Stability and the Distribution of Power." *World Politics*, 48: 239–267.

Pruitt, Dean G. (1969). "Stability and Sudden Change in Interpersonal and International Affairs." *Journal of Conflict Resolution*, 13: 392–408.

Pruitt, Dean G. and Jeffrey Z. Rubin (1986). *Social Conflict: Escalation, Stalemate, and Settlement*. New York: Random House.

Quester, George H. (1970). *Nuclear Diplomacy*. New York: Dunellen.

(1977). *Offense and Defense in the International System*. New York: Wiley.

(1989). "Some Thoughts on 'Deterrence Failures.'" In Paul C. Stern, Robert Axelrod, Robert Jervis, and Roy Radner (eds.), *Perspectives on Deterrence*. New York: Oxford University Press.

(1998). "The Continuing Debate on Minimal Deterrence." In T.V. Paul, Richard J. Harknett, and James J. Wirtz (eds.), *The Absolute Weapon Revisited*. Ann Arbor: University of Michigan Press.

Rapoport, Anatol (1964). *Strategy and Conscience*. New York: Harper and Row.

(1967). "Escape from Paradox." *Scientific American*, 217: 50–56.

(1968). "Chicken à la Kahn." *Virginia Quarterly Review*, 41: 370–389.

(1992). "Comments on 'Rationality and Misperceptions in Deterrence Theory.'" *Journal of Theoretical Politics*, 4: 479–484.

Rasmusen, Eric (1989). *Games and Information*. New York: Blackwell.

Reed, William (1998). "Selection Effects and Inference in World Politics." Paper presented at the 39th Annual Meeting of the International Studies Association, Minneapolis, March 17–21.

(2000). "A Unified Model of Conflict Onset and Escalation: Capabilities, Democracy, and Status Quo Evaluations." *American Journal of Political Science*, 44: 84–93.

Rhodes, Edward (1988). "Nuclear Weapons and Credibility: Deterrence Theory Beyond Rationality." *Review of International Studies*, 14: 45–62.

(1989). *Power and MADness: The Logic of Nuclear Coercion*. New York: Columbia University Press.

Richardson, James L. (1994). *Crisis Diplomacy: The Great Powers since the Mid-Nineteenth Century*. New York: Cambridge University Press.

Richardson, Lewis F. (1960). *Arms and Insecurity: A Mathematical Study of the Causes and Origin of War*. Pittsburgh: Boxwood Press.

Riker, William H. and Peter C. Ordeshook (1973). *An Introduction to Positive Political Theory*. Englewood Cliffs, NJ: Prentice-Hall.

Roth, Alvin E. (1985). *Game-Theoretic Models of Bargaining*. New York: Cambridge University Press.

Rousseau, David L., Christopher Gelpi, Dan Reiter, and Paul K. Huth (1996). "Assessing the Dyadic Nature of the Democratic Peace, 1918–88." *American Political Science Review*, 90: 512–533.

References

Russett, Bruce M. (1963). "The Calculus of Deterrence." *Journal of Conflict Resolution*, 7: 97–109.

Sabrosky, Alan Ned, ed. (1985). *Polarity and War: The Changing Structure of International Conflict*. Boulder, CO: Westview Press.

Sagan, Scott D. (1993). *The Limits of Safety: Organizations, Accidents, and Nuclear Weapons*. Princeton: Princeton University Press.

Samuelson, Paul A. (1938). "A Note on the Pure Theory of Consumer's Behaviour." *Economica*, 5: 61–71.

Sanger, David E. (1995). "Step is Strongest Taken by the US Against a Trading Partner." *New York Times*, May 17.

Sanger, David E. and Erick Eckholm (1999). "Will Beijing's Nuclear Arsenal Stay Small or Will It Mushroom?" *New York Times*, March 15.

Savage, Leonard (1954). *The Foundations of Statistics*. New York: Wiley.

Schelling, Thomas C. (1960). *The Strategy of Conflict*. Cambridge, MA: Harvard University Press.

(1966). *Arms and Influence*. New Haven: Yale University Press.

Schmidt, Helmut (1962). *Defense or Retaliation*. New York: Praeger.

Scoville, Herbert, Jr. (1981). *MX: Prescription for Disaster*. Cambridge, MA: MIT Press.

Selten, Reinhard (1975). "A Re-examination of the Perfectness Concept for Equilibrium Points in Extensive Games." *International Journal of Game Theory*, 4: 25–55.

Shy, John (1986). "Jomini." In Peter Paret (ed.), *Makers of Modern Strategy from Machiavelli to the Nuclear Age*. Princeton: Princeton University Press.

Simon, Herbert A. (1976). "From Substantive to Procedural Rationality." In S.J. Latsis (ed.), *Method and Appraisal in Economics*. Cambridge: Cambridge University Press.

Singh, Jaswant (1998). "Against Nuclear Apartheid." *Foreign Affairs*, 77: 41–52.

Siverson, Randolph M. and Michael P. Sullivan (1983). "The Distribution of Power and the Onset of War." *Journal of Conflict Resolution*, 27: 473–494.

Smith, Alastair (1995). "Alliance Formation and War." *International Studies Quarterly*, 39: 405–425.

(1996). "To Intervene or Not To Intervene: A Biased Decision." *Journal of Conflict Resolution*, 40: 16–40.

(1998a). "International Crises and Domestic Politics." *American Political Science Review*, 92: 623–638.

(1998b). "Extended Deterrence and Alliance Formation." *International Interactions*, 24: 315–343.

Smoke, Richard (1977). *War: Controlling Escalation*. Cambridge, MA: Harvard University Press.

(1987). *National Security and the Nuclear Dilemma*. Reading, MA: Addison-Wesley.

Smoker, Paul and Morris Bradley, eds. (1988). *Accidental Nuclear War*. Special Issue of *Current Research on Peace and Violence*, 11 (nos. 1–2).

Snyder, Glenn H. (1961). *Deterrence and Defense: Toward a Theory of National Security.* Princeton: Princeton University Press.

(1965). "The Balance of Power and the Balance of Terror." In Paul Seabury (ed.), *Balance of Power.* San Francisco: Chandler.

(1971). "'Prisoner's Dilemma' and 'Chicken' Models in International Politics." *International Studies Quarterly,* 15: 66–103.

(1972). "Crisis Bargaining." In Charles F. Hermann (ed.), *International Crises: Insights from Behavioral Research.* New York: Free Press.

(1997). *Alliance Politics.* Ithaca: Cornell University Press.

Snyder, Glenn H. and Paul Diesing (1977). *Conflict Among Nations: Bargaining, Decision Making and System Structure in International Crises.* Princeton: Princeton University Press.

Snyder, Jack (1984). "Civil–Military Relations and the Cult of the Offensive, 1914 and 1984." *International Security,* 9: 108–146.

Sobel, Joel (1985). "A Theory of Credibility." *Review of Economic Studies,* 52: 557–573.

Sorokin, Gerald L. (1994). "Alliance Formation and General Deterrence: A Game-Theoretic Model and the Case of Israel." *Journal of Conflict Resolution,* 38: 298–325.

Stein, Arthur A. (1982). "When Misperception Matters." *World Politics,* 34: 505–526.

Stein, Charles (1995). "US, Japan Reach Accord, Avert a Trade Battle." *Boston Globe,* June 29.

Stein, Janice Gross (1991). "Deterrence and Reassurance." In Philip E. Tetlock, Jo L. Husbands, Robert Jervis, Paul Stern, and Charles Tilly (eds.), *Behavior, Society, and Nuclear War,* vol. II. New York: Oxford University Press.

Steinbruner, John (1976). "Beyond Rational Deterrence: The Struggle for New Conceptions." *World Politics,* 28: 223–245.

Stromseth, Jane E. (1988). *The Origins of Flexible Response: NATO's Debate Over Strategy in the 1960s.* New York: St. Martin's Press.

Sudoplatov, Pavel (1994). *Special Tasks: The Memoirs of an Unwanted Witness.* Boston: Little, Brown.

Sullivan, Michael P. (1976). *International Relations: Theories and Evidence.* Englewood Cliffs, NJ: Prentice-Hall.

(1990). *Power in Contemporary International Politics.* Columbia: University of South Carolina Press.

Tirole, Jean (1988). *The Theory of Industrial Organization.* Cambridge, MA: MIT Press.

Tuchman, Barbara (1962). *The Guns of August.* New York: Dell.

Tversky, Amos and Daniel Kahneman (1981). "The Framing of Decisions and the Psychology of Choice." *Science,* 211: 453–458.

Tyler, Patrick E. (1997). "Control of Army Is Crucial Issue for China Rulers." *New York Times,* February 23.

References

US Department of Defense (1997). *Report of the Quadrennial Defense Review.* Washington, DC: Department of Defense.

US Department of Defense (1998). *Annual Report to the President and the Congress.* Washington, DC: Department of Defense.

van Damme, Eric (1983). *Refinements of the Nash Equilibria Concept.* Berlin: Springer-Verlag.

Van Evera, Stephen (1984). "The Cult of the Offensive and the Origins of the First World War." *International Security,* 9: 58–107.

(1990/91). "Primed for Peace: Europe After the Cold War." *International Security,* 15: 7–57.

Van Gelder, Timothy J. (1989). "Credible Threats and Usable Weapons: Some Dilemmas of Deterrence." *Philosophy and Public Affairs,* 18: 158–183.

Vasquez, John A. (1991). "The Deterrence Myth: Nuclear Weapons and the Prevention of Nuclear War." In Charles W. Kegley, Jr. (ed.), *The Long Postwar Peace: Contending Explanations and Projections.* New York: HarperCollins.

(1993). *The War Puzzle.* New York: Cambridge University Press.

(1997). "The Realist Paradigm and Degenerative versus Progressive Research Programs: An Appraisal of Neotraditional Research on Waltz's Balancing Proposition." *American Political Science Review,* 91: 899–912.

Verba, Sidney (1961). "Assumptions of Rationality and Non-rationality in Models of International Systems." In Klaus Knorr and Sidney Verba (eds.), *The International System: Theoretical Essays.* Princeton: Princeton University Press.

Vogel, Mike (1995). "Canada Once Eyed US Invasion." *Buffalo News,* September 17.

Von Neumann, John and Oskar Morgenstern (1944). *Theory of Games and Economic Behavior.* Princeton: Princeton University Press.

Wagner, R. Harrison (1982). "Deterrence and Bargaining." *Journal of Conflict Resolution,* 26: 329–358.

(1991). "Nuclear Deterrence, Counterforce Strategies, and the Incentive to Strike First." *American Political Science Review,* 85: 727–749.

(1992a). "Rationality and Misperception in Deterrence Theory." *Journal of Theoretical Politics,* 4: 115–141.

(1992b). "Reply to Comments by McGinnis, O'Neill and Rapoport." *Journal of Theoretical Politics,* 4: 485–491.

Walker, Stephen G. (1977). "The Interface Between Beliefs and Behavior: Henry Kissinger's Operational Code and the Vietnam War." *Journal of Conflict Resolution,* 21: 129–168.

Walt, Stephen M. (1999). "Rigor or Rigor Mortis? Rational Choice and Security Studies." *International Security,* 23: 5–48.

Waltz, Kenneth N. (1959). *Man, the State and War: A Theoretical Analysis.* New York: Columbia University Press.

(1964). "The Stability of the Bipolar World." *Daedalus,* 93: 881–909.

(1979). *Theory of International Politics.* Reading, MA: Addison-Wesley.

(1981). "The Spread of Nuclear Weapons: More May Be Better." *Adelphi Paper*, no. 171. London: International Institute for Strategic Studies.

(1993). "The Emerging World Structure of International Politics." *International Security*, 18: 44–79.

Ward, Michael Don (1982). "Cooperation and Conflict in Foreign Policy Behavior." *International Studies Quarterly*, 26: 87–126.

Weede, Erich (1976). "Overwhelming Preponderance as a Pacifying Condition Among Contiguous Asian Dyads, 1950–1969." *Journal of Conflict Resolution*, 26: 395–411.

(1981). "Preventing War by Nuclear Deterrence or by Détente." *Conflict Management and Peace Science*, 6: 1–8.

(1983). "Extended Deterrence by Superpower Alliance." *Journal of Conflict Resolution*, 27: 231–253.

Weingast, Barry R. (1996). "Off-the-Path Behavior: A Game-Theoretic Approach to Counterfactuals and Its Implications for Political and Historical Analysis." In Philip E. Tetlock and Aaron Belkin (eds.), *Counterfactual Thought Experiments in World Politics*. Princeton: Princeton University Press.

Wells, Samuel F., Jr. (1981). "The Origins of Massive Retaliation." *Political Science Quarterly*, 96: 31–52.

Wilkenfeld, Jonathan (1991). "Trigger-Response Transitions in Foreign Policy Crises, 1929–1985." *Journal of Conflict Resolution*, 35: 143–169.

Wilkenfeld, Jonathan, Virginia Lee Lussier, and Dale Tahtinen (1972). "Conflict Interactions in the Middle East, 1949–1967." *Journal of Conflict Resolution*, 16: 135–154.

Williams, J.D. (1954). *The Compleat Strategyst*. Santa Monica, CA: The Rand Corporation.

Wilson, Robert (1985). "Reputations in Games and Markets." In Alvin E. Roth (ed.), *Game-Theoretic Models of Bargaining*. New York: Cambridge University Press.

(1992). "Strategic Models of Entry Deterrence." In Robert J. Aumann and Sergui Hart (eds.), *Handbook of Game Theory with Economic Applications*, vol. I. Amsterdam: North-Holland.

Wohlstetter, Albert (1959). "The Delicate Balance of Terror." *Foreign Affairs*, 37: 211–234.

Wolfers, Arnold (1951). "The Pole of Power and the Pole of Indifference." *World Politics*, 4: 39–63.

(1962). *Discord and Collaboration: Essays on International Politics*. Baltimore: Johns Hopkins University Press.

Wright, Quincy (1965). "The Escalation of International Conflicts." *Journal of Conflict Resolution*, 9: 434–449.

Wu, Samuel S.G. (1990). "To Attack or Not to Attack: A Theory and Empirical Assessment of Extended Immediate Deterrence." *Journal of Conflict Resolution*, 34: 531–552.

Young, Oran R. (1968). *The Politics of Force: Bargaining During International Crises*. Princeton: Princeton University Press.

ed. (1975). *Bargaining: Formal Theories of Negotiation*. Urbana: University of Illinois Press.

Young, Robert J. (1978). *In Command of France: French Foreign Policy and Military Planning 1933–1940*. Cambridge, MA: Harvard University Press.

Zagare, Frank C. (1979). "The Geneva Conference of 1954: A Case of Tacit Deception." *International Studies Quarterly*, 23: 390–411.

(1981). "Nonmyopic Equilibria and the Middle East Crisis of 1967." *Conflict Management and Peace Science*, 5: 139–162.

(1984). *Game Theory: Concepts and Applications*. Beverly Hills, CA: Sage.

(1985). "Toward A Reformulation of the Theory of Mutual Deterrence." *International Studies Quarterly*, 29: 155–169.

(1986). "Recent Advances in Game Theory and Political Science." In Samuel Long (ed.), *Annual Review of Political Science*. Norwood, NJ: Ablex.

(1987). *The Dynamics of Deterrence*. Chicago: University of Chicago Press.

(1990a). "Rationality and Deterrence." *World Politics*, 42: 238–260.

(1990b). "The Dynamics of Escalation." *Information and Decision Technologies*, 16: 249–261.

ed. (1990c). *Modeling International Conflict*. New York: Gordon and Breach.

(1992). "NATO, Rational Escalation and Flexible Response." *Journal of Peace Research*, 29: 435–454.

(1993). "Review of *War and Reason: Domestic and Political Imperatives*." *American Political Science Review*, 87: 810–811.

(1996a). "Classical Deterrence Theory: A Critical Assessment" *International Interactions*, 21: 365–387.

(1996b). "The Rites of Passage: Parity, Nuclear Deterrence and Power Transitions." In Jacek Kugler and Douglas Lemke (eds.), *Parity and War: Evaluations and Extensions of "The War Ledger."* Ann Arbor: University of Michigan Press.

(1999). "All Mortis, No Rigor." *International Security*, 24: 107–114.

Zagare, Frank C. and D. Marc Kilgour (1993a). "Asymmetric Deterrence." *International Studies Quarterly*, 37: 1–27.

(1993b). "Modeling 'Massive Retaliation.'" *Conflict Management and Peace Science*, 13: 61–86.

(1995). "Assessing Competing Defense Postures: The Strategic Implications of 'Flexible Response.'" *World Politics*, 47: 373–417.

(1998). "Deterrence Theory and the Spiral Model Revisited." *Journal of Theoretical Politics*, 10: 59–87.

Index

CAMBRIDGE STUDIES IN INTERNATIONAL RELATIONS